THE UNION AND THE WORLD:
THE POLITICAL ECONOMY OF A COMMON EUROPEAN FOREIGN POLICY

The Union and the World

The Political Economy of a Common European Foreign Policy

Edited by

Alan Cafruny
Hamilton College

and

Patrick Peters
European University Institute

KLUWER LAW INTERNATIONAL
THE HAGUE / LONDON / BOSTON

A C.I.P Catalogue record for this book is available from the Library of Congress.

ISBN 90-411-0500-X

Published by Kluwer Law International,
P.O. Box 85889, 2508 CN The Hague, The Netherlands

Sold and distributed in the U.S.A. and Canada
by Kluwer Law International,
675 Massachusetts Avenue, Cambridge, MA 02139, USA

In all other countries, sold and distributed
by Kluwer Law International, Distribution Centre
P.O. Box 322, 3300 AH Dordrecht, The Netherlands

Printed on acid-free paper

Printed in Great Britain

Table of Contents

List of Contributors

Alan Cafruny is the Henry Bristol Professor of International Affairs at Hamilton College, New York and an External Professor of the European University Institute.

Federiga Bindi Calussi is a Ph.D. Candidate at the European University Institute in Florence, Italy.

Juliette Enser is an associate with the Weil, Gotshal and Mances Law firm in Brussels.

Marjoleine Hennis is a Ph.D. Candidate at the European University Institute in Florence, and a Lecturer at the University of Groningen in the Netherlands.

Thomas Grunert is a Principal Administrator in DG4 of the European Parliament in Brussels.

Sandrine Labory is a Research Fellow at CEPS in Brussels.

Kaisa Lahteenmaki is a Ph.D. Candidate at the University of Turku, Finland.

Sandra Lavenex is a Ph.D. Candidate at the European University Institute, Florence, Italy.

Michael Leigh is Principal Advisor in the Cabinet of Commissioner Hans Van Den Broek, in Brussels.

Jens Mortensen is a Ph.D. Candidate at the European University Institute in Florence, Italy.

Patrick Peters is Associate Professor of international commerce and finance at the University of Lima, Peru, and a Ph.D. candidate at the European University Institute in Florence.

Anthony Smith is a Ph.D. candidate at the London School of Economics.

Christopher Smith is a lecturer of international relations at the University of Aberdeen.

Sabrina Tesoka is a Ph.D. Candidate at the European University Institute in Florence, Italy

Amy Verdun is an Assistant Professor of European Politics at the University of Victoria, BC, Canada.

Bernard Winkler works for the Bundesbank in Frankfurt. He received his Ph.D. in Economics from the European University Institute in Florence.

Preface

The European Union deserves better. Its stature in international affairs is clearly handicapped by the inability or unwillingness of its member states to establish a common foreign policy. Struggling to find a balance between emerging federalism and remaining sovereignty, the Union behaves like a wounded animal in international diplomacy, weak because of its self inflicted wounds, but inhibited by its injuries from finding solutions for its long term problems. Nevertheless, the EU and its institutions – the parliament, the Court and the Commission – have engaged in unprecedented levels of foreign policy development in recent years.

The core idea behind this volume is that a communitarian foreign policy exists, but that it is difficult to model and difficult to theorize, because it occurs in so many different shapes and sizes. Foreign policy does not just refer to statements and Acts. The contributors to this volume describe and explain how foreign policy made by the Union why it has an impact on the World.

This book is neither Euro-skeptic nor Euro-phile. The contributors are scholars who have political views but do not necessarily agree with each other on how the Union does or should work. Some of the authors are skeptical about the achievements of the EU, while others are more optimistic about the historical achievements and potential of the Union. Our purpose in writing this book, however is dissatisfaction with the lack of scholarly attention to the real workings of institutions in the making of EU foreign policy. While the editors have not conditioned the contributors about the conclusions of the chapters, a common set of questions has been posed. This volume is the result of a year of scholarly work and debate.

We would like to thank our bright assistant at Hamilton College, Antonis Ellinas, for his research assistance, and Selma Hoedt, our publisher at Kluwer Law, who enthusiastically supported the idea and helped us to prepare the final manuscript. Hamilton College generously provided support for the project. Although many contributors are in one way or another linked to the European University Institute, the volume has been produced without any formal support of the EUI.

Alan Cafruny and Patrick Peters
Clinton, New York/ Florence, Italy
June 23, 1997

EU foreign policy:
From Maastricht to Amsterdam

Alan Cafruny and Patrick Peters

During a series of stormy transatlantic negotiations in 1973, US Secretary of State Henry Kissinger expressed his frustration with the European Community by asking "Who speaks for Europe?". In the ensuing 25 years, the European Union has clearly taken giant strides in the domain of a common foreign policy. While the institutional framework of the EU's common foreign policy is as confusing and as spread out over different institutions as it was in the 1970s, decision-making procedures have been streamlined, treaties have been implemented, and a Union has been proclaimed. Moreover, Europe's global stature has certainly increased during the past quarter century. A greatly enlarged Union now frequently speaks with one voice on a range of important economic and political issues. Although intergovernmental conferences such as Maastricht (1991) and Amsterdam (1997) continue to display and, at times, accentuate national rivalries, the scope of their policies and their impact on world affairs have increased dramatically. Nevertheless, despite these advances the much discussed "Monsieur PESC", a French initiative designed to eliminate uncertainty about who or which institution of the EU is responsible for foreign policy, has not elicited general support. The President of the Commission continues to struggle for recognition as the Union's spokesperson, while the Parliament, despite having benefited greatly from the Maastricht Treaty, presses to extend its leverage both in foreign policy and in the overall decision-making procedures of the Union. In short, Kissinger's question still lacks a satisfactory answer: It is still not clear just whom he should call if he wants to speak with Europe.

The theoretical literature in European Studies has not been notably more successful than Henry Kissinger in seeking to comprehend the complexities and ambiguities of the Union. Analyses of the Union's foreign policy with reference to the two dominant paradigms, realism and neo-functionalism, run the risk of intellectual rigidity and simplification.[1] While realists continue to portray the nation state as the dominant, unitary actor, and assert that the Union's foreign policy can be understood as a more or less straightforward bargain between the most powerful member states, neo-functionalists assume a tendency towards policy coordination and an erosion of individual state capacity. Yet the chapters in this volume indicate that functionalist and intergovernmental processes occur simultaneously and, indeed, tend to be mutu-

---

[1] On the realist tradition, see Milward (1992), Moravcsik (1991, 1993) and Taylor (1982). On functionalism, see Hodges (1986) and Groom and Heraclides (1985).

A. Cafruny and P. Peters (eds.), The Union and the World, 1–7

ally reinforcing: even as states remain formidable actors, the Union's own institutions also constitute an important explanatory variable in the conduct of foreign policy. In the idiomatic language of contemporary international political economy, the European Union is more than a regime, but less than a federation. Hence, the central question animating this volume is the extent to which the European Union has become an actor in its own right on the world stage. How is the Union's foreign policy made? In what areas does the Union have a strong claim to primacy? In what areas do the member states continue to hold sway? And, finally, what lies ahead for the Union's foreign policy?

If the complexities of the Union make it hazardous to render a satisfactory theoretical account of foreign policy, it is at least somewhat easier to describe the formal, institutional matrix of foreign policy. If Kissinger's successors want to speak with the Union, they usually start with the Commission, but quickly realize that they cannot ignore the Council of Ministers, the institution that embodies state sovereignty and national interest. The Commission is endowed with formal competency in some key areas, especially trade, but even here the Council informally plays a strong role in developments. The Council is an institution that is difficult to understand, with a hybrid and changing membership that does not formally initiate policy, and indeed seldom makes any decision. Most agreements reflect a compromise reached by anonymous bureaucrats and diplomats in committees of permanent representatives. The agenda is often set by the Commission, in consultation with the Parliament and, increasingly, under the watchful eye of the Court.

Hence, the Commission proposes, the Parliament mingles, the member states veto, the court judges, but eventually policy is legislated and executed. More importantly, much of this policy has an external dimension. A *communitarian* foreign policy is one that is either initiated or managed predominantly by the Union's institutions rather than the member states. For analytical purposes, it is important to distinguish between two types of communitarian foreign policy. One type is *decisional* in the sense that it results from a conscious decision-making process and is enshrined in treaty law or directive. In this type of policy the external impact is intentional. Examples include the EU Dollar banana ruling (see Chapters 2 and 11), custom agreements with third states (see Chapters 3, 5, 8), and the ACP/Lome Treaties (see Chapters 1 and 8). Such policies might arise primarily within the Union, or as a reaction to external policies. Examples of the latter include the EU opinion on the Helms-Burton Act (see Chapters 2 and 11), the fisheries disputes with Canada, and the EU's policy towards the war in former Yugoslavia (Chapter 7). A second type of policy is *structural*; the external impact of the Union's actions does not arise from law or directive, but results more or less indirectly from "domestic" political and economic processes. Examples of this type of policy include the Common Agricultural Policy (Chapter 14) the liberalization of the internal market (Chapter 11), asylum policy (Chapter 6) and anti-trust legislation. In practice, of course, the two types of policy are often overlapping. For example, the establishment of EMU is both a reaction to external monetary factors and a result of domestic developments; it is enshrined in legislation and directive, but will also greatly influence the international monetary regime.

Although many important areas of foreign policy have been brought under the purview of the Union's supranational institutions, it is important to recognize that the Union itself is the result of series of treaties, and not a constitutional convention as such – even if, arguably, an embryonic constitutional process has been launched.[2] Although the Treaty of Rome and subsequent documents such as the Single European Act certainly set in motion a process of integration, by definition these treaties also enshrine and, indeed, buttress national sovereignty.[3] The treaties underline the point that Europe's constitutional process is highly ambiguous, and follows a very different route from that of the federalist United States of America.

The Union makes foreign policy on the basis of articles 113, 228, 235 of the Treaty on European Union. Article 113 authorizes the Commission to make commercial policy for the Union; Article 228 allows active or reactive economic policy in foreign affairs, e.g. boycotts and embargoes. Article 235 is a safeguard article, under which the institutions can initiate legislation that was initially not foreseen in treaties. As a result of the Maastricht Treaty, a Common Foreign and Security Policy (CFSP) has been proclaimed, yet the practical results of this policy have been a disappointment because the member states have been unable to agree on the scope of the policy, and the retention of a *de facto* veto makes the decision-making process both cumbersome and conflictual.

Prior to the Maastricht Treaty on European Union (1991), the key areas of Union foreign policy were trade and agriculture. The Common Agricultural Policy (CAP), deemed necessary in the 1950s and 1960 but gradually having become more controversial, is an early example of how the common policy of the EU has influenced the international political economy of food (see Chapter 14). The common position of the Union in trade issues, especially in the GATT/WTO, is another prime example of the political involvement of the Union on the world stage. Surprisingly, this is generally considered one of the more successful examples of a common foreign policy, managed primarily by one of the core institutions, the Commission, albeit under the careful eyes of the Council. Can the Union expand the range of policies within the communitarian first pillar? The Union has now developed a common bargaining position mainly in areas of trade, commerce and economic cooperation, while it lacks a convincing stand in sensitive political and security issues such as defence cooperation, peacekeeping and diplomatic relations, which penetrate into the core of national sovereignty. In sum, in economic affairs the Union generally speaks loudly and with one voice. In political affairs, a *sotto voce* Union still struggles to be heard over the din of member states.

The case studies presented in this volume are designed to help students of European studies and international relations to understand the growing role of the EU in world affairs. Part I describes the evolution and contemporary functions of the key foreign policy actors – the Commission, the Court and the WEU – and considers the role of EU foreign policy within Europe's changing constitutional order. Part II discusses the Union's policy with respect to the most important issues of contemporary European international affairs: enlargement to the East, the war in former Yugo-

---

[2] The treaty of Amsterdam enhances this. See the Conclusion in this volume and Chapter 2.
[3] This has also been the principal argument of Milward (1992).

slavia, refugees and citizenship, and the Maghreb. Part III shifts the focus to economic and monetary issues, where the Union hopes to establish a single currency zone by 1999. In Part IV, the impact of the communitarian foreign policy with reference to several key industries and sectors is discussed.

PART I. LAW AND INSTITUTIONS IN THE MAKING OF EU FOREIGN POLICY

In Chapter 1, Patrick Peters argues that the Commission has proved to be a much more hybrid and important source for foreign policy than previously recognized. Several factors help to account for the Commission's increasing significance. Over-crowding within the Commission, weak leadership under President Jacques Santer, and regionalization of the portfolios have compelled the Commission to expand its activities greatly in the past five years. As a result of initiatives undertaken by individual commissioners, the Union has added a number of new foreign policy areas to its agenda. Peters argues that neither traditional functionalist nor foreign policy analysis satisfactorily explains a process that, at least in part, is driven by the internal, bureaucratic dynamics of the Commission itself.

In Chapter 2, Sabrina Tesoka argues that political scientists have neglected the role of the European Court of Justice in Europe's foreign policy. Several decisions of the Court have strengthened the external role of the Commission, and the constitutionalization of the third pillar will only enhance the role of the Court in matters of migration, refugees and justice. As a result of the Maastricht Treaty, the Common Foreign and Security Policy (CFSP) is subject to indirect scrutiny of the court. Moreover, judicial review of the Union's directives, many of which touch directly or indirectly on foreign affairs, is still exerted by the Court. International agreements are subject to judicial review, as are the foreign policy acts of the Council, including those in the second pillar. The association agreements are a further area where the court has maintained jurisdiction.

In Chapter 3, Michael Leigh considers the impact of eastern enlargement for EU institutions. He argues forcefully that the Union is playing a crucial role in the stabilization of Eastern Europe. An important issue in this relationship with the East has been the prospect for membership and the complex interlinkages between the Union and the Eastern countries. Moreover, not only did these countries aspire to become members; they have already implemented a large part of the so-called *acquis communitaire* of the EU. Leigh argues that the prospect of accession provides the EU with additional leverage to ensure that reform in Central and Eastern Europe remains on track, and that the deployment of its power resources in the East has enhanced the role of the Union as an independent actor. Notably, most of the negotiations between the East and the West are pursued at multilateral levels, through collective membership of organizations, or through Union bilateral relations. The establishment of the more important aid programmes on a communitarian platform has enhanced the role of the Union as an actor in Eastern Europe, making the Union perhaps the most important foreign policy actor for these countries.

In Chapter 4, Federiga Bindi argues that third countries (non-member states) as well as multinational corporations have a strong interest in lobbying the EU. She shows that lobbying has expanded greatly in recent years under the impact of the single market. The establishment of Brussels as a key nexus of lobbying activities in itself constitutes powerful evidence of the Union's expanded role in international affairs.

PART II. FOREIGN POLICY IN THE SECOND AND THIRD PILLARS

Pillars II and III refer to the CFSP and Home and Justice Affairs respectively. Perhaps the greatest foreign policy challenge for the Union will be to extend its diplomatic role beyond the economic sphere into these areas, which have traditionally been guarded jealously by the Member States. In Chapter 5, Thomas Grunert addresses the problems and issues arising from the Common Foreign and Security Policy as they pertain to the planned enlargement of the Union. Enlargement has several implications for the CFSP, notably the problem of national veto in an expanded Council. Therefore, enlargement and further elaboration of the CFSP will be mutually reinforcing processes and the Union faces the challenge of incorporating new members while simultaneously enhancing the communitarian dimension of external policy.

In Chapter 6, Sandra Lavenex notes that much of the contemporary debate on Western European asylum policies has concentrated on the exclusionary character of "safe third countries", with less attention being paid to its impact on neighbouring states. She argues that the harmonization of asylum and immigration policy has an important bearing on external relations. In particular, EU policy in these areas has greatly influenced the asylum policies of other European states. The adoption of the "safe third country" rule thus leads to the incorporation of a "wider Europe" into a new system of asylum cooperation, which not only shifts its borders eastwards but also weakens the international commitment to refugee protection.

The war in former Yugoslavia offered the EU an opportunity to expand its influence in world affairs. In Chapter 7 Alan Cafruny traces the history of European involvement, focusing on the interplay of national and supranational involvement. Although the inability of the EU to stop the war resulted in part from institutional limitations, Cafruny argues that failure also resulted from the inability or unwillingness of Europe's leaders to distinguish between aggressor and victim. Although difficult to quantify, Europe's failed policy not only showed that the United States remains a key player in European politics, but also greatly damaged citizen confidence in the Union.

In Chapter 8, Kaisa Lahteenmaki and Christopher Smith argue that the EU has established a very strong presence in the Mediterranean region through its trade and investment policies. Several factors have served to repair the historically troubled relationship between Europe and the Maghreb, foremost among them the growing integration on the basis of market forces and the dominance of European capital. Security relations now also play an important role in the relations between the two regions. The Barcelona conference of 1995 has served to institutionalize Europe's growing power in the Mediterranean region.

PART III. ECONOMIC AND MONETARY INTEGRATION

In Chapter 9, Amy Verdun shows that the tendency towards European monetary integration has become an integral part of external policy. In particular, the attempt to fix exchange rates has reflected the desire of Europe's leaders not only to prevent inflation, but also to augment the monetary power of the EU, particularly in relation to the United States. In Chapter 10, Bernard Winkler addresses political issues resulting from the planned monetary union. The key question, he contends, is whether a "double transfer" of monetary sovereignty will be acceptable and sufficient in the long run. He identifies potential pitfalls for the project of the EMU arising from national economic imbalances, but also opportunities. Price stability might not be achieved, because of lack of political legitimacy to strengthen supranationality, institutional cohesion and social harmony. A precondition for a strong monetary policy is a corresponding common fiscal policy.

PART IV. INTERNATIONAL TRADE AND INDUSTRIAL POLICY

In Chapter 11, Jens Mortensen provides an overview of the Union's developing role in international economic affairs. Given the problems of both EMU and CFSP, the common commercial policy remains the centre-piece of the Union's external policy. Like Patrick Peters (Chapter 1), Mortensen argues that competition among the various directorate generals in the Commission has resulted in additional fields of competence, thereby enhancing the external power of the EU.

The automobile industry remains central to the European economy. Sandrine Labory argues in Chapter 12 that technological advances have produced important structural changes in the industry. Flexible production techniques have greatly altered the approach to efficiency, which has led in turn to a change in the internal structure of firms. As a result of these changes, automobile firms have abandoned the strategy of "national champion" that prevailed in the 1970s and 1980s in favour of a single EU strategy. The shift away from the member-state level has enhanced the international position of Brussels as a venue for lobbying, and strengthened the hand of the EU as a global agent for European automobile manufacturing.

Anthony Smith argues in Chapter 13 that the Energy Charter Treaty (ECT) is a prime example of the collective power of the EU at the world level. The EU has sought to combine energy security with an EU-based foreign investment strategy in the former Soviet Union (FSU). Under the Lubbers plan, designed to strengthen links with the nations of the FSU, the ECT has facilitated a legal framework for investments in Transcontinental Gas. Besides providing opportunities for the member states to diminish dependence on Middle East oil, the ECT has made the EU a dominant force in the trade with the FSU. When fully implemented, the ECT has the potential to establish a strong basis for economic linkages between the EU and FSU.

In Chapter 14, Marjoleine Hennis shows that the Common Agricultural policy (CAP) is experiencing great turbulence under the impact of globalization of agriculture. The CAP not only greatly influences the nature of European farming and food prices, but also strongly influences the level of global food production. The European agricultural sector, with its complex system of subsidies, brings the Union into continuous conflict with its trading partners. Although the CAP represented the earliest successful supranational policy, Hennis suggests that renationalization of the CAP may be possible. Deregulation of the CAP as a result of budgetary pressures and the drive to make European agriculture more internationally competitive have compelled the states to adjust by compensating farmers at the national level for diminishing subsidies from Brussels.

In Chapter 15, Juliette Enser argues that the Commission has been the principal institution responsible for the development of a telecommunications policy. This is an example of a policy that has had both an internal and external effect. Internally, a sector that had been dominated by national monopolies has been transformed by global liberalization. The EU has emerged as a key actor in the trade negotiations within the framework of the World Trade Organization. More importantly for the EU, it was in the telecommunication case that the Commission obtained legal status, after the ECJ decreed that the members states and the Commission held joint responsibility for negotiating the General Agreement on Trade in Services (GATS).

Alan Cafruny and Patrick Peters argue in the Conclusion to this volume that although successive gains have been made in the establishment of a communitarian foreign policy, the implementation of policy occurs within the boundaries of two models – communitarian and intergovernmental. While intergovernmental foreign policy often occurs in areas belonging to the core of sovereignty, most successful European policies are found in the area of communitarian foreign policy. However, while both the Single European Act and the Treaty of Maastricht fostered significant expansion of the Union's foreign policy competency, the Amsterdam Treaty did not bring any new major developments in the communitarian foreign policy.

BIBLIOGRAPHY

Groom, A.R.J. and A. Heraclides (1985). "Integration and Disintegration". In Light, M. and A.R.J. Groom (eds) *International Relations. a Handbook of Current Theory*. London: Pinter.

Hodges, M. (1986). "Integration Theory". In Taylor, T. (ed.) *Approaches and Theory in International relations*. Longman.

Milward, A. (1992). *The European Rescue of the Nation-state*. University of California Press.

Moravcsik, A. (1991). "Negotiating the European Single Act: National Interests and Conventional Statecraft in the European Community". *International Organization 45*, winter.

Moravcsik, A. (1993). "Preferences and Power in the European Community: A Liberal Intergovernmental Approach". *Journal of Common Market Studies 31*.

Taylor, P. (1982). "Intergovernmentalism in the European Communities in the 1970s. Patterns and Perspectives. *International Organization 36*, autumn.

PART ONE

LAW AND INSTITUTIONS IN THE MAKING OF EU FOREIGN POLICY

CHAPTER 1

Dynamic interaction, conflict and policy development in the European Commission
How bureaucratic politics can explain the further development of a Communitarian Commission

Patrick Peters [1]

1.1. INTRODUCTION

The European Commission (CEC) has in the past years enhanced its relative position in the formulation and development of a Common Foreign Policy, and has occupied the foreground on several occasions. The institutionalized position of the CEC in the area of foreign policy is based on several articles in the treaty of Rome and the treaty on European Union,[2] also known as the Maastricht Treaty. With the approval of the European Council and with (the assent of) the European Parliament, the Commission is setting the agenda and developing aspects of a Common Foreign Policy in several areas, and it has progressively expanded its obligations and duties. Although a common foreign policy administered by the European Commission has not developed *de jure*,[3] in several areas a policy has already emerged *de facto,* and decisions are taken by the Commission in related fields of policy. The most obvious examples are the common commercial policy, trade-related policy and the administration of the Agreements with third countries, including Phare, Tacis and the Asian and Mediterranean programmes. This chapter does not argue that the Council is not the most important actor in foreign policy, or that intergovernmentalism is not an important source of foreign policy. It merely argues that the study of the Commission as a foreign policy actor has been underestimated and the dynamics within the Commission has received too little scholarly attention.

The much-discussed 'Common Foreign and Security Policy' (CSFP) is intergovernmental, and still under construction in the Intergovernmental Conference (IGC) that will probably lead to a final document after the Amsterdam European Council of 1997. At present an 'intergovernmental' 'troika' of three foreign ministers is conducting foreign policy in the name of the Council and the Union. No protagonistic role is

[1] The author thanks Federiga Bindi, Christopher Piening, Michael Smith, Glenda Rosenthal, Chris Hill, Alan Cafruny, David Allen and Femi Babarinde for comments on earlier drafts of this chapter.
[2] Arts 113, 228, 235 and 238 of the Treaty on European Union.
[3] Although some provisions for the development of a CSFP were made in the Maastricht Treaty, these provisions fall within the intergovernmental area of the second pillar. The Commission is not considered in either the second or the third pillar.

A. Cafruny and P. Peters (eds.), The Union and the World, 11–33
© 1998 *Kluwer Academic Publishers. Printed in Great Britain.*

officially established for the Commission. However – and this is the main argument of this paper – the Commission is not in the least withheld by the non-existence of a "Communitarian" foreign policy. Instances of foreign policy-making by members of the European Commission are numerous and consistent overall with the role of the Commission within the institutional framework. Communitarian foreign policy initiatives have rapidly increased in number over the past years, predominantly because of the influence and initiatives of dominant individuals in the Commission.

The European Commission that started in January 1995 and will work until 2000 is very different from the Commission that left with the departure of President Delors. The first and most obvious difference is the absence of Jacques Delors, a contemporary hero for Europhiles and the brain and muscles behind the relative success of integrating Europe over the past decade, by proposing the Single European Act (SEA), the Single Market, and European Monetary Union (EMU). The number of Vice-Presidents in the Santer Commission was reduced from six to two, and three new Commissioners from new countries – Austria, Sweden and Finland – were nominated. Moreover some senior Commissioners have left, together with Delors.[4] Many inexperienced new Commissioners were appointed. In the new Santer Commission, with a President that is much less dominating than his predecessor, more space is left for initiative by, and disagreement among, the individual Commissioners.

The European Community/Union has long had considerable disagreement among its dominant institutions – the Council, the Court, the Commission and the Parliament. This has been studied by several scholars. Another dimension has been added with the appointment of the Santer Commission, i.e. the internal disagreements and competition in agenda-setting that affect policy-making. The assumption that the European Commission is acting as a homogeneous actor without internal preferences is unfounded. Even a very superficial research of the speeches of the senior Commissioners and the EP would quickly show the differences between and within the institutions. Differences between member countries, represented in the European Council and the Council of Ministers, are even more broadly exposed but are accepted.

A virtually continuous series of episodes of conflict over the building of the European edifice emerges in all institutions, but disputes within the Commission are the least examined.[5] However, for Santer these conflicts and the lack of coordination of political initiatives of individual Commissioners show the need for a more important role for the President in the appointment of the individual Commissioners in the next Commission. The proposed future cap on the number of Commissioners proposed by the Commission is a result of this, and will be discussed in the IGC. A maximum has been proposed by the CEC of 20 Commissioners, independently of the number of countries. The variety of political priorities in the Commission has caused its policies to be much more extensive. However, the struggle over priorities has not paralysed the Commission; on the contrary, it has helped in expanding the duties and the agenda of the CEC.

---

[4]   Christopherson and Matutes.

[5]   It is clear that conflict and cooperation centre around the three largest members: the UK, Germany and France. Because of domestic uncertainties and lack of policy formation, Italy is normally excluded from the list of main protagonists.

In this chapter it is argued that the European Commission is a source of policy creation itself, mainly because of struggle between individual Commissioners and because of its agenda-setting capabilities. In the execution of day-to-day policy and by proposing initiatives, individual Commissioners and their leading civil servants are making policy; low-level policies that are influencing outcomes of larger policy areas, including the CFSP. The Commission is developing an embryonic foreign policy that can be considered truly "common" or "communitarian" for the EU, because of the supranational character of the Commission. This policy is supplementary to the Council and the officially approved policy of the Union in initiatives, agreements and treaties. This chapter tries to synthesize concepts of the neo-functionalist "spill-over theories" and the "bureaucratic politics theory" arguing that the consequences of internal decision-making on external policies can be independent from the proposed or intended purpose of the institutions as a whole. The policy neutrality of the Commission assumed explicitly by the intergovernmentalists is challenged. This chapter is a first attempt, and nothing more, to analyse dynamics within the Commission, a topic that has dominated the agenda of some journalists but has hardly attracted the attention of foreign policy analysts.[6,7] Several recent occurrences require further attention of the scholarly community.

Formally the Commission is not engaged in formulating external relations and foreign policy in first instance. All "projects" that the Commission undertakes have to be approved and delegated by the Council, sometimes after amendments and changes proposed by the EP. Over the years, the Council has obstructed several proposals for foreign policy development and initiated others; the expansion of the role of the Council in foreign policy has led to a follow-up by the CEC of these policies. Examples are the execution of the ACP treaty and the Tacis and Phare programmes which are now fully implemented by the Commission. Moreover, Commissioners, rather than a delegation of one of the intergovernmental institutions, tend to negotiate in the name of the Union. The Commission handles the bulk of the "management" of external relations as well as the execution (for now) of what is called the common trade policy. This role may diminish if it is formally agreed to continue to pursue the CFSP on intergovernmental terms by the enhanced position of the Secretary-General of the Council or by naming a "Mr PESC".

1.2. THE LEGAL BASIS FOR EXTERNAL RELATIONS, FOREIGN AND COMMERCIAL POLICY

The legal basis for Commission action on the basis of which external relations are maintained and established is the articles 113, 228, 235 and 238 of the Maastricht treaty. Article 113 is developing the so-called commercial policy, the area where the Commission has been most successful as an independent actor. Although the Council eventually decides on agreements, the Commission initiates, negotiates and maintains

---

[6] Further analyses will be given in *The Santer Commission* by Bindi and Peters, to be published in 1998.

[7] An exception is the recent article of Mark Pollack in IO, Vol. 51, No. 1, pp. 99–135.

these arrangements. This is the article that has provided the Commission with the authority to develop much of its agreements and that explains the development of an expanding package of international relationships. Art. 228 allows economic actions, including boycotts, embargoes and other measures, against third states. Art. 235 is a "catch-all" article: in the case that a policy has not been established by the treaty and certain action is deemed necessary for meeting the goals of the treaties, the Commission and the Council then have the authority to develop such a policy. This article is probably the largest infringement of the member states' sovereignty; it is commonly used for various political initiatives. Art. 238 allows the Community to conclude the previously discussed association agreements and other multilateral agreements. Articles 113 and 235 have shaped the foreign policy that is already in place and are mainly used by the Commission. The Commission has recently proposed to extent the independent role of the Commission, by further expanding its role of negotiator.[8]

The development of a communitarian foreign policy will neither start nor end with the conclusion of the IGC; a large bilateral and multilateral set of foreign policy has already developed, precisely because of these initiatives by the European Commission and the administration, based on the articles in the Maastricht treaty. This is the Commission-based foreign policy that will be examined in this chapter. The definition used for describing this particular type of foreign policy development is: "Any formal contact or agreement where the European Union is represented by the Commission and where a third actor or country is involved, and where a political or economic gain is intended by either side, or by groups, individuals or interests belonging to any of negotiating actors".

This definition includes expressions of policy or intended actions of future foreign policy that has not yet been formally established, including failed proposals or as yet unconcluded legislation. The responsibility for these policies should belong predominantly to the CEC.

1.3. TOWARDS A COHERENT THEORY OF COMMON FOREIGN POLICY ANALYSIS

For policy management, and for policy creation on the basis of the above-mentioned articles, the Council still has to give its approval. The Commission is allowed to manage, negotiate and execute relationships in the framework of the commercial and other policies. On a mandate approved by the Council it negotiates external commercial agreements in the WTO, as well as bilateral arrangements, applies EU's trade legislation, and proposes new legislation. Directorates I, IA and IB (Brittan, Van Den Broek and Marin) share responsibilities for external relations and DG VIII (Deus Pinheiro) is responsible for the relations with the Lome Convention and some specific development programs.[9] Important international trade agreements are adopted by the Council and require the assent of the European Parliament. Association agreements need the assent of the EP.

---

[8] *Financial Times*, "Brussels strives to call the tune on trade", 12 March 1997.
[9] http://Europea.eu.int/en/eupol/exrel.html

Common European Foreign Policy analysis is not a new area. Many scholars, including Ginsberg (1989), Hill (1983, 1996) and Risse-Kappen (1995) have studied the topic from different perspectives. While Ginsberg is providing an overview of foreign policy actions as an interaction between sovereign third states and the EC or sovereign third states and the EU, and while Hill examines foreign policy as the result of a bargaining process of the (dominant) states within the Union, Risse-Kappen sees foreign policy mainly as the EU influencing US foreign policy. Ginsberg (1989, p. 1) argues that foreign policy in the EC is a process of integrating policies and actions of the member states towards the outside world. Examining a total of 480 joint actions, he argues that bureaucratic politics is inherently dependent on élite actors. Ginsberg argues that although the Commission may achieve some independence, the eventual outcome of any policy rests on final approval or obstruction by these intergovernmental actors. While the present author largely agrees with this argument, the emphasis is different in this chapter. It being agreed that most actions can be overruled or obstructed, this still leaves space for analyses in the field of maintenance of diplomatic relations and on the matters of agenda-setting and implementation (Ginsberg 1989, p. 18). Hill and Nuttall, on the other hand, argue that the Commission has not yet won its struggle for legitimacy (Hill 1996; Nuttall 1996). While, according to Nuttall, the Commission has successfully participated in obtaining legitimacy as an independent partner, the Commission remains a unitary actor. Moreover, while legitimized, the Commission decided to keep a low profile, thereby obeying its role as subordinated actor. Nuttall (1996, p. 145) argues that '...the debate on the appointment of Mr Santer did not turn on the Commission position as a foreign policy actor...'. However, he does not make a distinction between sorts of actions, and the levels of involvement of the Commission. He also plays down the role of the European Parliament in the legitimization of the EC. Rather, the confrontations of the CEC and the EP, more than anything else, have showed that the CEC is considered a serious and occasionally an independent actor. This has been especially clear in the recent BSE affair.[10] The near-punishment of Commissioner Fischler and the rescheduling of portfolios in the BSE case have strengthened both democratic control by the Parliament and the role (and responsibility) of the Commission as an independent actor. Although the Parliament still cannot sack individual Commissioners, it has legitimized the Commission on several occasions. This is an aspect that is new in the Santer Commission, because of the parallel legislative periods of both institutions, which were introduced in 1995. It was neither up to the Council nor up to the individual member states to question this "democratic" procedure. Although an individual Commissioner was damaged, the whole Commission and the EP have reaffirmed their dualistic role and it has been established that both institutions have their own obligations and leverage over the agenda.

Risse-Kappen (1995) hardly mentions the EC communitarian foreign policy in his empirical work, but this is mainly caused by the area choice in his analyses. Risse-Kappen examines the European influence on US foreign policy: the EC as an institutional actor is hardly discussed. He argues, in a traditional neo-realist fashion, that the

---

[10] See *European Voice*, 27 February 1997 for a good analysis.

EC has not been a dominant player. He does argue that more research has to be done on the EU as an international actor, but does not identify the nature of that research agenda (Risse-Kappen 1995, p. 215). He argues that if EU member states have developed a foreign policy, that foreign policy is predominantly a member state-based policy and, for the case studies examined by him, this is true. So if there is any influence on world politics, and in this case on US foreign policy, it is still of the state at the member state level (ibid.). The principal argument of Risse-Kappen is that states are still the dominant actors in the development of foreign policy, but thereby merely influence the United States. The main criticism here is that he does not leave any space for an independent role of the European countries collectively, let alone of independent institutions or non-state actors. Many other explanations, liberal intergovernmentalism and the Keohane/Hoffman analysis of institutional change fail to address the same issue by examining dynamics only within and between state actors. The unitary foreign policy-maker is still an undisputed assumption in most contemporary FPA theory.

1.4. THE BUREAUCRATIC POLITICS MODEL

How can competition among, and initiatives emerging from, EC Commissioners be explained? The "Bureaucratic Politics" model has long been a tool to analyse the politics within organizations. Allison (1971) used this model to explain how dissident behaviour within the US administration, caused by conflicting interest of individuals and groups with several institutions of this administration, was leading to an outcome. He applied this to the cases of the Cuba Crises and the Korea war, two important cases of foreign policy analyses in the USA (ibid., p. 145). While examining the strength of this theoretical framework, an attempt will be made to apply it to the EU.

Allison argues that the basic unit of analyses is "governmental action as political resultant". A resultant is defined not as a solution to a problem, but rather as the outcome of conflict and compromise and confusion of officials with diverse interests and unequal influence (ibid., pp. 162–3). Moreover, it is political in the sense that the activity from which decisions and actions emerge is best characterized as bargaining along regularized channels between individual members of a government (or in this case of a polity – the CEC).

Any official action of a polity, in this case the Commission, includes the policy that has been developed on the initiative of interests, groups within administrations or by administrations opposing the other sources of power. In the analyses of the EU/CEC policy a distinction will be made between different sorts of actions of the EU members and groups, which differs slightly from Allison's analyses.[11] In the study of the EU, actions are to be categorized as:
1. Formal actions that reflect a combination of the preferences and relative influence of central players. Included in this group of actions are policies that the Commis-

---

[11] This is done to make the analyses possible in the case of the European Union, in which actors are operating in a different setting to the American institutions.

sion is required to do by order (of the Council) or treaty.
2. Formal actions that reflect influence of a subset of players (personal priorities and interest groups).[12]
3. Individual policy actions that translate into governmental policy actions.[13]

1.5. THE ORGANIZING CONCEPTS

The bureaucratic politics model has been used to analyse foreign policy since the end of the 1960s. The model tries to explain how opposing forces within an administration compete for an uncertain outcome. The realist "unitarian" or billiard-ball model analysis of policy units is set aside, and space is left for analysing dynamics within organizations. The outcome of this process with many actors bargaining for a favourable outcome can be compared with initial statements and priorities. The preferences of the EU are not merely the preferences of the dominant actors as argued by the liberal intergovernmentalists; rather there is a hybrid process of the three types of actions mentioned above.

Important questions to be asked by the scholar of CFP analyses (Allison 1971, p. 166) are:
1. Who plays?
2. Who has which priorities in policy-making?
3. What determines each player's relative influence?
4. How does the player combine stands, influence and moves to yield governmental decisions and actions?

Hence one must assess what players in the Commission are active in foreign policy development, what their agenda is, and how their personal agenda combines with other interests. One must also assess their formal standing and their influence on the agendas of other players. Examples of policy outcomes that will be examined here are all part of the common foreign policy of the Commission, and include:
1. The common commercial policy/the WTO negotiations.
2. The policy towards Eastern Europe.
3. The policy towards Latin America
4. The policy towards the Mediterranean
5. The policy towards Asia.
6. The policy towards the ACP/Lome Countries.

The policies mentioned here will not be discussed at length: only the relative change in priority or agenda-setting will be discussed. Moreover, the role of the foreign affairs Commissioners will be examined to the extent that they were responsible for changes in the priorities as perceived by the Commission.[14]

---

[12] This group includes actions that reflect the interests of the Commission as opposed to the EP or Council.
[13] This group of actions includes personal actions, reflecting the agenda of individual Commissioners, opposing each other.
[14] For an extensive description of foreign policy changes of the European Commission, see Peters and Bindi 1998.

1.5.1. Who plays: the actors

As argued above, the initiatives of Commissioners and most forms of interaction between Commissioners are extremely important for the formation of foreign policy. Three issues in particular determine the intensity of the relationship:

1. The leverage of the Commissioner over the overall agenda of the European Commission and the attention of the Commission to the portfolio of the Commissioner.[15] The Santer Commission, especially Pinheiro and Van Den Broek, are suffering from the relative saturation of their geographic areas. The EU's presence in the world[16] programme benefits areas other than the EU's traditional foreign policy areas, namely the ACP and Eastern Europe. Also Kinnock (TENs) and Thibault are benefiting from increased formal interest in their agenda.[17]
2. The interest of the Commissioner in developing the relationship with the geographic or functional area of his responsibility.[18] This has also to do with the perseverance of the Commissioner. Especially, the rise of the Trade Commissioner Brittan and the Commissioner with responsibility for competition placed their agenda on a higher standing.
3. The bargaining process with the appointment of the Commissioners: why Commissioners are appointed in a particular position, with a particular port- folio.

1.5.2. Who are the main actors in foreign policy?

The main actors in the Commission are the Commissioners and their staff, the *Cabinet*, which are mainly political nominees. A civil service that is relatively small compared to the national administration supports the Commissioners.[19] During the negotiations prior to the appointment of the Santer Commission a functional and geographic division was made between the Commissioners. The most important actors are the Commissioners involved in foreign policy. In the 1995–2000 Commission the members that are involved in policy-making are as follows.

1. Jacques Santer, President of the Commission since 1995 and former Prime Minister of Luxembourg.
2. Sir Leon Brittan, the senior British member (born 1939) and Vice-President since 1989. He has been a member of the British Conservative Party since 1974 and was

---

[15] This is mainly the relative position of the named Commissioner and his level of persuasion as to the agenda-setting.

[16] A priority in "the 1997 work program of the Commission". See Work Program 1997, CEC, Luxembourg.

[17] The TENs (Trans European Networks) have been a recurrent theme of interest, culminating at the Florence Summit and leaning heavily towards Kinnock's transport sector. The European Monetary Union is one of the dominant agenda points of the Council.

[18] This is the level to which the Commissioners can make the case that on issues that are touch both the functional and the geographical description of the Commission, the named Commissioner is dominant. See *Financial Times*, 4 November 1996, "Brittan and the East".

[19] The Commission has 17,000 employees. Excluding the B (assistants), C (secretaries) D (clerks) and L grades (translators), some 4,000 A level (academic) "functionaries" are part of the policy execution.

minister during most of the 1980s, including the portfolios of trade and home affairs.

3. Manuel Marin, a prominent member of the Spanish socialist party who has been a Vice-President of the European Commission since 1986.
4. Hans Van Den Broek, Christian Democrat and long-time foreign minister of the Netherlands. He succeeded Andriessen in 1993 in Delors III, but has not been appointed Vice-President. Joao de Deus Pinheiro, professor and Portuguese minister of foreign affairs.
5. Emma Bonino, Italian radical/social-liberal, a politician and human rights activist.

Moreover, a relatively important actor is the European Parliament. In the European Parliament the most important members are the Chairmen of the Committee on External Economic affairs (REX), Willie de Klerk, and the Committee on Foreign Affairs, Security and Defence Policy, Abel Matutes of Spain. Other important committees are the delegations to countries that have special priorities for the EU (applicant countries and large trading partners).

1.5.3. What determines each player's standpoint and relative influence?

The Maastricht Treaty greatly expanded the area that is open for foreign policy, even while most of this is intergovernmental. In the Treaty, several foreign affairs articles were added. Title V is the title where most arrangements provide for the development of a foreign policy. In what context did this change take place?

Most importantly, the Maastricht Treaty was heavily influenced by the occurrences in Eastern Europe and the fall of the Berlin Wall. The unification of Germany and the collapse of the "diplomatic" Berlin Wall have influenced greatly the set-up of this Treaty. Title V, article J states simply that: "...a common foreign and security policy is hereby established". Two points must be made here: firstly, the common foreign and security policy is mainly a matter for the Presidency of the Council, which rotates every six months; secondly, the Treaty describes no explicit role for the Commission. Notwithstanding the absence of the Commission in the Treaty's articles, the Commission got even more involved after the signing of the Maastricht Treaty. The "need" for a more active involvement of Europe in day-to-day policy and in the construction of a new order forced a proactive role on the Commission. Moreover, since the second Delors Commission, several other changes have occurred, and this has changed the dynamics within the Commission in the making of foreign policy.

1. *The number of Commissioners involved* in external relations has increased. Whereas Andriesen was powerful in Delors II, in Delors III his position was split between two Commissioners: Vice-President Brittan for the external economic policy and Commisioner Van den Broek for the external political policy. Moreover, Vice-President Marin became responsible for economic relations with Asia and Latin America, traditionally areas of the world ignored by the EU. Marin also became responsible for the institutional arrangements with the APC countries. At this time DG1A was created, and headed by Van den Broek. The diplomatic service of the European Commission, which established a strong institutionalized pres-

sure group within the EU, was taken seriously.

2. *More expansion along geographic lines.* In Santer I a geographic division was made, as the solely functional approach did not suffice. A total of four Commissioners was appointed in the area of foreign policy and was given geographic areas of concentration: Van Den Broek, Eastern Europe; Marin, the Mediterranean, the Middle East, Latin America and some of Asia. Sir Leon Brittan obtained the important trading partners –Japan, North America, and the Chinas – and Joao de Deus Pinheiro the Lome pact and the ACP countries. This division greatly enhanced the status of some Commissioners and some areas, and has led to a large extent to the competition mentioned above. Moreover, instead of two Commissioners making policy, four were now actively elaborating the policy and defending their agenda.

3. *Vice-presidents.* Importantly, in the Santer Commission the number of Vice-Presidents was diminished. Brittan and Marin were the only two that remained Vice-President. A real start was made with "ranking" seniority in the CEC. Van Den Broek and Pinheiro were not nominated Vice-Presidents when they replaced their countrymen in Delors III and Bonino was clearly the junior Commissioner, only nominated in Santer and second to Monti. No longer was it common to have all the large countries nominate at least one Vice-President and for some additional and exceptional heavyweights among the smaller countries' Commissioners to be nominated to the same rank.[20] Although the power and duties of Vice-Presidents were limited, the prestige remained important. It was clear that Marin and Brittan, being the Commissioners longest in service, together with Bangeman and Van Miert, had obtained somewhat more clout than the others. The nomination of senior and Junior Commissioners has become also an important issue with the expected further enlargement.

4. *Involvement of the President.* Whereas Delors himself did not really get involved in the policy coordination of external affairs, Santer became responsible for the development of the CFSP with Van den Broek. The coordination of foreign policy had become a Presidential affair in the Commission, thereby adding leverage over the agenda. A novelty was that Santer was getting involved as President with the development of a structure that could be expanded, but that formally did not belong to the agenda of the Commission. Notwithstanding the fact that CFSP was to be intergovernmental, the Commission was to have an executive position in the second intergovernmental pillar of the Maastricht Treaty.

5. Joao de Deus Pinheiro got responsibility for the ACP countries. This indicated two things: the importance of this area and the separation of this area from the overall political external policy: The ACP become high policy, and no longer a routine agenda point or obligation.

---

[20] Only Andriessen, Christopherson and Van Miert managed to become Vice-President. During the negotiations, Van Miert and Bangeman lost out against Brittan and Marin.

Table 1.1 Commissioners active in external policy

Commission	Delors II	Delors III	Santer
Delors	President	President	–
Santer	–	–	President, Common Foreign and Security Policy
Andriessen	External relations[21] and cooperation with other European countries	–	–
Marin	Fisheries	Cooperation and development. ECHO	Mediterranean, Middle East, Latin America, Asia
Matutes	Latin America and Asia	Energy, transport	–
Brittan	Competition	External economic affairs	North America, Asia, OECD, WTO
Deus Pinheiro	–	Relations with the European Parliament	ACP/Lome
Van den Broek	–	External political relations	Eastern Europe Common foreign and security policy
Bonino	–	–	ECHO[22]

Sources: Dinan 1994, p. 210; European Commission, 1995a, pp. 10–50.

Moreover, Bonino obtained the incoherent but important portfolio of ECHO and Fisheries, but was clearly not in the core group of foreign affairs Commissioners. Bangeman was included in foreign affairs in cases where industrial policy was involved; Van Miert only where anti-trust was considered.

1.6. WHY THE EXPANSION OF FOREIGN AFFAIRS IN THE COMMISSION?

Clearly Europe had to develop its position in the world; this was probably the single most important reason for the expansion of the FP agenda. On one hand, Europe was inward-looking and the successful Presidency of the Delors Commissions had not changed that. The large projects undertaken under the Delors Commission had to do with the dynamics within the internal Community, not with areas outside. The SEA, Europe 1992, Maastricht and the successful enlargement to include Spain and Portugal were important goals in the 1980s, as well as a hindrance to the development of an active foreign policy. Moreover, the Cold War prevented Europe from looking beyond the limits of the Atlantic alliance.

On the other hand, the geopolitics had shifted and Europe was able to develop a policy that could be different, thereby even opposing US policy. It was clear that the end of the cold war brought up several issues in which differences of opinion existed.

---

[21] Andriessen was the only Commissioner in Delors II in charge of foreign policy (Dinan 1994, Table 7.3, p. 210).
[22] ECHO is the European Office for Humanitarian Aid.

Several projects became important that led to direct confrontation with the interests of the USA, the main ones being as follows.

1. *Trade.* the successful WTO agreement in Marrakesh had established a new paradigm in trade. To a large extent the successful application of articles 110 and 113 in the treaty of Rome and the development of the common commercial policy had caused this round to have a positive outcome. The WTO developed out of this into a dynamic and fully-fledged organization, unlike the predecessor GATT. Firstly, this was symbolized by the ever-increasing membership of this organization; secondly by the relatively successful role played by the EU as negotiator for the twelve countries. These negotiations boosted not only the role of the EU, but also that of Leon Brittan, the Commissioner in charge and chief negotiator for the Commission.

2. *The enlargement to the East* became a more important issue. Not only was the EU the largest donor[23] and investor, but geopolitical considerations made the EU an important actor. Again Europe was facing the D-mark dilemma. If no policy could be developed along communitarian lines in this area, Germany alone would develop a policy. The development of the East and the issue of enlargement were considered so important that this merited the nomination of a single Commissioner. The East therefore was the first area where the community was allowed to coordinate its efforts on a communitarian basis. The European Council took tentative first steps in common foreign policy by requesting the Commission to define the conditions and procedures for joint action with regard to Central and Eastern Europe, the Middle East, South Africa, former Yugoslavia and Russia (Duff and Pinder 1994, p. 96).

3. The ACP/Lome treaty would be up for renewal and it was clear that the present privileged relation was politically and ideologically unsustainable. The Lome treaty, with all its merits, had never made these countries independent and, with the signing of the Uruguay round, no further exemptions could be explained for another regional pact. Moreover, the French power over this pact, which mainly benefited former French colonial interests, was diluted by enlargements. The Lome treaty goes back a long time, and the present treaty was signed for 25 years in 1975. It concerns countries, predominantly in Africa, that neither seized the opportunities of preferential access to European market nor experienced rapid growth by modernization and industrialization. A combination of mismanagement and a culture of dependency made these countries as fragile as they were in the 1960s. At the same time, other areas that suffered from similar economic backwardness (South East Asia) and political distress (Latin America) managed to improve their lot. France as the protector had in the meantime lost considerable clout. Whereas in the 1960s it could use the EC as an instrument of its own development policy, it was unable to do so in the 1990s. New former colonial countries had entered the community (Spain, Portugal, Denmark and the UK) that had very different views on trade as well as different regional priorities.

4. *Migration.* The migration from North Africa and near Asia, together with renewed

---

[23] This budget is larger than the EBRD budget of 1996.

energy security concerns, had put the Mediterranean on the agenda again. Migration has, especially in the early 1990s, dominated the agenda of many countries. This was partly caused by the consequences of the contemporary rise of unemployment and right-wing parties. This occurred in combination with the mutual anxiety of the Southern members of the EU as well as their non-member neighbours in the Mediterranean. The likely enlargement to the East was not the priority for either group, and the development of a Mediterranean policy became a prominent policy issue in 1992 and 1993. This culminated in a pressure for at least an equal treatment of the Mediterranean to the east.

5. *'Europe, the third power' syndrome.* Pressure was put on Europe to act on occasions when it was clearly unprepared, both politically and institutionally. Bosnia, the trade negotiations in the WTO, the Gulf War, and the more general issue of overall post-war security demanded a stronger presence of Europe. Additional Commissioners became involved with foreign policy because of a greater demand for policy; Europe was expected to play its part and could no longer hide behind the Atlantic alliance.

6. *Jobs and underemployment.* Although a minor institutional arrangement, the enlargement brought another three Commissioners into an already fragmented Commission. What jobs would they be given? the negotiations prior to the accession made it clear that the new countries required serious positions, and Austria succeeded in obtaining the important post of agriculture. Sweden and Finland settled for relatively unimportant positions.[24] However, this brought the issue of reform of the number of Commissioners on to the agenda of the IGC, and for the moment the increase in Commissioners merely let to the division of some portfolios. It is clear that the right of all countries to send their representatives to the Commission could not be sustained in a Union with 25 members. However, the delicate nature of this matter excludes a rational outcome in these areas, if not negotiated in the framework of a larger package deal.[25]

7. *The rise of Asia* as an emerging trade-block made that Europe had to pay attention to this area, whereas it was convenient to ignore it until the end of the Cold War. The liberalization or modernization of Asia, and the rapid growth of China in particular, meant that this was no longer possible. Moreover, it was clear that the United States, freed by the collapse of the Berlin Wall of its security concern, was gradually shifting its attention to the Pacific. Europe had to develop some strategy for this area, especially under pressure of German business and British politics.

Several of these issues that were confronting the EU at the same time led to the strengthening of foreign policy in the agenda. Some portfolios were greatly enhanced and it was clear that this was the area for ambitious politicians, because of the relative gains that could be achieved.

---

[24] Although the Finish Commissioner Liikannen has proved to be extremely effective in the transparency chapter of the IGC and in the reform of the personnel status.

[25] The preliminary results of the negotiations in the IGC show no significant alterations of this policy.

1.7. How do actors try to enhance their positions in the competition for initiatives in foreign affairs?

Since the gradual enhancement of the Commission position in foreign policy and the enhancement of the EU's strategic role in the world, internal agendas and priorities within the Commission have caused some regions to be prioritized over others. There was a gap between desired and allowed policy, and the Commission had developed the policy because of the impossibility of the Council managing day-to-day relations in trade and commercial policy. Tools of the development of these commercial policies include custom unions, economic assistance, trade policy (art 113), development aid and humanitarian action. Hence, the CFP will not only develop because of the negotiations in the IGC: there is a spill-over effect that is further enhancing the role of the Commission in the development of the common foreign policy, i.e. the maintenance of multilateral and bilateral agreements.

Still, some actors and some departments of the Commission are benefiting more from this increasing protagonism than others. The rise in stature of Brittan and Marin is inherently linked with the rise of Asia, Latin America and the Mediterranean on the external agenda at the expensive of the Lome countries and Eastern Europe. The failure of Van den Broek and Deus Pinheiro to emerge can be seen as a consequence of that selective decline.[26]

When studying the Commission it becomes clear that the Commissioners themselves are more politicians then executives and have a past, and often a future, in their own parties and in their home countries. This is true for at least three of the foreign affairs Commissioners. Van Den Broek is by far one of the most popular members of his Dutch Christian Democratic party, and this could mean being called back to the Netherlands to become party leader, vice-prime minister or premier in a future coalition. Marin, together with Solana and Maragall, belongs to a small group of socialists that are still active politicians after the change in government, and that could take ministerial positions in the case of a return of the socialists to power. Moreover, at the end of the Santer Commission he will still be only 50 years old, after serving 13 years in Brussels. The same goes, to a lesser extent, for Joao de Deus Pinheiro, who has been a long-term minister in Portugal, and is only 52. Although it is unlikely that most of the agenda will be driven by future job opportunities, it is also unlikely that these people consider this their last job and behave in a neutral manner regarding their home countries' politics and leadership opportunities.

1.8. The actors, their standpoints and the development of a common foreign policy

Foreign policy is not a zero-sum game. Hence, there is no limit on the expansion of foreign policy. For the European Union foreign policy is a relatively new, underde-

---

[26]   For analyses of the rise of individual Commissioners, see listed articles in the *Financial Times*, the *Economist* and the *European Voice*.

veloped and expanding area. Much can be gained overall for the Union, but particular interests have their time-frame and their own agenda. Moreover, within the administration, diverging groups of "functionaries" and Commissioners have their own ambitions and agendas that can sometimes be compatible with each other. Henceforth, continuous realignments will take place within the Commission. What are the agendas and the interests of the dominant forces?

1.8.1. Sir Leon Brittan

Since Delors III and throughout Santer, friction has occurred between Brittan and the rest of the Commission. Brittan has proved to be one of the stronger and more successful Commissioners, and has dominated the agenda in areas that are not directly included in his portfolio. Moreover, a strategist, but not a team player, Sir Leon has not always dealt with matters diplomatically. His open scepticism towards the entry of Poland into the EU not only enhances his own agenda, it also creates antagonism with Van Den Broek, Kohl and Germany.[27] His criticism of Chirac in the Middle East has unnecessarily created a stressed working relation with France. This is, of course, is admired in the UK.[28] The opposition of Sir Leon Brittan (and, for that matter, Commissioner Kinnock) to the measures for the stability pact have worked, but at the same time have damaged the position of Brittan in the Commission.[29] He managed successfully to oppose waste management projects that belong to the portfolio of Bjerregard, herself one of the weaker Commissioners, and the deadline for liberalization of Spanish Telecom, thereby conflicting with Van Miert. Other recent examples of interference outside his portfolio made Brittan clash with Van Den Broek and Papoutsis. Leon Brittan has extended his own work field, and was desperately needed by the Commission, especially before the Labour victory, as he was the only Commissioner that was still on speaking terms with the Conservative government (until May 1997) and with the Conservative Party (after May, 1997).

The European Commission agenda has created new areas of attention. Never has Europe had such an extended set of relationships with the rest of the world as at the beginning of 1997. These new relationships included Asia, Latin America and the Mediterranean.

The commercial and trade policy role has been a good example. Sir Leon Brittan's role in the trade negotiations has been a success, and it greatly enhanced his standing in the eyes of both the public and the EU.[30] His second success has been in establishing relationships with Asia. Whereas Asia was never previously on the agenda of Europe, over the past two years it had emerged and required a much larger institutional and diplomatic attention. This culminated in a meeting in March 1996 in

---

[27] *Financial Times*, 26 November 1996
[28] *Financial Times*, 22 November 1996
[29] *Financial Times*, 20 October 1996.
[30] For a good "day-to-day" description of the negotiations in the Uruguay round, see Croome 1995.

Bangkok.[31] Bringing Asia on to the agenda was important for Europe as well as for Sir Leon himself. Especially in the UK, the importance of Asia had become dominant in the ideological discussion on the direction of world trade. Foreign investment by, and trade with, this continent is on the rise, and mainly through Hong Kong, Asia and China, the continent became an important political issue on the British agenda from 1995 onwards as the hand-over to China of Hong Kong was imminent.

Moreover, the US had virtually monopolized the policies of the West towards Asia. The lack of attention of Europe was commercially unmerited and dangerous in a post-Cold War setting. Germany and other EU countries have seen their companies investing heavily in this area, and national governments and the EU have had to catch up in order to place Asia on their political agenda at the same level as it was on the business agenda. The EU eventually did so, and an ever-expanding bilateral agenda emerged from 1995 onwards. Trade and diplomatic missions to China,[32] Japan,[33] Korea[34] and other countries followed, headed by Sir Leon. Several issues emerged that made Asia more important for the EU. Trade-related issues as anti-dumping, intellectual property rights, investment, protectionism, aid and commercial deficits all raised the Asia agenda to the top of the list.

This emphasis on Asia is new to the Commission, and lessened the importance of other topics and areas. It fits well with the UK/US concept of responsibilities of government, that politicians should include business interests in their agenda, thereby following the agenda of strategic traders. Hence, China and the rest of Asia have become a new policy priority for the EU, and on a communitarian basis. The EU was at the same time promoting the entrance of China into the WTO, against the will of the US. Bilateral relations of the latter with China have declined after the insistence that institutional relations be set up with APEC and ASEAN.[35] Moreover, China uses contacts with the EU to ease US pressure on its human rights record and on its nuclear exports programme.

Another relatively successful project has been the new "Transatlantic Agenda". This agenda was set up to enhance mutual understanding and revitalization of the Atlantic alliance. After the EU–US summit directly following the European Council in Madrid, this document renewed the relationship of the EU with the US. Although it is in itself a vague document, offspring documents include a customs agreement with the US that was signed in November 1996.[36] Moreover, the Atlantic alliance is likely to remain the dominant concern for many years to come, because of the sheer size of the bilateral relations. Again, this area is in the portfolio of Sir Leon Brittan.

---

[31] For a short report on this meeting see http://www.asean.or.id/world/asempr1.htm, "The chairman's statement of the Asia-Europe meeting in Bangkok", 2 March 1996.

[32] In November 1996. See *European Voice*, 6 November.

[33] *European Voice*, 30 September 1996.

[34] Several agreements were signed in October 1996. *European Voice*, 6 November 1996

[35] See *European Voice*, "EU injects new dynamism into Asian Relations", 30 January–5 February 1997.

[36] This document is called "Agreement between the EC and the USA on customs cooperation and mutual assistance in customs matters". http://www.eurunion.org/partner/nta1296.htm

1.8.2. Vice-President Marin

Spanish Commissioner Marin has had his own major conference on the Mediterranean, similar to the one Sir Leon Brittan had on Asia, which has lead to a series of successive agreements. The Barcelona declaration on 28 November 1996 has led to a series of customs unions in the area, including those with Egypt,[37] Jordan, Lebanon, Turkey, Algeria, Tunisia, Israel and the Palestinian Authority.[38] The Barcelona Declaration emphasizes further cooperation and an equal amount of money to be spent in the future on this area as is spent now on projects for the East.[39] This emergence of this region on to the agenda can be explained both as a personal effort of Marin and as compensation towards the Southern countries for the "excessive" interest in Eastern Europe in the early 1990s. Eastern Europe, an area of foremost importance for Germany, but clearly competing with the interest of the South, became a reason for discontent among Southern members during most of the 1990s. As argued by Lahteenmaki and Smith in Chapter 8 of this volume, only in 1995 did this become a mature and developed relationship.

Similar success was achieved in another areas: in Latin America, agreements were signed with Mexico, the MERCOSUR (the trade bloc of Argentina, Brazil, Uruguay and Paraguay) and Chile. In 1996 a DG1B was set up to give administrative back-up and to provide departmental coordination[40] to Marin. Thereby the latter obtained similar status to Van Den Broek (DG1A) and Brittan (DG1). Marin clearly managed to achieve several successes with multilateral conference and cooperation agreements that enhance his portfolio and his leverage over the Commission's agenda and budget. Besides matters of commerce and trade, non-APC aid is also included in his portfolio.

1.8.3. Commissioner Van Den Broek

Since his nomination in Delors III, Van Den Broek has fought an uphill battle. He had to threaten resignation when Brittan and Marin opposed the formation of DG1A, his "brainchild", and only with the support of Delors was this opposition overruled and the foreign politics ministry created. His attempt to join the President at important meetings, as a true minister of foreign affairs, failed and no longer does he attempt to achieve this status.[41] At present President Santer represents the Commission alone or accompanied by the Presidency of the European Council or with members of the (intergovernmental) Troika. Although Van Den Broek obtained Eastern Europe as his area, which he asked for when re-appointed in the Santer Commission, it turned out to be a priority of yesterday. De Jonquieres argued that the enlargement to the East has been postponed several times now, and it seems unlikely that Poland and the Czech

---

[37] Egypt's custom union is still to be signed (in the second half of 1997).
[38] See the report on implementation of the Commission's work programme for 1996, 16 Oct 1996.
[39] Barcelona Declaration, 27–28 November 1995.
[40] http://europa.eu.int/en/comm/dg1b/mission.htm
[41] The Economist, 6 March 1993.

Republic will enter before 2003.[42] This has been one of the key programmes in Van Den Broek's agenda. In this context, Brittan was happy to explain that too much attention has been paid to the date of enlargement and not enough to the economic and institutional changes that it would require: a clear criticism on how Van Den Broek's agenda, going towards enlargement, took too little account of the economic conditions of the future member states. At the same time Van Den Broek's DG had agreements signed with Slovenia, Macedonia, Belarus, Ukraine, Uzbekistan and Armenia. However, the amount of money spend on the East is to be matched by the amount of money spend on the Mediterranean by 1998.

Van Den Broek on several occasions has attempted to enlarge the extent of his mandate. In May 1996 diplomats rebuked him for suggesting that the EU could take over peacekeeping in Bosnia. The Dutch Commissioner argued in a speech in late January 1997 that the three large member countries should take a larger role in foreign policy-making.[43] This led directly to opposition from politicians of other smaller countries and within the Commission. By early spring 1997 it was already clear that the nomination of a foreign policy representative would not be in the form of an enhanced Commissioner. Rather it would be bureaucrat, a high representative or an upgraded position for the secretary-general to the Council and working within the intergovernmental framework of the second pillar. In the draft presented by the Irish Presidency the Council's role in the CFSP would be highlighted.[44] If a "Monsieur PESC" other than Van Den Broek were named after the IGC, the setback for the Commission in foreign policy would affect him most, as all economic external relations would be excluded from the mandate.

1.8.4. Commissioner Deus Pinheiro

Prof. Deus Pinheiro's role is to reform the long relationship that Europe has had with the ACP countries. Deus Pinheiro, a junior Commissioner with ambition, has been only partially successful, as the pressure from countries and Commissioners is coming from both sides. Firstly within the Union, several countries would like to lower the status of the Lome treaty to the "normal" level of other regions. The Lome conventions date back to the beginning of the community. As the results of the successive Lome treaties have been extremely meagre, many EU member countries suffer from "donor fatigue". Countries have had enough of paying for "privileged" countries that no longer manage to attract attention or pity (since the end of the cold war) and have underperformed since the beginning. Secondly, Latin America and Asia have consistently been able to outperform the ACP countries, who suffer from mismanagement and political experimentalism. The results of the Treaty are not enough to continue within the present framework.[45] Whereas it is the mission of Marin, Van Den Broek and Brittan to expand foreign relations, it is the mission of Deus Pinheiro to shrink or

---

[42] *Financial Times*, 3 February 1997.

[43] NRC Handelsblad, 26 January 1997, *European Voice*, 30 January 1997.

[44] Draft treaty proposal of the Irish Presidency, http://www.europe.org

[45] *Economist*, "Wanted: some African Tigers", 30 November 1996.

rationalize the relationship. He argues in his "Green Paper" that the post-colonial period has finished, implicitly arguing that financial liabilities can no longer be claimed by former colonies. 2000 might greatly change the ACP–EU relationship, and Pinheiro is doing so by gradually cutting embassies, aid, and projects.[46] Deus Pinheiro is already "regionalizing" many offices, and eight of them have been downgraded.[47] The Green Paper produced by DG8, on relations between the European Union and the ACP countries is "*Una Crónica de una Muerte Anunciada*" stating *inter alia* that priorities have changed and the EU is rationalizing itself, under the pressure of high unemployment and the enlargement to the East. The Commission is making its priorities clear: a likely outcome of cuts and rationalization is to follow. Whatever the details of the outcome, the consequences are clear. The Commission will reshape its development cooperation on the basis of the Green Paper and will function much more in a responsive and less in an ideological way. Pinheiro's initiative will greatly affect funds that will be available to other areas of policy, and will mainly focus on the emerging areas of Marin, like the project Alfa, and Brittan's Asia projects.

1.9. THE BUDGET AND THE PEOPLE: PRIORITIES IN FOREIGN POLICY

Europe is spending a total of 5.79 billion ECUs a year (an ECU is about 20 per cent more than a dollar) on programmes related to "foreign action". The bulk of this money goes to direct assistance programmes in multilateral agreements. The ACP is still excluded from the "internal" budget, as it has its own source. Expenditure in the area of foreign relations is still increasing (unlike agriculture and structural funds) and is likely to expand in the 1998 budget.

Table 1.2 Foreign policy expenditure (billions of ECUs) per area in the 1996 budget year

Eastern Europe	1.76
Latin America, Asia and Southern Africa (Marin)	0.82
Mediterranean	0.88
Humanitarian Aid and food (ECHO)	1.23
Other forms of cooperation	1.1
ACP	3.3[48]
Total	8.1

Source: EU Budget 1996.

Outside the regular budget, the European Community is spending 13.3 billion ECUs

---

[46] *European Voice*, 30 September 1996. "Overseas Staff on the Move".
[47] Netherlands Antilles, Comorois, Djibouti, Gambia, Solomons, Sao Tome, Swaziland.
[48] This amount is not included in the budget of the EU, but kept in a fund. It averages 3.3 billion ECUs per year

over the years 1996 to 2000 on ACP countries, an average of 3.3 billion ECUs a year. The European Union is the biggest donor in the world of public development cooperation.[49] This is a total of 6.6 per cent of the Community's budget, not including administrative expenses of the more than 100 delegations abroad. A mere 62 million is available for the infant CFSP. Eighty-two per cent of the budget of 86 billion ECUs is taken by agricultural and structural subsidies.[50]

1.10. HOW DO PERSONAL ACTIONS AND INTERESTS CHANGE THE COMMON EUROPEAN FOREIGN POLICY? IS THE COMMISSION A POLICY-EXECUTOR OR A POLICY-MAKER?

Since the Maastricht Treaty foreign policy has become a day-to-day involvement for the CEC. No longer does it suffice to make foreign policy and to maintain external relations on a infrequent basis, as has been done by the Council, or on an *ad hoc* basis as done by the Troika. Henceforth, the expansion of the role of the Commission is likely to continue as the number of "special" relations increases. Whatever the Intergovernmental set-up of the CFSP after the IGC, there will be an undeniable role for the Commission and its staff. Only when a permanent agent will be named within the Council might the foreign policy of the Commission be at risk. The dynamics within the Commission are unlikely to change if the nomination procedures remain the same. With the "overcrowding" of external relations and with differing interest between Commissioners, competition will continue. The number of opportunities is likely to increase, especially if more countries become members of the EU, as they bring their own additional priorities. The Commission will continue to develop a foreign policy in the areas already entrusted to it: trade, the several bilateral agreements, humanitarian aid and multilateral cooperation. Moreover, these areas will become more important because of their nature in a post Cold-War setting. The regional focuses of the community are likely to increase rather than to diminish. Day-to-day policy will also be expanded because of the tendency of the relations to become more detailed, especially agreements covering technical subjects such as customs unions and trade negotiations. Still, there is space for the Commission to do more than simply be the "executor" of foreign policy. It is likely to be also a policy initiator in the context of expanding trade relations. A case in point is the Helms-Burton act, where the Council has sanctioned extended policy formation on a day-to-day basis by the Commission. Other examples where the European Commission was executing and formulating foreign policy was the Canadian Fisheries quarrel,[51] bringing the Helms Burton case before the WTO and the representation of the position of Europe in the negotiations on telecommunications and intellectual property in the WTO. The recent call of the Commission to become the sole negotiator in trade is convincing and will be discussed as a proposal in the IGC.

---

[49] Source: http://europe.eu.int/en/comm/dg19/graphfr/deprech.html (Budget of the Union on the web).
[50] Ibid.
[51] Bonino mainly handled this matter as Commissioner in charge of Fisheries.

Conclusions will be offered on the state of development of foreign policy by the CEC as an independent actor, and an attempt will then be made to assess the credibility of the bureaucratic foreign policy paradigm for the European Commission.

1.11. THE CEC: A FOREIGN POLICY ACTOR?

Of all the EU institutions, the difference between formal power and actual leverage on the formulation of policy is greatest in the Commission. While the Council remains the most important legislative institution, and while the Parliament has enhanced its legislative and political role in successive treaties, the Commission has quietly developed an institutional role that has not been sanctioned yet in the treaties. It has been like that in the pre-SEA period and in the pre-Maastricht period, before already established procedures were sanctioned. Treaty revisions usually incorporate legislation that was already common practice in policy-making in the years before.[52] In the first months after the ratification, it has to be assessed if the Treaty of Amsterdam will be a codification of practices that already sanction an increased role for the Commission, as has occurred during 1992–1997, or whether it will develop into a new institutional direction, where a different constitutional and intergovernmental structure is proposed for foreign policy development. The first analyses of the treaty show that the Commission has not been too successful. However, the role of the Commission in trade issues will be gradually expanded, notwithstanding the development of the CFSP in an intergovernmental direction.[53]

The European Commission has greatly enhanced its position in the past five years as an independent actor in foreign and commercial policy. Even if the treaty is developing as predominantly an intergovernmental strengthening, it is unlikely that the role of the Commission will diminish because of the dynamics described here and the need to have a daily follow-up of agreements.

1.12. TOWARDS A "BUREAUCRATIC POLICY" THEORY OF EUROPEAN FOREIGN POLICY

It has been argued in this chapter that several independent actors are identifiable in policy-making within the Commission, with different standpoints and interests. However, can bureaucratic politics be useful in explaining outcomes in policy-making within the Commission? The examples given were discussed under the headings of the individual Commissioners. It is clear that the Commissioners involved were not merely executing commonly agreed-upon policy, as personal agendas existed as well

---

[52] Although some new elements were included in the Maastricht Treaty: against the wishes of the Commission and the Dutch Presidency, the three-pillar structure was introduced. Moreover, Maastricht introduced the concept of subsidiarity, mainly to please the British.

[53] See *Financial Times*, 12 March 1997. After having lost its legal battle before the court to be the sole legislator, the Commission proposes a procedure that avoids the time consuming and lowest denominator compromise procedure that has been adopted until now. This together with the expansion of the Majority voting would enhance the Commission role as both executor of policy and agenda setter.

as particular interests and personal leverage in some matters. This became especially clear when examining the portfolios and the bargaining power of the senior Commissioners, Vice-Presidents Marin and Brittan. Vice-President Marin has exerted considerable leverage over the areas that are of particular interest to him and to his country: the Mediterranean and Latin America. Resources have successfully been allocated to these areas, and agreements have been finalized. As the Community is working with a minimal growth budget, sources for the Barcelona conference programmes and for the bilateral agreements with Latin America will compete with funds for the established programs in DG1A and DG8. The same occurred with projects of Vice-President Brittan: the maverick Commissioner has managed not only to overrule several member countries' agendas (France, Germany) during negotiations in the WTO, but also to obtain a large degree of autonomy in performing this task (he has requested even further autonomy, as sole negotiator).[54] Moreover, various initiatives have focused on expanding relations with the Asian countries, which ranks high on his personal ideological agenda (WTO, opening of markets) and fits neatly with the rhetoric of his country's foreign policy agenda. Moreover, the inroads into the agendas of other Commissioners are a clear sign of his expanding interest and leverage.

The case of Prof. Deus Pinheiro is clear cut. Deus Pinheiro obtained this portfolio in the negotiations prior to the Santer Commission, without being able to influence greatly the agenda or the distribution of portfolios. This limited leverage resulted in his obtaining a portfolio that few member states or interests are willing to fight for. It is clear that his portfolio will suffer from a budgetary point of view and as an agenda topic.

The case of Van Den Broek is more complicated. Although the Netherlands was able to secure a potentially important portfolio ("large" small country, senior outgoing Commissioner), the portfolio has suffered considerable setbacks over the past three years. The political result can to a large extent be explained by the limited leverage over the overall agenda and the clashing with other Commissioners' agendas and the leverage of other Commissioners over his portfolio. The lack of progress of the area involved (postponed enlargements, limited economic progress, instability, emergence of other areas) has also caused the spread of resources to other areas and the establishment of DG1B, which created for Marin an institutional back-up to the level of DG1. While the portfolio might not have suffered in absolute terms, it certainly has in relative terms. This has influenced greatly the standing of other proposals proposed by Van Den Broek. Further research on a case-by-case basis will assess to what extent this will lead to issue-linking and changes in relative interests and power (Peters and Bindi 1998). For now, the theory of bureaucratic politics described can be considered a promising method to examine the dynamics within the Commission. Moreover, it can be part of a methodology to explain better the outcome of the policy-making process of the Commission and, more generally, the European institutions. Is this an alternative to other, more elaborate theories such as intergovernmentalism or functionalism? It appears to be a promising tool for European Studies, but this area of analysis is underdeveloped and merits further research.

---

[54] *Financial Times*, 12 March 1996.

1.13. REFERENCES

Allison, G. (1971). *Essence of Decision*. Boston: Little Brown and Company.

Croome, J. (1995). *Reshaping the World Trading System*. WTO.

Dinan, D. (1994) *Ever Closer Union*. Boulder: Lynne Rienner Publishers.

Duff, A., J. Pinder and R. Price (eds.) (1994) *Maastricht and Beyond: Building the European Union*. London: Routledge.

European Commission (1995a). *The European Commission*. Luxembourg: Office for the Official Publications of the European Communities.

European Commission (1995b). Various documents. Luxembourg: Office for the Official Publications of the European Communities.

Ginsberg, R. (1989). *Foreign Policy Actions of the EC*. Boulder: Lynne Rienner Publishers.

Hill, C. (1983). *National Foreign Policies and European Political Cooperation*. London: Allan and Unwin/RIIA.

Hill, C. (1991) "The European Community, Towards a Common Foreign and Security Policy?" *The World Today*, November.

Hill, C. (ed.) (1996). *The Actors in European Foreign Policy*. London: Routledge.

Nuttall, S. (1996). "The Commission: the Struggle for Legitimacy". In: Hill, C. (ed.) *The Actors in European Foreign Policy*. London: Routledge.

Peters, P. and F. Bindi (1998) *Policy Making by the Santer Commission*. Forthcoming.

Pinder, J. (1994). *After Maastricht*. London: Routledge.

Risse-Kappen, T. (1995). *Cooperation among Democracies*. Princeton: Princeton University Press.

Viotti P.R. and M.V. Kauppi (1990). *International Relations Theory*. New York: Maxwell Macmillan.

CHAPTER 2

Judicial politics and EC external relations: the role of the European Court of Justice

Sabrina Tesoka

2.1. INTRODUCTION: (RE)DISCOVERING THE EUROPEAN JUDICIARY

The European Court of Justice (ECJ) is increasingly considered to assume a key role in European integration, not least by undertaking the task of giving "flesh" and substance to an "outline" Treaty, and by promoting, in a more or less explicit manner, a *"certain idea of Europe"* which it desires to promote.[1] In the years of so-called stagnation of the European integration process, the ECJ appeared to have played a "political" role through law, by rendering the Treaty effective even when its tenuous provisions had not been fulfilled as required by the Community, and in making secondary legislation effective even when it had not been properly implemented by the member states. In essence, European integration issues that could not be settled at a political level appeared to be removed to the judicial arena. The Court thus adopted an active part in the European integration process through the litigation which came before it, at time when progress towards forging a European Union through positive legislative harmonisation was hindered by institutional inaction and political opposition.[2]

In this respect, some legal scholars have provided precocious and original accounts of the role of the Court in the European integration process, emphasising the development of Community-based supranationalism.[3] Although asserting the importance of legal principles developed by the ECJ such as the supremacy and authority of EC law, these analyses have also examined the political, economic and social context within which the Court operates. However, such analyses have rarely engaged with a body of work on substantive policy areas[4] and have been rather reluctant to provide a less

---

[1] According to the former ECJ judge Pierre Pescatore, judges' motivation for embarking on the path of direct effect in *Van Gend & Loos* and the construction of a new Community legal order was related to their conception of Europe. As he put it, they had *"une certaine idée de l'Europe"* of their own (Pescatore 1983).

[2] This draws on Weiler's (1993) narrative of the growth of judicial activism.

[3] Legal scholars such as Eric Stein, Francis Snyder, Martin Shapiro and Hjalte Rasmussen, to name just a few. The now-classic analysis developed by Cappelletti *et al.* (1986) under the provocative title *Integration Through Law* is a key reference here. See also Weiler (1982).

[4] In this respect, works developed by Snyder (1985) on the Common Agricultural Policy and Bieber *et al.* (1992) on regulatory strategies are rather unusual.

35

A. Cafruny and P. Peters (eds.), The Union and the World, 35–54
© 1998 *Kluwer Academic Publishers. Printed in Great Britain.*

positive overall assessment of the contribution of the EC law[5] in general, and of the Court in particular.[6]

Alternatively, analyses of the Court "from the inside" have also been developed.[7] Such a perspective has naturally been interesting and useful in understanding questions such as how the judiciary works, what its priorities are, and where it considers its judicial activity is leading the EU, etc. However, it is worth remarking that such evidence must be treated with a certain cautious distance and objectivity. Furthermore, it needs to be adequately contextualised and theorised.

By contrast, political scientists have generally neglected the ECJ, assuming that the Community judiciary could be reduced to the role of a *"technical servant"*.[8] However, recent developments, which theorise about the transformations of the Euro-polity and (at last) take European institutions seriously, have provided a good starting point to depart from this rather primitive conception of the European judiciary.[9] Progressively, the deficit is being remedied. This new body of work generally acknowledges the function of the Court as a significant leading political force in building the Community. Concurrently, the judiciary's capacity to restructure legislative and political environments and to generate legislative processes and outcomes is also increasingly recognized.[10]

Nevertheless, much of the new political science work on the Court shows a marked preference for returning to some of the grand theories of integration, in particular neofunctionalism[11] and, to a lesser extent, intergovernmentalism.[12] This is all the more paradoxical since such a phenomenon occurs at a time when the trend for most political scientists is towards moving beyond the sterile controversy of neofunctionalism *vs.* intergovernmentalism.[13] It is clear that such an interest in "recycling grand theories" through the analysis of a newly discovered object of analysis, i.e. the Court, risks falling into several traps.

---

[5] Lately, however, some legal scholars have inspired new approaches which consider the disintegrationist trends of Community law. For instance, in a recent analysis Shaw (1995) appeared to break the conventional and immutable link between law and the integration process, and highlighted the strong disintegrationist elements in the present EU legal order. On this concept of fragmentary trends see also Harmsen (1994).

[6] In this respect, the critical work developed by the legal scholar Rasmussen (1986) constituted a rather original – and shocking – account of the ECJ.

[7] See writings by judges of the ECJ (Pescatore 1981, 1983; Mancini 1989; Due 1994).

[8] This expression was coined by Weiler (1982).

[9] See for instance Sbragia (1992), Jachtenfuchs and Kohler-Koch (1996).

[10] See Shapiro (1992), Stone (1995).

[11] For a neofunctionalist perspective on the Court see Burley and Mattli (1993) and Mattli and Slaughter (1995). See also current work which is being developed by Alec Stone Sweet and Wayne Sandholtz (1997).

[12] This refers to the intergovernmentalist or realist approach which has been developed by Geoffrey Garrett and Barry Weingast as regards the ECJ: "Ideas, Interests and Institutions: Constructing the EC's Internal Market" in Goldskin, J. and Keohane, R. O. (eds.): *Ideas and Foreign Policy. Beliefs, Institutions and Political Change*, Ithaca, NY, 1992, pp.173-206. Geoffrey Garrett, "International cooperation and institutional choice: the European Community"'s internal market", *International Organization*, 46, 2, Spring 1992. By the same author see also: "The Politics of legal integration in the European Union", *International Organization*, Vol. 49, No. 1, 1995, pp.171-181

[13] On the necessity to go beyond these major schools of thought, see Caporaso and Keeler (1993) and Haartland (1993).

First of all, such accounts simply aim at providing a theory-based explanation of traditional paradigms of the interface "law–integration" or the entanglement "member states–EU institutions". Such perspectives certainly possess a certain rhetorical and ideological force, but they appear to rely on rather debatable arguments which are not always substantiated by any empirical foundations.

Secondly, this kind of approaches tend to apprehend the ECJ as a political institution among others without any consideration, on the one hand, for the specificity of a judicial institution and, on the other hand, for the role of law. By doing so they completely miss the rather anomalous character of the role of judicial politics in the sphere of foreign policy. There is thus a danger that political science accounts of the Court of that kind slip into assessments of the Court without the law.[14]

Furthermore, focused on the rationality and instrumentality of their privileged key actors in the legal integration process – i.e. the state for intergovernmentalists; the ECJ, national courts and transnational interest groups for neofunctionalists – these theses both explain any development by the so-called objectives, strategies or tactics of the parties concerned.[15] For these reasons, they completely miss two crucial points: on the one hand, the institutional dynamism of the Euro-polity, and on the other hand, the impact of the ECJ as a "meaning-structure".[16] Neither neofunctionalist nor intergovernmentalist perspectives incorporate such variables in their analyses – or if they do so, their perspective is rather arguable.[17] It is clear that political analyses of the ECJ need to depart from such approaches and withdraw from intergovernmentalist

---

[14] Despite their differences, intergovernmentalist and neofunctionalist theses seem to have common weaknesses as regards their conception of law. In this respect, it is common knowledge that Garrett's approach provides a rather limited conception of law since it conceives it as an instrument for national governments. In this view, the ECJ is a watchdog of the founders of the treaties; its case law just reflects and protects the interest of the national governments. Paradoxically, Slaughter and Mattli do not really go beyond these limitations since they only apprehend the specificity of law under the following terms: remote from the "political sphere", law serves as a "mask and shield" for the political agenda of the ECJ and the other actors involved in the litigation process. The neo-functionalist view thus consists in perceiving the ECJ both as an actor with a clear supranationalist agenda and as a Trojan horse for national courts and transnational interest groups; this phenomenon of reciprocal interest revolves around the process of *spillover* and shift of loyalties.

[15] Against this view, I would argue that it is slightly simplistic to apprehend necessarily the impact of Community institutions in terms of strategic action and instrumental interest. By its very existence and activity, a given European institution influences its environment.

[16] This term draws on a neo-institutionalist or even constructivist concept. It refers to the impact of the ECJ as structuring its environment and producing norms and values.

[17] Recent works drawing on neo-functionalist precepts take into consideration some aspects of the problematical interaction between the ECJ and its environment. In this respect, they try to apprehend three major aspects of the legal integration process: the motives animating the actors, the dynamics of their interaction and the context within which they operate. However, they seem to over-emphasise the intentionality of the mutual influence between the actors concerned and tend to conceive it in a rather systematic way. In this view, the empowerment of the Court, national courts and transnational actors, and the subsequent changes induced by the integration process to domestic structures and institutions, appear to be slightly mechanical. This critique can be addressed to Sandholtz (1996) and Mattli and Slaughter (formerly Burley) (1995) and (1996).

and neofunctionalist models of integration.[18]

By focusing on the analysis of the ECJ as a significant institutional actor in EU foreign politics, this analysis will attempt to remedy two major lacunae in the existing political science literature on European foreign policy. Not only is the available material mostly focused on other institutional and non-institutional actors – member states, the Commission, the European Parliament, pressure groups, etc.[19] – but it also tends to remain informed by the never-ending and vain discussion between the tenets of the two prevailing models of European integration.[20] This work on the role of judicial politics in the EU foreign law and policy will thus necessarily attempt to make such a conceptual leap.

Last but not least, it should be clear that although it scrutinizes the specific role of the ECJ, the purpose of the present analysis is not to rehearse again legal scholars' considerations as regards the significant contribution of the Court *vis-à-vis* legal integration and Community law.[21] The study will rather consider the particular role of judicial politics in the external relations of the EU, and assess the Court's regulatory functions over the exercise of Union powers in the international arena.

The analysis will thus proceed in four steps. It begins by apprehending the role of judicial politics in the process of the "constitutionalisation" of the Community legal order and consider its implications for the activities of the ECJ in the domain of EC external relations. Secondly, it examines the various means by which the Court exerts its competence in the field of the international activities of the EU and reviews the existing mechanisms of control over the dealings of Community institutions and acts. It then traces the unexpected expansion of the ECJ's powers to review the international activities of the Communities. Consideration of the expanding competence of the Court will necessarily lead to some considerations as regards the limits and ambiguities of the Court's action in the domain of EC external relations in the light of its recent case law. By way of a conclusion, the analysis will deal with the future developments of these competencies in the sphere of foreign policy in respect of the increasing constraints on the Court's action as epitomized by some restrictive provisions of the Treaty on European Union.

2.2. Recasting the "Constitutionalization" of the Community's Legal Order

"If one were asked to synthesize the direction in which the case law produced in

---

[18] In this respect, Wincott's (1995) analysis has attempted to develop a neo-institutionalist analysis of the ECJ.

[19] For an example of this neglect of the role of the Court in Europe"s external relations see Hill (1996). Although it provides a good analysis of the role of the Member States and the Commission in foreign policy-making processes, it completely ignores the contribution of the EC Court.

[20] For a reassessment of these different theoretical perspectives on Europe's foreign policy, see Smith (1994).

[21] A cautious distance is needed as regards the frequent assumption that the case law reflects the social reality on the ground. In this respect, it is clear that legal scholars should beware of the dangers of doing *"law without politics"*, to paraphrase Shapiro (1981).

the Community has moved since 1957, one would have to say that it coincides with the making of a Constitution for Europe" (Mancini 1989).

The EC's constitutional achievements are largely due to the judicial interpretation of the EC Treaty as a constitution, and of the EC free trade rules as individual "market freedoms", primarily by the ECJ, purported by national courts in EC member states. Basically, the Court has become partially an autonomous "political actor", which has constitutionalised the Treaties and has instituted itself as a constitutional court.[22]

In a series of now renowned decisions, the European Court of Justice has established two major principles: the doctrine of direct effect and the doctrine of supremacy or primacy of Community law over national law. As a result, the Court converted the founding treaties – which under conventional law are binding only on the signatories, i.e. the national states, and only indirectly binding on their citizens – into a federal constitution enforceable on the members and directly binding on all the citizens of those states. In order to achieve such a transformation, the Court distinguished the structure of the Community from classical international structures (Shapiro and Stone 1994). It referred to a *"new international legal order"*[23] that evolved into a *"new legal order"*.[24] According to the ECJ, "the European Community is a Community based on the rule of law, inasmuch as neither its Member states nor its institutions can avoid a review of the question whether the measures adopted by them are in conformity with the basic constitutional charter, the Treaty".[25] In this perspective, EC law exercises constitutional functions as regards the European nation states and their citizens. These supranational constitutional guarantees include the principle of rule of law, horizontal and vertical separation of powers, democratic government, non-discrimination, transnational "market freedoms", fundamental individual rights and judicial review.

Needless to say, this gradual process of "constitutionalization" of the Community legal order has significant implications for the development of the Court's activities in the domain of the international activities of the Union powers (Hancher 1994). This unusual role of the ECJ naturally rests on the major functions of the Court. It is further reinforced by specific devices and the Court's different techniques of review of the relationship between Community and national norms on the one hand and international norms and agreements on the other.

---

[22] It is worth specifying that the ECJ is not a fully developed federal or appellate court. Individuals still have no right of appeal to the ECJ and the national court can decide whether a reference is necessary. In this respect, the Court''s judgements are still, at least in theory, given only on points of interpretations and validity, and much continues to be made of the division of responsibilities between ECJ and national courts.

[23] Case 26/62, *NC Algemene Transport on Expeditie Ondernemong Van Gend en Loos v Nederlandse Administratie der Belastingen*, 5 February 1963, ECR 1. According to the doctrine of direct effect, individuals may rely on their supreme Community law rights before their national court and have those rights protected by the national court. In this view, giving the maximum effectiveness of Community law implies empowering individuals to act as Community law enforcers.

[24] Case 6/64, *Costa v ENEL*, 15 July 1964, ECR 585. On this occasion, the Court proclaimed the supremacy of EC law over conflicting provisions of national law. This led to a transformation of Article 177.

[25] Case 294/83, *Les Verts*, [1986] ECR 1339, 1365.

2.3. THE JURISDICTIONAL COMPETENCE OF THE COURT IN THE DOMAIN OF EC EXTERNAL RELATIONS

The introduction of restrictive provisions as regards the jurisdictional competence of the ECJ in the domain of Common Foreign and Security Policy and in the sphere of Justice and Home Affairs would suggest some reluctance – if not opposition – on the part of the Member States as regards the process of "constitutionalization" of the Community legal order and the related empowerment of the European judiciary. The subsequent analysis will define the scope of the Court's jurisdiction over the Community action in the international arena and review the various mechanisms and devices which enable the Court to be and remain a significant institutional actor in this field, despite obvious increasing constraints on its activities. In this respect, it is clear that in the sphere of foreign affairs no less than in other policy areas it is worth while to check whether the Treaty on European Union affects existing jurisdictional competencies of the Court.

2.3.1 The Treaty on European Union

The Treaty on European Union not only formally introduced the principle of subsidiarity into the Community legal regime, but also set severe limits on Community legislative action in fields of Common Foreign and Security Policy and cooperation in the domain of justice and home affairs. In essence, these two new "pillars" of the Union are intergovernmental in nature.[26] Furthermore, Article L of Title VII (Final Provisions) clearly attempts to exclude these pillars from the Court's jurisdiction.[27] It is clear that the introduction of these severe restrictions on the jurisdictional competence of the Court constituted a serious warning against the so-called judicial activism of the Court in respect of Community action in the international arena. Concurrently, it also expressed the member states' awareness of the expanding agenda of the Court in their so-called *domaine réservé*. Nevertheless, somewhat more reassuring in respect to the preservation of the *"acquis communautaire"* in the sphere of external relations is the fact that the exception provided by Article L TEU cannot prevent the Court of Justice from incidentally reviewing CFSP decisions on their compatibility with Community law. For in accordance with Article M TEU, the Court will have to annul any decision taken in the context of the Community pillar if it contravenes Community law including essential procedural requirements of the EC Treaty. In this respect,

---

[26] As far as the specific case of CFSP is concerned, it is worth remarking that it is not pure intergovernmental cooperation. Although competence is not transferred to the Community, and although the Community process as such is generally excluded, there are a number of connecting points to the Community institutions. Basically, it allows member states to cooperate intergovernmentally within the context of the Union. The second pillar provides in Article J3(4) that "Joint action shall commit the Member States in the position they adopt and in the conduct of their activity". This is not limited to participation in international organizations and conferences. By the reference to the positions they adopt in the conduct of their activity, member states would be bound to defend those actions in international organizations and conferences.

[27] Nevertheless Article L acknowledges that the Court may also be given jurisdiction to interpret certain conventions, and to rule on their application, in the field of justice and home affairs – Article K3 (2) (c)

despite Article L, CFSP is subject to an indirect scrutiny of the Court whose effectiveness should not be underestimated.[28] More generally, the ECJ exerts clear functions of judicial review and interpretation of the Community acts in the international arena. As stated by Article 164 EC, the Court "shall ensure that in the interpretation and application [of the Community treaties] the law is observed". Such a regulatory function rests on specific mechanisms and devices.

2.3.2. Devices and mechanisms of judicial review

The Court enjoys competence to review international agreements and their compatibility with Community law both *a priori* and *a posteriori*. In the frame of a control *a priori*, the Court may be asked to examine the proposed agreements between the Community, third states and international organizations in accordance with Article 228(6) EC.[29] Such an opinion is binding. Where the opinion is adverse, the agreement may enter into force only in accordance with Article N of the Treaty on European Union.[30] As far as control *a posteriori* is concerned, this type of review may be activated in many and various ways.

Firstly, it may be activatedthrough a Commission complaint to the Court under Article 169. Basically, Article 169 establishes the liability of Member States as regards any infringements of Community law, irrespective of which state authority has occasioned the infringement through its act or its omission, even if it is a constitutionally independent body. Although cases concerning infringement of Community law are not spectacular, they have enabled the Court to rule on several kinds of excuses which the member states have invoked. It is also worth mentioning that a judgment of the Court under Article 169 declaring that the member state has not fulfilled its obligations resulting from Article 189(3) constitutes an important indication for the national courts that the State is in breach of this article. They are thus informed that they may be required to continue the examination of the case concerned in order to establish whether the state should be liable for damages. This central mechanism thus entails clear decentralized patterns.

Secondly, the Court's judicial control also concerns direct actions brought by Member States, the Council or the Commission or by natural or legal persons under Article 173 EC or Article 215 EC[31] challenging the alleged violation of international

---

[28] For a clear assessment of the foreign affairs system of Maastricht see Monar (1996).

[29] It is worth remarking that new Article 228(6) EC Treaty does not establish the right of the European Parliament to have checked the compatibility of an envisaged agreement with the Treaty by the ECJ. The fact that an institution, which under the assent procedure has been granted a power of co-decision as regards certain types of agreements, has still no access to the Court comparable to the other institutions and the member states in respect of this co decision procedure constitutes a major inconstitency in the TEU.

[30] This provision which currently deals with the proposals submitted to the Council for the amendment of the Treaties is thus a rather exceptional procedure.

[31] Article 215 EC addresses the question of the contractual and non-contractual liability of the Community.

law principles by Community institutions.[32] Article 173 of the EC Treaty entitles the ECJ to consider the legality of acts – other than recommendations and opinions – of the Council, the Parliament, the Commission and the ECB and to annul illegal acts perpetrated by them. It is worth remarking that the procedure under Article 173, challenging Community competence to conclude an international agreement, is a delicate issue since it seems that the case law of the Court on this matter frequently raises controversies.

In contrast, the third mechanism of review rests on the references by national courts to the European Court when a case before them raises a question of European law.[33] Clearly, Article 177 is one of the most interesting provisions of the Treaty.[34] The existing procedure of preliminary ruling is aimed at helping the national courts to overcome the difficulties arising out of the necessity to observe rules foreign to them. It is also aimed at guaranteeing an application of the Community law which is as homogeneous as possible, since decisions by the ECJ require the national courts to interpret national legislation in accordance with Community law. In the frame of Article 177, national courts or tribunals may thus seek references relating to the interpretation of international agreements and, in certain instances, as to the effects of such agreements on Community as well as national measures.

Furthermore, this procedure provides a viable alternative or complement at the Community level since it enables a more decentralized enforcement of non-implemented or inadequately implemented directives in national courts and involves individual litigants. As a result, individuals can then challenge both national and Community decisions which would otherwise be out of their reach since there is no direct access for individual litigants.[35] Equally, it has been the vehicle through which seminal Community concepts, such as direct effect and supremacy, have been developed. To some extent, this provision has also been used as a way to extend the Court's powers of review, as illustrated by the *Sevince* case where the ECJ justified its jurisdictional competence by referring to Article 177 since it enabled it to *"ensure the uniform application throughout the Community"*.[36]

Article 177 is clearly a mechanism through which national courts and the ECJ have engaged in a *discourse* and *dialogue* as regards the question of the appropriate reach

---

[32] In accordance with Article 173 EC any natural or legal person may institute proceedings against a decision addressed to that person or against a decision which, although in the form of a regulation or a decision addressed to another person, is of direct and individual concern to the former.

[33] The provisions which can be referred under the 177 procedure are the following: 177 (1) (a) concerning the interpretation of the Treaty; 177 (1) (b) relating to the validity and interpretation of acts of the institutions of the Community; 177 (1) (c) concerning statutes of bodies establishehd by an act of the Council.

[34] Every second case brought before the ECJ by now is a preliminary ruling.

[35] In the litigation phase, national courts assume two major tasks. First, they assume the control of legality of national rules under national law with the provisions of Community law. The national jurisdiction will thus interpret national law, particularly the provisions transposing the directive, thereby bridging the gap between national law and the directive which has not been adequately transposed. Secondly, national judges are frequently called upon to apply the measures of transposition of the provisions of the directive to a concrete case before him. Consequently, the national judge is entrusted with the task of the "judicial implementation" of the provisions of the directive. It is thus situated somewhere near the end of the "chain of implementation".

[36] case C-192/89 *Sevince*, [1990] ECR I-3461 at para. 11.

of Community law when conflicts between Community and national norms or international norms and agreements occurred.[37] In this respect, Article 177 EEC enables the ECJ to assume a dual role in the Community legal order since it combines a traditional judicial function with a clearly consultative/guiding role.

Concurrently, Article 177 EEC has also marked the advancing instrumentalisation of the ECJ – and Community law – for the resolution of national disputes. It is clear that contrary to the Supreme Court in the USA, the ECJ is not (yet) an important forum for interest groups. However, individual litigants, interest groups, agencies and national courts have increasingly used the opportunity provided by the preliminary ruling to reorient the national law in a direction corresponding as far as possible to their expectations.

The fourth mechanism that ensures the regulatory function of the ECJ results in fact from the line set out in the case law of the Court that attributed to Community instruments – the Treaty, some regulations and directives – "direct effect". This means that these provisions may be invoked, even without national legislation, as a legal basis for a claim before a national jurisdiction. In this respect, the question of the direct effect of an international agreement concluded by the Community on either the status of a Community or a national act has frequently arisen in national courts.

A fifth mechanism can be described as the *"effective judicial protection line"* (Prechal 1995). It is true that the Court has frequently used its case law to promote the idea that the power of review and the availability of effective judicial remedies constitute the "bottom line" of a Community based on the rule of law. Relying on this argument, the Court decided in 1991 that a member state is in principle liable for harm caused to individuals by breaches of Community law, including the non-implementation of directives. It thus ruled that the state owed compensation to those affected by its defects.[38] Needless to say, this rhetoric as regards the particular foundations of the Community – and the novelty of its legal order – also serves to draw the line between Community law, on the one hand, and international norms on the other. To some extent, it contributes to widening the gulf between these different legal systems, as illustrated by the following case which is an exemplar of the Court's position on this issue.

In Opinion 1/91 of 14 December 1991 on the Agreement establishing the European Economic Area (EEA), the Court emphasized the fundamental differences between the EEA and the Community. While the EEA established a normal intergovernmental organization, the EEC Treaty was said to constitute a constitutional charter of a community establishing a new legal order.[39] As a result, the interpretation and appli

---

[37] The nature of the relationship between national courts and the ECJ has changed over the years and is still evolving. The original conception referred to horizontal and bilateral relations. It connoted the idea that the ECJ and the national courts were separate and equal. In this perspective, it was for the national court to decide whether to refer a matter to the ECJ, which the European judiciary would then interpret. The relationship appears to be vertical and multilateral. The ECJ is in fact acting as a supreme court and has in effect enrolled the national courts as enforcers and appliers of Community law. As far as the multilateral character is concerned, the ECJ judgments which are given in response to the request for a ruling from one member state are increasingly held to have either a *de facto* or a *de jure* impact on all other national courts.

[38] Joined cases C-6/90 and C-9/90 *Francovitch and Bonifaci* [1991] ECR I-5357.

[39] OJ 1992 C136/1.

cation of the law of the EEA would certainly conflict with Community law. More specifically, as far as the Community rules on free movement were concerned, the machinery of courts provided for in the agreement was said to conflict with Article 164 of the EEC Treaty "and more generally, with the very foundations of the Community".[40]

As illustrated by the previous analysis, specific mechanisms and devices enable the Court to exert its jurisdictional competence in the field of the EC external relations. In the following section, the analysis will focus on the way the Court has addressed the question of its powers of review through its case law and has expanded the scope of its competence to review both international agreements and acts of EU powers in the international arena.

2.4. THE (EXPANDING) COMPETENCE OF THE EUROPEAN COURT OF JUSTICE

Treaty provisions have been used by the ECJ as a basis to justify broadly its power to apply or interpret international treaties or other overriding rules of public international law. In its case law, the ECJ has expanded the principle of rule of law and judicial review to all Union powers. In addition, the Court has adopted a very expansive reading of its jurisdiction to consider international agreements,[41] including agreements as regards matters which fall to the exclusive competence of the member states, or which are not necessarily dependent on the Community being party, or on its capacity to become party, to these agreements in international law. Such a jurisdictional competence signifies that the Court has the power not only to examine and eventually invalidate the international acts of Union powers but also to review acts of international organs which are involved in the implementation of these broadly defined international agreements. This expansion of the ECJ's jurisdictional competence to review international agreements is illustrated by the following significant examples.

2.4.1. Reviewing international agreements

In several preliminary rulings under the procedure of Article 177 EEC the Court has clearly expressed the view that it has the jurisdictional competence to review a given international agreement between the Community and one or more parties, but also to review acts which appear to be "directly connected" with the agreement concerned. In this perspective, the ECJ has asserted its jurisdiction to interpret the acts of the Councils established under a number of Association agreements.[42] Equally, it has concluded in the *Shell* case that a given recommendation from a Joint Committee in

---

[40] Para 46, OJ 1992 C136/1.

[41] The *Haegemann* ruling and subsequent judgments confirmed that international agreements, as well as the acts leading to their conclusion, could be treated as acts of the institutions and thus be subject to judicial control by the ECJ. Case 181/73 *Haegeman v. Belgium* [1974] ECR 449.

[42] See significant judgments such as Case 12/86 *Demirel v. Stadt Scwäbisch Gmünd* [1987] ECR 3719 and Case C-192/89 *Sevince* ECR I-3461.

the frame of a convention between the EEC and EFTA countries formed an integral part of the Community legal system – and could thus be reviewed by the ECJ.[43]

Furthermore, the ECJ, through its jurisprudence, has increasingly expressed its willingness to review agreements to which the Community was not even party. On this logic, it came to scrutinize the activities of the international organs which are implementing the agreements concerned. Needless to say, such an activist interpretation of the Court's competence has raised some objections on the part of the international bodies concerned, as in the case *SAT v. Eurocontrol* where the ECJ was confronted with a direct rejection of its jurisdiction in the international arena by an international body.[44]

Eurocontrol, a body entrusted with the administration of a Treaty concerning the safety of air navigation, was challenged by a German company, SAT. Basically, SAT refused to pay a tax set and collected by Eurocontrol for the use of certain traffic routes for the reason that the organization had abused its dominant position and thus contravened two major provisions of EC competition law – Articles 86 and 90 EEC. SAT thus sought the arbitration of the ECJ. In opposition, Eurocontrol simply asserted that as an international organization governed by international law it was not subject to the jurisdiction of the Court. Eurocontrol's claim that the ECJ's judgment could not be implemented was dismissed as irrelevant.[45]

The broadening of the ECJ's jurisdictional competence to review international agreements is also illustrated by the Court's case law as regards the question of the Community's competence to conclude international agreements and its implications for member states' margin of action in the international arena.

2.4.2. Reviewing acts of Community institutions in the international arena

The majority of Opinions sought under the Article 228(6) EC (previously Article 228 (1) EEC) procedure concerned the Community's competence to enter a particular agreement, and its consequences for member states. Generally, the question of the exclusive character of the Community's competence was at the core of the requests. In its various Opinions, the Court has elaborated two related tests: firstly, the need to preserve the institutional balance between the component parts of the Community institutions on the one hand and the balance of powers between the Community institutions, and secondly, the judicial protection as guaranteed by the Treaties.[46]

---

[43] More specifically, this case concerned a recommendation by the Joint Committee in charge of the administration and implementation of the Convention on a common transit regime concluded in May 1987 between the EEC and the EFTA countries. This recommendation, which was in turn incorporated into the German legislation, was challenged in the German courts and then referred to the ECJ. Case C-188/91 *Shell* [1993] ECR I-363.

[44] Case C-364/92 *SAT v. Eurocontrol* [1994] ECR I-43.

[45] See particularly the arguments developed by Advocate-General Tesauro, who relied on two lines of reasoning: first effective judicial protection and then the related requirement to ensure effective judicial control over delegated decision-making either by Community institutions or by the member states.

[46] Here the seminal Opinion is the Court's Opinion 1/76 on the Laying up Fund for Inland Waterways Vessels, [1977] ECR 741.

In this respect, Opinion 2/91 clearly addressed this issue of the proper division of Community and member state competencies in the international arena.[47] Relying both on Article 118(2) EEC and on certain statements of the Court in the 1971 *ERTA* judgement,[48] the Commission argued that it had exclusive competence to conclude Convention 170 on safety in the use of chemicals at work. Concurrently, it also argued that member states no longer had the right to undertake obligations with third countries which affect those rules. This view clearly contrasted with the German and Dutch governments' positions which held that the Community only had observer status as the ILO in these matters. In respect of the issue of the Community's power to conclude Convention 170, the Court concluded that Community competence could not be exclusive. The Court also emphasized the fact that the question of the scope of the respective competencies of the Member States and the Community within a given international area was to be decided by references to rules of Community law. As the Court asserted it, it was possible under Article 228(1) EEC (Article 228 (6) EC) *"to consider all questions concerning the compatibility with the Treaty of any agreement envisaged, and in particular the question whether the Community has the power to enter that agreement".*[49] Consequently, Convention 170 needed to be examined in order to know whether it included provisions affecting Community rules laid down in the relevant directives. If so, member states could not undertake such commitments outside the framework of the Community institutions. Furthermore, the Court considered that in accordance with Article 5 EC, obligations of the member states extended to the conclusion of international agreements or commitments "containing rules capable of affecting rules already adopted in areas falling outside common policies or altering their scope". Once the Community enters into an international agreement, the member states are thus precluded from doing anything capable of affecting that agreement or altering its scope.[50] As regards the question of the implementation of the Convention, the Court considered that the Community may act as the competent authority to be empowered to prohibit or restrict the use of hazardous chemicals on health and safety grounds but also attributed certain supervisory powers to national authorities.[51] Considering the fact that the Community could not under international

---

[47] Opinion of 19 March 1993. Convention No. 170 of the International Labour Organization concerning safety in the use of chemicals at work. [1993] ECR I-1061.

[48] Case 22/70 *Commission v. Council* (re ERTA) [1971] ECR 263. This case is the basis of the Court"s doctrine as regards the notion of "Community competence" in the sphere of external relations. Basically, such a term refers not only to explicit Community competence but also to the Community's implied powers. However, the ERTA doctrine has been slightly questioned by new TEU Articles 109(5), 130r(4) and 130(y), despite a declaration annex to the TEU. In essence, the new TEU provisions provide that, without prejudice to Community competence and Community agreements, member states have the competence to negotiate in international bodies and conclude international agreements in the fields of monetary policy, environment and development cooperation respectively. See Declaration on Articles 109, 130r and 130y of the Treaty Establishing the European Community (Nr. 10).

[49] Opinion of 19 March 1993 2/91. Convention No. 170 of the International Labour Organization concerning safety in the use of chemicals at work, [1993] ECR I-1061. It concerned the compatibility of ILO Convention 170 with the EEC Treaty.

[50] Opinion of 19 March 1993. Convention No. 170 of the International Labour Organization concerning safety in the use of chemicals at work. [1993] ECR I-1061, para 11.

[51] Para 34 of Opinion 2/91, ibid.

law conclude the ILO convention, it reached the conclusion that the unity and effectiveness of EC law could be guaranteed by a "close association between the institutions of the Community and the Member States both in the process of negotiation and conclusion and in the fulfilment of the obligations entered into".[52]

Recently, the Court has reiterated this position as regards Community's competence to enter a given agreement and its implications for the member states. In *Parliament v. Council* the case concerned the competence of the Council to adopt an act on development finance cooperation under the Fourth Lomé Convention.[53] The European Parliament argued that the act had been adopted on the wrong legal basis and that the Community had exclusive competence in financial matters. The Court ruled that where an agreement is concluded in an area of shared competencies, its negotiation and implementation required joint action by the Community and the member states. In this particular case, it was considered that even though funds were provided by the Member States, obligations *vis-à-vis* the ACP states had been undertaken by the Community.

As shown by the previous examples, the Court has put forward a broad conception of its competencies to review international agreements. In this respect, there is an ongoing debate as to whether the Court also enjoys the power to review the legality of the agreement itself. In accordance with the Court's case law, it seems that this is effectively the case. In the context of annulment proceedings brought by the French government under Article 173 EC, the Court was asked to consider the legality of an agreement procedure relating to the mutual enforcement of competition law concluded between the Commission and the government of the United States.[54] This bilateral agreement signed by representatives of the US and the EC competition authorities was defined as an "administrative measure" by the Commission. It was thus not adopted according to the procedure provided in Article 228 EEC, but at a meeting of the Commission in September 1991, and subsequently transmitted by way of a letter of October 1991 to the member states. In his Opinion of 16 December 1993, Advocate-General Tesauro considered the question of whether the Court was competent to examine the legality of the Community act purporting to conclude the agreement as well as the legality of the agreement itself. In his view, the ECJ could entertain a direct action seeking the annulment of the agreement itself.[55]

Although cases concerning the review of Community acts in the international arena are not spectacular, they have enabled the Court to expand the scope of its jurisdictional competence and exert clear regulatory functions as regards relations between Community powers and other states or international organizations. Concurrently, such cases have enabled the European judiciary to promulgate the precepts of the particular nature of the Community legal order and reassess the foundations of the Community

---

[52] Para 36 of Opinion 2/91, ibid.

[53] Case C 316/91 *Parliament v Council*, [1994] ECR I-625. Judgement of 2 March 1994. Advocate-General Jacobs had reached similar conclusions as regards the shared competences.

[54] Case C-327/91 *France v. Commission*

[55] In accordance with the jurisprudence of the Court, the Commission procedure leading to the signing of the agreement was as an "act" capable of review within the meaning of Article 173 EEC. Case 22/70 *Commission v. Council* (re ERTA) [1971] ECR 263 at para 42.

legal order (de Witte, 1994). It would be worth assessing the limits and ambiguities of the Court's action in this domain.

2.5. THE COMPLIANCE OF COMMUNITY INSTITUTIONS WITH INTERNATIONAL TREATY OBLIGATIONS OF THE EC: LIMITS AND AMBIGUITIES OF THE CASE LAW

The Treaty provisions are rather vague as regards the status and effects of international agreements in the Community legal system; the exception being that under Article 228(7) EC (228 (1) EEC) agreements concluded under these conditions are "binding on the institutions of the Community and on Member States". Furthermore, the TEU requires the EU to base its foreign policy on respect for international treaties, thereby promoting the idea that Community law and international law must mutually reinforce each other. Such a principle concerns the European Convention for the Protection of Human Rights (Article F) and the UN Charter; the Helsinki Final Act and the Paris Charter (Article J. 1); the Western European Union and NATO (Article J.4); the UN Security Council (Article J.5); and the UN Convention relating to the Status of Refugees (Article K.2). The EC Treaty also refers to the GATT and other international organizations (Article 229 EC); the Council of Europe (230 EC); the OECD (231 EC); and cooperation with international monetary institutions.

The constitutional significance of this principle of mutual reinforcement had already been asserted by the Court in its case law since it considered that international agreements binding on the EC operate within EC law as "an integral part of the Community legal system", as stated in the *Kupfeberg* judgment.[56] Such a principle was reaffirmed by the ECJ in its Opinion 1/91 on the Agreement establishing the European Economic Area. The Court found that "in principle" an international agreement providing for its own dispute settlement system is compatible with EC law, and that its decisions are binding on the EC institutions, including the EC Court.[57] EC membership of international agreements thus implies the submission of the EC to international disputes settlement systems, whose decisions will be binding on the EC not only under international law but also under Community law.

Paradoxically, the Court seems to have departed from this principle as regards international agreements which were legally accepted by both the EC and its member states, such as the GATT and the WTO Agreement.

2.5.1. The "banana judgement" and its consequences[58]

The EC Court's judgment of 5 October 1994, the "banana judgement", raised the issue of the compliance of Council regulation with international treaty obligations of the EC. This landmark case gave birth to the ECJ's doctrine regarding the relationship

---

[56] Case 104/81, *Kupferberg*, [1982] ECR, 3659 (para. 13).

[57] Opinion 1/91, European Economic Area Agreement 1, [1991] ECR 6079 at seq., at 6106.

[58] See comments on the "banana case" by Petersmann (1995).

between GATT norms and the Community legal system. (See the Court Second Judgement on 12.12.93 C-469/93). It concerned Germany's complaint against Council Regulation (EEC) No. 404/93 of 13 February 1993 on the common organization of the market in bananas. The German government argued that such a Community act was contrary to EC international treaty obligations under the GATT. The Court did not consider the German argument and clearly defended the Council's position. To some extent, such a ruling would suggest that majority decisions by the EC Council in clear violations of GATT rules, as determined by two independent GATT dispute settlement proceedings, may not be challenged by the EC Court, even though the EC member states and individual citizens request the Court to protect them from illegal discriminatory trade restrictions. Furthermore, it appears that the European Court of Justice seems to consider itself not to be obliged to comply with the rulings of another judicial system such as the one embodied by the GATT dispute settlement system. In short, the Court does not seem to acknowledge systematically the primacy of international law *vis-à-vis* the EC. Needless to say, the position of the Court has triggered very negative reactions within both the Community and the international arena.

The question of the compliance of Community institutions with international treaty obligations of the EC under mixed international agreements such as the GATT and the WTO Agreement remains a highly controversial issue. In this regard, one of the major critiques touches on the apparent special treatment which is granted to the EC Council. Such a trend would suggest that violations of international agreements such as GATT and WTO Agreement ratified by national parliaments in EC member states can be freely decided by a majority in the EC Council without effective parliamentary and judicial review.[59]

Another matter of dispute concerns the unsatisfactory expansion of the doctrine of direct effect in the context of international agreements. This question is all the more serious since it touches on the question of the level of judicial protection available for individuals within the Community. In this respect, it seems rather difficult to rely on international agreements in order to challenge acts of Community institutions. The question of direct effect also addresses the problematic relationship between Community law and international norms as well as between Community institutions and international organizations.

2.5.2. Direct effect of international agreements on the Community legal order

The Court, which is the only competent body to assess and interpret the criteria for direct effect, has pursued the expansion of this doctrine in the context of various agreements between the Community and other states or international organizations. However, it is highly doubtful whether this line of case law could be extended to other forms of international agreements or acts taken by international organs. For it is clear that, far from adopting a uniform and coherent position, the Court seems to promote a

---

[59] Eeckhout (1997).

differentiated treatment depending on the type of international agreements at issue.

In respect of mixed agreements, the Court appears to be very prudent. Clearly, it does not totally assimilate this type of agreement to Community agreements. Such a feature attests to the limits of the Court's "mandate" in the field of EC international relations; whether these boundaries are due to external constraints or self-restraining attitudes of the ECJ itself.

In the domain of the Association agreements between the EC and a number of states, the ECJ appeared to have developed its principle of direct effect in its case law concerning rights of free movement of workers under various Association agreements, and in particular the EEC–Turkey Association agreements.[60] In *Sevince*, the Court confirmed that decisions of the Council of Association could also be directly effective, provided that the obligations contained were clear, precise and unconditional.[61]

By contrast, the Court has persistently refused to accept that the GATT, while binding on the Community, did not have direct applicability in the sense that individuals could invoke certain articles of the GATT before their national courts to challenge the validity of Community acts. Needless to say, it has been subject to great criticism in the available literature. While the Court claimed that it could interpret agreement binding on the Community, it would not examine whether the validity of a Community act was impaired by international law unless the latter rule was binding on the Community and was capable of creating rights of which interested parties might avail themselves in a court of law.[62] In contrast to certain national courts which appeared to recognize the self-executing character of GATT, the Court refused to do so.

The major critiques of the Court's position in respect of the direct effect of international agreements concern the following points. First of all, the ECJ appears to impose its own conditions as to when rules are binding. Secondly, the European judiciary seems to ignore the common interpretation and application given to the agreements by some member states and their foreign counterparts. Against this, it is argued that the Court is not free to modify standards of interpretation and application established at the international level, even for reasons of uniform interpretation inside the Community. Despite these harsh criticisms, the ECJ has not entirely modified its approach to international agreements in general, and the GATT in particular, even though it has departed from its global evaluation of the binding nature of an international agreement and has focused more on the question of the assessment of the relevant individual rules and provisions.[63] It now recognizes a qualified version of the doctrine of direct effect for certain provisions in international agreements, but has not necessarily required that the substantive interpretation of intra-Community law must also be transposed to them.

With regard to direct actions brought by individual companies against Community institutions, the Court has recently considered the legality of Council Regulation

---

[60] Cases C-237/91 *Kus* [1992] ECR I-6781; case C-18/90 *Kziber* [1991] ECR I-199.

[61] Case C-192/89 *Sevince*, [1990] ECR I-3461.

[62] Cases 21 to 24/72 *Third International Fruit Company v. Produktschap voor Groenten en Fruit* [1972] ECR 1219.

[63] Case 17/81 *Pabst and Richarz v. Hauptzollamt Oldenburg* [1982] ECR 1331.

2176/84, the basic regulation on protection against dumped or subsidised imports from non-EC countries, as well as individual regulations applying anti-dumping duties to particular products as contrary to both Article VI of the GATT and the GATT anti-dumping code. Obviously, despite the process of "constitutionalization" of the Treaties, the Court is not prepared to recognize international legal guarantees of freedom of trade such as the ones imposed by the GATT, and to confer a "constitutional" dimension to these norms.

2.6. CONCLUSION: TOWARDS A FOREIGN POLICY CONSTITUTION?

Controversies over the decisions of the Court are neither novel nor unusual.[64] They were, however, for a long time the domain of a small group of lawyers, most of whom specialized in European or business law. It is true that the view that the judicial institution could be considered the "least dangerous part" of the Community has long prevailed. In this view, the Court could devote itself to its cases since it was "...hidden away in idyllic Luxembourg and blessed with the generous disinterest of the truly powerful and the mass media" (Stein 1981). Such a posture enabled the Court to pursue its "quiet revolution" and steadily to enhance and expand the scope of Community law provisions (Weiler 1994).

This has certainly been the case in the field of the EC external relations, where the Court has significantly expanded its jurisdictional competence to review Community acts in the international arena and has assessed international agreements. Treaty provisions have been used by the ECJ as a basis to justify broadly its power to apply or interpret international treaties or other overriding rules of public international law. In its case law, the ECJ has expanded the principle of rule of law and judicial review to all Union powers. In this respect, it has frequently addressed the question of the proper division of Community and member states' competencies in the international arena. In addition, the Court has adopted a very expansive reading of its jurisdiction to consider international agreements, including agreements as regards matters which fall to the exclusive competence of the member states, or which are not necessarily dependent on the Community being party, or on its capacity to become party, to these agreements in international law. Such a jurisdictional competence signifies that the Court has the powers not only to examine and eventually invalidate the international acts of Union powers but also to review acts of international organs which are involved in the implementation of these broadly defined international agreements. Last but not least, the Court came to assess the very legality of the agreement concerned by

---

[64] In this respect, the Court's jurisprudence and the growing visibility of the judiciary in the arena of political integration have engendered strong reactions on the part of both political actors and scholars. There were attacks by Chancellor Kohl in 1992 (see Weiler 1994). More recently, the UK government proposed that the 1996 IGC should allow decisions of the Court to be overridden by a majority vote in the Council of Ministers (Agence Europe, 3 February 1995, p. 3). See also Editorial: "Quis custodiet the European Court of Justice", *Common Market Law Review*, Vol. 30, 1993, p. 899. Among scholars, "unfriendly" positions are epitomized by works, for instance, by Rasmussen (1986) and Coppel and O'Neill (1992).

the adjudication.

While constitutionalizing the Community legal order, the Court has progressively defined and shaped the relationship between Community law and national law but also between Community law and international norms. In this respect, both the Court and Community law are progressively becoming more "visible". With the shift to majority voting in the post-SEA period, national governments, which no longer have the "veto guarantee", seem to be more willing to minimize the influence of the ECJ, as attested by the restrictive provisions of the Treaty of European Union. Recently, there have been escalating reactions to the decisions of the Court and it seems that the criticism is harsher than ever; political bodies call for a review of the powers of the Court, which have apparently "developed in a way quite different from the original intentions".[65] As attested by some reform proposals on the occasion of IGC 1996, member states are increasingly anxious to influence the approach of the Court.[66]

Concurrently, the ECJ is withdrawing from sensitive issues by adopting a lower profile. In this respect, it is clear that it is trying to develop some control over the Article 177 procedure and adopting an increasingly "filtering" approach as regards preliminary rulings. The Court's caution regarding the now-famous principle of direct effect is also an exemplar. Obviously, the ECJ has begun to exercise more positive control over its own jurisdiction. The well-known "come one, come all" strategy of the ECJ has led to practical and political problems for the European judiciary which are in fact driving the ECJ into a position of relative retrenchment. Its refusal of direct effect of GATT and WTO norms is also a cause of problems. Despite this current context of contraints and self-restraint, the impact of judicial politics on EC external relations remains significant. In this respect, some provisions of the TEU might play a crucial part in the (re)activation of the Court's constitutional action in this field.[67] However, this does not seem to be the option favoured by the new treaty of Amsterdam.

2.7. REFERENCES

Bieber, R., R. Dehousse, J. Pinder and J.H.H. Weiler (eds) (1992). *1992: One European Market? A Critical Analysis of the Community's Internal Market Strategy*. Baden-Baden: Nomos Verlagsgesellschaft.

Burley, A.M. and W. Mattli (1993). "Europe before the Court: A Political Theory of Legal Integration". *International Organization 47*, 1.

Caporaso, J.A. and J.T.S. Keeler (1993). "The European Community and Regional Integration Theory", Paper prepared for the Third Biennal International Conference of the European Community Studies Association, Washington D.C., 27–29 May 1993.

Cappelletti, M., M. Seccombe and J.H.H. Weiler (eds) (1986). *Integration Through Law*, Berlin, New

---

[65] Federal Chancellor Kohl, EC-Forum of the Gemeinschaftsausschuß der Deutschen Gewerblichen Wirtschaft of 5 October 1982, *Europe* No. 5835, 14 October 1992.

[66] See editorial comments, "The IGC 1996 and the Court of Justice", *Common Market Law Review*, Vol. 32, No. 4, 1995, pp. 883–892.

[67] This refers, for instance, to provision 228 a inserted by the TEU. This provision, which considers the question of economic sanctions against one or more third countries, is the first to provide for the use of Community instruments for foreign policy ends.

York: Gruyter.

Coppel, J. and A. O'Neill (1992). "The European Court of Justice: taking rights seriously?". *Common Market Law Review 29*, 69ff.

de Witte, B. (1994). "Rules of Change in International Law: How Special is the European Community?". *Netherlands Yearbook of International Law 25*, 299–334.

Due, O. (1994). "The Law-making Role of the European Court of Justice Considered in Particular from the Perspective of Individuals and Undertakings". *Nordic Journal of International Law 63*, 123–137.

Eeckhout, P. (1997). "The Domestic legal Status of the WTO Agreement: Interconnecting Legal Systems". *Common Market Law Review 34*, 11–58.

Haartland, J.M. (1993). "Beyond Intergovernmentalism: The Quest for a Comprehensive Framework for the Study of Integration". *Cooperation and Conflict 28*, No. 2, 1810–208.

Hancher, L. (1994). "Constitutionalism, the Community Court and International Law". *Netherlands Yearbook of International Law XXV*, 259–298.

Harmsen, R. (1994). "A European Union of Variable Geometry: Problems and Perspectives". *Northern Ireland Legal Quarterly 45*, No. 2, 109–133.

Hill, C. (ed.) (1996) *The Actors in Europe"s Foreign Policy*. London: Routledge.

Jachtenfuchs, M. and B. Kohler-Koch (eds) (1996) *Europäische Integration*. Opladen: Leske & Budrich.

Mancini, F.G. (1989). "The Making of a Constitution for Europe". *Common Market Law Review 26*, 595–614.

Mattli, W. and A.M. Slaughter. (1995). "Law and Politics in the European Union: a reply to Garrett". *International Organization 49*, No. 1, 183–190.

Mattli, W. and A. M. Slaughter. (1996). "Constructing the European Community Legal System from the Ground Up: The Role of Individual Litigants and National Courts". EUI Working Papers, RSC, No. 96/56.

Monar, J. "The Foreign Affairs System of the Maastricht Treaty: a Combined Assessment of the CFSP and EC External Relations Elements". In: Monar, J., W. Ungerer and W. Wessels (eds) The Maastricht Treaty on European Union: Legal Complexity and Political Dynamic. Brussels: European University Press; 139–150.

Pescatore, P. (1981). "La Carence du législateur communautaire et le Devoir de Juge". In: Rechtsvergleichung, Europarecht, Staastintegration – Gedächtnisschrift für L.-J. Constantinesco. Cologne: Cark Heymanns Verlag; 559–580.

Pescatore, P. (1983). "The Doctrine of Direct Effect: An Infant Disease of Community Law". European Law Review 8, 157.#

Petersmann, E.-U. (1995). "Proposals for a New Constitution for the European Union: Building-Blocks for a Constitutional Theory and Constitutional Law of the EU". Common Market Law Review 32, No. 5, 1123–1175, 1164ff.

Prechal, S (1995). Directives in European Community Law. A Study of Directives and Their Enforcements in National Courts. Oxford: Clarendon Press; quote at p. 10.

Rasmussen, H. (1986). *On Law and Policy in the European Court of Justice: A Comparative Study of Judicial Policy Making*. Dordrecht: Martinus Nijhoff.

Sandholtz, W. (1996). "Membership Matters: Limits to the Functional Approach to European Integration". *Journal of Common Market Studies*, Sept.

Sbragia, A.M. (1992). *Europolitics: Institutions and Policymaking in the "New" European Community*. Washington, DC: Brokings Institutions.

Shapiro, M. (1981). Courts: A Comparative and Political Analysis. Chicago: University of Chicago; 23.

Shapiro, M. (1992). "The European Court of Justice". In: Sbragia, A.M. (ed.) Europolitics: Institutions and Policymaking in the "New" European Community. Washington, DC: Brookings Institutions.

Shapiro, M. and A. Stone. (1994). "The New Constitutional Politics of Europe". *Comparative Political Studies 26*, No. 4, Jan., 397–420.

Shaw, J. "European Union Legal Studies in Crisis? Towards a New Dynamic", EUI Working Paper, RSC, No. 95/23, EUI, Florence, 1995.

Smith, S. (1994). "Foreign Policy Theory and the New Europe". In: Carlnaes, W. and S. Smith (eds) *European Foreign Policy. The EC and Changing Perspectives in Europe*. London: Sage Publications; 1–20.

Snyder, F. (1985). *Law of the Common Agricultural Policy.* London: Sweet & Maxwell.

Stein, E. (1981). "Lawyers, Judges and the Making of a Transnational Constitution". American Journal of International Law 75, 1.

Stone, A. (1995). "Constitutional Dialogues in the EC". European University Institute, Florence, RSC, Working Paper 95/38.

Stone Sweet, A. and W. Sandholtz. (1997). "European Integration and Supranational Governance". In: *Journal of European Public Policy*, 4:3, 297–317.

Weiler, J.H.H. (1982). "Supranational Law and the Supranational System: Legal Structure and Political Process in the European Community". European University Institute, PhD Thesis.

Weiler, J.H.H. (1993). "Journey to an Unknown Destination: A Retrospective and Prospective of the European Court of Justice in the Arena of Political Integration". *Journal of Common Market Studies 31*, No. 4, Dec., 417–446.

Weiler, J.H.H. (1994). "Journey to an Unknown Destination: A Retrospective and Prospective of the European Court of Justice in the Arena of Political Integration". In Bulmer, S. and A. Scott (eds) *Economic and Political Integration in Europe*. Oxford: Blackwell; quote at p. 158.

Weiler, J.H.H. (1994). "'Quiet Revolution': The European Court of Justice and Its Interlocutors". *Comparative Political Studies 26*, 510, quote at p. 524.

Wincott, D. (1995). "The Role of Law or the Rule of the Court of Justice? An 'Institutional' Account of Judicial Politics in the European Community". *Journal of European Public Policy 2*, 4 Dec., 583–602.

CHAPTER 3

EU enlargement and European Security

Michael Leigh

3.1. INTRODUCTION

The transition from dictatorship to democracy in central and eastern Europe and much of the former Soviet Union has, on the whole, been remarkably peaceful. Political changes as momentous as any since the Russian revolution have taken place with little bloodshed, with the exception of the tragic conflicts in Chechnya and Bosnia. The credit for this achievement goes principally to the forbearance of the peoples concerned who have put up with harsh conditions, often involving a sharp drop in living standards, without putting into question the reform process. They have used the ballot box to express discontent with the slow pace of reform or with its social and economic consequences. In most countries this has led to an alternation in power of different political parties as in long-established democracies.

The general maturity of electorates in most transition countries has prevented sudden reversals of policy and contributed to broad consensus on the goals of political and economic reform. Exceptions have occurred mainly where the reform process was "confiscated" by the previous ruling élite or where power has been captured by an autocratic or charismatic leader. In the comparatively few cases where governments have proved reluctant to accept the outcome of elections (Serbia) or have clung to power despite popular discontent (Bulgaria), demonstrations and strikes created pressure for change.

Refusal by the authorities to recognize the legitimacy of this pressure and to act accordingly did put into question the peaceful nature of the transition process. But in Bulgaria the popularity of the new president, Petar Stoyanov, of the then opposition Union of Democratic Forces, following his election in November 1996, enabled him to persuade the ex-communist Bulgarian Socialist Party to accept an early general election, held in April 1997. The political and economic crisis that began in early 1997 in Albania sprang from a specific problem, the collapse of pyramid investment schemes. The government, under pressure from the EU and the OSCE, acknowledged the legitimacy of public disenchantment by agreeing to call early elections, but there remains a considerable risk of instability.

The transformation of central and eastern Europe has taken place in a favourable international context. Despite internal political turbulence and dissatisfaction among the old guard, Russia's acceptance of the new situation in Europe as well as the continued engagement of the United States contributed significantly to the generally

A. Cafruny and P. Peters (eds.), The Union and the World, 55–64
© 1998 Kluwer Academic Publishers. Printed in Great Britain.

pacific nature of political change. But another crucial factor, on which this chapter concentrates, has been the success of the European Union in providing a focus for the ambitions of countries in central and eastern Europe.

3.2. THE BREAK WITH THE PAST

The desire of the political élites and informed sectors of the public in these countries to join the European Union, and NATO, reflected the search for security and for acceptance into the main current of European political and economic life. Taking the steps to qualify for membership in the "Euro-Atlantic" institutions became a major theme in the policy of most governments. This was questioned only in countries where the break with the mentality and methods of the communist past was particularly ambiguous. Even in these cases, however, the need to qualify for EU and NATO membership became a rallying cry for democratic political forces.

3.3. THE DEVELOPMENT OF "SOFT" SECURITY

While debates in the OSCE and elsewhere on a new post-Cold War security system in Europe have, so far, proved inconclusive, the EU has contributed greatly to what is often referred to as "soft" security. Soft security refers to the creation of a network of interdependence which favours cooperation and the peaceful settlement of disputes and which makes threats from a potential adversary less likely. Such security has been enhanced by the association of central and eastern European countries with the EU and the prospect this opened to them of EU membership. Indeed, some central European leaders claim privately that EU membership will do more to enhance their countries' security than would NATO's article 5 security guarantee, which remains to be tested.

By stimulating political and economic reform, encouraging efforts to overcome regional conflicts, for example over minorities, supporting the fight against international crime, and making the associated countries more attractive to foreign investors, the EU has also reduced the risk of internal political instability. The EU's contribution to security in this wider sense has less to do with the Common Foreign and Security Policy, established by the Maastricht Treaty, than with its active political and economic engagement in the countries concerned. If the EU succeeds in giving the CFSP a harder edge, it could in future play an important role in preventive diplomacy, crisis management and conflict resolution.

3.4. THE PROSPECT OF EU MEMBERSHIP

The EU's influence in central and eastern Europe became firmly established in 1993 when it accepted the goal of EU membership for these countries and spelled out in detail the conditions for eligibility. The EU indicated which applicants were concerned and defined a strategy to prepare them for membership.

The success of the EU in encouraging the development of a zone of stability in central and eastern Europe has aroused certain expectations which may be hard to satisfy in the short term. The Nordic countries and the United States, for example, have made no secret of their wish for the EU to step in to provide a security framework for the Baltic states, as they will not be part of the first wave of NATO enlargement. There have been calls for the EU to take its decisions on enlargement largely on the basis of security considerations.

This is understandable in geo-strategic terms. Yet the EU's first obligation is to ensure that the integration process which it embodies remains viable. Accordingly, applications for EU membership are judged on their individual merits, bearing in mind particularly the capacity of the applicant to implement the full *"acquis"* of the European Union. Insistence on the need for applicants to be properly prepared before they become members is not inimical to the goal of strengthening security. For, if the integration process ground to a halt under the weight of new entrants that may not be ready to assume the full obligations of membership, the EU would cease to contribute to security and stability in Europe.

Unfortunately this has been little understood in the United States, where few policy-makers are aware of the intricacies of European integration. For them, a quick fix, whereby the EU would pick up the pieces left by NATO's enlargement, seemed an attractive solution. Among EU member states themselves, of course, the degree of commitment to maintaining the momentum of integration varies considerably and some might see an extension of the EU's soft security umbrella as a higher priority.

To explain how the EU came to assume such a central role in the geopolitics of post-Cold War Europe, we shall examine briefly its reaction to the political changes which began with "new thinking" in the Kremlin in 1985 and, within four years, had spread throughout the former COMECON bloc. For decades the European Community had been largely boycotted by the communist countries at the behest of Moscow, which viewed it as "the civilian arm of NATO" and, thus, a potential threat to its control of its satellites in central and eastern Europe. When the Velvet Revolution occurred in Czechoslovakia in November 1989, the European Community had few contractual or trade links with its neighbours to the east.

Against this background and considering the complexity of decision-making among twelve and, from 1995, fifteen member states, the European Union's response to the overwhelming interest expressed by the transition countries was particularly decisive. It had to overcome lobbying on behalf of a number of declining industries which felt threatened by the prospect of free trade with low-cost producers to the east. But on the whole, broader considerations prevailed. By moving swiftly to offer a new form of association to the transition countries, with the prospect of accession, the (then) European Community gave a positive response to their desire to "re-join" Europe. The new agreements were innovative and wide-ranging, covering political dialogue as well as economic rapprochement. The name "Europe agreement" was chosen to symbolize their ambitious nature.

The EU's central role in supporting the transition process was reinforced by the designation of the European Commission to coordinate assistance from all the major industrialized countries and the international financial institutions through the G-24. Grant aid from the EU through the Phare programme and loans guaranteed by the EU budget provided a challenge to the international community to come up with additional support. This was a useful catalyst but meant that the G-24 did, at times, become bogged down in discussions on "burden-sharing".

As the Europe agreements were extended to an increasing number of countries and their pre-ambular clauses became more explicit about the ultimate goal of EU membership, the European Commission, together with successive Council Presidencies, worked out a "pre-accession strategy" whose main lines were approved at the Essen European Council in 1994. The centrepiece was a White Paper, published in 1995, which provided a guide for the associated countries to prepare for participation in the single market. Inspired by the White Paper which launched the "Europe without frontiers" campaign in 1985, the new White Paper helped the associated countries to set priorities in adapting their legislation to the requirements of the single market. It quickly became clear that establishing the administrative and legal structures for proper implementation and enforcement was just as necessary as the laws themselves.

The EU recognized that it was important for the associated countries to feel part of the European integration process in the period before membership would be feasible. The concept emerged of a systematic relationship between the associated countries and the institutions of the EU, known as the "structured dialogue". This brought ministers from the ten associated countries and the fifteen member states together for regular meetings covering all the main areas of EU activity. Cyprus also maintains this type of dialogue with the EU, as did Malta until it froze its application for membership, following the victory of the Labour Party in the 1996 general elections.

The heads of government of the associated countries are invited to be present at European summits as part of this process. While somewhat cumbersome, these arrangements have led to greater understanding by the associated countries of EU policies and procedures. Cooperation on foreign and security policy, through the participation of the associated countries in the system of European correspondents, has involved them in frequent exchanges of information, as well as joint declarations and *démarches* with the fifteen.

In 1993 the Copenhagen European Council endorsed the goal of membership for the associated countries. The prospect of eventual EU accession helped to build a consensus in most associated countries in favour of further political and economic reform.

At Copenhagen, the EU also set out the political and economic conditions that the associated countries would have to meet. These conditions concern the stability of institutions guaranteeing democracy, the rule of law and the protection of human rights, including the rights of minorities, the existence of a functioning market economy, the ability of the applicant country to compete in Europe's single market and the capacity of the applicant to take on the other obligations of membership. Another condition was that the Union itself should be in a position to absorb new members while maintaining the momentum of integration.

These conditions gave the EU a legitimate interest in the reform process in the applicant countries and a basis for drawing attention to shortcomings. Whenever privatization, for example, seemed to be lagging or to be taking place in less than transparent conditions, European Commissioners and officials raised difficult questions. At the same time weaknesses in democracy or in the protection of minorities became a valid subject for discussion without any appearance of undue interference in domestic affairs.

This dialogue intensified once applications had been made. The Commission began to prepare formal opinions on each application pursuant to article O of the European Union Treaty. This involved questionnaires and detailed responses on every aspect of the applicants' political and economic situation and their capacity to implement the *acquis* of the Union. Since Maastricht, this *acquis* has included not only traditional economic policies but also foreign and security policy and justice and home affairs. This means that the dialogue with applicant countries on their preparations for membership covers a wide field.

While the EU approved the principle of enlargement in 1993, uncertainties remain over its scope and timing. Experience suggests that the negotiations and subsequent process of ratification will extend over several years. The pace of negotiations will differ according to the complexity of the issues raised by each application. It is, therefore, virtually excluded that all the candidates will enter the EU at the same time.

The prospect of accession provided the EU with additional leverage to ensure that reform in central and eastern Europe remained on track. It fell to the Commission to warn the applicants that they could not afford to relax reform efforts in the confidence that accession would go ahead anyway at an early date for political reasons or that deficiencies in their preparations could simply be overcome by derogations or transitional periods.

The Commission also kept up pressure on the applicants to bring competition policy, state aid controls and trade policy into line with EU rules. At times, for example, applicant countries adopted measures which favoured a major foreign investor but which ran counter to EU rules. Such measures, the Commission argued, in the course of negotiations which were sometimes prolonged, ran counter to the Europe agreements and were unacceptable in countries which aspired to join the single market.

3.5. REGIONAL COOPERATION

Another theme in the pre-accession strategy, launched at Essen in 1994, is regional cooperation. It made little sense for the Union to offer the associated countries free trade if they erected or maintained barriers among themselves. Nor could the Union envisage enlargement to countries with unresolved conflicts related to frontiers, minorities or other potentially explosive political problems. The EU did not wish to import instability through enlargement. Thus EU support for regional cooperation, developed in the enlargement context, had spin off benefits for European security in general.

Having recently recovered their sovereignty, some associated countries at first balked at regional cooperation, which they perceived as reviving the old east European bloc. There were also fears that such cooperation could become an alternative to joining the EU, a kind of "poor man's common market". Some leaders stated bluntly that they did not feel that they belonged at all to an east European "region" whose only common feature was that it had previously been subject to Soviet domination. Most governments looked west in their trade relations. Indeed, even before the communist period, relatively little trade had taken place among the countries of eastern Europe. Scepticism was strongest in the countries which were most advanced in the reform process; the less advanced were only too happy to be included in regional arrangements which confirmed their common European destiny.

While some doubts still linger, most associated countries came to see regional cooperation as part of preparations for EU integration rather than as a second best alternative. It also promised benefits for trade and investment. Many of these countries are rather small and find it easier to attract direct foreign investment if they can also offer investors access to neighbouring markets. The reduction of trade barriers in eastern Europe also provided outlets for goods which could not be sold as easily in the more demanding markets of western Europe. Besides these trade benefits, regional cooperation created opportunities to concert policy towards the EU and to reduce bilateral tensions, notably over minority rights.

Sub-regional groupings (i.e. those involving some but not all the actors in central and eastern Europe) provide practical means to foster integration while reducing tensions, where they exist, and strengthening links among the participants. To be successful, however, they require a considerable degree of common purpose, and concrete projects which respond to real needs, such as the improvement of border crossing facilities or the modernization of customs services.

The groupings which developed during the 1990s differ greatly with respect to degree of institutionalization (generally rather low), the number and the homogeneity of the participants, their focus – political, economic or sectoral – and their relations with broader structures such as the EU and the OSCE. Member states have played a prominent role in developing these groupings, for example Denmark, Germany, Finland and Sweden in the case of the Council of Baltic Sea States; Austria and Italy in the case of the Central European Initiative; and Greece in the case of Black Sea Economic Cooperation.

Membership of such groupings varies considerably and comprises EU member states, applicants for membership, EEA countries, and New Independent States of the former Soviet Union. The European Commission is fully involved in the Council of Baltic Sea States and the Barents Euro-Arctic Council, while it is invited to attend meetings of the Central European Initiative and Black Sea Economic Cooperation, without being a member.

The Council of Baltic Sea States brings together EU members, associated countries (Estonia, Latvia, Lithuania, Poland), Russia, which is linked to the EU through a partnership and cooperation agreement, Norway and Iceland. By chairing the Council's key working group on economic cooperation and tailoring PHARE and TACIS programmes to promote regional cooperation, the Commission is helping to foster a sense of common interests in the region.

The Visegrad group promoted cooperation between Poland, Hungary and Czecho-slovakia in the early years of the transition process. Although it declined in importance after the break-up of Czechoslovakia, it gave rise to the Central European Free Trade Area, which remains one of the most concrete examples of sub-regional cooperation. Participants are expected to be World Trade Organization members, to be linked with the EU through Europe agreements and to negotiate free trade agreements with other CEFTA countries. Since its inception in March 1993, CEFTA has boosted trade considerably among members and is mentioned frequently by foreign investors as improving the investment climate.

The EU has supported CEFTA from the outset and has consistently advocated its extension to other associated countries. Slovenia became a member at the beginning of 1996 and Romania in July 1997. Bulgaria, Latvia, Lithuania and Ukraine were invited to the CEFTA summit in 1996 as observers. By bringing down trade barriers, CEFTA has a positive influence on competitiveness and growth, and helps prepare its members for accession to the EU.

Sub-regional cooperation provides a bridge between the EU, countries likely to be among the first to join the EU, and others. It allows Russia and Ukraine, for example, to develop common projects with applicants for EU membership. It should also enable the EU's different support programmes to contribute to projects in adjoining regions of member states, associated countries and independent states of the former Soviet Union.

The prospect of EU accession has proved effective in defusing regional tensions both in central Europe and in the Baltic sea region. There was initial scepticism about the added value to be obtained from the "Stability Pact" which began as a French initiative and became a "common action" under the Common Foreign and Security Policy. But it turned out to be a useful framework for pressing for basic treaties to be concluded which would normalize bilateral relations between Hungary and Slovakia and Hungary and Romania. Hungary's treaty with Slovakia was actually signed at the Stability Pact meeting in Paris in 1995 and ratified in 1996, the year in which Hungary and Romania signed their basic treaty.

The EU had a direct role in defusing the tensions which had arisen over the Gabcikovo-Nagymaros dam on the Danube. This project was perceived in Hungary as a communist white elephant which had been started largely for strategic reasons and which was harmful to the environment. It was perceived in Czechoslovakia, and later in Slovakia, as a legitimate project which would cater to the country's energy needs, facilitate traffic on the Danube and even, in some respects, safeguard the natural environment. The issue became highly politicized, tensions rose and there were fears that they could escalate into direct confrontation.

The European Commission funded detailed technical studies and brokered an agreement between the parties to take the case to the International Court of Justice in the Hague. The work of EU experts also helped Hungary and Slovakia agree on how the Danube waters should be shared out pending a court judgment. This largely depoliticized the issue and reduced tensions.

As part of its role in analysing the preparedness of candidates for membership, the EU kept the political situation in the associated countries under constant review. In the case of Slovakia, the EU frequently drew the government's attention to weaknesses in democracy and the protection of minorities in a number of *démarches* and declarations. It was reassuring for the Hungarian minority to know that the EU, as well as the OSCE and the Council of Europe, was attentive to its situation. This also reduced any feeling in Hungary itself that it had to take strong measures in favour of the minority.

The EU has played a significant role in reducing tensions in the Baltic. Despite Russia's reluctance to participate in the Baltic round table set up under the Stability Pact, this initiative did lead to contacts between representatives of Russia, on the one hand, and Estonia, Latvia and Lithuania on the other. The EU offered support through its PHARE and TACIS programmes for cross-border projects which address common concerns.

As Estonia, Latvia and Lithuania are applicants for EU membership, the European Commission scrutinized closely policies regarding non-citizens and minorities to ensure that they were up to European standards. At the same time, the EU's dialogue with Russia provided a framework to stress the importance of its concluding agreements with these countries which would confirm borders and provide the basis for good neighbourly relations.

3.6. THE FIGHT AGAINST ORGANIZED CRIME

Another field in which the EU potentially has much to contribute to security is the fight against organized crime. Drug trafficking, illegal arms sales, illegal immigration and its exploitation, trade in human beings for prostitution, and money laundering are the downside of a more open society, with fewer barriers to the free movement of people. These problems have developed considerably in central and eastern Europe and the New Independent States since the end of the Cold War. Organized crime originating in Russia has penetrated many neighbouring countries. If unchecked, its spread could undermine public confidence in democratic institutions.

These problems are international by nature and cannot be prevented by the action of individual states alone. The EU's intergovernmental conference devoted considerable attention to strengthening cooperation on justice and home affairs and applying to it Community rules. But progress proved difficult because these areas, while having a major international dimension, are often still perceived as essentially the domain of national authorities.

Despite the difficulty in bringing these areas fully within the EU's purview, they have become a major theme for regional cooperation. Combating international crime was one of the priorities for joint action identified by the Visby summit of the Council of Baltic Sea States in 1995, on the basis of a plan put forward by Commission President Jacques Santer. The Commission has confirmed that Phare funds are available to support "third pillar" and related projects, and this will become an increasingly important field in the run-up to EU enlargement.

3.7. BORDER MANAGEMENT

Difficulties have been encountered by some applicant countries in managing borders, especially their eastern borders, because of the inadequate training of civilians, in an area traditionally the domain of the military, a shortage of personnel, low pay and a lack of economic development in border regions – encouraging corruption – and inadequate infrastructure. These deficiencies facilitate crime and are compounded by weak legislation and enforcement.

The EU can do much to strengthen border management in advance of accession and to bring it up to EU standards. This will be necessary to enable new member states to participate fully in the single market. The greatest needs include training for customs officers, the police and other experts, help with legislation and investment promotion in border regions. A multi-country drugs programme based in Riga is under way which could serve as a model for future action.

3.8. THE IMPACT OF ENLARGEMENT ON RELATIONS WITH THE EU'S NEIGHBOURS

The accession of ten countries in central and eastern Europe and of Cyprus would affect significantly the EU's geo-strategic situation. Its population would increase from 370 million to 470 million, its common frontiers with Russia and Turkey would be extended, and Belarus, Ukraine and Moldova would be immediate neighbours. The Baltic would become virtually an EU lake, with the important exception of the Russian coastline around St Petersburg and Kaliningrad. The EU would also have a major presence on the Black Sea. The stability of this new hinterland would become a major interest of the EU.

Yet this hinterland is a region of considerable volatility, which will demand the EU's attention. The countries concerned will be major economic partners of the enlarged EU and will wish to participate in the wider process of European integration. Turkey's application for EU membership, which it lodged in 1987 and on which the Commission issued an opinion in 1989, is still on the table. Other applications for membership cannot be excluded.

But the criteria for eligibility established in Copenhagen in 1993, including the political conditions relating to democracy, the rule of law and the protection of human rights, and the enhanced *acquis* emerging from the intergovernmental conference make further enlargement in the foreseeable future, beyond the eleven countries now involved in the pre-accession strategy, problematic. The impact on the EU's institutions, common policies and resources would be overwhelming.

The enlarged EU will thus need to develop a concept for managing relations with its eastern neighbours. Just as the Barcelona Conference launched the idea of a new Euro Mediterranean partnership and the Cannes summit backed this up with new resources for cooperation, the enlarged Union will have to consider how to involve neighbouring countries in the integration process.

The existing Union has had the foresight to create a network of partnership and cooperation agreements with Russia and other independent states of the former Soviet Union and to establish a customs union with Turkey, pursuant to the 1964 Ankara agreement. These contractual links, and the flows of trade and investment they have favoured, provide a basis for the further development of relations. But considerable diplomacy, tact and creativity will be needed to develop a pan-European concept to guide the external relations of the enlarged Union.

The natural corollary to the EU's role in promoting good neighbourly relations and internal stability would be a more overt role in "harder" forms of security. This raises complex questions related to the Common Foreign and Security Policy and the respective functions of the EU, the Western European Union and NATO. But, as indicated above, the EU is already contributing significantly to preventive diplomacy and conflict resolution and its effectiveness should increase with the improvements in the CFSP to be incorporated in the Treaty of Amsterdam.

3.9. CONCLUSION

This chapter has sought to demonstrate that the EU's response to political changes in central and eastern Europe and its preparations for further enlargement have contributed to stability and security in Europe. There is now no immediate perceived threat to the survival and the value systems of countries in central and eastern Europe, although it is easier to make this judgement when sitting in Florence or Brussels than in Riga or Prague. This sense of relative security is mainly due to the end of the Cold War and associated geopolitical changes. But it is fragile and vulnerable to external and internal sources of instability, which may not be easy to predict.

The EU has succeeded in reducing the risk of such instability by creating a network of interdependence and by supporting political and economic transition in practical ways. The offer of membership of the EU, subject to certain conditions, has greatly enhanced the EU's capacity to encourage policies and practices favouring political stability and to discourage others.

Trade liberalization, economic assistance, support for democratic institutions and the fight against organized crime in central and eastern Europe are policies which the EU conceived as part of its pre-accession strategy but which have spilled over into gains for security, notably "soft" security. Support for sub-regional cooperation, coupled with bilateral links, enables the EU to build bridges with countries unlikely to become members, at least in the foreseeable future, and thus to reduce the risk that enlargement will create new divisions in Europe.

If the EU succeeds in giving the CFSP a harder edge, this will allow it to play a more direct role in preventive diplomacy, crisis management and conflict resolution. By stressing that the enlargement process is a comprehensive one, involving all applicant countries, whatever their state of preparedness and the likely timing of their accession, the EU has adopted an approach which should enhance the security and stability of Europe as a whole.

CHAPTER 4

The cost of staying out of the European Union: Third states and foreign multinationals lobbying The EU decision-making process

Federiga M. Bindi Calussi

4.1. INTRODUCTION. THIRD COUNTRIES AND MNCS: EUROLOBBYISTS AMONG OTHERS?

To third countries and multinational corporations (MNCs) the European Union either is a feared "Fortress Europe" or represents new potential for investments and trades: MNCs and third countries thus need information, in order to (try to) influence those aspects of the Single Market which may concern them. In other words, they may need to rejoin the wide club of Eurolobbyists. In the European Community in 1970 there were about 300 Eurogroups;[1] in 1992 there were about 3,000, with more then 10,000 people involved,[2] and the figure is still increasing: this explosion can also be explained by institutional and policy changes.With the White Paper (1985) and the Single European Act (SEA, 1987), EC institutions obtained a new and powerful decision-making role *vis-à-vis* the twelve member States, thus initiating the recovery from the "Eurosclerosis" of the 1970s and early 1980s. The SEA changed the decision-making process: with the "cooperation procedure" the EC decision-making process became quicker and more incisive, but also more spread among institutions.[3] As Eckstein (1967, p. 208) showed, there is a direct relationship between the establishment of lobbies and the effective existence of a decision-making power. This appears to be confirmed by the Eurolobbying phenomenon: Europe-wide Interest

[1] See Economic and Social Committee (1980). In this text, the term "Eurogroup" refers to a pressure group whose aim is to influence the EU decision-making process, during one (or several) of its phases. Such a definition focuses on the locus of the lobby action; consequently, a single group can potentially be a local/national/European etc. pressure group, according to which decision-making process, at a given time, it ultimately intends to influence (local/national/European etc.). For example, the Italian industrialists' association, Confindustria, can act as a local or regional pressure group when it aims to influence a local provision; it can perform as a national pressure group when it tries to influence a national piece of legislation; or it act as a Eurogroup when it tries to influence EU pieces of legislation or policy.
[2] Commission CEE: *Un Dialogue ouvert et structuré entre la Commission et les groupes d'intérêt*, Doc. SEC(92) 2272 *final*, of 2.12.1992
[3] In addition to the changes in the legislative process, the SEA gave a mandate to proceed with the implementation of the EC Commission's White Paper of 1985. On the basis of the White Paper, 287 measures had to be taken, before 31 December 1992, in order to complete the Single European Market. Such measures have a direct effect on business and trade as well as on the everyday life of European citizens.

65

A. Cafruny and P. Peters (eds.), The Union and the World, 65–91

groups have existed since the early 1950s in industrial sectors such as coal, steel and agriculture, the fields then included in the Treaties. However, prior to the Single Act, much of the lobbying was done through national political and administrative channels, as member states had (and used) the possibility of blocking any legislation by use of the veto in the Council. Since the new "cooperation procedure" was introduced by the SEA, all proposals related to the creation of the Single Market had to be adopted on a qualified majority vote (QMV) basis: it didn't take long for interest groups to realize how much of the decision-making power was on its way to Brussels, and thus to respond to this new situation. The situation has been further changed by the Maastricht Treaty, as the new procedure (Art 189b) strengthens the position of the EP in influencing Eurolegislation.

The first Eurogroups to respond – attracted by the "1992 myth"[4] – were groups involved in economic activities, MNCs above all. However, as the SEA also introduced new EC fields of competence, such as environment or social policy, new kinds of groups also became active, such as promotional groups or territorial groups, of which *third states* are an example (see Andersen 1992, Andersen and Eliassen 1991, Garder 1990, Lowe 1989, Mazey and Richardson 1991, Nonon and Clamen 1991, Nugent 1991, Petite 1989, Sidjanski and Ayberk 1991, Wallace 1990).[5] As a consequence of the decision to act at the European level, most Eurogroups establish a permanent Secretariat in Brussels: proximity to EU institutions allows easier access to information and the establishment of informal contacts with EU decision-makers (Sidjanski and Ayberk 1991, Bindi 1993). The following two sections deal with non-EU states and MNCs lobbying the EU; in the last part of the chapter we shall analyse the peculiarities of Eurolobbying, quoting cases relevant linked to third states and MNCs.

4.2. THIRD STATES LOBBYING THE EU

Third states (i.e. non-EU member states) attach a great deal of importance to their

---

[4] The advantages expected from the complexion of the Single Market contributed to create a sort of "1992 myth" which further explains the "explosion" of Eurolobbying since the mid-1980s (Cecchini, 1988)

[5] Elsewere (Bindi, 1996), Eurogroups are divided into four kinds according to the *kind of shared interest*:

• *Economic Eurogroups* are related to the economic sectors (capital and workers) of the society and (can) gain a financial benefit from their European activities: they comprise professional organizations, trade unions, groups involved in trades, etc. They can be divided into the following sub-types: *European (con)federations, national organisations, single firms.*

• *Public interest groups* are concerned with the promotion of topics which may affect large sectors of the society; they are groups defending consumers' rights or the right to public health, groups against nuclear power, etc.

• *Promotional groups* aim to promote special causes or ideas, of political, cultural, religious, etc. origins. Promotional Eurogroups have lately become very influential. They can be *political movements* as well as *think tanks.*

• *Territorial groups* aim to promote the interests of a territorial entity, this being an EU member state *region, town* or *county*, a *third state*, or even an *international organization.*

Not to be confused with these four categories of Eurogroups are the so-called *professional lobbyists*, who can be hired by Eurogroups on a permanent or *ad hoc* basis, according to their means and/or needs.

relationships with the EU, so that more than 130 states have a diplomatic mission to the EU in Brussels, in addition to their embassy to the Kingdom of Belgium. Bigger states may even have *ad hoc* EU offices which follow specific issues (trade, agriculture, etc.); smaller states that cannot have two diplomatic missions usually create an EU department within their embassy to the Kingdom of Belgium.

The interests of third states differ, but most non-EU states are mainly interested in trade and political relationships. To achieve them both, the first step is to establish a formal link to the EU. From Art 210 TEC, the European Union has in fact legal personality[6] and can thus negotiate agreements with states and international organizations. The agreements that can take place between the EU and a third state can broadly be divided into three kinds (Gautron 1994, p. 51):

1. membership
2. association agreements
3. trade and cooperation agreements.

Each category can be subdivided: for instance, association agreements can be classified as preferential agreements and non-preferential agreements.[7] The TEU deals with external agreements in various articles: in art 228 TEC it supplies the internal mechanism to conduct external agreements; with art 238 TEC it establishes that "the Community may conclude with one or more states or international organisations agreements establishing an association involving reciprocal rights and obligations, common action and special procedure"; arts 131–136a TEC deal with the associations of non-European countries and territories which have special relations with Denmark, France, Holland and the UK; art 113 TEC applies to agreements with states or international organizations in the field of commercial policy. According to the new Amsterdam Treaty art 113 TEC may be used also in agreements related to services and intellectual property.

The Maastricht Treaty extended the use of the procedures ex art 228 TEC to all cases where the TEU "... provides for the conclusions of agreements between the Community and one or more States and Treaties", including agreements in the field of commercial policy (i.e. ex. 113 TEC). The formula where this treaty provides for in 228(1) TEC refers to the art. 113, 130m, 130r, 130y, 238 TEC which all refer to art 228 TEC as the procedure to be followed in the conclusion of agreements by the Community. But the EC's external competencies are not limited to those areas. Art 126(3), 127(3), 128(3) and 129(3) TEC provide for the EC to foster cooperation with international organizations and third states and, furthermore, the EC has implied powers to enter into international agreements in many areas in which it has internal

---

[6] Such ability has been reinforced over the years by the ECJ's judgments: for instance, in *Commission v. Council* (AETR case, 31/3/1971) the ECJ established that the member states can no longer negotiate with third parties in the fields where common rules exist within the (then) EEC. Other cases interesting in this context are the *Advice* 1/75 of 11/11/75 on the common commercial policy; the *Kramer* Judgment (14/7/1976); the *Advices* 1/76 of 26/4/77 and 1/91 (see Gautron 1994, 211–212).

[7] Preferential agreements include several free-trade agreements (also on specific products); the EEA agreement; cooperation conventions such as Lomé; and several agreements having as objective the establishment of a free trade area or a custom union. Non-preferential agreements include tariff agreements; trade agreements (e.g. *nation plus favorisée*); trade cooperation agreements; framework agreements on trade and economic cooperation (see Gautron 1994, p. 213; Depondt 1995, p. 147).

legislative competence. In other words – disregarding art.109 TEC – the provisions of art. 228 are for general applications in all cases where the EC exercises its competence in international agreements.

Furthermore with the Maastricht Treaty, the role of the Commission in negotiating such agreements has been partially diminished to the extent that now, from art 228 EEC, the Council formally oversees the negotiation of agreements, using the example of what already existed concerning agreements in the field of commercial policy (art 113 TEC). On the other side, the European Parliament is given more standing, notably though the extra assent procedure indicated in the latter part of para 3.[8] However, the EP is still excluded from commercial agreements, as well as from the possibility to appeal to the ECJ.

Obviously, the kind of agreement a state has with the EU is relevant in lobbying the EU itself; much effort on the part of third states is thus employed in negotiating such agreements. For instance, during EEA negotiations[9] the EFTA officials first focused on EC Commission and Council, but later gave prominence to the European Parliament, in view of both debate and vote. Such lobby action lasted several months: as a first step, contacts with MEPs were established, particularly with the EP's President Egon Klepsh, whose role was decisive in the vote. In fact, in order to adopt an Association Agreement, the absolute majority of the votes is needed in the EP.[10] Therefore it is necessary that most MEPs actually be present in the Plenary room: an unusual situation. So Klepsh – under request of EFTA officials – used a "technical trick" in order to verify the number of MEPs in the room before asking for a vote: the EEA agreement was thus adopted by the Parliament with 351 votes in favour, 16 against (the Greens) and 17 abstentions.[11]

But how are the relationships between the EU and third states? We shall now look at them in terms of geography.

---

[8] "...agreements establishing a specific institutional framework by organizing cooperation procedure, agreements having important budgetary implications for the Community and agreements entailing amendament of an act adopted under the procedure referred to in art. 189b shall be concluded after the assent of the European Parliament has been obtained". Art 228,3 EEC, 2nd para.

[9] Juridically based on art 238 EEC, the EEA agreement foresaw the founding of a *European Economic Area* (EEA) which – as from 1 January 1993 – should have given rise to the widest free trade area of the world, involving 19 countries (EC plus EFTA countries), thus 380 millions citizens and 42.4 per cent of global trade. EEA institutions can be seen as "asymmetrical institutions", where the EEA itself is almost a kind of extension of the EC Single Market. The EEA agreement is constituted by 129 articles, 1000 pages (mainly annexes), plus about 12,000 pages of *acquis communautaire* (i.e. EC legislation) which EFTA countries must implement. Future EC legislation will also have to be implemented by EFTA countries, without them having a real say on it (Sæter 1991).

EFTA representatives are in fact to be consulted by the Commission in the preliminary phase of the legislative process but they will not be able to vote on it. The EEA institutions are the following: Council of Ministers, Joint Committee, Court of Justice (independent of, but linked to, the ECJ), Parliamentary Committee and Consultative Committee. They shall hold periodic meetings: the Council every six months, the Joint Committee once a month. The Presidency shall alternate between EC and EFTA every six months. The EEA agreement is constituted by 129 articles, 1000 pages (mainly annexes), plus about 12,000 pages of *acquis communautaire* (i.e. EC legislation) which EFTA countries must implement. It is only a marginal agreement today, as Finland, Sweden and Austria opted for EU membership.

[10] i.e. 314 votes.

[11] *Agence Europe*, 9, 29 & 30/10/1992.

4.2.1. Western Europe

Little of Western Europe remains out of the EU: only Norway, Switzerland, Iceland and small states such as Monaco, San Marino, Liechtenstein, the Vatican and Andorra. Norway twice negotiated membership of the EC/EU; both times (1972 and 1994) membership was rejected by the population in a referendum. Yet the EU remains Norway's most important partner, from both an economic and a political point of view. Norway is in fact the only non-EU and non-WEU (Western European Union) country to be a member of NATO, and, of the former EFTA countries, it was the one most closely linked to European Political Cooperation (EPC).[12] It and Liechtenstein being the only members of the EEA outside the EU, Norway has to cope with the fact that – as the former Norwegian Minister for Foreign Affairs, Thorvald Stoltenberg, put it – "...staying outside it [the EU] we remain without influence on the decisions that certainly will have a bearing upon us" (Stoltenberg 1992).

Consequently, there is strong determination on the part of the Norwegian government to keep a strict and good relationship with the EU. In any case the Commission has made clear that "Norway has decided to stay out twice, and having decided that on its own, it's their problem"[13].

The Norwegian Government, given that there continues to be good cooperation among the Scandinavian countries – for instance a meeting of the Ambassadors to the EU takes place weekly – had initially hoped that Sweden, Finland and Denmark would act as representatives of Norwegian interests in the EU, as was the case with Denmark before Sweden and Finland joined the EU. However, Nordic cooperation seems to have been penalized by the last EU enlargement: in fact, it is seldom that the EU Scandinavian countries defend the interests of Norway, unless of course if Norwegian interests either coincides with, or hides their own interests. However, there are cases, like the "war of the herrings", where Sweden did not only not defend Norway's position, but rather assumed the role of defender of "EU interests" against Norway[14].

Given this situation, Norway had to reorganize its links with the EU to defend and promote its interests on its own. The patterns described below about Norway are quite representative of other European countries such as Switzerland, and of non-European countries such as Japan, South Korea or the United States (which will be dealt with in detail below), etc.

The Norwegian Mission to the EU Commission employs 28 people, representing 9 of the 19 Norwegian ministries: Agriculture, Environment, Transport, Finance, Energy, Work, Social Affairs, Foreign Affairs and Local Affairs. The function of the EU Embassy is both to send home information on EU politics and activities and to inform EU institutions on the most relevant Norwegian events. Each of the officials is responsible for his own field, including keeping good relationships with EU officials. Norway is allowed to send four *stagiaires* to the Commission each semester, in

---

[12] With observer status at the WEU and a high degree of collaboration with the EPC (Church 1990, p. 415).

[13] Interview.

[14] The question is related to fishing of herrings in the Norwegian sea. Of course Sweden had its own interest in playing the "European difensor" role. (Cf. *Sole 24 Ore,* 2.4.1996)

addition to a number of Norwegian public officials who work for the Commission, for a period generally of three months. One official of the Embassy is charged with following the plenary meetings of the European Parliament. Twice a year the MEPs belonging to the EP commission charged with the relationships with Norway are invited to visit the Storting (the Norwegian Parliament) and on such occasions are usually escorted by the Norwegian Ambassador to the EU. Relationships with the COREPER also exist, although Norway tends to rely on bilateral relationships with EU states. In Brussels there are offices of NHO, LO, the Norwegian Trade Council and 15 other Norwegian companies including *Norsk Hydro* and *Statoil*.[15]

Switzerland is a country whose relationships to the EU – and to international organizations in general – are rather puzzling. Switzerland signed the *Stockholm Convention* on January 4, 1960 creating the *European Free Trade Association* (EFTA). Then followed its EFTA counterparts in creating the EEA, perceiving it as a first step to membership into the EU. However, when a federal referendum resulted in a "No" to the EEA, the Swiss Government stated first that membership was not on the agenda anymore, then asserted that EU membership was not on the short term agenda, but it was still on the long term agenda. Indeed, the Federal Government is investing an impressive amount of money in financing pro-EU activities and researches (showing to have learnt the Norwegian lesson: first mobilize public opinion, then apply). The actual Swiss' behavior after the "No" to the EEA has been rather puzzling: after the negative referendum, spurred by its business organization *Vorort,* the Government started to negotiate bilateral agreements with the EU. So, for instance, Switzerland finally negotiated an agreement on customs cooperation with the EU but, at the same time, no agreement was made on haulage transportation.[16] Furthermore, on January 1, 1998 a major reform to the taxation of holdings will be introduced, in order to make Switzerland more competitive than the EU member states for the constitution of holdings[17].

4.2.2. Eastern Europe

The USSR recognized the EC only in 1988. Just one year later, its former satellites aimed to become part of the EC itself. Indeed – at least concerning the Central and Eastern European Countries (CEECs). In the Amsterdam Council (16–17/6/1997) the European Heads of State and Government restated their commitment to enlarging the Union to eastern Europe by noting "...that, with the successful conclusion of the IGC, the way is now open for launching the enlargement process ... the Commission in its *Agenda 2000* communication will draw the main conclusions and recommendations ... and [will] give its views on the launching of the process ... enabling the actual opening

---

[15] Norsk Hydro (Hydro Egri and Hydro Aluminium), Statoil, Det Norske Veritas Classification, Dyno Industrier, Elsafe, Montin, Nycomed, Noral, Norske Skog, Norway Foods (names given by the Norwegian Trade Council)

[16] It was the last European state of a certain importance to negotiate a custom cooperation agreement! *Sole 24 Ore,* 10.6.1997

[17] *Sole 24 Ore,* 5.6.1997

of negotiations as soon as possible after December 1997..."[18] According to the *Agenda 2000* communication[19] negotiations with Poland, Hungry, Czech Republic, Slovene, Estonia and Cyprus and the EU will begin negotiations in January 1998, and they will likely become members around the years 2005–2010 – this is also the wish of the EU. Economic and trade agreements were signed as early as 1988 (Hungary and Czechoslovakia), 1989 (Poland) and 1990 (Bulgaria and Romania), and replaced by association agreements in 1992 (Hungary and Poland), 1993 (Czech Republic, Slovak Republic, Bulgaria and Romania) and 1996 (Slovenia). With Albania, the Baltic states and Russia there are still only trade agreements.

Economic and trade agreements were signed as early as 1988 (Hungary and Czechoslovakia), 1989 (Poland) and 1990 (Bulgaria and Romania); such agreements were then "upgraded" to association agreements (the so-called *Europa-agreements*) respectively in 1992 (Hungary and Poland) and 1993 (Czech Republic, Slovak Republic, Bulgaria and Romania) and (Slovenia) 1996. With Albania, the Baltic states and Russia there are still only trade agreements. However, on March 23, 1997, Russian President Boris Yeltsin declared to President Clinton that one of Russia's objectives was to be finally recognized as a "fully European" state by adhering to the EU. The concept was further reaffirmed in July 1997 by Prime Minister Viktor Tchernomyrdine who – in front of an astonished Commissioner Hans Van den Broek – declared that "all of Russian's activities aim, *moment venu*, to join the EU."[20] Russia, together with the CEECs, is part of *ad hoc* EU programs such as *Phare* or *Tacis*.

Last, but not least – as will be discussed later in the chapter – Eastern European countries, thanks to their association agreements with the EU (and cheap skilled labour), can represent an interesting gateway to the EU to third states companies. Indeed, it is interesting to note how in Poland, of the top ten private investment companies, four are American companies, one Australian, one Swiss and two MNCs[21].

4.2.3. Mediterranean Area

The relationships with Greece, Spain and Portugal evolved into membership in the 1980s.[22] Turkey, Cyprus and Malta – which have also applied for membership[23] –

---

[18] *Presidency Conclusions* in General Secretariat of the Council of the European Union, 1997

[19] The *Agenda 2000* communication was presented by Jacques Santer to the European Parliament Plenary in Strasbourg on the 15.7.1997. Besides enlargement, Agenda 2000 discusses the future of structural funds, of the CAP and of the EU budget. For a detailed analysis, cf. Bindi and Peters, *The Santer's Commission*, forthcoming 1998.

[20] *Le Figarò*, 19.7.1997

[21] The correct order is: Fiat (ITA); Ebrd (MNC); Polish-American Enterprise Fund (US); Pepsico (US); Ing Group (NL); Coca-Cola Amant (AUS); Int. Finance Co. (MNC), Nestlè (CH); Philip Morris (US). (*Sole 24 Ore*, 20.5.1997)

[22] Greece joined in 1981, Spain and Portugal – after 7 years of negotiations – in 1986.

have association agreements with the EU. Also, there is a cooperation agreement with San Marino. As for the other side of the Mediterranean, there are agreements covering the fields of agriculture, energy, industry, distribution trades, infrastructure, education and training, health, environment and scientific cooperation with the Maghreb countries (Algeria, Morocco[24] and Tunisia), the Mashrek countries (Egypt,[25] Jordan[26], Lebanon and Syria), Israel, Gaza Strip and the West Bank (Mathijansen 1995, pp. 376–377), while a cooperation agreement with the States of the Gulf was signed in 1988 (Boudant-Gounelle 1989, p. 206).

4.2.4. *United States of America*

The relationship between the USA and the EU is rather ambiguous: one the one hand, both sides claim to attach great importance to closer cooperation and to a strengthening of their relation, and on the other hand they are involved in what seem petty disputes, threats, retaliation measures, counter-retaliations, etc. (Mathijansen 1995, pp. 372–373). In any case, since the USA and the EU are each other's largest trading partners,[27] partnership goes on. In November 1990 a *Transatlantic Declaration* was adopted, under which both parties affirm their determination to strengthen their partnership, which includes the need to inform and consult each other, to strengthen the multinational trading system, mutual cooperation in various fields such as research in medicine, environmental protection, etc., and the development of a consultation procedure.[28] Among other things, the principle of semestrial meetings between the President of the USA and the Presidents of the EU Council and of the Commission is reaffirmed. In one such meeting (Madrid, 1995), Clinton, Santer and Gonzales set out a *Framework for Action* with four major goals: promoting peace, stability, democracy and development around the world; responding to global challenges (fighting international crime, drugs trafficking and terrorism; protecting the environment; etc.); contributing to the expansion of world trade and closer economic relations; building bridges across the Atlantic (working with business people, scientists, etc.). The main object of the *New Transatlantic Agenda* is the establishment of a transatlantic marketplace designed to eliminate trade barriers and to expand trade and investment opportunities and to create jobs on both sides of the Atlantic (AMCHAM 1997, p. 279). In November 1995 a *Transatlantic Business Dialogue (TABD)* was also launched (see section 4.3). Indeed, the USA appears to be the most effective lobbyist among third

---

[23] Turkey has been rejected for the moment by the Commission. With Malta and Cyprus negotiation could take place in the near future, although the 1996 elections in Malta returned the Labour party, which opposes membership. A Customs Union has been signed with Ankara.

[24] Morocco has also applied for membership!

[25] An association agreement called a Euro-Mediterranean Association Agreement with Egypt is currently being negotiated. Negotiations started in January 1995.

[26] A Euro-Mediterranean Association Agreement has been signed in 1997.

[27] US–EU trade flows amount to more than $250 annually. The EU is the US's largest export market, accounting for over 20 per cent of total US exports; more than half of the sales of American overseas affiliates ($818 billion) are in the EU (AMCHAM, 1997: 279)

[28] A similar agreement was adopted between the EU and Canada, also in November 1990.

states, on the one hand due to the means employed, and on the other one to the US lobbying-oriented political culture.[29] The US diplomatic mission to the EU is the biggest in Brussels, with more than 50 officials dealing with different topics. In addition, a number of bodies are effectively part of the US lobby: the *TABD*; the EU Committee of the American Chamber of Commerce in Belgium (AMCHAM) and its new baby, the European–American Industrial Council (EAIC); the AMCHAMs in the various countries in Europe (coordinated by the European Council of the American Chamber of Commerce, ECACC); and the *US Industry Coordinating Group* (USICG). These are considered in more detail in section 4.3.

4.2.5. Asia

A paper entitled *Towards a New Asia Strategy* was elaborated and approved during the German Presidency in July 1994 (Nugent 1995, pp. 81–82). The EU has ratified a number of trade agreements (usually sectoral) with India, Pakistan, Sri Lanka, Bangladesh, Macao, Mongolia, Thailand, and China.[30] There is a cooperation agreement with the ANSEAN countries (Indonesia, Malaysia, the Philippines, Thailand, Brunei). The framework for a cooperation agreement was been agreed in October 1996 with South Korea, while a Joint EC–Japan Declaration was adopted in 1991 foreseeing cooperation in the fields of trade, environment, industry, scientific research, social affairs, competition policy and energy, followed by an agreement on auto-limitation of car imports valid until 31 December 1999 (Mathijansen 1995, pp. 373–374; *Documentation Française* 1992, p. 138). Such an agreement, which does not have the force of international law although it was notified to GATT, it is in fact a "gentleman's agreement" setting out the elements of consensus. It has being a major issue for a long time for both Europeans and Japanese. Finally, it was possible to agree a voluntary export restraint (VER) on the part of Japan in exchange for a number of things, such as the Commission's ceasing to authorize recourse to art 115 TEC, i.e. the possibility for a member state to adopt measures in trade policy in case of urgency (used, for instance, by Italy to limit Japan's cars imports). But the EC committed itself to imposing no restrictions on Japan's investments or on free circulation of Japanese products in the EC, while there was no commitment on the part of Japan to limit its EC transplant production (production or assembly in the EC by Japanese companies). Ironically, while the European automobile industry, with the exception of Peugeot-Citroën, reacted positively, Lindsay Halstead, Chairman of Ford Europe, attacked

---

[29] To Americans lobbying is a well-known process, considered useful for democracy. Toqueville in its *Democracy in America* (1835) saw the role played by groups as the basis for democracy; the verb "to lobby" was invented in the USA (the term "lobby" in fact originally referred, in the US experience, to a room where parliamentarians and others could talk). In 1830, representatives of interest groups began to visit the American Congress in order to contact and try to influence American congressmen, quickly becoming known as "lobbyists"; consequently, a lobbyist is a person who – whether being paid or not, whether a member of the group or simply delegated by it – tries to influence the adoption (or rejection) of a piece of legislation *(US Federal Act*, 1946, sect. 308(a)).
[30] China recognized the EC in 1975 and concluded the agreement in 1978, subsequently renewed with the exception of the period 1989–1991.

both the Commission and the British Government for encouraging Japanese car makers to invest in Europe (Andersen 1992, pp. 309–314). In fact, Halstead was the only one to see the Trojan horse: he felt that the Japanese MNCs would adopt the strategy of producing directly in Europe (see section 4.3). This episode also threw some light on the Japanese lobby strategy: the Japanese in Europe are quiet and difficult to penetrate, but this does not mean that they are not moving: they are simply long-term lobby investors. Their invasion of the US market is a good example: in the US, Japan started in the late 1970s to finance universities and think-tanks, they invited influential (or potentially influential) people to visit Japan, making sure to provide them with the best hospitality and paying them generously for their time. In contrast to the Americans, who know how to intervene bottom-up in the decision-making proc-esses, Japanese's strategy is to intervene from the top down in the socio-political hierarchy, and to follow the "3S" rule: *Sleep, Silence, Smile*. Their presence in Europe had increased four-fold by the early 1990s (Nonon and Clamen 1990, pp. 195–202).

4.2.6. Latin America

Relationships with Latin America have been developing since the beginning of the 1980s, especially since Spain and Portugal became members of the EC. The EU has established relations with the *Rio Group* countries (Argentina, Brazil, Colombia, Mexico, Peru, Uruguay and Venezuela), the countries of Central America (the *San José dialogue*) and *Mercosur* and the *Andean group* (Bolivia, Colombia, Equador, Peru and Venezuela). A more ambitious agreement with Mexico on political, com-mercial and economic co-operation is being negotiated, but, at the time of writing, the finalization of the agreement has been suspended on the issue of human rights, a clause which is nowadays "standard" in all agreements with thirds states[31].

An issue marked in the last years by tension was the trading of bananas. Indeed, it is more of interest to the US which was adversely affected by this rather than Cen-tral/Latin American. In the last replacement of import regimes in certain EU member states with a single EU-wide system, preference was given to bananas produced in the ACP countries, thus "discriminating" against the so-called dollar-bananas produced in Central America which had previously entered half of the member states without restrictions. After failing to get satisfaction through bilateral negotiation, several banana-producing countries joined the US in filing a complaint with the WTO[32].

4.2.7. Africa

There are two relevant cases: the Lomé Convention and South Africa. As soon as Mandela was elected President of South Africa negotiations began, culminating in a Cooperation Agreement which, besides aiming to boost cooperation in trade and

---

[31] *L'Echo,* 23.6.1997
[32] Calingaert, 1996: 154

development, deals with the questions of democracy and human rights. It also represents the essential groundwork for a Free Trade agreement between the EU and S. Africa.[33]

The Lomé Convention concerns the so-called ACP (African, Caribbean and Pacific) countries, i.e. some 70 states, mainly former colonies of EU member states. Signed for the first time in 1964 as the *Yaounde I* Convention, replaced by Yaounde II in 1971, it was then transformed into Lomé I in 1975, followed by Lomé II, III and IV every five years (the last one for ten years). If Yaounde I was still marked by the paternalistic approach of most of the European countries towards their former colonies, the Lomé Conventions aim to establish a kind of partnership between developing countries and the Community; they thus establish commercial, industrial and financial relations between the EU and the ACP countries. These countries enjoy, among other things – without reciprocity for the EU member states – free entry into the EU of most of their agriculture products and all industrial products originated there.[34] Furthermore, the Convention touches the principles of human rights and respect for human dignity: art 5 of the Convention even specifies the various categories (non-discriminatory treatment; fundamental human rights; civil and political rights; economic, social and cultural rights). It also decrees that financial resources may be allocated for the promotion of human rights in the ACP countries through specific schemes.[35] Finally, the Lomé Convention establishes paritarian institutions: the EU–ACP Council of Ministers, the EU–ACP Ambassadors' Committee; the paritarian EU–ACP Assembly.

4.3. MNCs LOBBYING THE EU

We can define an MNC as an organization having operations in a number of countries, the ownership of the MNC determining its origin – an American, Japanese or German MNC, etc.[36] Obviously, regarding strategies *vis-à-vis* the European Union, it is important whether an MNC is of EU origin or not. Section 4.4 looks at methods of lobbying for both EU-owned and non-EU-owned MNCs; this section essentially deals with originally non-EU MNCs, with particular emphasis on American and Asian ones.

The EU is the largest trading bloc in the world, with 15 members and 371 million people, and has the highest GNP per head ($21,150 *vs.* $15,807 in NAFTA, $14,000 in APEC and $1,680 in ANSEAN). It is hence a very desirable market. Indeed, US exports to the EU amount to $1,032 million (*vs.* $865 from the EU to the US), while Japan's exports to the EU are worth $592 million (EU exports to Japan amount to

---

[33] The EU is S. Africa's most important trading partner, taking more than 40 per cent of its exports and providing 33 per cent of its imports: a total of 15 billion ECUs (Nugent 1995, pp. 80–81).

[34] Between 95 and 98.5 per cent of ACP exports can have free access to the EU (*Documentation Française* 1992, pp. 141-144).

[35] Nugent (ed), 1995: 390-393

[36] According to the *Concise Oxford Dictionary of Politics*, a multinational corporation (MNC) exists where "clear managerial coordination and control together with some elements of ownership link legally distinct business operating in several countries".

$318 millions) (Nagel and Spencer 1996, pp. 12–13). However, despite the trade liberalization process of recent years within GATT (today WTO), it is not always easy for produce to enter the EU, due to non-tariff barriers, anti-dumping or anti-subsidies duties, etc. The completion of the Single Market increases this difficulty, as it establishes common rules that non-EU MNCs also have to respect if their products are to circulate within the Union: EU *technical standards* can thus could turn into *technical barriers* for MNCs. For instance, an anti-pollution directive can have adverse effects on imports. Also, in many fields, the EU has tended to protect its own products *vis-à-vis* foreign ones, for instance by introducing *quotas* (e.g. the mentioned case concerning the Japanese car industry), or *subsidies* to its own producers (subsidies of agriculture products are one of the major and long-standing disputes between the US and the EU).

It is much more difficult to lobby the EU institutions as an outsider than as an insider. The above-mentioned "war of herrings" in the Norwegian Sea, for instance, shows how industries can benefit from being supported by their own member state. So, one possibility is for an MNC to push its own government to institute preferential agreements with the EU. For instance, Norway and Switzerland, soon after having said "No" respectively to the EU and the EEA – spurred by their business organizations – started to negotiate bilateral agreements with the EU. In particular, the Swiss business organisation, *Vorort*, worried by the negative consequences on exports of the joint effect of EU technical barriers and the strong Swiss franc, is pushing for an agreement providing equal treatment to workers in Switzerland (on the basis of reciprocity) and the abolition of the much criticized (by the EU) limit of 28 tonnes for transportation by road.[37]

However, as mentioned above, bilateral agreements first of all do not cover all the trading areas (for instance fisheries and agriculture are usually excluded); secondly, with the exception of ACP countries, non-European states are always given a less favoured status than that granted to European ones. So additional strategies are needed: first, establish a Euro-office in Brussels; second, transplant into Europe.

Until a few years ago, MNCs used to coordinate their European activities from their headquarters in nearby capitals, mainly London and Amsterdam. Today, specific "Euro-offices" are increasing being established in Brussels. In addition, MNCs try to become members of one or more Eurogroups. Among the firms having an *ad hoc* lobby office in Brussels are Fiat, Ferruzzi, Elf-Aquitane, Rhone-Poulenc, Bull, Philips, Exxon, ICI, Shell, IBM, Siemens, Mercedes, Dassault, Monstanto, British Steel and British Coal (Richardson and Mazey 1991, Love 1990, Petit 1990, Butt Philips 1992). Alternatively, firms may decide to hire a professional lobbyist to look after their interests.[38] The duties and objectives of the MNCs' Brussels offices are similar to those of other groups: to gather and send information to the headquarters and to represent the MNC *vis-à-vis* EU institutions. How much a firm can achieve by being in Brussels is illustrated by a report – quoting official EU sources – that the decision taken in 1987 not to deregulate air transport was mainly due to Air France's

---

[37] *Il Sole 24 Ore*, 5 April 1996.
[38] See *Intermediarie*, 28 Nov. 1988.

lobbying of EC and national institutions.[39] The very first MNC to establish in Brussels was the Italian Ferruzzi, which opened a Euro-office in 1968 so to keep abreast of progress in the Common Agriculture Policy (CAP). The Ferruzzi-Europa office, which initially employed two officials, now employs as many as ten, and has managed to make the lobbying of EU institutions a kind of "partnerial activity", to the extent that Ferruzzi, where relevant, does not hesitate to propose new policies to the Commission.[40]

However, such successful lobbying can rarely be achieved by MNCs whose only goal is to sell their products in the EU, without having something to give in exchange. In other words, to have an office in Brussels is indeed useful, but only if one has plants in the EU. The winning strategy is thus to *transplant*. In fact, art. 58 TEC states that "Companies and firms formed in accordance with the law of a member state and having their registered office, central administration or principal place of business within the Community shall, for the purpose of this chapter [Chap. 2 – right of establishment] be treated in the same way as natural persons who are nationals of member states .....". The article therefore does not distinguish between firms and companies whose source of capital is EU or non-EU. In addition, member states are truly sensible to working places. While American MNCs have long had branches in Europe, Japanese and South Korean MNCs started to transplant only in the 1980s, following a number of anti-dumping cases on electronic supplies. However, although differences exist between the member states, the average cost of labour is not cheap (except for Portugal and Greece). One solution is to choose the UK, which has attracted the lion's share of the foreign MNCs locating in the EU in the past 40 years. One-third of all inward investments to the EU are in the UK, with £220 billion invested in manufacturing; 3,500 companies from the US and 200 from Japan have located in the UK (i.e. 39% of Japanese and 41% of US investments overseas) (Nagle and Spencer 1996, p. 16). Korean MNCs are not far behind, with 154 companies located in the UK (against 29 in Belgium).[41] Japan is thus worried about South Korea, as it is doing what Japan did 30 years ago, with the difference that South Korea – like Taiwan – was much faster in investing abroad. The South Korean government in fact assists and subsidizes its companies in order to increase their capacity.[42] Both South Korean and Japanese MNCs started by assembling their products in Europe, then directly produced them on the territory, thus employing European materials.

In contrast to most other EU countries, the UK has welcomed, even courted, foreign investors. Foreign firms can use their British locations as a springboard into Europe: their products are considered "European" as long as they use between 60% and 80% European components. However, the other EU countries worry about the effects of these transplant factories on their industries: the feeling is that Britain has

---

[39] *Le Monde*, 8 April 1990.
[40] *Intermediarie*, 28 Nov, 1988. For instance, the 1980 EC subventions to soya production were specifically "tailored" to Ferruzzi's needs (see *Le Monde Affaires*, 8 April 1989).
[41] Korea Foreign Trade publication – Brussels Office, 1996.
[42] South Korean MNCs are fewer but bigger than Japanese ones. While Japanese companies concentrate on one sector, Korean companies deal with virtually everything (e.g. Samsung deals with suitcases as well as aircrafts).

stabbed its European economic allies in the back in return for jobs, regional regeneration and transfer of technology. The decision of Hoover to rationalize its European
operations and close its plants in Dijon to concentrate production in Glasgow, for
instance, was the catalyst for much debate about Britain's stance on the Social Chapter. Britain was thus branded the "Taiwan of Europe" by an aggrieved French Government, which has argued that the UK has sought to achieve an unfair competitive
advantage in keeping employment costs artificially low. The truth is that Britain,
along with an aggressive strategy in getting companies into its territory, can offer
fiscal attractiveness and lower social expenses to foreign MNCs, since the UK is self-
excluded from the Social Protocol attached to the Maastricht Treaty. Figures show in
fact that labour costs in the UK (wage plus non-wage) are lower then the EU average,
being almost on a par with Spain and Ireland and just above Greece and Portugal. In
any case, foreign MNCs also have branches elsewhere in the EU: for instance, Ford's
"world car" Mondeo is assembled in Ghent (Belgium), the four-cylinder engine being
made at plants in Bridgend (UK) and Cologne (Germany) and manual transmissions
in Halewood, Merseyside and Cologne. Indeed, the car industry is one of the major
domains for foreign MNCs in Europe. For instance, in the Japanese case, Toyota,
Nissan, Isuzu, Mitsubishi, Suzuki, Daihatsu and Honda all have plants in the EU,
either alone or jointly with European companies (for example Honda has a stake of 20
per cent in British Rover, Daihatsu has a joint venture with Italian Piaggio, holding 51
per cent of it, and Mitsubishi is in a joint venture – 33.3 per cent each – with Netherlands Car and Volvo (Nagle and Spencer 1996, p. 16). The EU is also the biggest
market for South Korean cars,[43] and among the US car companies in Europe are Ford,
General Motors, Chrysler and Morgan Stanley.

There are other fields where foreign MNCs have substantial interests in the EU,
one of them being electronics. For example, Toshiba has created Toshiba Consumer
Products Italia Spa; Nippon Electric Glass and (German) Schott Glaswerke make
glass for cathode ray tubes for televisions in Wales (UK), their main customer being
the Sony television plant at Bridgend in Wales, which previously imported the components. Japan's Sharp is conducing R&D on word processing and microwave
technology in Wales, while the Swiss company Ascom chose Wales on account of its
flexible labour force and good labour rates and a workforce with an ability to learn
new skills (Nagle and Spencer 1996, p. 144).

Finally, the collapse of the Iron Curtain at the end of the 1980s and the subsequent
involvement of the EU in Eastern Europe, which – as mentioned above – led to the
signing of association agreements with all of the Central and Eastern countries
(CEECs), unveiled new possibilities to foreign MNCs. In fact, by virtue of the association agreements, a free market is to be established between the EU and the CEECs:
as a consequence, foreign and EU-owned MNCs are relocating their branches to
Eastern and Central Europe, as educated workers can still be hired there at low rates
(in contrast to Asia).

To "go European" gives three main advantages to foreign MNCs: direct entry to
EU markets; the possibility of acting as big "national" groups in lobbying the EU

---

[43] *Il Sole 24 Ore*, 14 Nov. 1996.

governments; and the possibility of joining European (con)federations through which to act. Besides acting on their own, "Europeanized" MNCs can associate with other groups sharing the same kinds of interests, i.e. they can join a sectoral Euroconfederations in their field(s) of interest. This gives them a two-fold advantage: on the one hand, common strategies *vis-à-vis* EU institutions can be developed; on the other, the existence of a sectoral Eurogroup means - especially for the Commission - having a single referent for a given field. Hence, General Motors and Ford are for example members of ACEA, the association of *European Car Constructors*; CEFIC (*European Chemical Industry Federation*) has among its members, alongside national chemical federations from both EU and EFTA countries, MNCs involved in the field of chemicals (Andersen 1992, pp. 170–171); and the *European Convention for Constructional Steelworks* has members from Australia, Canada, Japan and the United States. According to Lowe, the members of a standard Eurogroup represent 30 per cent of global production in a given field. However, Asian MNCs are on average still behind in this aggregating process at the European level (Lowe, 1983, p.40).

Americans have their own forums too, namely AMCHAM (*American Chamber of Commerce*) and EIAC. The EC Committee of AMCHAM – created in 1963 and reformed in 1985 – today unites 140 American enterprises (mainly manufacture, services, legal or general consultants) which have created an impressive network, extremely helpful in lobbying EU institutions as soon as the "soft pencil stage" (the first drafting phase) of Euro-legislation takes place. Twenty-one people –14 full-time and 5 *stagers* – work in AMCHAM's office, which makes of it one of the biggest Eurofederations in Brussels. Only companies (i.e. no associations) belong to AMCHAM; in fact these are the European companies of American MNCs.[44] Twenty-five per cent are lawyers or consultants[45] (which to be accepted have to present references from three US companies) and a maximum of 5 per cent are non-US companies (e.g. Northern Telecom from Canada; Pharmacia, Upjohn and Smith Kline Beecham from the UK). AMCHAM has good coordination with the US Government, though claiming it receives little support: there is a representative of the US Diplomatic Mission to the EU in each of AMCHAM's Working Groups, and there is a meeting at the executive level every one to two months. AMCHAM is affiliated to the US Chamber of Commerce and to other business organizations. Furthermore, it works in coordination with the AMCHAMs in the various EU member states and can thus organise a "pan-European" lobby with meetings with national ministers etc.; as AMCHAM representatives put it: "for each topic there is in fact the 'proper' member state, in other words a member state which is more receptive to AMCHAM's ideas". There is a particular link with the UK government; however, since AMCHAM supports further EU integration, relationships with Major's government were not so good.

While 15 per cent of AMCHAM's work is done at the request of the Commission or the EP, the Council is still the problem since "it is not democratic and there is no

---

[44] They include American Express, Apple, AT&T, Avon, Chrysler International, Coca Cola, Colgate, DHL, Disneyland Paris, Exxon, Ford, Hewlett Packard, IBM, Kellogg's, Levi Strauss, McDonald's, Microsoft, Nike, Texaco, Time Warner, etc.
[45] Baker & McKenzie, Ernst & Young, Hill & Knowlton, etc.

transparency".[46] Finally, AMCHAM has also created "its own ERT"[47]: the *European-American Industrial Council* (EIAC). Founded in 1993, EIAC is a grouping of Senior Executives from among the largest MNCs of US parentage which deploy substantial resources and investments throughout Europe. The current members represent over 1.1 million European jobs, sales in excess of 170 billion ECUs and investments of some 45 billions ECUs. The main priority of EIAC is "to improve the competitiveness of the European marketplace". Where "advisable", it provides timely recommendations and support to those developing and overseeing public policies, particularly in fields affecting operations of European companies of American parentage. Among the current members of EIAC's Steering Group are Franco Mariotti (Hewlett Packard), Juergen Aumueller (American Express Europe), Vito Baumgartner (Caterpillars Overseas); David Badger (Mars), and Uwe Washer (General Electric Europe). Mariotti and Baumgartner are "issue leaders".[48]

4.4. How MNCs and third states can influence the EU decision-making processes

If an MNC or a third state wants to (try to) influence EU legislation or policies, it must follow the basic rules of Eurolobbying. This section thus deals with Eurolobbying – the methods and the resources – highlighting the means employable by foreign MNCs and/or third states, with reference to particular cases.

In 1966, Stanley Hofmann introduced the distinction between high politics and low politics as regards to the EC policy process; Bulmer (1994), recalling Lowi (1972), talks about constitutive policies – those affecting the overall architecture of the European Union, i.e. the constitutional–legal order, the geographical parameters and other broad questions. Whatever the term, Eurolobbying can indeed aim to influence two different kinds of EU decision-making process: the legislative process and the wider EU decision-making process (for which we will borrow Bulmer's concept of constitutive policies). An example of a legislative process is the car-emissions standards directive; an example of lobbying on constitutive policies is the role played by the Social Partners in negotiating the Social Protocol in the Maastricht Treaty (Bindi, 1994). For each kind of lobbying, we find similar patterns as well as peculiarities. What follows is a brief description of the most salient elements of Eurolobbying.

---

[46] Interview. See also Butt Philips (1992), pp. 45–47; Andersen (1992) pp. 97–98.

[47] The European Round Table (ERT), founded in 1983, is a peculiar and very influential Eurogroup, comprising 45 Chief Executives from the main European enterprises, taking parting in ERT on a personal basis. ERT has a Secretary General based in the Brussels-located Secretariat. ERT members meet both in plenary sessions and in working groups; these deal with topics such as education, youth activities, employment and R&D. In the words of the ERT's Secretary General: "The challenge in Europe is to build a new environment in which business can flourish... so that prosperity can spread across the continent" (Richardson, K., "Europe's industrialists help shape the Single Market", *Europe*, EC Commission office, Washington, DC, December 1989). According to its Chairman: "I would consider the round table to be more than a lobby group as it helps to shape policies..." (interview to Wisse Dekker, *Europe 2000*, March 1990, Vol. II, No. 2).

[48] EAIC information package.

In lobbying the Euro-legislative process, the most important factor is *technical knowledge*: the small number of EU officials, as compared with the great volume of material they have to deal with, does not in fact allow EU institutions to keep many specialists working on a permanent basis. Therefore it is essential for the Commission and the European Parliament to be able to ask Eurogroups to provide them with technical knowledge.[49] If a Eurogroup manages to get a good reputation for the quality of its work,[50] the Commission and the Parliament will *motu proprio* contact it again in the future. Everything that can inform the decision-maker is perceived as useful: seminars, conferences, press conferences and, mostly, reports. These reports – also known as best advices – are dossiers which, in the shortest and easiest possible way, contain high-level technical information and analysis. Letters are also used as a means of lobbying, but are really useful only when a good relationship already exists between the Eurogroup and the decision-makers. In addition, it is very important that a group keep good contacts with the press, as this has the double advantage of making the group known to public opinion and to decision-makers. It is particularly important to be quoted by *Agence Europe*, the so-called bible of EU decision-makers. In addition, most Eurogroups have their own publication(s); a few Eurogroups even own nationwide newspapers or radio/TV channels.

The EU decision-making process is complex and overlapping, therefore a lobbyist has to monitor at the same time different EU institutions and, if possible, the national level. This means that it is essential to have a perfect knowledge of all the phases of the legislative process and of the EU institutions. The two golden rules in EU lobbying are therefore to know exactly *who does what when* and to act *the sooner the better*. To the lobbyist, the most important phase of the EU legislative process is the first, "soft pencil" stage, i.e. the one going from the Commission's Green Paper to the Council's first reading, as afterwards it is far too difficult to achieve results, due to the voting system. Hence, relations between Eurogroups and EU officials are at all levels, from desk officers to Director Generals up to Commissioners: these last, however, are usually used only when problems are of a political nature. In this last case, the Eurogroup's highest representatives will meet the other party.[51] Two kinds of relationships can in fact be distinguished, although they are strictly linked: formal and informal. For instance, the European Round Table (ERT)'s report *Agenda for Action* (ERT 1984a) – to which Lord Cockfield's *White Book* of 1985 owes much – was presented by the

---

[49] Parlement Européen, Commission du Reglement, de la Verification des Pouvoirs and des Immunitées: *Propositions a l'intention du Bureau Elargi sur une reglementation de la representation d'intérêts auprès du Parliament Européen*, Doc. FR\DV\214\214673 – PE 200.405/def. of 8.10.1992: 2; Commission CE: *Conunication de la Commission: Un Dialogue ouvert and structure entre la Commission and les groupes d'intérêt*, Doc. SEC(92) 2272 final, of 2.12.1992:1; Corbett and Jacobs 1990, pp. 222–223; 1992, pp. 245–246.

[50] Quality depends on the accuracy and objectivity of the work (Meynaud 1960, p. 186)

[51] An unwritten code of Eurolobbying distinguishes between the different circumstances and their roles, so that there is mutual agreement about when it is permissible to talk about business and when it is not. Social happenings such as dinners, shows, etc. (a perfect time is during the EP's plenary session in Strasbourg, especially on Wednesday and Thursday nights) are considered a good way of meeting interesting people. *Petit-déjeuners*, lunches and dinners are estimated as midway between work and pleasure meetings, and seem to be perfect for gaining informal agreements.

then ERT Secretary General Wisse Dekker in January 1985 in a European tour of public conferences and private meetings. Another ERT report focusing on the future of the Community, *Reshaping Europe* (ERT 1991), was similarly promoted by ERT's members in conferences and debates with top National and European decision-makers. One should not be surprised, then, that in the Maastricht Treaty topics such as "Trans-European Networks" (arts 129b TEC, 129c TEC, 129d TEC), industrial politics (art 130 TEC) and education and professional training (art 126 TEC) are very close to the ERT's proposals.

There is no evidence that to be of the same nationality provides a preferential channel when relating to up to A3-level EU officials, but from level A3 up (where officials are political appointees) and with higher decision-makers it does count. However, it is essential to speak several foreign languages fluently and to be well acquainted with the cultural background of the political actors one has to deal with.[52] How much the cultural and political elements matter is shown for instance by the initial difficulties faced by Norwegians in approaching Eurolobbying. In Norway – a country characterized by societal corporatism[53] – the interest groups model is in fact opposite to the EU's: there is a more rigid and partitioned concept of political bargaining than in most of the EU countries, so that interests representation is still based mainly on official channels. This means a difficult starting point for understanding and influencing the EU decision-making process, and a complex conversion to a lobby environment which is marked by different cultures, languages and behaviours, and which is at the same time vertical and horizontal, inter-institutional, national and supranational (Bindi 1993).

The characteristics of the institutional framework in which a group acts combine in determining the group's behaviour (Truman 1970, pp. 501–535; Eckstein 1960, pp. 407–421). Eckstein (1960, pp. 15–39) argues that pressure groups tend to adjust the form of their activities not so much to the formal (constitutional) structure of the governments as to the distribution of effective power within a governmental apparatus. Eurogroups select their major target on the basis of two main considerations: (1) which EU institution(s) have the major powers in their field(s) of interest; (2) the Eurogroup's means.

The first target of Eurogroups is clearly the Commission, especially where lobbying on the legislative process is concerned. The Commission is in fact the only EU institution able to introduce formally new Euro-legislation and to modify it all along the legislative path. Moreover, the Commission is open to Eurogroups as this is useful to it from at least four points of view:

1. Eurogroups supply the Commission with specialized information, as well as with

---

[52] Interviews. See also *Science & Vie Economique*, No. 74, July–Aug. 1991; *Libération Europe*, 4 May 1990; *Management Today*, July 1989; *International Management*, June 1988; *Le Monde Affaires*, 8 April 1989; *La libre enterprise*, 20 July 1990; Rolfes (1989); *The European Citizen* No.8, 1991; Nonon and Clamen (1991); Nugent (1991), Corbett and Jacobs (1992); Andersen (1991); Garder (1990); Lowe (1989)

[53] Societal corporatism is a system in which the State recognizes (or even creates) a limited number of groups to which it guarantees the monopoly of representation in the given sectors, though asking them to keep a certain control on the selection of leaders and on the requests of the groups themselves (see Schmitter 1974, 1977; Lembruch 1977)

news which can help the Commission in meeting its function as "guardian of the treaties"

2. if the Commission manages to show that its own positions are supported by (influential) Eurogroups, this will put it in a stronger position *vis-à-vis* the Council
3. if, on the contrary, the Commission did not bother to consult Eurogroups it would risk facing strong opposition in the Council, as the most influential groups would then try to exert their influence on the latter body
4. if a well-known Eurogroup supports the Commission's positions, this will help the Commission to defend European interests against national ones (Nugent 1991, pp. 233–234).

Each Eurogroup, according to its field(s) of interest, has its own selected partners in the Commission: car constructors mostly deal with DGs II, IV, XIII and XXIII; agriculture-related groups with DG VI; and so on, the goal being to sit on one of the several hundred consultative committees organized by the Commission.

The Single European Act introducing the new cooperation legislative path, and the Maastricht Treaty the joint decision-making procedure (procedure ex. art 189b EEC), made the European Parliament more appealing to Eurogroups than before. Nevertheless, even if an increasing number of Eurolobbyists attend the EP's work (committees and/or plenaries), the Parliament still appears as a "second-best chance", being lobbied only if the groups have enough means to do so without penalizing their work with the Commission. This is also why several groups, such as UNICE, employ professional lobbyists to monitor the EP, hence organizing lobby actions only when the Parliament deals with subjects which are really relevant to them. There are groups, such as EUROMETAUX, that pay no attention to the European Parliament. There are also groups, such as the trade unions, that hold special relationships with selected political groups and/or MEPs, whom they may have supported during the electoral campaign. This is not generally the case, however, for third states and MNCs. For instance, AMCHAM – which admits that some 15 per cent of its work is done at the request of the Commission or the EP, and that it has good relationships with several MPEs – tries to avoid specific links with a given party, as "in the long term such preferential links could prove to be difficult". One should not forget the important role that MEPs' assistants, as well as commissions and political groups' officials, can play. Often, it is more worth while for a Eurogroup to lobby an MEP's assistant than the MEP himself. Assistants, in contrast to MEPs, are usually based in Brussels and thus easier to meet; moreover, MEPs usually trust their subordinates, who often end up in preparing even the voting list for them.

Finally, the Council does not generally provide easy access to Eurogroups, so that only a few of them are really able to influence it. The secret nature of the Council's work does not help in learning about its internal mechanisms, and – contrary to what happens with the Commission – the Council's working groups are composed exclusively of people designated by member states, thus cutting out almost all possibilities for Eurogroups to send their own experts. Furthermore, the chances of succeeding depend on having good contacts at political and administrative levels in all EU member states. In such a perspective, the Council appears as an easier target for MNCs having branches in several EU member states. However, even the powerful

AMCHAM does not manage to get into the Council. In fact, AMCHAM – working in coordination with the AMCHAMs in the different member states – manages to organize a "pan-European" lobby, with meetings with national ministers and other decision-makers. However, the Council is considered an obstacle since "it is not democratic and there is no transparency"; thus AMCHAM's policy is not to act after the common position is reached.

As a consequence, it may be easier for MNCs to block than to promote a piece of legislation through the Council, through a particular good ally. Nevertheless, this possibility should not be overemphasized: for instance, when in the winter of 1988–1989 a major debate took place about the installation of catalytic converters in small cars, a measure that represented a penalty for French car constructors, these did not manage to agree on a common position, being convinced in any case that the French government would exercise its veto in the Council meeting. However, German car constructors supported the converters, thus joining Danish and German environmental groups, and together these managed to gain the support of the European Parliament and of public opinion. Therefore France could not impose its veto, and the legislation was adopted: a clear example of how the ability of a single – even a "big" and "important" – country to exercise its veto in the Council should not be taken for granted.

The political relevance of the Eurogroup's leaders and their ability to create overlapping alliances are crucial when the problems dealt with are of a political nature, for instance when they concern constitutive policies. In such cases, in fact, the possibility "to make a phone call" or to visit without formalities an EU Commissioner or a national minister is decisive. In such circumstances elements such as political closeness, nationality, or even personal interests indeed count.[54] A clear example of how much personal relationships and the ability to build overlapping (trans-party and transnational) coalitions count is given by the role played by ETUC's Secretary General Emilio Gabaglio on the occasion of the Intergovernmental Conferences (IGCs) of 1991, when a trans-party and transnational lobby to allow the so-called Agreement of 31 October on Social Policy introduced as an opt-out the Social Protocol in the Maastricht treaty (Bindi 1994).

In Eurolobbying, financial means, although helpful, are not the most important factor. Lobby actions such as the financing of electoral campaigns are limited to a small number of MEPs, mainly in the agriculture, trade union, and industrial fields (Bowler and Farrel 1991), while the financing of Europe-wide information or propaganda campaigns is discouraged by the difficulties of so many different languages and cultural and political habits. Corruption (*tout court* or not) does not seem to be part of Eurolobbying either. On the contrary, it was in reaction to a new and more aggressive way of lobbying that the European Parliament first, and the Commission afterwards, began to work on possible lobbying legislation. When the tobacco MNC Philip Morris gave a diary as a present to the members of the Commission of the European

---

[54] It is interesting to note how several observers regard international youth organizations as a means to get potential future leaders to know each other, so as to collaborate better if and when they become national/EC decision-makers. For instance, the long-time friendship of Kohl and Mitterrand seems to have started in their common experience in the European Movement when still young.

Parliament dealing with a problem related to tobacco, the President of the Commission obliged fellow members to send it back: this is probably just an anecdote, but it helps in understanding the high deontological professional code of EU officials and MEPs. It was in fact to guarantee the respect of such deontology that Jean Monnet wanted the (then) ECSC's officials to receive very high salaries. What really counts for a Eurogroup is to be able to get what can be described as a psychological advantage over the Commission. The main way to do so is to be able to present its own interests as European interests. And this is exactly the major problem that third states and MNCs have to face. Since the 1970s, the Commission has showed a clear preference for Europe-wide groups against national ones, an attitude that has been changing only recently: the Commission is in fact very keen on its role as defender of the Community's interests (Nugent 1991, pp. 233–234). Ferruzzi, an MNC that can reasonably claim to have a "partnerial activity" with EU institutions,[55] failed in 1984 in its battle over bio-ethanol precisely because it was too openly linked to it as a single firm. Ferruzzi in fact launched an aggressive campaign in favour of the so-called green oil through its *Il Messaggero*, a well-known Italian national newspaper, thus causing sharp reactions on the part of the Italian oil group ENI (Ente Nazionale Idrocarburi), which in turn attacked the green oil through its newspaper, *Il Giorno*. As a consequence – although several national ministers seemed favourable to green oil and an "expert group" was created – the Commission finally said "no" to bio-ethanol. Another kind of psychological advantage over the Commission can be achieved by employing the EEIG juridical framework, the Commission's "pet"; for instance, EUROELETRIC (European Committee of Electric Supply Industry) – which was one of the first to be transformed into an EEIG in 1990[56] – reports how, since then, the Commission has become much more receptive to the group's input.[57] However, this, too, can be a problem for foreign MNCs, above all for Asian ones, as they like to run their European branches on the same internal organization patterns as the home ones: for instance, they prefer to take non-unionized workers

In conclusion, third states and foreign MNCs need to influence the EU decision-making processes if they want to be competitive in the Single Market. This is not easy to be do, but it is far from impossible, especially if the rules of Eurolobbying are followed: in other words, if representatives from third states and foreign MNC's want to succeed in Eurolobbying, they have to be able to adapt to the multinational, multicultural and multilevel political environment of the EU.

---

[55] Ferruzzi does not hesitate, where relevant, to propose new policies to the Commission: for instance, the 1980 EC subventions to soya production were specifically "tailored" to Ferruzzi's needs (see *Le Monde Affaires*, 8 April 1989; *Intermediarie*, 28 Nov. 1988).

[56] *Agence Europe*, 27 Sept. 1991; *Le Monde*, 23 Sept. 1991. See also EUROELETRIC Annual Report 1991.

[57] For instance, EUROELETRIC was asked to join the European Electricity Professionals' Consultative Committee (CCPE) and solicited by DG XVII to outline a possible future for the energy sector in order to reduce the greenhouse effect (EUROELETRIC Report of Activities 1991, pp. 3–12).

4.5 Conclusions

As Calingaert (1996) clearly explains in his book, world economic relations are increasing purely a US/EU issue, especially where trades are concerned. This could turn into an increased partnership between the two entities, or into a commercial war, as sometimes appears to be the case. The way two major events will develop in the next years will deeply influence these relationships: the introduction of a single currency (the *Euro*) within a *European Monetary Union* (EMU), and enlargement of the EU to the East. In addition there is a third issue which is increasingly becoming a source of tensions between the EU and the US, which is antitrust laws.

As mentioned, according to the *Agenda 2000* communication, negotiations with Poland, Hungary, the Czech Republic, Slovenia, Estonia and Cyprus shall begin in January 1998, and they will likely become members around the years 2005–2010. For MNCs this means that they have one more reason to transplant in such countries. Eventually, one could even hypothesize that in the case of an MNC having substantial investments in an Eastern European country, the government of that country would have serious motivation to defend the MNCs interests in negotiations with the EU. Not surprisingly, it has been mentioned how for instance, in Poland, of the top ten private investment companies four of them are American companies, one Australian and one Swiss.

As for the EMU, the schedule predicts that in early 1998 the decision about its *ins* and *outs* will be taken. As from January 1st, 1999, Stage Three of EMU will begin. The conversion rates of the currencies of the participating countries will be irrevocably fixed, the Euro will become a currency in its own right and the ECU basket will cease to exist. Member states will issue new public debt securities in Euros and foreign exchange operations will be in Euros. Euronotes will be gradually introduced along with national ones until – July 1, 2002 at the latest – the changeover to the Euro will be completed in participating states[58]. The shift to the Euro will have major implications, both economically and politically. Indeed the debate is growing both in and out of Europe[59]. If, in 1996, a leading Italian politician – returning from a professional trip in the US – could report that "even in the highest spheres, almost nobody is concerned by the Euro. They do not believe it, therefore they simply do not care about it"[60], the situation has since progressed. A debate is also taking place in the US as well. According to Calingaert (1996, p. 180), "the establishment of the EMU will have two consequences that will potentially increase the EU's economic influence and power: First, as discussed in Chapter 8, the single currency may emerge as an alternative reserve currency to the dollar. Second, it might create a major voting bloc ... in the IMF, potentially larger than that of the US ....'"

Finally, there are the antitrust policies. The EC's rules on competition are found in *Title V* of the TEC and more precisely in art 85–94 TEC[61]. They prohibit "the

---

[58] EC Commission (1996)
[59] Just as an example, cfr. two commentary, one on La Libre Belgique (28.6.1997): *Euro contre Dollar*, and the other on *International Herald Tribune*, (27.6.1997): *Americans, if Wise, Should not Knock the Euro*.
[60] Interview.
[61] The procedure to be followed is set out in the so-called Regulation 17. (Mathjiasen, 1995: 241-244)

prevention, restriction, or distortion of trade" and the abuse by undertakings of a "dominant position"[62]. In addition, *Regulation 4064/89* sets out the rules concerning merging. Strictly legally speaking, such rules are confined to the Internal Market, but in practice this is not the case. Indeed, one realizes that, before the end of the cold war, the application of the principle of non-interference in one state's internal affairs was strictly adhered to, but now that principle is no longer followed. From a defense and security policy point of view this was symbolized by the Kuwait War of 1990. In international trade this was exemplified by legislation such as the Helms–Burton Law or the application of the EU antitrust legislation to the (American) Boeing–McDonnell Douglas affair[63].

The Boeing–McDonnell Douglas affair – the merging of two companies neither one residing in the EU, but affecting trades in the EU – risked creating a commercial war between the US and the EU, with France as the most belligerent partner. An agreement was signed between the US and the EU regarding the application of their competition laws. This agreement contains provisions on exchange of information, consultation, notification and other procedural aspects; it also provides for co-operation in cases where they apply their competition rules to related situations. Both the US and the EU agreed to take into account the important interests of the other party[64]. Indeed, in the past, US and EU regulators have never come to opposite conclusions about a major merger. However, while the US competition watchdog – the Federal Trade Commission – had given its green light to the 10-billion-ECU ($14 billion) merger of Boeing and McDonnell Douglas[65], the EC Commission threatened to block it, supported by many EU member states, *in primis* by France's President Jacques Chirac. Chirac openly protested to the US for putting pressure on some EU member states to convince the Commission to give its green light. In reply, Bill Clinton answered that he hoped to avoid a commercial war, but he was "worried by the reasons lying behind the Europeans"[66]. As a matter of fact, the merger was going to affect Airbus, the European consortium that is the only non-American competitor in the field[67]. The hard line taken by the Europeans started a furious few weeks of commercial negotiations and political lobbying on both sides of the Atlantic[68]. Eventually, the Commission approved the merger after Boeing's decision to drop a series

---

[62] Church and Pinnemore, 1994: 136-142

[63] Other recent but less famous non-EU cases where the Commission has given its approval include the acquisition by the American Tyco International of ATD, a firm settled in Bermudas (June 1997), and the joint venture of the American Universal with the CLT-UFA group for their activities in Poland (February 1997). (*Les Echos*, 1.7.1997)

[64] Mathjiasen, 1995: 247-248. However, France challenged the powers of the Commission to enter such agreement which was thus annulled on 9.8.1995 (Case *C - 327/91, France vs. Commission*)

[65] *International Herald Tribune*, 3.7.1997,*European Voice*, 10-16.7.1997 and 24-30.7.1997

[66] Chirac protested against the US for putting pressure on some EU member states in order to convince the Commission to give its green light. As a reply Bill Clinton answered that he hoped to avoid a commercial war but the he was "worried by the reasons lying behind the Europeans" (*Sole 24 Ore*, 18.7.1997)

[67] *International Herald Tribune*, 3.7.1997

[68] *International Herald Tribune*, 3.7.1997. Interesting enough, the two firms were assisted by one of the best lawyer firms in Brussels, the *Van Bael & Bellis*.(interview)

of exclusive agreements to supply planes to American Airlines, Delta Airlines and Continental Airlines[69].

4.6. REFERENCES

AMCHAM EC Committee (1996). *Business Guide to EU Initiatives 1996*, Bruxelles, AMCHAM EC Committee Ed.

AMCHAM EC Committee (1997). *EC Information Handbook 1997*, Bruxelles, AMCHAM EC Committee Ed.

Andersen, C. (1992). *Influencing the European Community. Guidelines for a Successful Business Strategy.* London: Kogan-Page.

Andersen, S. and K.A. Eliassen (1991a). "European Community Lobbying". *European Journal of Political Research 20*, 173–187.

Andersen, S. and K.A. Eliassen (1991b). "European Trade Union Influence in the EC", Handelshoyskolen BI working paper, 1991/44.

Andersen, S. and K.A. Eliassen (1991c). "National Corporativism and the Challenges of the European Communities", BI, Sandvika, Working Paper 1991/45.

Andersen, S. and K.A. Eliassen (1992). *Det Nye Europa: Den europeiske unions inmstitusjoner og politikk.* Oslo: TANO.

Andrews, W.G. (1991). "Corporatist Representation In European International and supranational Organisations", paper presented at the XVth World Congress of the International Political Science Association, Buenos Aires, 21–25 July.

Antola, E. (1990). "EFTA and its Limits". in Wallace, H. (ed.), *The Wider Western Europe. Reshaping the EC/EFTA Relationship.* London: Pinter, for the Royal Institute of International Affairs.

Belmont, C. and L. Belmont (eds) (1989). *The New Commission: Policies, Priorities and Personalities.* Brussels.

Bindi, F.M. (1993). "ETFA and Norway: EC lobbyists, too!". *NUPI-Notat N500*, November 1993, Oslo.

Bindi, F.M. (1994). "Economic Eurogroups and the EU Decision-making Process". Paper presented at the IX Conference of Europeanists, Chicago, 31 March–2 April, 1994.

Bindi, F.M. (1996). "The Eurogroups, the European Union and the EU Legislative Process". NUPI Report 201, Oslo, (N. 201, March 1996).

Bindi Calussi, F. M. and Peters, P. (eds.) (1998). *The Santer Commission,*. forthcoming.

Boudant, J. & Gounelle M. (1989). *Les grand dates de l'Europe communautaire*, Larousse, Paris.

Bowler, S. & Farrel D. M. (1991). *MPEs and Interest groups: A survey of the 1989 Parliament*, ECPR Joint Sessions, Essex, March 1991.

Bulmer, J.S. (1994). Institutions, Governance Regimes and the Single European Marke: Analyzing the Governance of the European Union, paper presented at the ECPR Joint Working Session, Madrid, 17–22.4.1994.

Butt, Philip A. (ed.) (1991). *Directory of EC Pressure Groups in the European Community,* Harlow, Longman, 1991.

Calingaert, M. (1996). *European Integration Revisited. Progress, Prospects and US Interests*, Westview Press, Colorado.

Cecchini P. (1988). *Il Costo Della Non-Europa*, EC Publications.

Church, C. (1990). "The Nordic States and their ETFA Policies". *Journal of Common Market Studies 28*, No. 4, June, 401–430.

Church & Pinnemore (1994). *European Union and European Community*, Prentice Hall, Hemel Hempstead.

Commission CE: Comunication de la Commission: Un Dialogue ouvert and structure entre la Commission and les groupes d'intérêt, Doc. SEC(92) 2272 final, of 2.12.1992.

(EC) Commission (1996): *When will the Euro be in our pockets?* Official publications of the EC, Luxem-

---

[69] *European Voice*, 1 24-30.7.1997

bourg.

(EC) Commission, SEC(96) 1225 final: Scope of the Codecision procedure. Commission report under art. 189(8) of the Treaty.

Corbett R. & Jacobs, F. (1990) *The European Parliament*, Longman, London.

Corbett R. & Jacobs, F. (1992, 2nd ed) *The European Parliament*, Longman, London.

Delors, J. (1992). *Le Nouveau Concert Européen*. Paris: Odile Jacob.

(La) Documentation Française (1992). *L'Europe des Communautes*, Paris.

Economic and Social Committee (1980). *Les Groupements d'interest Europeens et leur relactions avec le CES*, Bruxelles, Editions Delta.

Eckstein H. (1960). The determinants of pressure groups, in Eckestein & Apter (1960).

Eckstein H. (1967). *Pressure Groups politics: the Case of the British Medical Association*, Stanford University Press, Stanford.

EFTA (1987). *The European Free Trade Association*. Geneva: EFTA Secretariat.

Eliassen, K.A. (1991). "Nordic EC Membership – The Question of When". BI, Sandvika, Working paper 1991/4.

Eliassen K.A. (ed.) (1996). *Norsk Forsvarindustri. Utfordringer og fremtidig veivalg*. Bergen: fagbokforlaget.

ERT (1984). *Europe 1990. An Agenda for Action*, Brussels.

ERT (1991). *Reshaping Europe*, Brussels.

EUROELETRIC *Report of Activities 1991*, Bruxelles.

European Round Table (1984a). *Europe 1990: An Agenda for Action*. Brussels.

European Round Table (1984b). *Missing Links*. Brussels.

European Round Table (1991). *Reshaping Europe*. Brussels.

Fagerberg, J. (1990). "The Process of Economic Integration in Europe. Consequences for EFTA Countries and Firms". NUPI-Notat 428, Oslo, June.

Ferrer, C. (1990). *An Agenda for Europe: UNICE's Priorities for the '90s*. Vienna: European Chemical Convention.

Garder J. (1990). *Effective Lobbying in the EC*, Kluwer and Law Taxation Publishers, Deventer – Boston.

Gautron (1994). *Droit europeen*, Dalloz, Paris.

General Secretariat of the Council of the European Union: Intergovernamental Conference. Amsterdam European Council Draft Treaty, Bruxelles, June 1997, doc. CONF/4001/97/CAB/EN.

Hegtun, H. *Kampen for Fred*. Oslo: Aschehoug.

Hoffman S. (1966): "Obstinate or Obsolete: The fate of national State and the case of Western Europe", in *Daedalus*, vol. 95,1966, pp. 862– 915.

Keohane, R.O. and S. Hoffmann (1990). "Conclusions: Community Politics and Institutional Change". In Wallace, W. (ed.) *The Dynamics of European Integration*. London: Pinter.

Keohane R.O. and S. Hoffmann (1991). "Institutional Change in Europe in the 1980s". In Keohane, R.O and S. Hoffmann (eds) *The New European Community. Decisionmaking and Institutional Change*. Oxford: Westview Press; 1–84.

Laursen, F. (1990). "The Community's Policy Towards EFTA: Regime Formation in the European Economic Space (EES)". *Journal of Common Market Studies 28*, No. 4, June, 303–325.

Lembruch, G. (1977). "Introduction: Neo-Corporativism in Comparative Perspective". In Schmitter, P.C. and G. Lembruch (eds) *Patterns of Corporatist Policy-Making*. Beverly Hills: Sage.

Lembruch, G. "Liberal Corporativism and Party Government. Concluding Remarks: Problems for Future Research on Corporatist Intermediation and Policy-making". In Schmitter, P.C. and G. Lembruch (eds) *Trends Towards Corporatist Intermediation*. Beverly Hills: Sage.

Lowe, B. (1989). *How to Keep Abreast and Wield Influence*, Club de Bruxelles editions, Bruxelles.

Lowi T. (1972). "Four System of Policy, Politics and Choice", in *Public Administration Review*, Vol. 32, No. 4, pp. 298– 310.

Macleod, I., Hendry, D., Hyett, S. (1996). *The External Relations of the European Communities*, Clarendon Press, Oxford.

Malary, J.H. (1991). "The EC Policy-Making Process in the Field of Energy: An Analysis with a View to Norwegian Interests". In Austvik, O. G. (ed.) *Norwegian Gas in the New Europe*. Oslo: NUPI-Vett & Viten.

Martens, H. (1984). *Euroorganisationerne – Set fra Europa*. Kobenhaven: Seminarrapport–Institut for Samfundsfag og Forvalting.

Mathijasen, R.S.R.F. (1995). *A Guide to the European Union Law*, Sweet & Maxwell, London.

Mazey S. & Richardson J. (1991). *Lobbying Styles and European Integration*, ECPR Joint Session, Essex, 3/1991.

Mazey S. & Richardson J. (1993). *Lobbying in the European Community*, Oxford University Press, Oxford.

McLean, I. (ed.) (1996). *Oxford Concise Dictionary of Politics*, Oxford University Press, Oxford.

Meynaud J. (1960). *Les groupes de pression internationaux*, Lausanne, Etudes de Sciences politiques.

Michalski, A. and H. Wallace (1992). *The European Community: The Challenge of Enlargement*. London: Royal Institute of International Affairs.

Nagle G. & Spencer K. (1996). *A Geography of the European Union*, Oxford University Press, Oxford.

Nell, P.G. (1990). "EFTA in the 1990s: The Search for a New Identity". *Journal of Common Market Studies 28*, No. 4, June, 327–358.

Nonon J. & Clamen M. (1991). *L'Europe et ses couloirs: Lobbying et Lobbyistes*, Parigi, Dunod.

Nugent N. (1991). *The Government and Politics of the EC*, MacMillan, London.

Nugent, N. (1992). "The Deepening and Widening of the European Community: Recent Evolution, Maastricht and Beyond". *Journal of Common Market Studies 30*, No. 3, September, 311–328.

Nugent N. (1996). *The Government and Politics of the European Union*, 3rd ed., Westview Press, Oxford.

NUPI (1991). EOS-avtalen, Hvor hender det? No. 13, 11 November, Oslo.

Parlement Européen, Commission du Reglement, de la Verification des Pouvoirs and des Immunitées: Propositions a l'intention du Bureau Elargi sur une reglementation de la representation d'intérêts auprès du Parliament Européen, Doc. FR\DV\214\214673 - PE 200.405/def. of 8.10.1992.

Pedersen, T. (1991) "EC–EFTA Relations: An Historical Outline". In Wallace, H. (ed.) *The Wider Western Europe. Reshaping the EC/EFTA Relationship*. London: Pinter, for the Royal Institute of International Affairs; 13–30.

Petite M. (1989). "Les Lobbies Européens", in *Pouvoirs*, 48/1989.

Richardson K. (1989). "Europe's Industrialists help shape the Single Market", in *Europe*, EC Commission office, Washington DC, December.

Rolfes R. (1989). "Manouvering the Euromaze", in *Across the Road*, 1989.

Sæter, M. and Knudsen O.F. (1991). "Norway". In Wallace, H. (ed.) *The Wider Western Europe. Reshaping the EC/EFTA Relationship*. London: Pinter, for the Royal Institute of International Affairs.

Sæter, M. (1965). "Hva er integrasjon?". *Internasjonal Politikk 4*, 366–390.

Schmitter P.C. (1974) "Still the Century of Corporativism", *Review of Politics*, 36(1), pp.85-131.

Schmitter P.C. (1977). "Modes of Interest Intermediation and Modes of Societal Change in Western Europe", *Comparative Political Studies* N.10, pp.7–38.

Sidjanski D. & Ayberk U. (eds.), (1990). *L'Europe du Sud dans la CE*, Paris, P.U.F.

Stalvant, C.-E. and Hamilton, C. (1991). "Sweden". In Wallace, H. (ed.) *The Wider Western Europe. Reshaping the EC/EFTA Relationship*. London: Pinter, for the Royal Institute of International Affairs; 194–214.

Steiner, J. & Woods, L. (1996). *Textbook on EC Law*, Blackstone Press Ltd., 5th ed., London.

Stoltenberg, T. (1992). Paper presented at the conference "Norway and Europe", Oslo, 28 September, organized by NUPI (Norwegian Institute of International Affairs), PRIO (International Peace Research Institute), Norwegian Institute for Defence Studies, The Fridtjof Nansen Institute.

Traité de Maastricht: mode d'employ. Paris: UGE, 1992.

Truman D.B. (1970). *The Governmental Process: Political Interests and Public Opinion*; 2nd ed., New York, A.Knopf.

Tyszkiewicz, N. (1987). *UNICE's Position and Role in the Completion of the Internal Market*. WP, College d'Europe, Brugge.

Tyszkiewicz, T. "Les patrons européens construissent l'Europe". In *Politique Industrielles*; 217–223.

Tyszkiewicz, T. (1990). "UNICE: The Voice of European Business and Industry in Brussels". IREC Conference, 28–30 September.

US Federal Act, 1946, sect. 308(a).

Valen, H. (1995). "L'affaire de la UE dans la politique norvegiénne". In *Revue Internationale de Politique comparée 2*, No. 1, 111–134.

Van Schendelen, R. (ed.) (1993). *National Public and Private EC Lobbying.* Newcastle upon Tyne and Dartmouth.

VG (1991) *Norge og EF.* Oslo.

Wallace, W. (ed) (1990). *The Dynamics of European Integration*, Pinter, London.

Wallace, H. (ed.) (1991). *The Wider Western Europe. Reshaping the EC/EFTA Relationship*, Pinter Publishers for the Royal Institute of International Affairs, London.

PART TWO

FOREIGN POLICY IN
THE SECOND AND THIRD PILLAR

CHAPTER 5

The European Union's Common Foreign and Security Policy and Enlargement: Consequences for the East and the Atlantic Alliance

Thomas Grunert[1]

5.1. INTRODUCTION

Between now and the early years of the next century, the European Union will be involved in a phase of almost continuous negotiation. The Intergovernmental Conference (IGC) in Turin on 29 March 1996 opened this process; the role of the IGC has been seen to be pivotal because of the task it has been given – amending the Treaty on European Union and preparing for enlargement.

The main purpose of the conference was institutional reform with a view to future enlargements of the European Union and the deepening of political union. While diplomacy and defence were not the only subjects at issue, questions relating to these have been at the heart of the debate. The changes to be made to the Common Foreign and Security Policy (CFSP) are particularly important against the background of the modest results achieved in the CFSP area to date and the necessary adaptation of the CFSP mechanisms in view of further enlargements.

A first analysis of the results of the Amsterdam summit, which concluded the IGC on 18 June 1997, shows that this goal has not been achieved: modest reform of CFSP and an even more complicated decision-making mechanism, the postponement of the crucial institutional adaptation (weighting of votes in the Council, number of Commissioners, etc.), indispensable for enlargement, as well as an extremely vague commitment to integrate (when the time comes) the WEU into the EU, have to be interpreted as a sign of stagnation of the political process rather than as a decisive leap forward.

The enlargement of the Union, and as a logical consequence of the WEU, is one of the major challenges that the member states must meet at the end of this century and the beginning of the next. The three most recent new members, with their historical policies of neutrality, have raised the issue of "variable geometry". The growing diversity of the Union will bring its relevance more than ever to the fore. Similarly, NATO's internal debate on its own enlargement is by no means irrelevant to the Union.

---

[1] The author accepts sole responsibility for the views expressed in this chapter, which do not necessarily reflect the European Parliament's position.

A. Cafruny and P. Peters (eds.), The Union and the World, 95–112
© 1998 *Kluwer Academic Publishers. Printed in Great Britain.*

The pressing need for the provisions of the CFSP to be revised arises above all from the somewhat disappointing outcome of their implementation. The Union's institutions and the various reflection groups engaged in preparing for the IGC have drawn up a number of reports and studies which, with minor variations, come to the same conclusion: "laborious implementation",[2] "serious powerlessness",[3] "a great deal of progress to be made".[4] Even the Council, the main actor in the CFSP, admits that implementation is "varied".[5]

It must be borne in mind, however, that the CFSP is an ongoing process, and that barely two years passed between its entry into force and the opening of the Conference. During this time the Union has been present at the great events on the international stage, at least in the capacity of a donor or an adviser. The progress made must be emphasized all the more since foreign policy and, *a fortiori*, defence are part of what the member states regard as their private domain.

Nevertheless, the prospects for implementation of a CFSP that is worthy of the name remain uncertain. The tragedy of former Yugoslavia will always be there as a blot on a record which would in any case have been mixed. In former Yugoslavia, as in other parts of the world, the Union spared no effort in humanitarian or financial terms, but the political benefits have, for the most part, been extremely limited. The press summed up the Dayton Accord, which put a stop to the hostilities in the former Yugoslav republics, as "an American plan with European financial support". The diplomatic activities of the 15 are often confused and ineffective, although experience in this area dates not from the end of 1993, but from the early 1970s. Without denying the progress that has been made, one is forced to conclude that the record of the CFSP looks thin, particularly by comparison with that of the economic aspect of external relations. And yet, in view of what is at stake, no concessions should be made here; a failure in the area of political union would be damaging to the Union as a whole.

There is no doubt that the reform of the CFSP is a precondition for enlargement and will have major consequences with regard to the integration of the applicant countries into the European and Atlantic security structures. Although it is likely that the EU enlargement negotiations will start in early 1998, it remains unpredictable whether and when they can be concluded and what impact this process will have for the further development of CFSP and a European Security and Defence Identity (ESDI) in the framework of the Atlantic Alliance.

---

[2] Report by the Commission for the Reflection Group in preparation for the 1996 Intergovernmental Conference, May 1995 (ISBN 92-827-4176-1).

[3] Second report by the high-level group of experts on the CFSP (chairman: Mr Durieux), "The common foreign and security policy on the eve of the year 2000", 28 November 1995 (PE 214.986 of 10 January 1996).

[4] Report of the Council of the European Union on the operation of the Treaty on European Union, 6 April 1995 (SN 1821/1/95 rev.).

[5] European political cooperation (EPC) was initiated by the Hague European Council of 2 December 1969.

5.2. SECURITY AND DEFENCE IN THE CFSP FRAMEWORK

Under Article J.7 of the European Union Treaty agreed in Amsterdam on 18 June 1997, "the common foreign and security policy shall include all questions relating to the security of the Union, including the progressive framing of a common defence policy, which might lead to a common defence, should the European Council so decide". According to the new Treaty, "the Western European Union (WEU) is an integral part of the development of the Union providing the Union with access to an operational capability.... It supports the Union in framing the defence aspects of the common foreign and security policy. The Union shall accordingly foster closer institutional relations with the WEU with a view to the possibility of the integration of the WEU into the Union, should the European Council so decide."[6]

Two declarations relating to the WEU, annexed to the Maastricht Treaty,[7] set out the practical details of the organization's tasks:

- *developing its dual relationship with the Union on the one hand and the Atlantic Alliance on the other.* The principle of including the WEU in the mechanisms of the CFSP is clearly set out, the first of the two declarations stating that the organization "will be developed as the defence component of the European Union".
- *developing its operational capacity.* In a declaration of 24 June 1992, the member states of the WEU, meeting in Petersberg, stated their intention of providing the organization with genuine operational capacity so that it could meet the requirements of the Treaty.

According to the European Commission, "the dimension of the common policy which concerns security and defence has not yet really taken shape".[8] Apart from the cautious terms in which the old and the new Union Treaties are couched, a number of the provisions bear witness to the incomplete nature of arrangements in this area: the CFSP "shall not prejudice the specific character of the security and defence policy of certain member states and shall respect the obligations of certain member states which see their common defence realized in NATO, under the North Atlantic Treaty and be compatible with the common security and defence policy established within that framework".[9]

Likewise, Denmark was authorized as a result of the Edinburgh European Council not to take part in the adoption and implementation of decisions and actions by the Union having implications for security and defence. This "opting-out" provision has been confirmed by the results of the Amsterdam summit. The new Treaty does not include a commitment to mutual solidarity which would pledge the member states to military involvement in the defence of one or more other member states. Article V of the WEU Treaty, which contains such an obligation, was not incorporated. On the other hand, "Petersberg" missions, i.e. humanitarian aid, peace-keeping or crisis-

---

[6] Conference of the Representatives of the Governments of the member States: Draft Treaty of Amsterdam (CONF/4001/97), 19 June 1997, Article J.7.
[7] Treaty on European Union, Office for Official Publications of the European Communities, Luxembourg, 1992.
[8] See footnote 2.
[9] See footnote 5.

management operations and peace-making, are now part of the Union's Treaty.[10]

The place of the WEU in the European security and defence structure is not well defined. Several questions remain unresolved, as described below.

5.2.1. The WEU's relations with the Union and with the Atlantic Alliance

The WEU has the dual role of being the defence component of the European Union and the European pillar of NATO. A number of practical measures have been introduced with the aim of facilitating this dual relationship; they include harmonizing working methods and synchronizing the times and venues of meetings. However, despite some progress, the distribution of roles between the organizations remains unclear.

According to the Commission, the relationship between the WEU and the European Union "has not worked satisfactorily". Cooperation between the Councils and secretariats, exchange of information and consultation between the Commission and WEU have, it is true, made real progress. But a lot remains to be done: "the respective presidencies have different timetables.... The WEU is usually represented at NATO meetings but rarely at meetings of the Council of the European Union. Document exchange and reciprocal attendance at meetings by the two secretariats must be improved."[11]

Ultimately, the Commission says, "the use made of the WEU to date in joint actions undertaken under the CFSP has been restricted to the provision of a surveillance force for the administration of Mostar". The Union therefore seems reluctant to use the services of the WEU, particularly as the incorporation of its provisions into those of the CFSP has not yet been finally settled.[12]

The relationship between the WEU and NATO has included an interesting initiative: at the NATO summit in Brussels in January 1994 the idea of setting up Combined Joint Task Forces (CJTFs) was raised. The Atlantic Alliance would allow NATO resources to be made available to the WEU for emergency operations for which only the WEU would bear responsibility. These would therefore be "separable but non-separate" forces which could be temporarily taken from NATO. The Berlin Atlantic Council of 2 and 3 June 1996 authorized the adoption of declarations annexed to the acts enabling the studies needed for the CJTFs to be set up. These presuppose a reform in the command mechanisms of the Alliance allowing the European components to be clearly identified with a view to carrying out operations under the control of the WEU. The European pillar of NATO is only sketched in: the practical details still have to be worked out and other aspects of the reform of the structures of both NATO and the WEU addressed.

It is to be hoped that these initiatives will help to clarify the distribution of roles between NATO and the WEU, which is not always well defined.

---

[10]   Amsterdam Draft Treaty, Art J.7.2.
[11]   See footnote 2.
[12]   See footnote 2.

5.2.2. Incorporating the WEU in the structure of the CFSP

Three main options have been proposed, as follows.

(a) *Short-term merging of the WEU with the EU.* The WEU would cease to exist and the dual structures for security (CFSP) and defence (WEU) would be done away with. The Petersberg missions and a collective undertaking on defence would be incorporated in the Treaties.

(b) *Continuing the convergence of the Union and the WEU,* with increased subordination of the latter to the former, by the establishment of binding legal–political links. This second option would pave the way for the first, but would mean a *gradual* incorporation of the WEU into the Union.

(c) *Preservation of the WEU as an autonomous body.* A "reinforced partnership" between the Union and the WEU would be achieved by strengthening the links between their secretariats, coordinating their presidencies or holding joint summits. Preserving the intergovernmental character of the security and defence policy would mean that the asymmetry between the composition of the WEU and that of the Union could be retained. Despite their differences, all the member states would then be able to take part in shaping the European security and defence identity.

The outcome of the IGC confirms that the option of continuing the convergence of the EU and the WEU is seen as the most realistic approach. However, it cannot be predicted whether a step-by-step integration of WEU into the EU will be achieved in the foreseeable future. On the other hand, it is obvious that if EU enlargement takes place within the next 10 years (including the Baltic States), it will be much more difficult to provide the Union with a military/defence identity.

5.3. THE ENLARGEMENT DEBATE

The question of enlargement currently dominates all conceptual considerations of a new European security architecture. Among the various questions still to be settled, the most important is the kind of conceptual linkage that should be established between the enlargement of the Atlantic Alliance on the one hand and the enlargement of the European Union and the Western European Union on the other. While a conceptual linkage between the enlargement of NATO and the EU is generally accepted, problems start when it comes to tackling the question of "who and when". In both cases, different answers will probably be found for the European Union and for NATO.

With respect to the European Union, the question of "who" was settled in principle by the European Council in June 1993. The European Union could therefore begin the enlargement process by admitting the relevant countries individually or in groups, and a country benefiting from a Europe agreement but not included in the first wave of enlargement would have no reason to fear being left outside definitively.

However, the European Union has a major problem as regards the time framework of its enlargement. The question whether NATO enlargement should on the whole precede the enlargement of the European Union or vice versa is still unresolved. On the other hand, there is a growing consensus that the first wave of NATO enlargement, presumably with the Czech Republic, Hungary and Poland, should coincide with the 50th anniversary of the Atlantic Alliance in 1999.

In fact, enlargement of the EU may be less problematic in the security field, but as it depends on so many factors and conditions in economic, financial, structural and organizational terms, it is very unlikely to be achieved prior to enlargement of NATO.

As regards NATO, the option that the Alliance will and should enlarge is almost unquestioned. The problem of NATO enlargement is "who and when". As long as NATO remains ambiguous on the question of "who", any approach to admit new members in a series of waves may be regarded by other countries as a signal that there will be no second wave of admission to follow the first.

Russia's persistent opposition to NATO enlargement, despite the 14 May 1997 agreement on the NATO–Russia Founding Act, and uncertainties with regard to its political future will continue to have an impact on the debate concerning the timetable and the choice of countries for NATO enlargement.

5.3.1. The candidates

5.3.1.1. NATO enlargement

At present, consultations are taking place in the framework of an intensified dialogue between NATO and each of the 12 states which have explicitly asked to become a member of NATO. These states are: Albania, Bulgaria, the Czech Republic, Estonia, the former Yugoslav Republic of Macedonia (Fyrom), Hungary, Latvia, Lithuania, Poland, Romania, Slovakia and Slovenia. NATO is also conducting an intensified dialogue with Ukraine, its main purpose being to extend cooperation in the framework of the Partnership for Peace with a view to Ukraine's becoming a member of NATO at a later stage or to concluding a special agreement similar to the NATO–Russia Founding Act. In other countries which participate in the North Atlantic Cooperation Council and the Partnership for Peace programme, a political debate about the option of NATO membership is evolving without so far having reached concrete results (Austria, Sweden, Finland, Moldova).

5.3.1.2. European Union enlargement

The candidates for membership of the European Union in the next enlargement phase are: Bulgaria, the Czech Republic, Estonia, Hungary, Latvia, Lithuania, Poland, Romania, Slovakia, Slovenia (all of which have concluded Europa agreements with the EU) and Cyprus. Official applications for membership have also been submitted by Switzerland and Turkey, but it is unlikely that these two countries will be considered as serious candidates for the next enlargement of the European Union. Malta's application has been frozen since the change of government in 1996.

5.3.1.3. WEU enlargement

Potential candidates for membership of WEU are obviously the European NATO member countries that are not yet full members of WEU, namely Norway, Turkey, Iceland and Denmark, as well as the member states of the European Union that have opted so far for observer status in WEU and are invited to become full members, namely Denmark, Finland, Austria, Sweden and Ireland. The other candidates are the 10 "associate partners" who already participate in WEU at various levels, namely Bulgaria, the Czech Republic, Estonia, Hungary, Latvia, Lithuania, Poland, Romania, the Slovak Republic and, since June 1996, Slovenia.

The groups of countries that want to become members of NATO, EU and WEU are virtually identical. All the countries that applied for EU membership are at the same time candidates to become members of WEU, apart from Switzerland, Malta and Cyprus. The countries that have officially applied for NATO membership have also submitted an official application to become a member of the European Union with the exception of Fyrom, which, however, has also mentioned interest in becoming an EU member. Among the European NATO members that are not members of EU and WEU (Iceland, Norway, Turkey), only Turkey has explicitly mentioned its interest in becoming a full member of both groupings. From this very fact derives Turkey's opposition to NATO enlargement, in case this would not be met by Turkey's admission to the European Union and WEU (see below). Denmark is a special case, being a full member of NATO and EU and having so far rejected the invitation to become also a full member of WEU. However, a debate has started in Denmark on the issue of WEU membership.

5.3.2. NATO enlargement

In December 1994, NATO Foreign Ministers initiated a study to examine the questions related to the inclusion of new members in the North Atlantic Alliance.[13] The study has served to clarify the "why and how" of enlargement and what NATO and possible new members will need to do to prepare to join. The "who and when" of enlargement have not been addressed because this is still too controversial.

As regards the principles of enlargement, all new members will need to accept and conform with the principles, policies and procedures adopted by all members of the Alliance at the time that new members join. Willingness and ability to meet such commitments would be a critical factor in any decision to invite a country to join.

In particular, the Alliance wishes to avoid a situation where a new member might "close the door" behind it to admissions in the future of other countries that may also aspire to membership. States which have ethnic disputes or external territorial disputes must settle them by peaceful means in accordance with OSCE principles. Resolution of such disputes would be a factor in determining whether to invite a state to join the Alliance. Finally, the ability of prospective members to contribute militarily to collective defence and peace-keeping and other new missions of the Alliance will be a factor in deciding whether to invite them to join.

According to the NATO point of view, the enlargement of NATO is a parallel

---

[13] Study on NATO Enlargement, NATO General Secretariat, Brussels, September 1995.

process with, and will complement, that of the European Union. The maintenance of the linkage of NATO and WEU membership is considered to be essential, because of the cumulative effect of security safeguards extended in the two organizations. The enlargement of both organizations should, therefore, be compatible and mutually supportive.

An eventual broad congruence of European membership in NATO, EU and WEU would have positive effects on European security. Therefore, the Alliance should, at an appropriate time, give particular consideration to countries with a perspective of EU membership, and which have shown interest in joining NATO, in order to consider how they can contribute to transatlantic security within the Washington Treaty and to determine whether to invite them to join NATO.

The NATO enlargement study gives broad consideration to the Alliance's relations with Russia. The authors argue that NATO enlargement threatens no-one and is not directed against Russia or any other state. As a consequence, inviting new members into the Alliance would contribute to enhanced security for the whole of Europe, which is in Russia's interest as well. Against this background, the NATO–Russia Founding Act[14] is seen from a NATO perspective as the cornerstone of a new, inclusive and comprehensive security structure in Europe. This view is obviously not shared by most of the Russian authorities.

In June 1997, it became evident that Poland, Hungary and the Czech Republic will be in the first wave of NATO enlargement, given the fact that they are the closest to having fulfilled the accession criteria. Three other countries have been considered for inclusion in this group, namely Slovenia, Romania and Slovakia. Slovenia basically fulfils all the criteria outlined in the NATO enlargement study. Romania is increasingly considered to be a candidate for an early enlargement wave, mainly due to the fact that the country has a new president and a new government whose democratic attitudes and commitment to reform are uncontested, and in view of the country's successful shaping of good relations with its neighbours (for example the Hungarian–Romanian Treaty of 1996), which also settles the minority question. Slovakia has been considered because of its geopolitical situation, but the internal political situation in the country (partial disrespect of the rule of law, unresolved minority questions, etc.) does not make it very likely that Slovakia will be included in an early NATO enlargement.

Who else will be admitted to NATO, and when, is an open question. In principle, there is agreement that the ten WEU associate partners should be considered as potential candidates for joining the Alliance.

5.3.3. EU enlargement

The European Council at Copenhagen in June 1993 agreed that: "The associated countries in central and eastern Europe that so desire shall become members of the

---

[14] Founding Act on Mutual Relations, Cooperation and Security between NATO and the Russian Federation, NATO–Russia Summit Document, Paris, 27 May 1997.

Union. Accession will take place as soon as a country is able to assume the obligations of membership by satisfying the economic and political conditions. Membership requires:

- that the candidate country has achieved stability of institutions guaranteeing democracy, the rule of law, human rights and respect for and protection of minorities
- the existence of a functioning market economy, as well as the capacity to cope with competitive pressure and market forces within the Union
- the ability to take on the obligations of membership, including adherence to the aims of political, economic and monetary union.

The Union's capacity to absorb new members, while maintaining the momentum of European integration, is also an important consideration in the general interest of both the Union and the candidate countries.

Against this background, the Union has developed a comprehensive pre-accession strategy. The main features of this strategy include:

- structured relations with the institutions of the Union
- development of the Europe agreements
- financial assistance under the PHARE programme
- preparation for integration into the Internal Market.

The actual timetable of enlargement will depend primarily on the progress made by the individual countries in their preparation for membership. There is a general feeling that EU enlargement will not take place before 2002: the European Policy Centre forecasts 2003 as an optimistic target. A Chatham House paper hazards 2005 or later. Moreover, ratification of accession treaties cannot be taken for granted.

The next enlargement, like all past enlargements, and like the creation of the original European Communities, concerns the basic objective defined in Article A of the Treaty as the "process of creating an ever-closer union among the peoples of Europe". Since the Union's fundamental aim is to promote peace, security and stability among Europeans, the effects of enlargement should first be judged on that criterion. Peace, security and stability are more difficult to quantify than the economic aspects, but they are vitally important for the countries of Central and Eastern Europe and for the existing members of the Union. In this context, the future relations between the EU, WEU and NATO have to be considered as well as the NATO enlargement debate.

After the conclusion of the IGC in Amsterdam resulting in the postponement of major institutional adaptations of the Union's Treaty to a significantly enlarged Union, EU enlargement before 2005 appears to be very unlikely.

5.3.4. WEU enlargement

In fact, all full members of the Western European Union (WEU) are also members of NATO. If the EU takes new members on board, it is likely that they will also apply for full membership of the WEU, the WEU being "an integral part of the development of the EU" (art J4, Maastricht Treaty).

At present, the WEU has four different types of membership: full members, associate members (the European NATO members that are not EU members), associate partners (the Visegrad countries, Bulgaria, Romania and the Baltic states) and observers (the EU members that are not full WEU members, namely Ireland, Sweden, Finland, Austria and Denmark). All the associate partners are applicant countries for full membership in the EU and have (formally or informally) shown interest in full WEU membership. WEU membership implies security guarantees according to Article V of the Brussels Treaty and hence a mutual defence commitment, which would go further than the commitment expressed in Article V of the Washington Treaty. Thus, full WEU membership is theoretically equivalent to NATO membership in the event of an external aggression towards the territory of a member state.

From the EU's and its member states' point of view, accession to the Union should be accompanied by membership of the WEU, for the sake of internal homogeneity and as a positive element to further the integration process. Hence, there does not seem to be a political obstacle to the full integration of the applicant countries into the Western European security alliance, as soon as they become full members of the EU.

Against this background and the fact that the military commitments of WEU are, according to art 4 of the WEU Treaty, transferred to NATO, it appears to be only logical that full WEU membership finds its equivalent in NATO membership. However, the debate about enlarging WEU appears to be less controversial than the debate about NATO enlargement; i.e. Russia seems to have fewer problems in accepting the accession of the former Warsaw Pact countries to WEU than to NATO. A psychological element may explain the differentiated approach of the Russian position: NATO is still seen as a relict of the Cold War era based on American supremacy, whereas the EU integration process is rather considered a "natural" development not directed against Russian interests and without major military or security implications.

With NATO enlargement approaching, it is indeed necessary now for WEU and the EU to consider more thoroughly the criteria for a conceptual link between WEU's enlargement eastwards and the enlargement of the European Union and NATO. The essential question is whether the goal of a broad congruence of membership in NATO, the European Union and WEU should be followed as a strict rule or replaced by a more flexible approach without invalidating the ideal underlying that principle.

A first objective to be pursued by WEU might be to grant the ten associate partner countries the status of associate members. This would be a further step in preparation for their full membership of WEU, to which they expect to accede as candidates for membership of the European Union. While such a step could be taken in a relatively short time, it would simultaneously require acceptance that all European members of NATO including Turkey, Norway and Iceland be granted full membership of WEU. The report concludes that such a measure would be a first step towards helping to achieve the aim of more congruence between NATO, WEU and the European Union by giving all European NATO countries the possibility of participating in the structures of the CFSP without being full members of the European Union. Admission of the ten WEU associate partner countries as associate members would also require a number of arrangements with NATO, in particular with respect to the Combined Joint Task Forces (CJTF) concept and to security arrangements. Thus, it should also be considered as a measure to prepare for their subsequent accession to NATO. The most delicate problem that would arise for WEU, however, would be what to do if NATO decided to grant full membership only to a limited group of Central European countries, whereas others of this group had been already admitted to WEU. The subsequent difficulty lies in the fact that the security guarantees laid down in art V of the WEU Treaty have genuine value only on the basis of NATO's military capabilities and structures.

However, opponents of the "linkage theory" argue that in the same way as NATO cannot accept a Russian veto on its enlargement, the link between the security safeguards contained in Article V of the WEU Treaty and in Article V of the NATO Treaty cannot lead to the acceptance of an American veto which may limit Europe's freedom of decision regarding the enlargement of European organizations.

The WEU Assembly notes that early NATO enlargement to take in only a few select Central European countries without paying careful attention to the security requirements of other Central European countries could be detrimental to the stability of the region. Further, it is emphasized that NATO enlargement should not be rushed through in order to make the 50th anniversary of the Atlantic Alliance in 1999 a more triumphant occasion.

5.4. PROBLEM AREAS

5.4.1. Relations with Russia

As mentioned above, any kind of NATO enlargement needs some sort of overall agreement between NATO and Russia on their relationship in the framework of a new cooperative security order in Europe.

To meet Russian concerns over NATO enlargement, proposals have been made to limit the new membership to Poland, the Czech Republic, Hungary and Slovakia and to create for the three Baltic states a special security zone including Finland and Sweden as a regional structure of the OSCE. The subsequent accession of the Baltic states, Finland and Sweden as European Union members to WEU and beyond that to NATO would in principle be admissible.

There are two important factors with regard to Russia's involvement in the NATO enlargement process: on the one hand, Moscow must not be allowed to have a veto on enlargement; but on the other, it has to be involved in European security structures. Former US Defence Secretary, Mr Perry, declared in September 1996 that NATO is building a circle of security in Europe and he believes that Europe cannot be secure unless Russia is inside that circle, working together with the Alliance. To this end, a number of proposals have been made:

(a) a charter that would put relations between NATO and Russia on a formal and legally binding footing

(b) provisions for cooperation in the fields of crisis management and conflict settlement

(c) provisions for mutual representation at NATO headquarters in Europe and at

Russian military headquarters
(d) cooperation with regard to a common tactical anti-missile defence system
(e) cooperation between NATO and Russia on armament technology.

With regard to the so-called "strategic partnership" between NATO and Russia, NATO has proposed that this partnership should contain three parts: the first dealing with principles, the second with procedures for consultation between NATO and Russia on European security, and the third with those areas in which there is scope for cooperation. Moreover, according to the Pentagon, Russia could be involved in virtually everything NATO does, the only exception concerning its collective defence obligations based on Article V. This formula would enable Russia to take part in a host of NATO committees and forums for military planning purposes. This would also mean that Russian liaison officers would be accommodated at every level of the Alliance's command structure, with permanent offices for them and their NATO counterparts in each other's headquarters.

To ease Russian concerns about NATO enlargement, the US Secretary of State, Ms Albright, suggested during her visit to NATO on 18 February 1997 that NATO and Russia should start work immediately on setting up a joint military brigade. Furthermore, she suggested envisioning a NATO–Russia joint council that would promote a regular dialogue on major security issues, reach concerted decisions wherever possible and seize opportunities for joint action. This formula appeared to be a delicate compromise between Russia's stated desire for joint decision-making procedures and the Western preference for a looser form of consultation. In another move intended to reassure Russia, NATO arms control experts agreed early in February 1997 on a new position which will be presented formally to the Vienna talks on conventional forces in Europe (CFE). To meet Russian concerns, this new position, for the first time, clearly accepts the principle of limits on the arsenals of individual countries as well as regions.

The NATO–Russian Founding Act, signed on 14 May 1997 by NATO Secretary General Solana and Russian Foreign Minister Primakov, can be seen as a compromise which takes into account Russian concerns and NATO's ambitions. Under the terms of the Act, NATO and Russia will consult and coordinate regularly and, where possible and appropriate, act jointly – as they are doing in Bosnia now. The Act has five principal sections, as follows.

- The preamble notes that NATO and Russia do not consider one another adversaries and cites the sweeping transformations in NATO and Russia that make this new relationship possible.
- Section I lays out the principles governing the relationship, e.g. restatement of the norms of international conduct in the UN Charter and OSCE Helsinki Final Act and explicit commitments, such as respecting the sovereignty, independence and territorial integrity of states and settling disputes peacefully.
- Section II creates a new forum called the NATO–Russia Permanent Joint Council for NATO–Russia meetings and describes how this Council will function.
- Section III describes a range of issues that NATO and Russia will discuss, including conflict prevention, peacekeeping, prevention of the proliferation of weapons of mass destruction and exchange of information on security policies and defence

forces.

- Section IV describes the military dimensions of the relationship, including NATO's December 1996 statement that it has "no intention, no plan and no reason" to deploy nuclear weapons on the territory of new members. On the other hand, it is recognized that NATO will require adequate infrastructure on new members' territories, commensurate with NATO's defence and other missions.

Mechanisms to foster closer military-to-military cooperation between NATO and Russia, including the creation of military liaison missions in the respective headquarters, are part of the agreement.

All in all, NATO retains its full prerogatives. While Russia will work closely with NATO, it will not work within NATO. The Act makes it clear that Russia has no veto over Alliance decisions and NATO retains the right to act independently when it so chooses.

The Act has no direct impact on NATO enlargement. The Madrid Summit in July 1997 extended invitations to the first countries to begin accession talks. Those countries admitted will have the full rights and responsibilities of Alliance membership and the door to membership will remain open to all emerging European democracies.

Despite the relatively high degree of Russian involvement in NATO affairs as a result of the Founding Act, Russia's concerns about NATO enlargement have hardly been eased.

5.4.2. Russia's view

Russia reluctantly joined Partnership for Peace (PFP) in June 1994. In May 1995, NATO and Russia agreed on a broad, enhanced dialogue and cooperation beyond PFP. However, since 1995, the issue of NATO enlargement has become one of the most salient items on the political agenda in Russia. According to Mr Arbatov, Chairman of the Defence Committee of the Duma, and "moderate democrat", there is a broad national consensus in Russia against enlargement. In Arbatov's view, enlargement would trigger new fears of isolation and enhance the Russian paranoia of encirclement. It would also undermine Russia's relations with the West and the position of the democrats in the country. Only the Russian nationalists such as Zhirinovsky seem to hope that NATO enlargement will happen (although they think it is bad for Russia) in order to strengthen their own position at home. In other words, from a Russian perspective, NATO enlargement and, to a minor extent EU/WEU enlargement, would have a negative impact on European security.

According to Russian sources, the consequences of the NATO enlargement debate are already visible in their country at various levels:
(a) the new military strategy places greater emphasis on nuclear deterrence
(b) the number of Russian troops will be increased from 1.5 million to 1.7 million and the military service time is likely to be extended.

Moreover, if enlargement were to be realized, other negative consequences for European security would follow:
(a) the START treaty would have little chance of being ratified

(b) the ratification of the Open Skies treaty (OS) would be in doubt
(c) Russia might claim a revision of the INF treaty
(d) Russia would take a tougher stance with regard to the renegotiation of the CFE treaty
(e) Russia would enhance its relations with the other CIS members and presumably try to create a new military alliance (including Belarus and maybe the Ukraine).

All in all, Russia does not see any need to integrate the former Warsaw Pact countries into the Western Alliance, as the Cold War and the division of Europe into politico-military blocks are over. Furthermore, the fact that Russia is not invited to join NATO makes the Russians even more suspicious. Russian sources predict that NATO expansion will also have a negative impact concerning Russian relations with the new NATO member states, and might lead to a new military build-up in the country. As a consequence, in the event of NATO enlargement, there would be a risk of a new bipolarization of the European continent and, hence, a threat to European security.

5.4.3. The Baltic problem

The Baltic states' accession to NATO is definitely their prime objective in the security field. All three governments are convinced that membership of the Atlantic Alliance is the only vehicle that can furnish them with a dissuasive element and enhance their stability, both of which are indispensable for maintaining a balance in their societies and for their economic and social development. However, they are aware that they will not be part of the first wave of NATO enlargement, for reasons given above. As a result, the Baltic states are now aiming at early membership of the European Union and of WEU. In a coordinated approach, they have clearly stated that they hope to become members of the European Union in 2001. There is no doubt that the entry of the three Baltic States to the European Union and their accession to WEU would strengthen their security position on the international stage, especially as they would simultaneously continue with their consistent efforts to improve relations with their neighbours and further their trilateral cooperation on security and defence.

In economic terms, an integration of the three Baltic states into the European Union would not pose any major problems given the small size of the countries. For this reason, representatives of the United States have suggested granting early membership of the EU to the Baltic states in order to compensate for not granting them early membership of NATO. On the other hand, one can argue that EU membership for the Baltics would give them the right to accede concurrently to WEU, and hence the security guarantees laid down in Article V of the WEU Treaty would apply to them. However, it is obvious that these guarantees have genuine value only on the basis of NATO's military capabilities and structures. In order to avoid such a contradictory situation, Mr Rühl, former Under-Secretary of State in the German Defence Ministry, has suggested creating a special security zone including the three Baltic states, Finland and Sweden as a regional structure of the OSCE. The subsequent accession of these five countries as EU members to WEU and beyond that to NATO would in principle be admissible. While the NATO states would in due course seek to reach an understanding with Russia on this subject, they would not accept that Russia had a veto. NATO and the European Union would respect Russia's sovereign right to organize a security and defence community together with other CIS members, in the same way as they are entitled to expect Russia to recognize their own common security and defence organization as contributing to stability in Europe.

5.4.4. The Turkish problem

As mentioned above, Turkey is a problem country, being a full member of NATO and at the same time aiming at full membership of the European Union and of WEU. For obvious reasons, full membership of EU and WEU has not yet been granted to Turkey and the perspectives of the country's full integration into both are uncertain.

In recent months, Turkey has reacted strongly to the European Union's unwillingness to consider seriously its full membership in the near future. After a meeting with NATO Secretary General Solana in early February 1997, Turkey's President, S. Demirel, officially confirmed that Turkey would veto expansion of NATO if his country were not included in plans for enlargement of the European Union. Turkey's Deputy Prime Minister and Minister for Foreign Affairs, Ms Ciller, stated in October 1996 that "enlargement processes of NATO, the EU and WEU should evolve in a parallel manner ... it is not realistic or justifiable that Turkey, an ally of the West for 44 years, is denied the European perspective while, at the same time, we are expected to enter into additional Alliance commitments, when NATO's enlargement is concluded".

It cannot be denied that there is a certain risk that Turkey, if the political élites in the country feel excluded from the European integration process, could reconsider its present geostrategic and political loyalties. What is in particular disturbing for the Turkish pro-European integration élites is the prospect that potential new members of NATO from Central and Eastern Europe may gain EU membership ahead of Turkey, which has been a loyal ally of the West for so long. Moreover, the entrance of Cyprus to the European Union could increase Turkish frustrations.

Most political analysts, however, believe that Turkey in the end would not veto NATO enlargement, in order not to undermine its good relations with the United States and given that the general decision to expand NATO was taken unanimously by the 16 Alliance members, including Turkey.

5.5. CONCLUSIONS

The enlargement of NATO, the EU and WEU is on the agenda for the end of this century and the beginning of the next. Despite the fact that there is no formal link between an enlargement of NATO and an enlargement of EU–WEU, candidate countries of Eastern Europe see their relations with the West in a much more integrated way. Moreover, it is hardly conceivable, given the military dependence of

WEU on NATO, that a country would become a member of WEU without joining the Atlantic Alliance at the same time. According to the American Ambassador to NATO, Robert Hunter, the US would have "serious problems" if the European Union gave the WEU instructions and this included countries not belonging to NATO. Accordingly, he believes that if WEU accepted new full member states which were not NATO members it would then have to renounce Article V on mutual assistance.

According to official statements, NATO enlargement is on track; a number of Central and Eastern European countries, namely Hungary, Poland and the Czech Republic, have been invited at the NATO Summit on 8–9 July in Madrid to join the Alliance. The 50th anniversary of NATO in 1999 is envisaged as the accession date. According to Ms Albright, membership negotiations should be completed by the end of this year in order to allow time for enlargement to be debated and ratified by the national parliaments of the NATO member states in the course of 1998. Accession would come into effect by April 1999.

One can only speculate about further enlargement phases of the North Atlantic Alliance. Much depends, of course, on Russia. During recent months, Russia has increasingly campaigned against NATO enlargement, arguing that the enlargement of the Alliance would destabilize the political and military balance in Europe. However, Russia recognizes that it cannot veto NATO expansion, for the sake of the continuity of positive relations with the Western Community. Moreover, the NATO–Russia Founding Act provides Russia with a considerable degree of involvement and influence in Alliance affairs.

However, despite the general consensus with regard to NATO enlargement, it is not completely unchallenged within the Western community. One of the most influential US strategists of the Cold War period, George Kennan, for example, thinks that expanding NATO "would be the most fateful error of American policy in the entire post-Cold War era".[15]

As regards WEU, all member states of the European Union which are not yet WEU members are invited to become full members. This concerns the four neutral member states of the European Union plus Denmark. In Finland, Austria and Denmark, the debate on the utility of WEU membership is gaining momentum. In Sweden and Ireland, the debate is starting. For all these countries (apart from the Alliance member, Denmark), NATO membership is much further away but is not categorically excluded any more by many political forces.

With regard to enlargement of the European Union, it is likely that this will happen after the first wave of NATO enlargement. All the EU applicants from Central and Eastern Europe, including the Baltic republics, are also applying for NATO membership and have mentioned interest in WEU membership. For Cyprus, Malta and Switzerland, NATO or WEU membership does not seem to be an issue.

As regards the successor states of Ex-Yugoslavia, only Slovenia is at present a serious candidate for NATO, EU and WEU membership.

Apart from Russia, it is at present Turkey and the Baltic republics that are creating

---

[15] *Financial Times*, 19 Feb. 1997.

headaches in the enlargement debate, Turkey unsuccessfully knocking at the door of the EU and WEU in order to become a full member and the Baltic republics aiming at being among the first new members of NATO, which is reluctant to admit them in view of strong Russian opposition and the fragile political situationin Russia.

To conclude, one could certainly state that the NATO enlargement debate is far from being finished. It gained a new momentum during 1996 and has continued after the Madrid NATO summit of 8–9 July 1997 to consider candidates for a second enlargement round, to work on a special agreement with the Ukraine and to assess the impact of the Founding Act on Russia perceptions with regard to future security structures in Europe. Its implication for European security (positive, negative or neutral) depends on a large number of circumstantial developments and cannot be assessed or predicted.

It is also difficult to predict the implication of EU enlargement for European security: in principle, it should have a positive impact for all parties concerned, as it would stabilize the democratic process and the economic transition of the applicant countries. Moreover, WEU membership could give them the assurance of security guarantees and open the door to NATO membership for those who will not be included in the first wave of the Alliance's enlargement. On the other hand, this would mean that the EU member states would have a real defence commitment towards countries which previously have been part of the "Soviet empire". In the event of a new bipolarization, the EU would have quite a burden to carry.

5.6. REFERENCES

Agence Europe (1996). Europe Documents: "State of Progress in Preparing for EU Enlargement". Brussels, 9 August.

Asmus, R.D. *et al.* (1995). "NATO Expansion: The Next Steps", *Survival 37*, No. 1, Spring, 7–39.

Commission of the European Communities (1995). "Report by the Commission for the Reflection Group in Preparation for the 1996 Intergovernmental Conference". May, ISBN 92-827-4176-1.

Commission of the European Communities (1995). Commission White Paper on "Preparation of the Associated Countries of Central and Eastern Europe for Integration into the Internal Market of the Union". COM(95) 163 final, 3 May.

Commission of the European Communities (1996). Commission Opinion: "Reinforcing Political Union and Preparing for Enlargement". COM(96) 90 final, 28 February.

Conference of the Representatives of the Governments of the Member States (1997). "Draft Treaty of Amsterdam". CONF/4001/97, 19 June.

Council of the European Union (1995). "Report on the Operation of the Treaty on European Union". 6 April (SN 1821/1/95 rev.).

European Parliament, Directorate General for Research (1995). Working Paper on "Prospects for a Common Foreign and Security Policy – Preliminary Review". Brussels.

European Parliament, Directorate General for Research (1996). Information Note on "Enlargement". Brussels, June.

European Parliament, Directorate General for Research (1996). Working Paper on "The CFSP on the Eve of the Intergovernmental Conference". Brussels.

European Parliament, Directorate General for Research (1997). "Note on Enlargement of NATO and the European Union". Brussels, February.

European Parliament, Directorate General for Research (1997). "Enlarged Community: Institutional Adaptations". Working Paper, Brussels, June.

European Parliament, Task Force on the Intergovernmental Conference (ed.) (1997). "Briefing on the 1996 IGC and the Enlargement of the EU". Luxembourg, 27 May.

"Founding Act on Mutual Relations, Cooperation and Security between NATO and the Russian Federation". NATO–Russia Summit Document, Paris, 27 May 1997.

High-level Group of Experts on the CFSP (chairman: Mr Durieux) (1995). "The Common Foreign and Security Policy on the Eve of the Year 2000". 28 November (PE 214.986 of 10 January 1996).

Kugler, R.L. (1996). *Enlarging NATO – The Russian Factor*. Rand.

NATO General Secretariat (1996). "Study on NATO Enlargement". Brussels, September.

North Atlantic Assembly (1996). "The Enlargement of the Alliance". Draft Special Report, Brussels, May.

Pinder, J. (1997). *Enlargement and the CFSP: Political Consequences*. Brussels: TEPSA.

Reflection Group (chairman: Mr Westendrop) (1995). Report, 5 December (SN 520/1/95 rev. 1).

Treaty on European Union, Office for Official Publications of the European Communities, Luxembourg, 1992.

WEU Assembly (1997). "Enlarged Security: the Security Problems Posed by the Enlargement of NATO and the European Insititutions". Colloquy, Athens, March.

WEU Assembly (1997). "Proceedings of the 42nd Session, December 1996". Paris.

CHAPTER 6

Transgressing borders: the emergent European refugee regime and "Safe Third Countries"[1]

Sandra Lavenex

6.1. INTRODUCTION

Traditionally, the European Community´s external relations were based on commercial policy, on development aid and – with European Political Cooperation – on foreign and security policy. In the 1990s, however, they have been increasingly extended to include policies relating to the fields of justice and home affairs that belong to the third pillar of the European Union.

This chapter gives an introduction to this new field of foreign policy as it has evolved, particularly in relations with the countries of Central and Eastern Europe. The focus is on the questions of immigration and political asylum,[2] which are becoming increasingly important in the context of the establishment of a common European refugee regime based on the redistributive principle of "safe third countries". It is maintained that these processes affect the EU and its external relations on three levels. At the domestic level, the inclusion of neighbouring countries in this new set of policies amounts to an interference in these countries' internal and foreign affairs, since they are bound to align their own policies towards foreigners. At the European level, these developments affect the conception of a common foreign and security policy and change the conditions for future enlargement. At the global level, the emergent European refugee regime profoundly transforms the traditional system of political asylum and weakens the principles, norms, rules and procedures of the international refugee regime.

The evolution of this new field of European cooperation is briefly summarized below, and an overview of its central institutional and legal features is given. These findings are then subjected to more thorough analysis and interpretation with regard to their implications for the EU, its neighbours and overall international relations. Finally, the main implications are summarized from the point of view of the Union's external relations.

---

[1] This chapter was completed in June 1997.
[2] In political debate, the distinction between the issues of voluntary immigration and political asylum as an involuntary form of immigration has become blurred. In this chapter, the term "immigration" is used according to its hitherto dominant meaning in European negotiations, and refers only to the territorial entry rules that affect third country nationals.

113

A. Cafruny and P. Peters (eds.), The Union and the World, 113–132

6.2. THE EVOLUTION OF THE EUROPEAN REFUGEE REGIME: FROM INTERGOV-
ERNMENTAL NEGOTIATIONS TO COOPERATION UNDER THE THIRD PILLAR

For many years, refugee policy was characterized by a clearly separated dual structure of policy-making at the international and national levels. At the international level, political asylum was codified in an international regime, based on the Geneva Convention (GC) on the Status of Refugees of 1951, together with the New York Protocol of 1967 and the activity of the United Nations High Commissioner for Refugees (UNHCR) acting as a guardian of the treaty. The core elements of this international regime are the general principles of international solidarity and cooperation for the protection of refugees, the norm of non-refoulement[3] and the other provisions of the treaty, as well as the rules and decision-making procedures laid down by the UNHCR Executive Committee.[4] However, within this general system of cooperation, the right to grant asylum is left to the discretion of the sovereign nation states. In Western Europe, all states have implemented the right to asylum in their respective aliens and refugee laws.[5]

What we observe in Europe today is the incremental transformation of the international refugee regime into a regional system of redistribution for asylum-seekers that redefines the relationship between the "national" and the "international". This section will retrace the evolution of this transformation process.

European cooperation in refugee and immigration matters was induced in the context of the internal market project, originally as a subordinate side-aspect of the abolition of internal border controls. It orginated in two more or less parallel intergovernmental processes between the European Ministers of the Interior, which developed outside the Community framework in the Schengen and TREVI groups. Whereas "Schengen" views itself as a sort of pilot project for the implementation of the internal market going back to the initiative of a limited number of member states,[6] "TREVI" refers to an informal cooperation process in the fields of internal security and public order which began during the mid-1970s. The prospect of the abolition of checks at the internal borders led these groups to elaborate compensation measures regarded as necessary for the safeguarding of internal security. Apart from regulations on the fight against drugs, terrorism, international crime, as well as general police and judicial cooperation, these include provisions relating to the entry, treatment and expulsion of non-EC citizens and asylum-seekers. The central results of these parallel negotiation processes are, on the one hand, the Schengen Implementation Agreement of 19 June

---

[3] This norm (art 33 GC) prohibits the forced return of refugees in situations where persecution or other dangers are imminent.

[4] This definition is oriented along Krasner's (1983) classical definition of international regimes as "sets of implicit or explicit principles, norms, rules, and decision-making procedures around which actors' expectations converge in a given area of international relations".

[5] For an overview see Hailbronner (1992), ECRE (1994).

[6] The First Schengen Agreement on the Gradual Abolition of Checks at the Common Borders of 14 June 1985 goes back to an initiative taken by Kohl and Mitterand and was signed by France, Germany and the Benelux countries. All EU member states except the UK and Ireland have joined this initiative.

1990[7] and on the other the Dublin Convention on the State Responsible for the Examination of an Asylum Claim of 15 June 1990,[8] together with the draft Convention on the Crossing of External Borders.[9] These agreements converge almost completely in their provisions with regard to third country nationals.[10] Having been framed as measures of internal security, they follow a defensive logic. Thus they aim at the intensification of control standards at the external borders, the adoption of common visa-requirements, harmonized policies towards illegal immigrants and the sanction of carriers who enable their entry. With regard to asylum seekers, the central provision of the Schengen and Dublin Conventions is the determination of the responsibility of a single signatory state for the examination of an asylum claim (see section 6.3.1).

While the Dublin and the Schengen Agreements did not have a thorough harmonization of immigration and asylum policies in mind, they set the demarcation lines for the future European and domestic reforms. They triggered (supported by the transformations in Eastern Europe and the emergent crisis in the former Yugoslavia) a far-reaching dynamic, which, on the one hand, reflected the increased importance of these policy fields and, on the other, called for a more substantive harmonization for these agreements to function.

In the Treaty on the European Union, the issues of immigration and asylum were incorporated for the first time as "matters of common interest" into the framework of the Community (art K.1 TEU). The list of these matters reflects the context of their political salience. It comprises the questions of asylum, the crossing of external borders, immigration, drugs, and fraud, as well as judicial, customs and police cooperation. This "third pillar", however, leaves these topics to the field of intergovernmental cooperation and brings no real substantive institutional changes.[11] In these areas, the Council may adopt joint positions and actions, as well as drawing up conventions. The two major innovations are the right to initiative of the Commission and the involvement of the European Parliament, which shall be regularly informed and consulted on the principal aspects of the activities in these areas (art K.3 TEU). Major reforms of this institutional framework are foreseen in the Treaty of Amsterdam concluded in June 1997. Accordingly, the issues of asylum and immigration shall

---

[7] Reproduced in Pauly (1993), p. 187ff. This agreement could finally enter into force with the functioning of its information system on 26 March 1995. With the Treaty of Amsterdam of June 1997 the Schengen Agreement has been incorporated into the Treaty on the European Union. Flexibility clauses have been introduced for the UK and Ireland.

[8] Printed in EC Bulletin 6 (1990), pp. 165–172. The Convention finally entered into force on 1 September 1997.

[9] Although it was drafted in 1990, the signing of this convention had to be postponed due to disputes between Great Britain and Spain over the status of Gibraltar.

[10] With the entry into force of the Dublin Convention, the equivalent provisions of the Schengen Agreement have become obsolete (art 142 SA).

[11] The operative structure of the Justice and Home Affairs Council is divided into four levels: at the top the Council of Ministers for Justice and Home Affairs, then the Committee of Permanent Representatives (COREPER), the so-called K4 Coordinating Committee (according to art K4 TEU) and the different steering groups on asylum and immigration, police and customs, and judicial control. This structure has absorbed earlier groups such as the *ad hoc* group on immigration, but mainly comprises the same institutional actors as before.

be transferred to the First Pillar of the Union. However, this will occur only after a transitional period of five years after the entry into force of the revised treaty. Then, the Commission will have the sole right of initiative and the Council will take a decision concerning the competences of the European Parliament and the introduction of qualified majority voting.

Until now, the initiatives of the supranational bodies have had little impact on the Council's line of policy. While this institution's scope of harmonization for a common asylum and immigration policy is largely reactive and limited to mostly procedural measures for combating illegal immigration and limiting the numbers of asylum seekers, the European Commission[12] and the European Parliament[13] strive towards a much more comprehensive strategy. This strategy – which places the global dimension of the migration issue in a long-term perspective – consists of three elements: the addressing of the root causes of migration via a common foreign policy, the management of migration flows via both immigration rules and provisions for the protection of refugees, and the integration of legal immigrants in the host societies.

6.3. ELEMENTS OF THE EMERGENT EUROPEAN REFUGEE REGIME: LEGAL AND IN-STITUTIONAL PROVISIONS

The core element of the emergent European refugee regime is the institutionalization of a system of negative redistribution based on the principle of "safe third countries", which aims at the relief of domestic asylum procedures in the EU member states through the limitation of access and the adoption of responsibility rules. However, while originally restricted to the EU, recent developments point at the enlargement of this regime through extension to Central and Eastern European states which will have to adopt corresponding policies.

This system of redistribution is based firstly, on the Schengen and Dublin Conventions (SC and DC), and secondly on the respective resolutions and declarations of the Council in the framework of the third pillar.

---

[12] While its first proposal for a coordination of national asylum procedures of 1988 (Draft Directive Com (1988) 640) was rejected by the European Council over considerations of sovereignty, the European Commission has enhanced its activities in matters of asylum and immigration in the wake of Maastricht. In 1991, it issued two communications to the Council and the European Parliament on immigration and asylum which were intended to take into account the increased political and social importance of these issues (Sec (91) 1857 final and Sec (91) 1855 final). The most recent communication of the Commission to the Council and the European Parliament was presented in the framework of the Maastricht Treaty and dates from 23/2/1994 (Com (94) final). It represents the most complete document of the European Union on migration to date and addresses for the first time the issues of immigration and asylum in a joint approach. It also forms the basis for the development of a new comprehensive strategy which faces the global dimension of the migration issue in a long-term perspective (see Fortescue 1995, De Jong 1995).

[13] The central initiatives of the European Parliament are the Vetter report of 23/2/1987 (Document A2-227/86/A and B), a resolution criticizing the inhumane asylum practices in several member states from the same year (Document B2-512/87 of 18/6/1987), and two reports on the harmonization of asylum and immigration policies from 1992 (Document A3-0337/92/A and B of 5/11/1992 and Document A3-0280/92 of 2/10/1992).

6.3.1. The "safe third country" principle in the Schengen and Dublin Conventions

Under the pressure of an increasing number of asylum seekers, the Schengen and Dublin Conventions implemented in the European Union a system of redistribution for asylum seekers that aims at the relief of domestic asylum procedures; this is effected through the adoption of more restrictive entry measures (visas, border checks, required documents, carrier sanctions) and the setting up of a system of unique responsibility for the examination of an asylum claim among the contracting parties. This system is based on the principle that only the state with which the asylum seeker has had his first contact is responsible for the examination of his claim. Such contact can be established by the issue of a residence permit, an entry or transit visa; the legal presence of a close family member; or, in the absence of one of these, simply the first physical contact with the territory (arts 4–8 DC, arts 28–38 SC). The asylum procedure, then, follows the respective national laws (art 3 DC, art 32 SC). This rule, which specifies that an asylum claim will be examined by only one contracting party, requires first the state's agreement to take back an asylum seeker if it is regarded as being responsible for the examination of his claim, and second the mutual recognition of the outcome of the status determination procedure. This recognition implies the existence of a certain degree of convergence in the status determination criteria. Thus, the emergent European refugee regime is based on the assumption of common standards of refugee protection that would justify the loosening of the exclusive responsibility of the sovereign states under international law and the transfer of this responsibility to third countries that are deemed to be safe.[14]

As fundamental differences in the various domestic material and procedural asylum laws became clear, the member states recognized the need for a more thorough harmonization of their regulations. However, the flagging efforts to harmonize the interpretation of the refugee definition of article 1A Geneva Convention show the reluctance of the member states to deepen their transfer of sovereignty.[15]

6.3.2. The extension of the use of the "safe third country" rule under the Third Pillar

The further course of cooperation in the matters of asylum and immigration under the third pillar of the Maastricht Treaty follows to a high degree the logic of action reflected in the above-mentioned intergovernmental agreements. The first results of this cooperation are the London Resolutions of 30 November–1 December 1992.[16] These resolutions are also directed towards the relief of domestic asylum procedures through the harmonization of instruments that are apt to limit access to asylum proce-

---

[14] The use of the safe third country rule is not completely new. However, while its application has been a common practice since the 1980s, it has been harmonized and systematized with these agreements.

[15] After several years of negotiations, the member states finally agreed on a draft harmonized definition of a refugee on 23/11/1995 that reflects the "lowest common denominator".

[16] Conclusions of the Meeting of the Ministers Responsible for Immigration, 10518/92, London 30/11–1/12/1992.

dures. The first resolution refers to the adoption of accelerated asylum procedures in "manifestly unfounded" cases, where there is clearly no substantive issue under the 1951 Geneva Convention, or no substance to the applicant´s fear of persecution in his or her own country, or when the claim is based on deception. In the second, more incisive resolution, the use of the "safe third country" rule is extended to include all countries also outside the Community that are deemed to be safe. Provided that these countries have ratified the 1951 Geneva Convention, and thus supposedly respect the norm of non-refoulement, an individual may be returned without examination of his claim if he or she may have had the opportunity to lodge an asylum application there. This opportunity is given when the asylum seeker has had contact with the territory of the third country, even if only in transit.[17] Finally, the London conclusions on countries in which there is generally no serious risk of persecution foresee the adoption of accelerated procedures for individuals coming from so-called safe countries of origin, which shall be listed according to common criteria.

These resolutions are the direct continuation of the logic of negative redistribution reflected in the 1990 treaties. While the adoption of accelerated procedures for "manifestly unfounded" cases and persons coming from "safe countries of origin" tends to minimize the procedural guarantees of legal protection for asylum seekers,[18] the "safe third country" rule prevents access to an asylum procedure for large groups of refugees altogether by extending the system of redistribution outside the EU to all potentially safe countries. As the resolution signifies that its application has priority over the Dublin Convention, the latter applies only if an applicant cannot be returned to a safe country outside the Community. In contrast to the international treaties of Schengen and Dublin, however, this resolution raises two problems. First, it neutralizes the question of responsibility as it omits to fix the conditions of readmission and the duty of granting access to asylum procedure for the third country in question. Given that international law derives a responsibility of readmission only for the states' own citizens, there is no legal basis for these states to agree to take back a third state national. Furthermore, the resolution does not take into consideration the specific needs of an asylum seeker as compared to an illegal immigrant when being returned; i.e. the specification of the need to provide him or her with access to fair and equitable asylum procedures in order to avoid refoulement. Given the fact that many of these "safe countries" had not participated in the international refugee regime before, they are only now starting to implement specific asylum regulations (see section 6.5.1).

In summary, when compared with the rules and procedures that guide intra-Union cooperation (Schengen and Dublin Agreements), this extension of the safe third country rule violates both basic requirements of the emergent European refugee regime mentioned above: firstly, the consent of the readmitting state to take back and examine the claim of an asylum seeker, and secondly, the requirement of a certain

[17] The possibility to return a person who has merely transited a third country contrasts with article 7, Dublin Convention, according to which a person's stay in the transit zone of an airport does not establish a responsibility of that state to examine his or her asylum claim.

[18] In particular, these accelerated procedures restrict the time-limits for requests and appeals, limit the possibilities for appeal, inhibit the consultation of legal advisers or NGOs, and often prevent the asylum seeker from being heard individually by the competent bodies for the examination of his or her claim.

degree of equivalence of procedural and substantive status determination criteria.[19]

The next section turns to the practical aspects of the implementation of the safe third country rule and the incorporation of matters belonging to the third pillar into the EU´s external relations. The documented extension of the emergent European refugee regime will be analysed with regard to its political and legal implications in the last section of the chapter.

6.4. Incorporating "Wider" Europe: the Implementation of the Safe Third Country Rule

In order to extend the system of redistribution which is at the core of the emergent refugee regime to other European countries, both the European Union and its member states have engaged in a variety of multilateral and bilateral activities. In general, these efforts aim at meeting the abovementioned shortcomings of an extension of the emergent regime by providing a legal basis for the readmission of third state nationals and the development of common standards of border controls and in the fight against illegal immigration and refugee protection. These can be roughly divided into three groups: firstly, activities within the context of the Schengen and the Dublin Agreements; secondly, measures adopted within the third pillar of the European Union; and thirdly, other bilateral activities between the member states and third countries. In addition, a number of intergovernmental conferences bringing together both EU and other European states complement these processes.

6.4.1. The extension of the Schengen and the Dublin Conventions

The Schengen and the Dublin Conventions setting up a system of redistribution that is based on the safe third country rule were originally limited to EU member states. However, the interest of some of these countries in including third parties became evident at a very early stage. Given its membership in the Nordic Union, Denmark had an immediate interest in the adhesion of the Nordic non-EU states to the convention. However, it was found that the linkage of this treaty with the Community's single market restricted full membership to the EU member states. Instead, a parallel convention was drafted for the participation of Norway, Sweden and also Switzerland that is virtually the same as the original. With the delay in the coming into force of the Dublin Convention, however, these parallel agreements have been suspended and are only now re-entering the negotiations. However, their use will be limited to the EFTA countries.

In the Schengen group, the incorporation of non-EU countries has already material-

---

[19]   See also Achermann and Gattiker (1995), Hailbronner (1993), Kjaergaard (1994) and the statements of Amnesty International; The Standing Committee of Experts in International Immigration, Refugee and Criminal Law; and UNHCR.

ized more concretely. A readmission agreement was signed with Poland on 29 March 1991 which aims at the return of illegal immigrants who enter "Schengenland" via Poland. In contrast to earlier bilateral readmission agreements, this agreement also applies to nationals of third states including asylum seekers who passed through Polish territory, and thus corresponds to the redistributive mechanism of the Schengen and the Dublin Conventions (Czaplinski 1994, p. 641). By fixing a legal commitment for readmission, this agreement makes a decisive step in the implementation of the safe third country rule.

Moreover, the Schengen states are currently negotiating a possible adhesion of the EFTA states Norway and Iceland in order to be able to incorporate the Nordic Union into their group. Although according to official statements the drafting of parallel agreements with these states should not create a precedent, the future will show to what extent the participation of third states will be extended.

6.4.2. Activities of the European Union

In the framework of the third pillar, the conclusion of the London Resolution on safe third countries triggered the adoption of further measures in order to ensure its implementation. After their meeting as the Council of Justice and Home Affairs on 30 November–1 December 1993, the competent EU ministers issued a plan of action in which they stated the need to consider the matters of asylum and immigration in the EU's external relations. For this purpose, general guidelines for the adoption of bilateral or multilateral readmission agreements should be elaborated and eventually linked to the "European", "Association" and "Cooperation" Agreements of the Community and its member states with third countries (European Parliament 1995, p. 7).

The first steps in this direction were the adoption in late November 1993 of common principles for the conclusion of readmission agreements with third countries, the recommendations in 1994 of the Council on a specimen bilateral agreement between a member state and a third country,[20] and the guiding principles to be followed in drawing up protocols on the implementation of readmission agreements, agreed upon in July 1995.[21,22]

Apart from these specific measures aimed at implementing the London Resolution on safe third countries, the issues of asylum and immigration have entered the field of EU external relations in much broader terms. On the European Council in Essen in December 1994, the heads of government decided generally to give the issues of the

---

[20] Council Recommendation of 30 November 1994, printed in Official Journal of the European Communities C274 Vol. 39 of 19 September 1996. For a critique see the European Parliament Report by Claudia Roth of 20 July 1995, EP Doc A4-0184/95.

[21] Council Recommendation of 24 July 1995, printed in Official Journal of the European Communities C274 Vol. 39 of 19 September 1996.

[22] It is important to note that with these recommendations the Council omits using one of the tools foreseen in art K.3TEU and thus avoids possible claims for legal obligations or democratic control (see European Parliament 1995, p. 8).

third pillar more weight in the structured dialogue and to integrate cooperation in asylum and immigration matters in the strategy of pre-adhesion to the Union. With regard to the EU's general external relations, a reference to the need for cooperation with the aim of preventing illegal immigration can be found in several agreements concluded by the Community and its member states with third countries. As at February 1996, such a clause figured in the agreements with the Baltic states, Slovenia, Armenia, Azerbaijan, Belarus, Georgia, Kazakhstan, Kirghizstan and Russia. In the agreements with Egypt, Jordan, Lebanon, Morocco and Tunisia, a dialogue on problems related to illegal immigration is foreseen as part of the social dialogue. In addition, these agreements foresee cooperation facilitating the resettlement of individuals who are to be repatriated as a consequence of their illegal status. In the light of the Justice and Home Affairs Council decision of 23 November 1995 on incorporating readmission clauses in mixed agreements with third countries,[23] it is to be expected that such clauses will appear in many such future agreements.[24]

Although the Europe agreements signed with all countries of Central and Eastern Europe do not contain any clause mentioning asylum as such, they provide, by reason of their Association Council and Committee meetings, fora in which subjects such as asylum can be discussed between individual countries and the EU Commission, the Presidency and the member states. Associated states may participate in the Justice and Home Affairs Ministers Council, the K-4 Coordination Committee and some of the subordinate working groups.

Regarding the decision to include the issues of the third pillar in the strategy of pre-adhesion, both the Council and the European Commission have started programmes aimed at putting forward this cooperation. While the activities of the Council under the Irish Presidency concentrated on the fight against drugs and the smuggling of immigrants as well as the general tightening up of border controls with modern technologies, the Dutch Presidency concentrated especially on asylum and sought to promote the implementation of the safe third countries rule through legislative adaptations in these countries. Apart from these activities of the Council, and partly as a complement to these, the task force "third pillar" of the European Commission is trying to build up a sensitivity to the needs of refugee protection and to support the introduction of fair and equitable asylum procedures. Its emphasis lies on the development of adequate institutional frameworks for dealing with refugees and asylum seekers, the implementation of appropriate asylum procedures and related measures, including training for personnel and the development of adequate documentary and information sources. For this purpose, the scope of existing, mainly economically oriented financial cooperation programmes such as PHARE[25] and TACIS[26] has been

---

[23] "Mixed agreements" are agreements signed between the EU and its member states on the one hand and third countries on the other hand.

[24] See Answer of the European Commission of 13/2/1996 to the questions raised by the Member of Parliament Philippe de Coene (H-0116/96).

[25] PHARE stands for "Poland, Hungary Aid for Reconstruction" and was originally designed to provide economic assistance in the reform of agriculture, ecology, finance, industry, infrastructure, the social sector and education.

extended to provide assistance related to matters belonging to the third pillar.[27] These measures are believed to complement the work of the structured dialogue.

The increasing role of immigration and asylum matters in the Union´s external relations poses a direct challenge to the current institutional settings, as it calls for very close coordination between the three pillars, most notably between the second (Common Foreign and Security Policy) and the third pillar, and, through the use of such programmes as PHARE and TACIS, derives new competencies for the European Commission in a formerly purely intergovernmental field of action.

6.4.3. Bilateral activities

Since the opening up of the Eastern bloc, Western European countries have demonstrated an increasing interest in the limitation of immigration from the East and, accordingly, the enhancement of border controls. The activities, on the one hand, concentrate on the conclusion of readmission agreements for the implementation of the safe third country rule at the domestic level and, on the other, aim at the transfer of funds and technology for the fight against illegal immigration and the adoption of compatible asylum regulations.

Although the conclusion of readmission agreements is not a new phenomenon, the scope and target of these agreements has changed radically. While the first generation readmission agreements between Western European states of the 1950s and 1960s were restricted to the duty of readmiting own state nationals who had entered the territory of the contracting state illegally,[28] the new generation follows the example of the abovementioned Schengen–Poland agreement. These agreements aim at the facilitated expulsion of third country nationals, including, although it is often not mentioned explicitly, asylum seekers on grounds of the safe third country rule. The driving intention is again to combat illegal immigration and to limit the intake of asylum seekers.

The conclusion of such agreements spreads rapidly and moves ever further east-

---

[26] TACIS is a cooperation programme agreed upon at the European Council in Rome in 1990, set up to assist the newly independent states of the former Soviet Union; it corresponds broadly to the aims of the PHARE programme.

[27] The decision to use PHARE funds is based on the conclusions of the so-called Langdon Report, which was issued at the request of the European Commission following the conclusions of the European Council in Essen in December 1994 on the strategy of pre-adhesion for the countries of Central and Eastern Europe.The report that was finalized at the end of 1995 sets up the priorities for this strategy and determines the matters to be financed within the PHARE framework. These are: firstly, the combat of illegal immigration and the enforcement of border controls; secondly, asylum; and thirdly, the combating of drugs (see Doc SEK (96) 86). A particular PHARE programme already under way and relevant to asylum issues is the Baltic Eastern Border Management Programme, which aims to assist Estonia, Latvia and Lithuania to improve the level and management and control of their Eastern borders. In addition, a comprehensive programme which will also address migration and asylum issues is currently in the early phases of preparation in Poland. Finally, the Commission is preparing a multi-country PHARE programme concerning issues pertaining to the Third Pillar which aims at fostering interregional cooperation in these fields.

[28] Although this duty is already a norm of customary international law, these agreements aimed at facilitating the procedures of return (see Schieffer 1996, p. 4).

wards. Given the implementation of the safe third country rule in its constitutional reforms of 1993 and its geographical position, Germany has taken the lead in the conclusion of such agreements. Since 1993, it has signed such treaties with its eastern neighbours (with Poland on 7 May 1993 and the Czech Republic on 9 November 1994). Furthermore, it concluded readmission agreements with Romania (24 September 1992), Bulgaria (9 September 1994 and 7 September 1996), Croatia (25 April 1994), the Federal Republic of Yugoslavia (10 October 1996) and Bosnia (20 November 1996);[29] but also with non-European countries such as Vietnam (21 July 1995), Pakistan (December 1995) and Algeria (January 1996). Considering that many asylum seekers come from these countries, these agreements concentrate on the readmission of own state nationals and thus facilitate the expulsion of rejected asylum seekers.[30] These agreements do not consider the special needs of asylum seekers, i.e. their access to equitable asylum procedures and their protection against refoulement. This is especially salient in the case of Austria, which has concluded such a readmission agreement with Hungary, although this country applies the Geneva Convention of 1951 with a geographical limitation to "European" refugees. Agreements of this kind have also been concluded by the Benelux countries, France,[31] and the Nordic countries.[32] In sum, the propagation of these new instruments is still spreading and proceeds by "passing the buck" of refugee protection further and further to the east (see section 6.5).

Apart from these legal measures, the EU member states have also engaged in a variety of bilateral cooperation processes in the fields of justice and home affairs that focus on the fight against illegal immigration in general, the improvement of border controls, the establishment of centralized institutions dealing with immigration control, and, to a lesser extent, legal counselling for the adoption of compatible immigration and asylum regulations. In general, it appears that these efforts are along geographical lines: while the Scandinavian countries concentrate on the Baltics, Germany and, to a lesser extent, France and the Netherlands cooperate mainly with the Central European countries and Bulgaria.[33]

---

[29] In parallel, the German government has in the 1990s been negotiating bilateral and multilateral agreements with Eastern European countries concerning organized crime, terrorism, and police and customs cooperation (German Parliament, Bundestagsdrucksache 13/6447, Antwort des Parlamentarischen Staatssekretärs Eduard Lintner, 26 November 1996).

[30] See the paper prepared by a member of the German Ministry of the Interior (Schieffer 1996).

[31] A highly sensitive confidential readmission agreement was signed in summer 1994 with Algeria, a major refugee-sending country, which was not made public until its revelation by *Le Monde* on 22 October 1994 (see *Migration Newssheet*, November 1994, No. 140).

[32] For an overview of the multitude of readmission agreements see Inter-governmental Consultations 1995, annex I.

[33] See European Parliament 6 June 1996. In Germany, for example, the financial transfer in the context of the readmission agreement with Poland was split up into 49 per cent for border security, 38 per cent for the police and only 13 per cent for the establishment of an asylum infrastructure. See Bundestagsdrucksache 13/6030 of 30 October 1996.

6.4.4. Overarching intergovernmental consultations

These bilateral and multilateral activities are occuring in the context of the intergovernmental consultations among Western and Eastern European governments that started shortly after the fall of the Iron Curtain in early 1991. The first conference on the fight against illegal immigration among the ministers of justice and home affairs of the 24 states of Council of Europe as well as other Eastern and South-eastern European countries took place in Vienna in January 1991. It was followed by the Berlin Conference in October of the same year, at which political and legal precautions against mass emigration to the West, as well as common steps against the smuggling of illegal immigrants, were adopted. The follow-up conference took place in Budapest together with seven international organizations in February 1993. It concentrated on immigrant smuggling and information exchange on illegal migrations, and introduced the plan to conclude readmission agreements and to enhance border controls. The so-called Budapest Group[34] was set up to examine the possibility of an enlargement of the readmission agreement between the Schengen Group and Poland to include other Central and East European countries. However, this plan to find a multilateral solution was soon dropped and the conclusion of bilateral agreements was favoured.[35] Since then, various intergovernmental conferences between Western and Eastern European countries, including international and non-governmental organizations, that dealt with the issues of immigration and asylum have taken place.

In the next section, these findings will be analysed and interpreted in view of their impact on Central and East European neighbouring states, their role as part of the Union's external relations, and their relationship with the international refugee regime.

6.5. TRANSGRESSING BORDERS: NATIONAL, EUROPEAN AND INTERNATIONAL IMPLICATIONS OF THE EUROPEAN REFUGEE REGIME

The transgression of the Union's borders induced by the extension of the cooperation in refugee and immigration matters affects its relations with its neighbours on three levels. At the domestic level, the EU's neighbouring countries are compelled to adapt their asylum and immigration policies to a new set of principles, norms, rules and procedures that have been negotiated in closed intergovernmental fora composed of the EU ministers of the interior. At the European level, these processes touch the question of the EU's external relations and that of European integration, i.e. the development of an autonomous and consistent European foreign policy. Finally, at the global international level, the transformation of European refugee and immigration policies has an important impact on the international refugee regime and the idea of refugee protection as such. These three levels are analysed in more detail in the following subsections.

---

[34] This group consists of the states assuming the presidency of the EC, the Schengen Group and EFTA, the Czech Republic, Poland, Slovakia and Hungary (*Migration Newssheet*, March 1993).
[35] See *Migration Newssheet*, April 1993.

6.5.1. The domestic level: political and legal implications of the extension of the emergent European refugee regime

While, for the EFTA countries, being incorporated into the system of redistribution for the treatment of asylum seekers through being labelled as "safe third countries" is in line with a common tradition in refugee and immigration matters, as is an overall trend among Western industrialized countries towards the adoption of restrictive policies, this move has major implications for the domestic politics of Central and East European countries. Unlike the Western countries, these "new" democracies lack experience of immigration and refugee protection in the post-War era and are only now joining the international refugee regime. Starting from the early 1990s, all Central and Eastern European Countries have now ratified the Geneva Convention of 1951.[36] Although the first generation of asylum regulations implemented in the early 1990s followed very general and generous guidelines,[37] the Central and Eastern European countries are currently experiencing a wave of restrictive reforms that tend to imitate the legislation of the West. At the end of 1996, the Slovak[38] and Bulgarian[39] asylum laws had adopted the notion of safe third countries; a similar reform was on the way in Hungary and the Czech Republic.[40] Altough not formally regulated, the use of this instrument is also an administrative practice in Slovenia and Romania. Poland, which up to now does not apply the safe third country rule, will follow the trend. According to its "national strategy for integration", a new law on foreigners is being developed in the light of a future accession to the EU "which will prevent the abuse of asylum procedures". This law will be "in accordance with the general trend in implementing stricter asylum policy in the EU member states".[41] The context in which this project is presented in the document illustrates the guiding logic behind it: it stands under the heading "Protection of the EU's external borders" – together with the issues of combating illegal immigration, organized crime, terrorism and drugs. Correspondingly, these states have started once more, after the fall of communism, to tighten their border controls and are increasingly introducing visa requirements for their eastern and southern neighbours.[42] Among those discriminated against are the associated states of Romania and Bulgaria, which still need visas for the EU. This situation

---

[36] Hungary in March 1989, though with a geographical limitation to Europe; Poland and Romania in late 1991, the (later) Czech and Slovak Republics in 1992 and Bulgaria in May 1993 (see European Parliament 6 June 1996). The three Baltic countries joined during 1997.

[37] In Poland the law of 29 March 1963 on foreigners as amended by Decree of the Minister of the Interior of 31 December 1991, in the Czech Republic act no. 498 of 16 November 1990 concerning regugees as amended by act no. 317 of 8 December 1993, in the Slovak Republic the same legislation as in the Czech Republic of 1990, in Bulgaria the decree no. 208 of 4 October 1994 for the adoption of ordinance for granting and regulating the refugee status (see UNHCR/Centre for Documentation and Research, Executive Committee, Update on Regional Developments in Europe, EC/46/SC/CRP.24 of 18 March 1996).

[38] Law of 14 November 1995, see Hoskova (1996).

[39] Law no. 208/1994 of March 1994, see Hottmeister (1996).

[40] See *Migration Newssheet*, June 1996 (No. 159) and UNHCR, "Summary of UNHCR Activities in Central Europe", October 1996, p. 5.

[41] Polish Committee for European Integration, National Strategy for Integration, January 1997, p. 57.

[42] See *Migration Newssheet*.

hinders their prospects for future EU membership.

These adaptation processes stand in a direct relationship with the designation of some of these states as "safe" by their Western neighbours and the subsequent conclusion of readmission agreements. The adoption of these instruments is currently spreading all over the continent. In the light of its readmission agreement with Germany of 7 May 1993, Poland concluded a similar agreement with the Czech Republic four days later, with Slovakia, the Ukraine and Romania in July and with Bulgaria in August of the same year. Similar agreements are planned with Russia and the three Baltic states.[43] But the self-transplanting dynamics of these instruments do not stop here: Lithuania and Latvia plan the adoption of the safe third country rule while Latvia made the ratification of the Geneva Convention directly conditional on the implementation of preconditions such as the establishment of readmission agreements with Belarus and Russia. The same strategy was implemented by the Czech Republic in the wake of its readmission agreement with Germany and by Hungary with respect to Austria. Again, both these states have propagated this instrument eastwards to their own neighbours, and these again with their neighbours, so that today one can speak of a "domino effect" (Kumin 1994, p. 13); a chain of readmission agreements that shifts the "burden" of illegal immigrants and refugees ever further from the West towards the countries of emigration.[44]

These processes are not enacted in a purely voluntary fashion. These countries realize that the EU is particularly interested in cooperation regarding the entry of foreigners, while other matters of the third pillar are less subject to cooperation (Handl *et al.* 1996). They also complain that they are now affected by rules for which they were not allowed to participate in the decision-making process. They realize that they function as a filter for the EU, although they would still consider themselves merely as transit-countries for migrations to the Union (Inotai and Nötzhold 1996). However, the willingness to adopt this legislation is used as leverage for the request of financial transfers. Faced with major opposition from the Polish government to the "export" of its immigration problem (expressed by a representative of the Polish government quoted in *Migration Newssheet* of March 1993), Germany finally linked the adoption of the readmission agreement with a financial transfer of 120 million Deutschmarks. Similarly, the consent of the Czech Republic finally depended on aid of 60 million Deutschmarks.[45] In return, the nationals of these states were exempted from visa requirements for Germany.

The reluctance of these states to be incorporated into this new system of redistribution for asylum seekers became very clear at the meeting of the ministers of the interior of six Central and East European countries in Prague on 16 March 1993, where a multilateral solution to deal with the flow of asylum seekers expected to result from the introduction of the safe third country notion in Germany was sought.[46] An alternative

---

[43] See *Migration Newssheet*, June 1993 (No. 123).

[44] For an overview of the panoply of readmission agreements, see Inter-governmental Consultations December 1995.

[45] See *Migration Newssheet*, March 1993 (No. 120), June 1993 (No. 123), September 1994 (No. 138); and Initiative Gegen das Schengener Abkommen 1993, pp. 6ff.

[46] See *Migration Newssheet*, April 1993.

proposal for multilateral readmission agreements was issued that condemned the emerging chain of bilateral readmission agreements and the use of the safe third country rule towards countries that had not been consulted before.[47] This rule not only interferes with the respective countries' home and justice affairs, but also touches on the field of foreign policy, as these countries are now compelled to secure their own borders towards their eastern neighbours and to adopt in their turn restrictive entry measures and visa requirements. However, the resulting adaptations must be interpreted in the light of the linkage of the questions of immigration and refugees with the prospects of an adhesion to the European Union. This point is discussed in the next subsection.

6.5.2. The European frame: foreign and security policy, enlargement and integration

The European Union's activities towards its eastern neighbours in the fields of the third pillar touch the question of integration in two respects. First, they represent a new area of external relations that modifies the conventional concepts of foreign and security policy and that of conditionality for adhesion to the Union. Second, at the institutional level, this new field of cooperation might have an influence on the Union's profile as an autonomous foreign policy actor.

As mentioned in the introduction, the EU's external relations were originally based on purely economic considerations. However, with the changes in Central and Eastern Europe, a "new conditionality" (Weber 1995, p. 198) entered the EU's foreign policy that put increasing emphasis on political requirements for economic cooperation. Although initially separated formally from the question of EU membership, these criteria were almost directly linked to the strategies of pre-adhesion. However, these concepts remain fuzzy. In its post-Maastricht report on enlargement, the Commission noted that "the European political identity" as a condition for membership combines geography, history, culture, ideas, values, and historical interaction (European Commission 1992). This political conditionality was then immediately adopted in foreign policy instruments such as the PHARE programme[48] and the Cooperation and Association Agreements that gave equal billing to political liberalization – human rights, democracy, civic freedoms – and to economic liberalization of markets, trade, and investment regimes (Weber 1995).

However, while these criteria concern only the fundamental freedoms of own citizens, the linkage of the questions of immigration and asylum with these foreign

---

[47] Budapest Group: Readmission Agreements, extract from the Report of the Expert Group on the Five Themes Selected for Examination by the Budapest Group. Third Meeting of the Budapest Group, Zurich, 14–15 September 1995; printed in Inter-governmental Consultations December 1995. See also UNHCR, Regional Bureau for Europe, International Symposium on Protection of Refugees in Central and Eastern Europe, April 1996 (Vol. 1, No. 1).

[48] PHARE would only provide assistance to countries that would make "clear commitments regarding the rule of law, respect for fair elections in the course of 1990, and economic liberalization...." (European Commission 1990).

policy instruments represents a new dimension as it touches the respective countries' own external relations and their policies towards aliens. As a result, these countries are compelled to adopt restrictive approaches to immigration, to build up corresponding standards of policing and control and to set up an infrastructure for the adoption of refugees and asylum seekers.

Apart from adding these requirements to the conditions for future membership, these strategies are part of a broader context that links them to the question of international security. They are the expression of a new conception of a common foreign and security policy, based not so much on traditional military and ideological preoccupations as on the idea of "societal security" (Waever 1993) and the potential threats of immigration.[49] Defined as "the sustainability, within acceptable conditions for evolution, of traditional patterns of language, culture, association, and religious and national identity and custom" (Waever 1993, p. 23), this concept includes subjective threats represented by immigration, but also by the idea of a European citizenship that challenges the national identities (Waever, 1996). This context is already reflected in the motivation behind the cooperation among EU member states since the 1980s and the conceptualization of the issues of immigration and asylum as matters of "internal security" (see section 6.2). It can be interpreted as the compensation for an increasing willingness to integrate and abolish internal borders. With this integrationist impact, the question emerges of how far these policies towards potential immigrants not only help to create a sense of community inside but also establish a common focus for the EU's external orientations. However, it seems that, given the overall protectionist character of these processes, it is much more the member states than the Union as such that dictate the course of action. Nevertheless, by using such programmes as PHARE and TACIS for the pursuit of its own ideals of a comprehensive asylum policy (see section 6.4.2), the European Commission might be able to enhance its own profile in the relations with Central and Eastern Europe.

6.5.3. The international context: implications for the international refugee regime

Finally, at the international level, the implications of the emergent European cooperation system in refugee matters for the international refugee regime will now be discussed.

As mentioned in the introduction, the international cooperation for the protection of refugees was originally characterized by a clear separation of a general framework of principles, norms, rules and procedures at the international level, and specific traditions and legislative provisions at the national level. With the evolution of European cooperation in these matters, this clear distinction has been blurred by the adoption of a set of intergovernmental decisions that redefine the refugee question. The central characteristics of the new frame of refugee policy in Europe are its linkage with the question of internal security, its confusion with the problems of illegal immigration and abuse of asylum procedures and, finally, its conception in defensive,

---

[49] On the new conception of threats to European security, see also Clarke (1996).

reactive terms as a problem of policing and controlling rather than in human rights terms.[50]

While the Schengen and Dublin Agreements have been much criticized with regard to their restrictive entry measures – visas, required documents, carriers sanctions – and the downgrading of standards of legal protection for asylum seekers,[51] the incorporation of other European countries into this system of redistribution has had major detrimental effects on the international protection of refugees in general. In contrast to the Schengen and Dublin Conventions, the inclusion of Central and Eastern European countries through bilateral readmission agreements lacks the underlying requirement of some sort of common background in the handling of refugees and the common agreement to set up a system of responsibilities for the examination of asylum claims. Apart from the fact that many of the so-called safe third countries have not yet implemented a functioning system of legal and administrative refugee protection, these agreements do not take into account the special situation of asylum seekers in contrast to illegal immigrants. The responsibility of the receiving state to afford access to fair procedures for the determination of refugee status and the granting of asylum is not mentioned in these agreements (UNHCR 1994, 1996; Kumin 1994). The failure to provide some sort of legal protection for refugees in the application of the safe third country rule and the lengthening chain of readmission agreements hold the danger of producing "orbit" situations, i.e. situations in which refugees are sent from state to state trying to find one that is willing to examine their asylum claims.[52]

In summary, European cooperation has not responded to the global principles of international refugee protection based on the ideas of international solidarity and burden-sharing, but has established a system more of burden-shifting or negative redistribution that shifts the responsibility for the protection of refugees towards the refugee-producing countries of the east and the south. Coupled with the downgrading of legal guarantees in the domestic implementation laws and the general underestimation of the difficulties of other European states in taking in asylum seekers, these developments are likely to increase the risk of refoulement, and thereby to violate the core of the international refugee regime.[53]

---

[50] On "frames" in European refugee policy, see Lavenex (1997).

[51] See e.g. Pauly (1993), Meijers *et al.* (1991), Miles and Thränhardt (1995), and the respective statements and press releases by UNHCR and Amnesty International.

[52] A study conducted by a German humanitarian NGO in Poland in October 1996 on the implementation of readmission agreements reveals that out of 122 persons who were readmitted from Germany on the grounds of the safe third countries rule and who now were in detention waiting for expulsion in Polish prisons, only six had had the opportunity to submit a formal asylum request, although all 122 had expressed their claim for political asylum (press release of the Forschungsgesellschaft Flucht und Migration, 11 Nov. 1996, Bonn).

[53] Prominent examples of the downgrading of procedural guarantees include the legal fiction of "international zones" in airports and other borders, in which access to national jurisdiction is denied, the increasing discretionary power of unskilled border officials and airline personnel, and the cutting of opportunities for judicial review.

6.6. Conclusions: Immigration and Refugees. A new field of foreign policy?

Originally limited to the aim of realizing the single market project, cooperation among the EU member states in asylum matters has triggered the development of a regional refugee regime based on the perception of the refugee problem as a threat to internal security, and establishes a new system of negative redistribution for the handling of asylum claims. By diminishing the individual commitment of the single nation states to provide protection, this regional cooperation system weakens the international refugee regime. Apart from these legal and ideological considerations, however, these developments also have an important external political dimension as they transcend the Union's borders and lead to the progressive incorporation of other European states.

Having been linked to the strategy of pre-adhesion for future membership in the European Union, the questions of asylum and immigration have entered the field of foreign policy. As a priority of the Dutch Presidency in the first half of 1997, they now play an increasing role in the relations with Central and Eastern European countries under the third pillar. This not only has transforming effects on the concept of refugee policy in itself, but also modifies the traditional understaning of foreign policy and the priorities of the European Union in its external relations. Reaching far beyond the traditional requirements for EU membership concerning economic welfare and cilvil liberties, these processes not only affect the realm of internal security, border controls, police, asylum and immigration, but also influence the respective countries' own foreign policies towards their eastern neighbours and third state nationals. In general, the emergent European refugee regime establishes a "buffer zone" at the Union´s borders that minimizes its exposure to refugee inflows from the east and the south (Toth 1995).

While one might find signs of a deepening integration in this new field of common foreign policy, the analysis reveals a much more protectionist attitude on the part of the member states that can be interpreted as the expression of their anxiety to protect their national boundaries. The present developments can be seen as a sign neither of more integration nor of the evolution of an independent, supranational identity of the Union as foreign policy actor. Rather, this new field of foreign policy is a genuine example of the member states' concern to secure their national sovereignty and cultural identity in the sense of "societal security".

6.7. References

Achermann, A. and M. Gattiker (1995). "Safe Countries: European Developments". *International Journal of Refugee Law 7*, No. 1, 19–38.

Buzan, B. (1993). "Introduction: The Changing Security Agenda in Europe". In Waever, O. *et al.* (eds) *Identity, Migration, and the New Security Agenda in Europe*. London: Pinter; 1–14.

Carlsnaes, W. and S. Smith (eds) (1994). *European Foreign Policy. The EC and Changing Perspectives in Europe*. London: Sage.

Clarke, M. (1996). "Future Security Threats and Challenges". In Pappas, S. and S. Vanhoonacker (eds) *The*

European Union's Common Foreign and Security Policy. The Challenges of the Future. Maastricht: European Institute for Public Administration; 65–76.

Czaplinski, W. (1994). "Aliens and Refugee Law in Poland – Recent Developments". *International Journal of Refugee Law 6*, No. 4, 636–642.

De Jong, C. (1995). "Proactive Policies with Regard to Situations of Pass Influxes". In Perrakis, S. (ed.) *Immigration and European Union: Building on a Comprehensive Approach*. Athens: Sakkoulas; 139–143.

Dunstan, R. (1995). "Playing Human Pinball. The Amnesty International United Kingdom Section Report on UK Home Office 'Safe Third Country' Practice". *International Journal of Refugee Law 7*, No. 4, 606–652.

ECRE (European Consultations on Refugees and Exiles) (1993). "Promotion of Refugee Protection in Central and Eastern Europe, Report on Activities October 1992-June 1993". London.

ECRE (1994). "Asylum in Europe". London.

ECRE (1995). "Sichere Drittstaaten". *Mythen und Tatsachen*, London.

European Commission (1990). "The Development of the Community's Relations with the Countries of Central and Eastern Europe". Communication to the Council and the European Parliament, Brussels, 1 Feb.

European Commission (1992). "Europe and the Challenge of Enlargement". Report to the European Council, Lisbon, 24 June.

European Parliament (1995). Report on "Entwurf einer Empfehlung des Rates betreffend den Musterentwurf eines bilateralen Rücknahmeabkommens zwischen einem Mitgliedsstaat der Europäischen Union und einem Drittstaat" by Claudia Roth (C4-0006/95), A4-0184/95 of 20 July.

European Parliament (1996). "Documentation on Asylum and Migration in the CCEEs". Committee on Civil Liberties and Internal Affairs, PE 166.088 or EN (2), 6 June.

Fortescue, A. (1995). "Opening Statement". In: Perrakis, S. (ed.) *Immigration and European Union: Building on a Comprehensive Approach*. Athens: Sakkoulas; 7–9.

Hailbronner, K. (ed.) (1992). *Asyl- und Einwanderungsrecht im europäischen Vergleich*. Köln: Bundesanzeyer.

Hailbronner, K. (1993). "The Concept of 'Safe Country' and Expeditious Asylum Procedures – A Western European Perspective". *International Journal of Refugee Law 5*, No. 1, 31–65.

Handl, V., C. Konecny and J. Poesch (1996). "Tschechische Republik". In Weidenfeld, W. (ed.) *Mittel- und Osteuropa auf dem Weg in die Europäische Union. Bericht zum Stand der Integrationsfähigkeit*. Gütersloh: Bertelsmann Stiftung; 242.

Hottmeister, F. (1996). "Grundzüge des bulgarischen Asyl- und Flüchtlingsrechts". *Zeitschrift für Ausländerrecht und Ausländerpolitik 16*, No. 3, 135–139.

Hoskova, M. (1996). "Das neue slowakische Asylrecht". *Zeitschrift für Ausländerrecht und Ausländerpolitik 16*, No. 3, 129–134.

Initiative gegen das Schengener Abkommen (ed.) (1993). "Materialien zum Export der Politik der Inneren Sicherheit und der Flüchtlingsabwehr nach Osteuropa". Bonn

Inotai, A. and J. Nötzhold (1996). "Ungarn". In Weidenfeld, W. (ed.) *Mittel- und Osteuropa auf dem Weg in die Europäische Union. Bericht zum Stand der Integrationsfähigkeit*. Gütersloh: Bertelsmann Stiftung; 236f.

King, M. (1993). "The Impact of Western European Border Policies on the Control of 'Refugees' in Eastern and Central Europe". *New Community 19*, No. 2, 183–199.

Kjaergaard, E. (1994). "The Concept of 'Safe Third Country' in Contemporary European Refugee Law". *International Journal of Refugee Law 6*, No. 4, 649–655.

Krasner, S.D. (ed.) (1983). *International Regimes*. Ithaca and London: Cornell University Press; 3.

Kumin, J. (1994). "Praxis der Drittstaatenregelung und Asyl in Europa". Paper presented at the Bundesfachtagung of the Diakonisches Werk, 8 June.

Lavenex, S. 1997: "'Hidden' Governance in Europe: The Impact of Intergovernmental Negotiations on the Transformation of Asylum Policies in France and Germany". Occasional Paper of the Human Capital and Mobility Network, No. 29, Colchester.

Meijers *et al.* (eds) (1991). *Schengen. Internationalization of Central Chapters of the Law of Aliens, Refugees, Privacy, Security and the Police*. Utrecht: Kluwer.

Miles, R. and D. Thränhardt (eds) (1995). *Migration and European Integration: the Dynamics of Inclusion and Exclusion.* London: Pinter.

Pauly, A. (ed.) (1993). *Les accords de Schengen: Abolition des Frontières Intérieures ou Menace pour les Libertés Publiques?* Maastricht: European Institute for Public Administration.

Polish Committee for European Integration (1997). "National Strategy for Integration". *Monitor of European Integration,* special edition, Jan.

Toth, J. (1995). "Humanitarian Security and Involutary Migration in Europe". In Dunay, P. *et al.* (eds) *New forms of Security. Views from Central, Eastern and Western Europe.* Aldershot: Darmouth; 150–165.

Schieffer, M. (1996). "The Readmission of Third Country Nationals within Bilateral and Multilateral Frameworks". Paper presented at 4th colloquium, "Schengen and the Third Pillar of Maastricht" at the European Institute of Public Administration, Maastricht, 1–2 Feb.

UNHCR (1994) "Readmission Agreements, 'Protection Elsewhere' and Asylum Policy". Brussels, August.

UNHCR (1996) "Considerations on the 'Safe Third Country' Concept". Paper presented at the EU Seminar on the Associated States as Safe Third Countries in Asylum Legislation, Vienna, 8–11 July.

Waever, O. *et al.* (eds) (1993). *Identity, Migration, and the New Security Agenda in Europe.* London: Pinter.

Waever, O. (1993). "Societal Security: The Concept". In Waever, O. *et al.* (eds) *Identity, Migration, and the New Security Agenda in Europe.* London: Pinter; 17–40.

Waever, O. (1996). "European Security Identities". *Journal of Common Market Studies 42,* No. 1, 103–132.

Weber, S. (1995). "European Union Conditionality". In Eichengreen, B. *et al.* (eds) *Politics and Institutions in an Integrated Europe.* Berlin: Springer; 193–220.

CHAPTER 7

The European Union and the war in the former Yugoslavia: the failure of collective diplomacy

Alan Cafruny

7.1. INTRODUCTION

The break-up of Yugoslavia from 1991 to 1995 precipitated the bloodiest armed conflict in Europe since 1945. More than 145,000 people, the great majority civilian, died in the conflict while 2.5 million were driven from their homes as a result of "ethnic cleansing" carried out primarily by Bosnian Serb and Croat forces. By February 1997, 630,000 Bosnians were registered as refugees in the member states of the European Union (EU), half of them in Germany.[1] The war also led to the first NATO combat engagement in the history of the Alliance; the deployment of armed forces under the banner of the Western European Union (WEU); the participation of German combat forces (fighter pilots) as a result of constitutional changes allowing German participation outside NATO; the first United Nations (UN) peacekeeping intervention in Europe; and the establishment of an International War Crimes Tribunal under the auspices of the United Nations Security Council.

The EU's policies had a great impact on the war and the subsequent "cold peace" resulting from the Dayton Peace Accords of November 1995. Conversely, the project of European Union was also greatly influenced by the war. The Treaty of Maastricht was signed in December 1991 as the Serbian-dominated Yugoslav National Army (JNA) laid seige to Vukovar and Dubrovnik, and four months after the EC had brokered a ceasefire between the JNA and Slovenia. The Maastricht Treaty called for the establishment of a common foreign and security policy (CFSP), committing EU members to "an ever closer union". The war thus presented the EU with the opportunity to establish a precedent for the peaceful resolution of ethnic and territorial claims in an era of state dissolution as well as to strengthen the communitarian dimension of foreign policy. Yet, as the International Commission on the Balkans, a distinguished group sponsored by the Carnegie Endowment, recently concluded (Carnegie Endowment for International Peace 1996, p. 56):

---

[1] "EU Torn Over Sending Home War Refugees," *European Voice*, 16–22 Jan. 1997, p. 7. Data on casualties are from Carnegie Endowment for International Peace (1996), pp. 6–7. The Bosnian Government provides an estimate of 300,000 killed.

A. Cafruny and P. Peters (eds.), The Union and the World, 133–150

Looking back five years later, it can be argued that few things have done more to dampen public enthusiasm for the cause of European integration than the inadequacy of European attempts at peacemaking in former Yugoslavia.

Section 7.2 of this chapter describes the progressive engagement of the member states of the EU in Yugoslavia, from 1990, when the intra-republican conflicts began to intensify, until the spring of 1997. It details the political and diplomatic strategies which EU negotiators adopted independently and in conjunction with other institutions and actors, including the Organization of Security and Cooperation in Europe (OSCE), the UN, the United States, and Russia, to resolve conflicts in Slovenia and Croatia, and to prevent war in Bosnia. Section 7.3 analyses the EU's response to the war in Bosnia which began in April 1992. Unwilling to distinguish between aggressor and victim or to sever relations with Serbia, the EU adopted a position of neutrality. The resulting political paralysis gradually led the EU to define its commitments towards former Yugoslavia in humanitarian terms. Section 7.4 discusses the relationship between national interests and rivalries in Europe, and the difficulties in forging a common policy towards Bosnia. The member states established several novel common institutions and policies in response to the war. At the same time, however, the war clearly demonstrated that the CFSP will continue to be shaped by the interests and objectives of the most powerful states, and that the ability of these states to project their power, either collectively or individually, will depend on support from the United States. In Section 7.5, some lessons are drawn from the EU's failure in former Yugoslavia, and the implications of the war for the future of the Union are assessed. If the limits to a communitarian policy reflected institutional and logistical problems, they were also a function of moral and intellectual failure: the EU's decision to view its international obligations in essentially humanitarian terms was in fact a thinly disguised exercise in *realpolitik*.

7.2. THE EU CONFRONTS A CRISIS

Yugoslavia occupied an idiosyncratic position within the Cold War bipolar system. Josip Tito's decision to pull Yugoslavia, the only communist country not liberated by the Red Army, out of the Warsaw Pact enabled Yugoslavia to receive favourable treatment from the West in the form of substantial foreign aid and loans, membership of the Bretton Woods organizations, and association agreements with the EEC and EFTA. Yugoslav citizens enjoyed freedom of movement and many became "guest workers" in Western Europe, especially in Germany.

Thus one of the legacies of Yugoslavia's special position was engagement in the post-War global economic boom on relatively favourable terms. As Yugoslavia's economy became increasingly dependent on the West, it adopted extensive measures of liberalization. But the decentralization of economic decision-making tended to reinforce the trend towards ethnic nationalism as power was increasingly devolved to individual republics. The global economic recession of the 1980s served to intensify the political and economic contradictions of market socialism. Confronted with an international debt exceeding $20 billion, a contraction of export markets in Western Europe, and the return of "guest workers", individual republics pursued their own methods of dealing with the resulting economic and political turmoil.[2] Serbia's political leadership opted for nationalism and the reassertion of Serbian hegemony over the rest of Yugoslavia (see, *inter alia*, Silber and Little (1996) and Pesic (1996)). In reponse, Slovenia and Croatia put forward proposals for a looser federation.

The victory of President Anton Marcovic in the 1990 federal elections offered Yugoslavs a final chance to preserve the federation. But Marcovic's strategy of rapid liberalization and privatization in the context of mass unemployment and hyperinflation lacked popular support. Shock therapy was unable to compete with the project of Greater Serbia amid similar, if less virulent, strains of ethnic nationalism that were breaking out in all consitutuent republics.

Thus the precipitating cause of the break-up of Yugoslavia was Serbia's decision to revise its relationship with other republics. As early as 1987, Serbian Communist Party chief Slobodan Milosevic had concluded that the way to maintain his power base within the collapsing socialist system was by redefining himself and the Yugoslav Communist Party in terms of Serbian nationalism. The drive to realize a project of Serbian hegemony included the enactment of martial law in Kosovo, Serbianization of the JNA, violation of the federal constitution including refusal to accept a Croatian President, and the looting of the federal budget. In July 1990, the parliaments of the Slovenian and Croatian republics responded by declaring their sovereignty and right to secession, and their governments suspended federal laws in February 1991.

As relations among the republics deteriorated in the first half of 1991, both the EU and the United States proclaimed their support for federal Yugoslavia in accordance with the Helsinki Principles of the CSCE. Both were preoccupied by events in the USSR, and believed that encouraging secessionist tendencies in Yugoslavia would have a spill-over effect there and, perhaps, elsewhere in Europe. The United States was, in addition, heavily engaged in the Persian Gulf, while the EU was entering the last stages of extremely delicate Maastricht Treaty negotiations in which the terms of monetary union were at stake. Consequently, neither the EU nor the United States took preventive measures or seriously considered Slovenian and Croatian proposals for transforming what was essentially a one party state into a democratic confederation. President of the Commission Jacques Delors and Luxembourg Prime Minister Jacques Poos travelled to Belgrade in May 1991, offering an association agreement and $4 billion in aid for the preservation of federal Yugoslavia, declaring that the Community would provide no political or economic support to breakaway republics.[3] US Secretary of State James Baker's meeting with Slobodan Milosevic in Belgrade in June left Serbian generals with the impression "that the United States had no intention of stopping them by force. It might isolate them and make them pariahs, but that, they concluded, was an acceptable risk" (Zimmerman 1996, p. 137).

On 25 June war broke out when, responding to Slovenia's declaration of independ-

---

[2] On the relationship between economic crisis and political disintegration see Woodward (1995) and Ramet (1996).
[3] On the role of the EU see Weller (1992), Hoffmann (1996), Gow (1997), Edwards (1997).

ence and occupation of border posts, Serbian units of the former Yugoslav defense forces (JNA) attacked the provisional Slovenian militia, triggering the involvement of the CSCE and the EU. The crisis offered the EU a means of restoring its rank after having played a subordinate role to the United States during the Persian Gulf War (Wood 1993). At the same time, the United States, unwilling to undertake strong commitments in a region no longer considered a vital sphere of influence, acquiesced to Jacques Poos' bold assertion that "This is the hour of Europe. It is not the hour of the Americans."

Within days of the outbreak of fighting, the EPC Secretariat[4] sent missions to Yugoslavia in response to the invitation of the federal government to join its negotiations with Croatia and Slovenia. Under the terms of the Brioni Declaration of 8 July, the JNA was withdrawn from Slovenia and the Slovenian militia was disarmed; Croatia and Slovenia declared a three-month moratorium on independence, and EC monitors were sent in to monitor compliance. On 25 September a general arms embargo was imposed on all republics, including Bosnia, through the UN Security Council.

The EC's mediation ended the fighting between the JNA and the Slovenian militia, and effectively severed Slovenia from the rest of Yugoslavia; an outcome that was not unwelcome to Milosevic, whose project was based on a concept of "Greater Serbia" and not on a return to the *status quo ante* (Zimmerman 1996, pp. 145–146; Woodward 1995, pp. 168–169). The ceasefire also served to free up JNA troops for the attack on Croatia, where local Serb militias, closely supported by Belgrade, had proclaimed a "Republic of Serbian Krajina". The EC asserted a principle of the inviolability of internal borders, stating a determination "never to recognize changes of frontiers which have not been brought about by peaceful means" (Weller 1992, p. 553). On 1 September the negotiation of a ceasefire agreement allowed EC monitors – five of whom would subsequently be shot down by Serbian forces – to be sent into Croatia, but the ceasefire did not hold. As a result, Yugoslavia, Austria, France and other countries requested the involvement of the UN Security Council. After the Serb destruction of Vukovar and conquest of Eastern and Western Slavonia, on 11 February 1992 UN Special Envoy Cyrus Vance eventually negotiated a ceasefire and the stationing of UN peacekeeping forces in Krajina.

In September 1991 the EC convened a Peace Conference on Yugoslavia's future, and established an Arbitration Commission, chaired by Robert Badinter, to make recommendations on the recognition of sovereignty of the various republics. The EC's envoy to the peace conference, Lord Peter Carrington, sought to secure agreement on a loose confederation of all the republics along with the protection of minorities and the principle of the inviolability of borders. The Badinter Commission was charged with making recommendations on recognition of the sovereignty of the republics. However, before the Commission could render an opinion, Germany declared its intention on the eve of the Maastricht IGC ceremonies unilaterally to recognize

---

[4] European Political Cooperation (EPC) was established in the early 1970s in order to develop a machinery for the coordination of external policy. Consisting of a Secretariat and permanent representatives, and chaired by the country occupying the Council Presidency, its role was expanded under the SEA until superseded by the machinery of CFSP under the terms of the Treaty of Maastricht.

Slovenia and Croatia. Anxious to obtain concessions from Germany in the Maastricht Treaty and reluctant to break ranks, Britain and France eventually acceded to this diplomatic *fait accompli* before the recommendations of the Badinter Commission were issued. The Commission eventually reported that recognition should be granted only to those republics which respected minority rights and where self-determination represented popular will. It declared that Slovenia and Macedonia had met the conditions, but expressed reservations about Croatia's treatment of Serbs living in Krajina. Thus the EC recognized Croatian independence despite the fact that Croatia did not establish a "special status" for minorities.[5] A ceasefire was eventually brokered as a result of UN intervention by Special Envoy Cyrus Vance. Under the terms of the Vance Plan, UN Protected Areas were established in Serb-controlled parts of Croatia and a UN Protection Force (UNPROFOR) of 10,000 was introduced.

5.3. WAR IN BOSNIA

Croatian independence placed Bosnia in an untenable position. By the spring of 1992 the JNA had withdrawn its heavy weapons to Serbia, and Bosnian Serb paramilitary forces were mobilizing in conjunction with the JNA. At the same time, Croatian forces were also planning a programme of expansion and ethnic cleansing in Herzegovina. Croatian President Franzo Tudjman met with Serbian President Slobodan Milosevic in September 1991 in what was widely considered to be a plan to divide territorially Bosnia-Herzegovina between Croatia and Serbia (Woodward 1995, p. 172; Ramet 1996, p. 50).

Bosnian president Alija Izetbegovic had publicly warned that Croatian independence posed a grave danger to Bosnia, whose survival had always depended on a federal Yugoslavia in which Croatia served as a counterweight to Serbia. In September 1991, four Serb autonomous regions were proclaimed in Bosnia; 5,000 JNA troops were dispatched to these regions along with a steady infusion of arms, including tanks and heavy artillery. Izetbegovic had asked the USA and EU not to recognize the secessionist republics until a comprehensive settlement including Bosnia could be reached, and (naively) allowed the JNA to remain on Bosnian territory in order to prevent conflict (Zimmerman 1996, p. 191). However, once the EU's intent to recognize Croatia was clear, Bosnia also petitioned the international community for recognition on 22 December, and appealed unsuccessfully for a UN peacekeeping force along Bosnia's borders. On 9 January 1992, a "Serbian Republic of Bosnia-Herzegovina" was proclaimed.

The Arbitration Commission stated that in order to achieve international recognition Bosnia must demonstrate that self-determination reflected the will of the majority and provide guarantees of minority rights. Accordingly, Bosnia held a referendum on 1 March 1992. Sixty-three per cent voted in favour, but the Serbs, representing 32 per

---

[5] Greece maintained that "Macedonia" refers exclusively to its own northern province. Accordingly, at Greece's insistence, the EU withheld recognition until the provisional name of "Former Yugoslav Republic of Macedonia" was adopted. 500 American troops were sent to this republic in 1991.

cent of the population as against 44 per cent Muslim and 17 per cent Croat, boycotted it. The EU then proceeded to recognize Bosnia on 6 April. In the meantime, however, both Croatian and Bosnian Serbs had begun to prepare for large-scale war. In February 1992 Lord Carrington requested that the Portuguese presidency convene a conference on Bosnia's future. On 18 March in Lisbon representatives of all three groups agreed in principle that Bosnia would become a single state but composed of three "constituent units", or ethnically-based cantons, having a veto over national policy. However, after returning to Sarajevo and consulting with members of the government and SDA, Bosnian president Izetbegovic rejected the agreement.

Although Izetbegovic's rejection of the Lisbon agreement has often been cited as a reason for the war, in fact the ethnic cantons envisioned by the Lisbon agreement amounted to a plan for partition. Given Bosnia's "patchwork quilt" of ethnicity, any such plan inevitably would provoke ethnic cleansing.[6] Moreover, given the subsequent record of the Bosnian Serb leadership, it is highly unlikely that it would have accepted the Lisbon plan. In any case, by the time Bosnia achieved international recognition, Bosnian Serb irregular troops had already begun mobilizing throughout the country under the control of Radovan Karadzic, the self-proclaimed president of the "Serb Republic of Bosnia Herzegovina", and Ratko Mladic, commander of Bosnian Serb forces. As war erupted throughout Bosnia, UNPROFOR's mandate was extended to Bosnia.

By the summer of 1992, Bosnian Serb units, closely supervised and supported by Belgrade, had overrun 70 per cent of Bosnian territory, laid siege to most major Bosnian cities, including Sarajevo, and carried out a savage campaign of ethnic cleansing and extermination. In the autumn of 1992 Bosnian Croats, similarly, embarked on their own project of territorial conquest and ethnic cleansing, leaving the Bosnian government in control of less than 20 per cent of its territory.

In August 1992 a special conference was convened in London, and a negotiating team chaired by Carrington (later David Owen and Carl Bildt) representing the EU and Cyrus Vance (later Thorsten Stoltenberg) representing the UN was established in Geneva. The London Conference identified Serbia as the aggressor, and called for UN peacekeepers to guarantee the territorial integrity of Bosnia. However, at the Geneva Peace Conference Vance and Owen repudiated the conclusions of the London Conference, introducing instead the concept of "three warring factions" and thereby granting Bosnian Serb and Croat insurgent forces the same status as that of the Bosnian government. In October 1992, 8,000 UN troops were sent to Bosnia in order to facilitate food shipments to major cities under Serbian assault, including Sarajevo. Britain and France provided large contingents to UNPROFOR, which eventually

---

[6] The phrase "patchwork quilt" is used by Ramet (1996). For a general critique of partition as a solution to ethnic conflicts see Kumar (1997). The most comprehensive study of ethnicity in Bosnia is that of Golubic *et al.* (1993). The authors conclude: Our demographic analysis of Bosnia-Herzegovina demonstrates that ethnic dominance is clearly not an acceptable criterion for any division or subdivision of the country.... We fear that [the Vance–Owen] artificially derived set of provinces, whose sole justification appears to be military disengagement, will actually magnify the difficulty in realizing Owen and Vance's own stated long term goals. The primary deficiency of the current Owen–Vance peace proposal is the attempt to appease the radical perpetrators of the war."

expanded to some 22,000 troops, but these forces were constrained by rules of engagement which limited the use of force to the protection of the humanitarian aid mission.

As the war continued, and the scope of atrocities and ethnic cleansing carried out became known, American and EU views began to diverge. By the end of 1992 the United States had identified the Bosnian Serbs as aggressors, and called for more robust action, including arming Bosnia and the use of air support. The EU, reflecting the views of Britain and France, rejected the use of force unless the United States was willing to provide its own troops. Through the European Community Humanitarian Organization (ECHO), the EU provided substantial amounts of humanitarian assistance. In order to secure access to the civilian population, the EU sought to maintain a position of neutrality, arguing that taking sides would endanger UNPROFOR troops and, eventually, threatening to pull out troops if the United States sought to provide arms to Bosnia.

In June 1993 the United States introduced a resolution to the UN Security Council to end the arms embargo on Bosnia. Britain and France (along with Russia) abstained, and the resolution did not pass; further initiatives were stifled by the threat of French and British vetoes. But the arms embargo had a devastating impact on the ability of the Bosnian government to defend itself. Prior to the war, the JNA had secured virtually complete control over heavy weapons in Bosnia, and continued to maintain supply lines to Bosnian Serb forces. Table 7.1 indicates the extent to which the enforcement of an arms embargo against all parties benefited the Serbs (and later Croats). At the outbreak of war Bosnian military forces had two tanks; Bosnian Serbs had 300 and consistently maintained close logistical ties to the JNA (International Institute for Strategic Studies 1993, *The Independent* 2 May 1995, p. 11).

Table 7.1. The balance of military forces in former Yugoslavia, May 1995

	Troops	Tanks	Artillery	Aircraft*
Croatian Government	99,600	173	900	35
Bosnian Croat army	50,000	75	200	6
Bosnian Serb army	80,000	330	800	32
Serbia/Mont. Government	90,000	630	1,500	399
"Republic of Serb Krajina" army	40,000	240	500	17
Bosnian Government	90,000	40	n.a.	–

*Planes and helicopters.
Source: *The Independent*, 2 May 1995, p. 11.

The unwillingness of EU and UN negotiators to identify the Serbs as aggressors led them to adopt a position of neutrality with respect to the Bosnian Serbs and the Bosnian government. Assuming that the conflict was rooted in irreconcilable ethnic and religious differences, and that the partition of Bosnia was inevitable, they repeatedly advanced plans for ethnically-based provinces linked in a loose federation, and maps were revised to take account of Serb territorial conquests, thereby encouraging ethnic cleansing. The willingness to re-draw maps to take account of Serbian territorial conquests encouraged the Croats to seek an accomodatation with the Bosnian

Serbs, resulting in an anti-Muslim front in June 1993 which included military cooperation, a meeting between Tudjman and Milosevic on 16 June, and a Serb–Croat
plan for partition of Bosnia, which became the basis of the Owen–Stoltenberg Plan of
20 August (Ramet 1996, p. 251).[7] This plan would have granted 52% of Bosnia to the
Serbs, 30% to the Bosnian government, and 18% to the Croats. The plan was opposed
by the United States, and ultimately rejected by the Bosnian government.

5.3.1. The entry of the US and the formation of the "Contact Group"

By the beginning of 1994 it was clear that the EU was unable or unwilling to do more
than contain the war within the borders of former Yugoslavia and provide aid to the
victims on terms acceptable to the Serbs. A negotiating strategy based on ethnic
partition but lacking enforcement could not bring the war to a halt and, indeed, tended
to encourage ethnic cleansing. The humanitarian effort had become a means of
"managing" the war. Humanitarian aid workers were compelled to facilitate ethnic
cleansing while lightly-armed UNPROFOR troops were forced to witness massive
human rights violations and war crimes, and even to become hostages of the Serbian
forces.[8]

The failure of the strategy of ethnic partition led to the marginalization of the EU in
favour of the more active involvement of the UN. Initially this took the form of the
protection of "safe areas", based on a UN initiative which both the United States and
the EC initially opposed. In April 1993, the UN Security Council had declared
Srebrenica, which had been under heavy artillery fire, as a UN-protected safe area,
and subsequently decreed that Sarajevo, Tuzla, Zepa, Bihac, and Gorazde should also
be treated as safe areas free from armed attack. At the same time, Bosnian soldiers
within these areas would be required to surrender their heavy weapons, although this
was never strictly enforced. The concept of safe areas illustrated the central contradiction in Western policy: the use of threats/negotiations in the absence of the credible
use of force. In the end, the safe areas became increasingly overcrowded as a result of
Serbian ethnic cleansing, short of food and medical resources, and under indiscriminate shelling. They were also not protected with credible forces. When the Serbs
carried out their "final solution" in Srebrenica in July 1995, expelling 23,000 Bosnian
Muslim women and children and killing thousands of men, Dutch forces which
numbered 429 immediately capitulated (Honig and Both 1996, Human Rights
Watch/Helsinki 1995).

The conjunction of several factors in early 1994 marked a new phase in the war,
culminating in the establishment of a "Contact Group" comprising the US, Russia,
Britain, France, and Germany. The Serbian bombing of a marketplace in Sarajevo in

---

[7] In September 1993 the European Parliament strongly condemned the Owen–Vance strategy of ethnic
partition, noting that it "constitutes an extremely dangerous precedent" which condones "the destruction of
a multi-ethnic society in Bosnia-Herzegovina and legitimizes the violent aggression that has taken place
there". "Resolution on the Situation in Bosnia-Herzegovina", *Official Journal of the European Communities* C 268/160, 4 Oct. 1993.

[8] Rieff (1995) provides a compelling first-hand account of the politicization of humanitarian aid.

February 1994 vividly illustrated the defects of the "safe area" strategy and generated increased international pressure for the use of air power against Serb forces, especially in the United States. At the same time, the new government of Eduard Balladur and Jacques Chirac in France accepted the need for stronger use of force and, hence, American participation. They recognized that the alternative might be America's unilateral lifting of the arms embargo coupled with the substitution of Islamic peacekeepers in the event that the British and French should withdraw their forces. The formation of the Contact Group thus signified the advent of a more traditional diplomacy in which EU actions were clearly dependent on American military power. The centerpiece of this diplomacy was the establishment of US-brokered federation between Croatia and Bosnia. The federation permitted more light arms to flow to the Bosnian military forces, and thus helped to change the balance of power on the ground. President Clinton declared a "no fly" zone around Sarajevo, demanding that the Serbs withdraw their heavy weapons, and presented the Serbs with a "take it or leave it" plan which would effectively give them 49 per cent of Bosnian territory. Karadjic's rejection of this plan, coupled with continuing attacks on safe areas, led to the incremental use of air power under NATO's southern command, against Serb targets.

The efforts of the Contact Group to forge a Muslim–Croat alliance gradually produced a new military situation and, by the summer of 1995, the situation on the ground was transformed. With the fall of Srebrenica, Zepa, and Gorazde, the Serbs realized longstanding war aims. The Croatian offensive in the Krajina, which led to the expulsion of 200,000 ethnic Serbs from their homes, represented the denoucment of the Serbo-Croat war of 1991. At the same time, the Bosnian Army showed that even without heavy weapons it could defend existing government territory and, with help from Croatia, reconquer territory in northwestern Bosnia. Finally, President Jacques Chirac reacted strongly to the Serb seizure of UN soldiers in July 1995 in response to NATO air action against the Serbs, leading to a NATO-led operation, "Deliberate Force", which damaged the Bosnian Serb military infrastructure and helped Bosnian and Croatian forces. The changed military situation, coupled with the effects of the embargo on Serbia, gave Milosevic stronger incentives to pressure Karadzic and Mladic, now both indicted war criminals, to negotiate a settlement.

In Dayton in November 1995, the United States, under the leadership of Richard Holbrook, brokered a peace accord which was signed by Izetbegovic of Bosnia, Tudjman of Croatia, and Milosevic of Serbia on behalf of the "Republika Srpska", the self-proclaimed Bosnian Serb state. The Dayton accords upheld the principle of a unitary, multi-ethnic Bosnia, and committed all parties to participation in the new federation, including upholding of the rights of ethnic minorities, democratic elections at the state and local level, and prosecution of war criminals. The accords were guaranteed by the presence of some 50,000 NATO troops, including 15,000 US troops, and OSCE monitors. In practice, however, NATO has been unwilling to enforce the terms of the agreement. Bosnia has moved progressively closer to a *de facto* partition, and, tragically, little more than might have been obtained by Izetbegovic at Lisbon in March 1992. The role of the EU has been limited to seeking to maintain civil order in Mostar, a city divided among Bosnian and Croat militias, the provision of aid, and administering the international presence, under the auspices of former Swedish Prime Minister, Carl Bildt. Strong British and French contingents remain in Bosnia, but these are considered to be national deployments under NATO command (Human Rights Watch/Helsinki 1996).

7.4. NATIONAL INTERESTS AND THE CFSP

At the outset of the Yugoslav crisis, there was a strong commitment to unity among the member states caught up in the general euphoria of Maastricht, coupled with an insistence that Europe should play the leading role in the war. The history of EU engagement shows that Europe's attempt to pursue a communitarian policy, largely independent of the United States, gradually gave way to the re-nationalization of policy. The formation of the Contact Group in early 1994, however, signified the eclipse of the communitarian approach in favour of the strongest member states, which had themselves surrendered the initiative to the United States.

Yet, the impulse towards a communitarian policy was always very weak. Even at the outset, the CFSP expressed and reinforced national rivalries, as vividly illustrated by the internal power struggle over German recognition of Croatia. Moreover, although American involvement was crucial to the Dayton Agreements, European power and interests remained very important. The shape of those agreements clearly reflected a European agenda. America's entry into the war did not represent a substantive change in the nature of international intervention, but rather was used to promote a settlement on essentially European terms.

7.4.1. German recognition

Germany's decisive role in the EC's decision to recognize Slovenia and Croatia in January 1992 has generated a storm of controversy.[9] Although Germany initially followed the US and EC consensus on the inviolability of the federation, as the war progressed in Slovenia and, especially, Croatia, there was a great deal of support in Germany for recognition of these republics. This support derived from several domestic sources, including the presence of Croatian *émigrés*, the recent experience of reunification, strong support from Bavarian Catholics as the Serb assault on Croatia intensified, and, perhaps, Chancellor Kohl's desire to play a stronger international role in the wake of reunification (Crawford 1993). Prior to the Maastricht Conference, Chancellor Kohl declared Germany's willingness to recognize the republics unilaterally, thereby placing great pressure on other EC members, and especially Britain and France.

French and British interests were formulated within a framework which included an strong fear of Germany in the immediate aftermath of reunification, the desire to

---

[9] Critics of German policy include Glenny (1991, 1993). See also, *inter alia*, Woodward (1995), Moore (1992), Grieger (1994), Wood (1993) and Ash (1993).

maintain longstanding strategic and economic ties with Serbia, and a more cynical assumption that the remains of former Yugoslavia would inevitably be divided between Croatia and Serbia. In the case of France, additionally, there was strong support for the principle of human rights, although this co-existed uneasily with France's more "realistic" calculations of self-interest.[10] Ultimately France and Britain endorsed Germany's position on recognition, in part to maintain the appearance of EC unity but also because each wanted something at Maastricht: Britain desired the opt-out from EMU, while France was pushing hard to secure a deal on EMU by 1999.

Criticism of Germany reveals less about the realities of an imploding Yugoslavia than it does about fears of German revanchism in the immediate aftermath of the fall of the Berlin Wall. The harshest criticism of Germany emanated from Britain and France. French Foreign Minister Roland Dumas claimed that Germany bore a "crushing responsibility in the speeding up of the crisis" (Lepick 1996, p. 79). Critics argued that recognition was premature for two reasons: first, it ignored the reservations issued in the Badinter Report concerning Croatia's human rights record with respect to the Serbian minority of the Krajina and thereby failed to prevent Serbo-Croat conflict; second, it served to provoke both the Bosnian Serbs and the JNA, thereby making war in Bosnia inevitable. As Misha Glenny wrote in December 1991:

> Once Croatia and Slovenia are recognised, the Muslims and Croats of Bosnia, the Albanians in Kosova and the Albanians and Macedonians is Macedonia will suddenly be part of a state dominated by Belgrade and the Army. All these groups (with the possible exception of the unarmed Albanians in Kosova) will demand the severing of links with Yugoslavia and the recognition of Bosnia and Macedonia as independent states. Using the Serbian population in both states as its agent, the JNA will take the war to these republics. Recognition...will definitely mean war in Bosnia and probably in Macedonia unless a substantial UN peacekeeping force is put into place before it happens Glenny 1991, p. 15).

This general line was echoed by Serbian propaganda, which depicted German intervention in terms of the "fourth Reich" and a repeat of Nazi support for the Ustashe regime during World War II, and evidence of Germany's historical economic "sphere of influence" in the Catholic Balkans. Conscious of their declining role in Europe, both French and British leaders (especially with the victory of pro-EC forces over Margaret Thatcher) strongly attacked Germany, even as they acquiesced to the German position and appeared to be moving in the same direction. Hence German "bullying" for recognition came to be seen as a cause of the subsequent war in Bosnia, and also alarming evidence of a German revanchist foreign policy, in relation not only to Britain and France but also to the United States, which had also counselled against early recognition.[11]

Although domestic politics played a role in Germany's decision to recognize Croatia, recognition also resulted from the belief of the German foreign ministry that Yugoslavia had already collapsed, not as a result of secessionist movements, but

---

[10] On French policy see especially Lepick (1996) and Wood (1994). On British policy see Gow (1996).

[11] See the particularly trenchant account of British Foreign Office indignation in Almond (1994).

rather as a result of Serbian legal and military provocations, including the brutal assault on Vukovar. As indeed all the EC foreign ministers had in fact acknowledged, once Serbia staged what amounted to a *coup d'état* on 1 October, when it excluded all republics but Serbia and Montenegro from the presidency, it was clear that the Yugoslavian constitution had been abandoned. By this time the German Foreign Ministry had concluded that "the JNA was not only unable to prevent interethnic conflict but that as part of the Serbian war of conquest and expulsion, it even abetted these clashes initially, then intervened, and finally took the lead in them" (German Foreign Ministry 1993, p. 2). Non-recognition, moreover, "had an increasingly adverse effect on the efforts to bring about peace; it only reinforced the Serbian leadership's expectation that the international community would accept a Greater Serbian policy of force under a Yugoslav guise" (ibid., p. 3). Recognition, on the other hand, allowed the conflict to become internationalized, thereby making possible the entry of UN peacekeepers and EC ceasefire-monitors. While the EC did finally elicit some guarantees from the Croatian President Tudjman concerning treatment of ethnic Serbs, this fell short of the guarantees asked for by the Badinter Commission. Yet prolonging the Badinter process would only have encouraged further Serbian aggression, while, regardless of human rights guarantees, the ethnic Serbs of the Krajina and Eastern Slavonia, highly mobilized by Serbian paramilitary groups, were unlikely to settle for anything less than "anschluss" with Serbia.

In retrospect, recognition probably did encourage the JNA to agree to a ceasefire in Croatia, as arranged by Special Envoy Cyrus Vance in January 1992. This ceasefire, of course, was by no means permanent because it did not resolve the question of Serbian minorities in Croatia; Serb militias were not disarmed and minority rights of Serbs were not guaranteed. Germany's subsequent policy in former Yugoslavia does not, however, support the contention of German revanchism. If anything, chastened by the criticism of Genscher's policy, Germany by the beginning of 1992 retreated to a position of passivity alongside France and Britain. The problem with German policy was not the recognition of Croatia, but that it applied the principle of non-aggression selectively; if the threat of recognition itself was not sufficient to deter Serbian attacks in Croatia, it was demonstrably insufficient in the case of Bosnia. The principles which Germany championed in the case of Croatia and Slovenia – self-determination against the project of Greater Serbia – were not applied to Bosnia-Herzegovina, whose recognition was not accompanied by military or political guarantees. Germany's brief period of activism may have served as a pretext and justification for Serbia's attack on Bosnia, but did not in itself provoke it. In contrast to the British and French desire to maintain ties to Serbia at all costs, German policy did initially seek to distinguish between aggressor and victim. Once Germany joined the Franco-British consensus on neutrality, it was no longer possible for the EU to identify Serbia as the aggressor. Tragically, the strategy of ethnic partition as envisioned in the various Vance–Owen and Owen–Stoltenburg plans would be pursued in Bosnia, with devastating results. EU unity, and later transtlantic unity, was obtained at the price of the dismemberment of Bosnia.

7.4.2. US–European Relations and the War in Bosnia

US–EU relations played a central role in all phases of the war. As noted above, the United States offered strong support for federal Yugoslavia, even after war with Croatia broke out, and then encouraged the EU to take the lead. As late as December 1991 the United States opposed recognition, eventually following suit only after the EU's formal recognition on 15 January 1992. Once the principle of self-determination was established, however, the United States moved ahead of the EU in encouraging Bosnian statehood.

American policies were, however, inconsistent with Administration rhetoric. The United States adopted a rhetorical position that differed substantially from that of Europe. During the 1992 campaign Bill Clinton strongly criticized the EU for failing to distinguish between aggressor and victim. The United States also sought to lift the arms embargo on Bosnia. Both collectively and individually, the member states of the EU, now joined by Russia, argued that arming Bosnia would widen the conflict and provoke greater involvement from Serbia. Britain and France declared their intention to withdraw UNPROFOR troops should the arms embargo be lifted. The United States countered with a "lift and strike" alternative in which Bosnia might receive arms and air strikes would deter greater Serbian involvement, but backed down when Britain and France threatened to withdraw UNPROFOR troops and jeopardize the humanitarian aid mission. Nevertheless, as Christopher Bennet (1995) writes:

> "Though Clinton's most ambitious projects were shelved by European opposition, whatever action the international community did take – airdrops to besieged Muslim communities, the NATO ultimatum ordering the Serbs to pull back from Sarajevo, the shooting-down of four Serb war planes and the Croatian–Bosnian Accord – was all US-inspired.

The US-brokered accord between Croatia and Bosnia of March 1994 provided a new source of military supply for Bosnia, although heavy weapons, airplanes, and tanks were still not permitted. Close American cooperation with the Bosnian–Croat alliance would eventually pave the way for the Dayton Peace Accords. On the one hand, the Bosnian Army proved incapable of liberating Sarajevo. At the same time, the brutal Serb assaults on Srebrenica, Zepa, and Gorazde eliminated these areas as negotiating issues. A joint Croat–Bosnian offensive (Operation Storm) in northwestern Bosnia threatened to liberate that whole region, including Banja Luka, from Serb control, while Croat forces overran the Krajina and captured Western Slavonia (Operation Flash), thereby resolving on the ground most of the important remaining disputes between Croatia and Serbia.

In this context, the Dayton Agreements served to preserve the battlefield *status quo* and, indeed, may even have prevented the Bosnian Army from exploiting its successes on the battlefield and recovering more territory.[12] As an exercise in *de facto* partition, Dayton constituted an outcome not dissimilar from the EC's original plans nor, for that matter, from what must have been contemplated by Presidents Milosevic and

---

[12] Albert Wohlstetter, "A Photo-Op Foreign Policy", *The Wall Street Journal*, 23 October 1996, p. A22.

Tudjman in 1991 and 1993.

US leadership in 1994 was acceptable to Europe because it did not challenge Europe's own core objectives. The presence of British and French troops on the ground (and the threat to withdraw them) in Bosnia had greatly limited America's room for manoeuvre. America's eventual willingness in the autumn of 1994 to contemplate the use of greater force against the Serbs secured European cooperation in the form of the Dayton negotiations. But the practical result of Dayton is the victory of ethnic nationalism and partition: Bosnian Serbs remain in control of their territory; they have signed economic accords with Serbia; war criminals have not been apprehended by NATO troops; Croatia continues to hold sway in large areas of Herzegovina, including West Mostar. An embargo on heavy weapons to Bosnia, a central element of European strategy, remains in force. Europe's dependence on American leadership clearly illustrates the limitations of CFSP, but it does not indicate that British, French, and German power in southeastern Europe has been eclipsed.

7.5. CONCLUSION: PROSPECTS FOR CFSP

The EU's policy towards former Yugoslavia provides few grounds for optimism concerning the establishment of a communitarian policy when key issues of national security are at stake. With the benefit of hindsight, it is clear that the attempt to develop a common policy collided with calculations of national interest. The communitarian aspects of policy quickly gave way to a more traditional European diplomacy of "lowest common denominator", which in turn led eventually to the reassertion of America's role in European security. The guiding principle of European diplomacy was not the defence of human rights against Serbian (and later Croatian) aggression, but rather containment of the war and the provision of limited humanitarian assistance to its victims.

The EU nonetheless undertook several important initiatives that might be considered central to an embryonic CFSP. The establishment of ECHO in 1992 and the provision of large-scale humanitarian aid,[13] the development of an unprecedented degree of collaboration and consultation, and the participation of European military forces under WEU and national flags in all phases of the war clearly signalled the presence of the EU as a key actor in world affairs. None of these initiatives, however, prevented large-scale war or helped to secure a peace that offered the hope of a unified, multi-ethnic Bosnia. The provision of humanitarian aid had costs as well as benefits. The policy itself promoted two objectives that were unrelated to humanitarian aims: appeasing European public opinion as the scope of Serb and Croat violence became known; and maintaining diplomatic leverage in relations with the United States while not risking large numbers of casualties. Europe's UNPROFOR troops were compelled to observe passively large-scale atrocities against civilians, and to

---

[13] In 1995 ECHO provided 692 million ECUs to projects in 50 countries and is now "a well-established feature of the Union's external relations policy...." (Ole Ryborg, "Creating an ECHO That Will Be Heard Around the World", *European Voice*, 24–30 Oct. 1996, p. 17).

tolerate attacks on their own forces. Humanitarian assistance to displaced populations also indirectly facilitated the policy of ethnic cleansing. Bosnian Serb forces reportedly siphoned off 40 per cent of food and fuel. On 20 December 1994 the *Christian Science Monitor* reported that "the Karadzic war machine is literally fuelled by UN aid" (p. 18). Above all, EU and later transatlantic unity was achieved by adopting a position of neutrality, even as an arms embargo greatly impeded the ability of the Bosnian government to defend itself.

7.5.1. Politics and political will

During World War II, Yugoslav's partisan movement fought for the principle of multi-ethnic unity against two especially virulent fascist movements: Serbia's cetniks and Croatia's ustashe. The Yugoslav federation that resulted from the victory of the partisans, who received substantial if reluctant support from the West, was deeply flawed. Yet, even as Yugoslav communism self-destructed, the legacy of citizenship based on *demos*, and not *ethnos*, survived within all republics, and continued to compete against the cetnik and ustashe revivals, most forcefully within Bosnia itself.[14] Had the EU supported this principle of citizenship, it is possible that Yugoslavia might have survived as some sort of voluntary confederation or that the break-up might have been managed more peacefully. If war could not have been avoided, Bosnia might have been able to defend itself and maintain a commitment to multi-ethnic democracy, rather than experience ethnic partition.

Could the EU have acted differently? At the outset, the EU would have had to recognize, as Germany did, the central role which Serbia played in provoking secessionist pressures. Concerted economic and political pressure would have needed to be brought to bear on Belgrade to assuage Slovenian and Croatian fears of Greater Serbia. If this pressure proved insufficient, then the EU would have needed to issue credible military threats against Serbia. After war broke out in Bosnia, Europe would have needed to lift the arms embargo on Bosnia while holding the main forces of the JNA at bay.

Europe's room for manoeuvre was greatest at the outset of the conflict. As the war widened, the constraints on active political and military engagement became greater, although certainly not insurmountable in principle. Resistance to military intervention on the part of the French and British general staffs reflected longstanding ties to Serbia; greatly exaggerated fears of Serbian military prowess; warnings that support for Bosnia might provoke Russia involvement on behalf of the Serbs; and an undercurrent of anti-Muslim sentiments. Most of these arguments also resonated strongly in an increasingly isolationist United States where, ironically, the military leadership was most strongly opposed to American military engagement.

Yet European public opinion was broadly favourable to greater intervention, especially by the fall of 1992 when the extent of Serb and Croat atrocities became known. However, no major party in France, Germany, or Britain advocated the use of

---

[14] See especially Denitch (1993).

force against Bosnian Serbs and (after 1993) or Croats or called for the lifting of the arms embargo on Bosnia. American proposals for an International War Crimes Tribunal received strong support from France as well as all the permanent members of the UN Security Council, but the Tribunal had no direct bearing on the course of the war. The contention that all "warring factions" bore responsibility for the war justified a policy that eschewed military intervention in favour of humanitarian aid, and encouraged opponents of such intervention to seek to discredit the Bosnian government and army. Yet, in retrospect, the obstacles to military intervention were exaggerated in both the United States and Europe; the success of limited air strikes of 1994 and 1995 against Bosnian Serbs indicates that the "lift and strike" alternative proposed by the United States was militarily and politically viable and would not have endangered the relief effort. Of course, to overcome the formidable obstacles to greater involvement would have required stronger leadership and political will in Europe's most important capitals as well as in Brussels.

Failure of the international community to enforce the provisions of Dayton suggests that, as the trend towards *de facto* partition continues, Bosnia itself remains highly vulnerable to both Croatian and Serbian territorial designs, even as it also becomes more susceptible to religious fundamentalism and intolerance. Even the claim that the EU has contained the conflict within the borders of former Yugoslavia is premature. EU administration of Mostar has not led to Bosnian–Croat political reconciliation or the return of Muslim refugees to their homes in Western Mostar. NATO troops and International High Representatives Carl Bildt and Carlos Westendorp have not enforced key provisions of the Dayton Accords, including the right of return for refugees and the arrest of leading Serb and Croat politicians indicted as war criminals by the International War Crimes Tribunal. The unravelling of the Dayton Agreements and the development of stronger ties between Bosnian Serbs and Bosnian Croats and, respectively, Belgrade and Zagreb suggest that a *de jure* partition might lead to future instability.

The failure of the EU in former Yugoslavia has contributed to a greater sense of realism concerning EU foreign policy. The problems in dealing with large-scale crises on the basis of an imperfect and still ambiguous Union have generated more modest proposals for CFSP, including "coalitions of the willing", as evidenced in the humanitarian mission to Albania of April 1997; and the call for a "Monsieur PESC" or "foreign policy czar". French power and interest remain central to these proposals. Partly as a result of its experience in Bosnia, France has recognized that a CFSP cannot accomplished without American support, and has accordingly begun to re-evaluate its role within NATO.

Most analyses of EU policy towards Bosnia have emphasized the salience of institutional constraints and problems of national interest in order to explain why Europe failed to prevent the war. To be sure, institutional problems and national rivalries present formidable obstacles to a common policy, but they do not explain the failure of the nations of the EU, either individually or collectively, to mobilize against ethno-national aggression in defence of human rights. As the founders of the European Economic Community recognized, European unity is essentially a political project. If the establishment of a common external policy depends on more efficient institutions and concerted leadership, it also requires the political will to expand human rights and democracy not only within the member states, but throughout Europe and the rest of the world.

7.6. REFERENCES

Almond, M. (1994). *Europe's Backyard War: The War in the Balkans*. London: Heinemann.

Ash, T.G. (1993). *In Europe's Name: Germany and the Divided Continent*. London: Jonathan Cape.

Bennet, C. (1995). *Yugoslavia's Bloody Collapse: Causes, Course and Consequences*. New York: New York University Press; 203.

Carnegie Endowment for International Peace (1996). *Unfinished Peace: Report of the International Commission on the Balkans*. Washington, DC.

Crawford, B. "German Foreign Policy After the Cold War: The Decision to Recognize Croatia". Center for German and European Studies, Working Paper 2.21, University of California at Berkeley, Aug.

Denitch, B. (1993). *Ethnic Nationalism: The Tragic Death of Yugoslavia*. Minneapolis: University of Minnesota Press.

Edwards, G. (1997). "The Potential and Limits of the CFSP: The Yugoslav Example". In Regelsberger, E. et al. (eds) *Foreign Policy of the European Union: From EPC to CFSP and Beyond*. Boulder: Lynne Rienner Press.

German Foreign Ministry (1993). "Recognition of the Yugoslav Successor States: Position Paper of the German Foreign Ministry". Bonn, 10 March.

Glenny, M. (1991). "Germany Fans the Flames of War". *New Statesman and Society 4*, 20 Dec.

Glenny, M. (1993) *The Fall of Yugoslavia: The Third Balkan War*. London: Penguin.

Golubic, S., S. Campbell and T. Golubic (1996). "How Not to Divide the Indivisible". In Ali, R. and L. Lifschultz, *Why Bosnia? Writings on the Balkan War*.

Gow, J. (1996). "British Perspectives". In Danchev A. and T. Halverson (eds) *National Perspectives on the Yugoslav Conflict*. New York: St Martins.

Gow, J. (1997). *Triumph of the Lack of Will: International Diplomacy and the Yugoslav War*. New York: Columbia University Press.

Grieger, W. (1994). "Towards a Gaullist Germany? Some Lessons from the Yugoslav Crisis". *World Policy Journal 11*, Spring.

Hoffmann, S. (1996). "Yugoslavia: Implications for Europe and European Institutions". In Ullman, R.C. (ed.) *The World and Yugoslavia's Wars*. New York: Council on Foreign Relations.

Honig, J.W. and N. Both (1996). *Srebrenica: Record of a War Crime*. London: Penguin.

Human Rights Watch/Helsinki (1995). *Bosnia-Herzegovina: The Fall of Srebrenica and the Failure of U.N. Peacekeeping*. Vol. 7, No. 13, Oct., New York.

Human Rights Watch/Helsinki (1996) *Bosnia-Herzegovina: A Failure in the Making – Human Rights and the Dayton Agreement*. Vol. 8, No. 8, June, New York.

International Institute for Strategic Studies (1993). *The Military Balance 1993 4*. London: Brassey's; 73–74.

Kumar, R. (1997). "The Troubled History of Partition". *Foreign Affairs 76*, Jan./Feb.

Lepick, O. (1996). "French Perspectives". In Danchev A. and T. Halverson (eds) *National Perspectives on the Yugoslav Conflict*. New York: St Martins.

Moore, P. (1992). "Diplomatic Recognition of Croatia and Slovenia". *Foreign Affairs 72*, No. 1.

Pesic, V. *Serbian Nationalism and the Origins of the Yugoslav Crisis*. Washington, DC: US Institute of Peace.

Ramet, S.P. (1996). *Balkan Babel: The Disintegration of Yugoslavia From the Death of Tito To Ethnic War*. Boulder: Westview Press.

Rieff, D. (1995). *Slaughterhouse: Bosnia and the Failure of the West*. New York: Simon and Shuster.

Silber, L. and A. Little (1996). *Yugoslavia: Death of a Nation*. London: TV Books.

Weller, M. (1992). "The International Response to the Dissolution of the Socialist Federal Republic of Yugoslavia". *The American Journal of International Law 86*.

Wood, P.C. (1993). "European Political Cooperation: Lessons from the Gulf War and Yugoslavia". in Cafruny, A.W. and G. Rosenthal (eds) *The State of the European Community, Volume 2: The Maastricht Debates and Beyond*. Boulder, Colorado: Lynne Rienner Press.

Wood, P.C. (1994). "France and the Post-Cold War Order: The Case of Yugoslavia". *European Security 3*, No. 1.

Woodward, S.L. (1995). *Balkan Tragedy: Chaos and Dissolution After the Cold War*. Washington, DC: The Brookings Institution.

Zimmerman, W. (1996). *Origins of a Catastrophe: Yugoslavia and its Destroyers – America's Last Ambassador Tells What Happened and Why*. New York: Times Books.

CHAPTER 8

Europeanization of the Mediterranean region: the EU's relations with the Maghreb

Christopher J. Smith and Kaisa Lahteenmaki

8.1. INTRODUCTION

The relationship between Europe and the Maghreb is long on historical experience and short on cultural understanding. The region is often characterized as a historic cross-roads between north and south, and a centre of cultural and economic exchange (Melasuo 1994, Latter 1991, Aliboni 1993, Spencer 1993). In the contemporary context, however the image of the cross-roads has been replaced by that of the gateway, where gatekeepers police the boundary between the two spheres, and the nature of exchange has become dominated by the unidirectional flow of culturally encoded messages that, in one way or another, seek to enframe the Maghreb as a non-threatening reflection of Europe encrypted in the post-war experiences of integration and commercialization.

The primary mechanism of influence flowing from Europe to the Maghreb can be situated firmly in the intellectual realm of ideas. In the post-1945 era the Maghreb has been enframed in successive waves by the European ideas of colonialism, nationalism, socialism and, now, by regionalization and globalization. A specific example of the current manifestation of this encompassing European influence on the Maghreb is the encouragement of Maghrebi regional integration through the Arab Maghreb Union (consisting of Tunisia, Algeria, Morocco, Libya and Mauritania), which we characterize below as a form of reactive regionalization.[1] The theoretical framework offered here is provided by the interleaved processes of regionalization and globalization enframing the Europeanization of the Maghrebi region.

We begin by discussing the relationship between regionalization and globalization and by outlining the way in which they combine to contribute to the emergence of reactive regionalization. We then move on to discuss the shape and scope of European

---

[1] Although Libya and Mauritania are members of the AMU, they are often treated as "exceptional" cases. Libya has been generally shunned by the EU since 1986 because of its suspected complicity in international terrorism; as such it has undergone a period of EC sanctions and has been excluded from the Euro Maghreb agreements for the time being. Mauritanian exceptionality comes from its geographical status as a non-littoral Mediterranean country which interacts with the EU primarily through the Lomé development aid process.

A. Cafruny and P. Peters (eds.), The Union and the World, 151–171

Union's external relations and the development of the EC's Mediterranean Policy. Lastly we discuss the political economy of EU–Maghrebi relations in light of the notions of hegemony and of civilian power. In an overview of the EC's Mediterranean Policy, the nature of the emerging EU as a foreign policy actor, encompassing the possibility of a CFSP shaped by current institutional boundaries and by ongoing globalization, becomes clearer.

8.2. GLOBALIZATION AND REACTIVE REGIONALIZATION – EUROPEAN ENFRAMING OF THE WESTERN MEDITERRANEAN

8.2.1. Reactive regionalization and the AMU

Regionalism is the mechanism through which the current phase of the European enframing of the Maghreb is taking place. It is important to uncover the nature of the process which constructs European integration as the major catalytic element in the spread of regionalism, both as a concept and as a political strategy. How has the process sparked off other regionalisms?

An explanation of the concept of regionalism must be grounded in an understanding of the changing nature of the twin pillars of traditional international relations: the international political system built around the concept of sovereignty, and the international economic system built around the concepts of production and exchange through trade. The Westphalian model of sovereignty is under attack. Sovereignty still maintains the affirmation of cultural identity, but it has lost meaning as power over the economy (Cox 1996, pp. 305–306 [original, Cox 1992]). Economic power, due to the changing nature of relations of production and the demise of financial exchange controls, has begun to seep beyond the controlling boundaries of the traditional Westphalian state towards a variety of intermediate destinations above and below the state.

In the realm of international trade, relationships can be characterized as increasingly adversarial. Within this trade framework, actors now aim neither to seek complementarity nor simply to compete, but to maximise market share. As Drucker notes:

> complementary trade seeks to establish a partnership. Competitive trade aims at creating a customer. Adversarial trade aims at dominating an industry. Complementary trade is a courtship. Competitive trade is fighting a battle. Adversarial trade aims at winning the war by destroying the enemy's army and its capacity to fight (Drucker 1989, p. 129).

The upshot of these changes to the traditional political and economic pillars of the international system is, in essence, highlighted by the process of regionalism. International political economy has been restructured by these changes, and regionalism can be seen as a major political response to such developments. From this basis, Cox constructs a simple model which suggests that these emerging political and economic developments (which we will characterize below as globalization) encourage macro-regionalism, which in turn encourages (rich state) micro-regionalism, which in turn encourages (poor state) micro-regionalism. For Cox,

> Macro-regions are political–economic frameworks for capital accumulation and for organising interregional competition for investment and shares of the world market. They also allow for development through internal struggles of different forms of capitalism. Macro-regionalism is one facet of globalization, one aspect of how the globalizing world is being re-constructed (Cox 1996, p. 306).

Unlike the 1930s, however, the current macro-regionalist groupings are not narrowly nationalistic and autarkic. The contemporary trilateral division, based on the EU, NAFTA and ASEAN, simply cannot exist in the old way as multinational corporations have sought to position themselves commercially within each politico-geographic grouping. Technical standards may vary from region to region, but the same producers supply each region through product differentiation strategies. In any case, patterns of trade are no longer matched by patterns of long- or short-term capital movements and, as such, the world's currency regions are not the same as the world's trading regions (Pettman 1996, p. 206). This renders 1930s style autarky improbable; instead, macro-regionalism encourages micro-regionalism. New layers of sovereignty are encouraged below the level of the traditional Westphalian state, classic examples being Catalonia, Lombardy, Bavaria and, perhaps more contentiously, Scotland. Crucially, when considering the Mediterranean, the third level of Cox's model is highlighted, namely the encouragement of (poor state) micro-regionalism. Across the shores of the Western Mediterranean this process seems to have occurred in two ways.

In the security realm, initiatives such as the 5+5 accords and, to some extent, the CSCM process can be seen as sub-regional approaches by small groups of Mediterranean littoral countries to enmesh the Maghreb, or the countries of the Southern Mediterranean shore, more generally in cooperative behaviour structures. A further example would be the movement of private finance capital from businesses and individuals in Southern Europe to the countries of the Maghreb.

At the macro-regional level, the EU has encouraged specific trade and aid regimes with the Maghreb countries through the maintenance of the Mediterranean Policy of the EC and, latterly, through the explicit strategy of the creation of the "partnership institution", the Arab Maghreb Union. European integration thus plays an important role in the encouragement of regionalism on a global scale, through example setting in the areas of prosperity, democracy and market-efficiency, and by rewarding the creation of economic and fiscal stability. The process of integration encourages the emergence of world-wide mirror-images of itself.[2]

This process facilitates interaction between institutionally and organizationally similar partners because regional formations are based on largely shared values and aspirations in relation to economic prosperity and political stability. One such underlying value is acknowledgement of the process of global interdependence requiring common action in the management of common problems.

Thus, a key factor in the establishment of the AMU in Marrakesh in 1989 was the role played by the European integration process, both as a macro-regional hegemon

---

[2] On regionalism and reactive regionalization, see e.g. Hurrell (1995) and Cox (1992).

and as a conveyer of global values and attitudes. The EU has set an example for regional integration and cooperation and it has encouraged and cajoled other regions to follow this example. EU pressure, linking market access and development aid issues with the ability of the recipient countries to undergo major programmes of structural adjustment, structures the desire for further integration, which then becomes increasingly internalized by Maghrebi elites. Regionalism thus comes to be viewed as the only way of addressing what were perceived to be intractable sub-regional problems.

Economic goals form the centrepiece of sub-regional ambitions in the AMU, though it is also envisaged that defence and security issues will be included in the process. For example, under Article 15 of the Marrakesh Treaty, member states "commit themselves not to permit on their respective territories, any activity harmful to the integrity or the political system of any one among them" (Kerdoun 1994, p. 135.) The prospect of setting up a common defence regime, however, appears rather optimistic, although Article 14 of the Treaty clearly sets out to establish a certain solidarity by stating that "any act of aggression aimed at one of the member countries will be regarded as an act of aggression against all other members". Moreover, on the basis of Article 3 of the Treaty, the Council of the AMU decided in its meeting in Tunis in January 1990 to provide for coordination and cooperation in the defence sector among all member countries.

8.2.2. Regional uncertainties

Such bold objectives, espoused in the brief period of optimism after the Cold War, were to prove susceptible to the instabilities in Middle Eastern politics. The height of this initial hurdle thus became a contributory factor to the stalling of the AMU process. In circumstances of instability, ambitious objectives tend to be jettisoned to make way for practical politics in the short term. The internal problems of the AMU member countries do not yet lend themselves to common solutions in the field of security. Though the stated aims of defence and foreign policy coordination and cooperation would increase stability and build confidence in the region, political circumstance and the lack of political will among the participants appear to preclude such far-reaching cooperation. Indeed, as the Europeans themselves discovered at the beginning of their own process of state-led regionalism, the only feasible starting point is the collective attainment of modest functional economic goals.

In this light, the question of "singularity or differentiation" in terms of the Mediterranean as a security complex, or as a set of interrelated complexes, emerges. Can the Maghreb be differentiated from other sub-regions of the Mediterranean such as the Mashreq, with its deeply divisive political and strategic cleavages between Israel and many of its neighbours? On balance, though the Mediterranean displays a far-reaching interdependence, manifested in security terms by reaction to the Israeli–Palestinian dispute, and in reaction to outside intervention in the region, it can be argued that concrete sub-regional integration projects such as the AMU are an important first step in a wider process.

A further factor causing regional uncertainty, given its potential influence on EU Mediterranean policy, is the internal European conundrum of "widening and deepening". In the post-1989 period, the European Union has become increasingly attracted by Eastern Europe, causing frustration in Mediterranean governments who felt overlooked in the rush to rapprochement between the EU and the former socialist countries.[3]

Though such concerns are justified since economic advantages have not been equally distributed, as financial aid to one region is often seen in terms of a zero-sum loss by the other, this problem should not be exaggerated. The inclination of the European Union to support development towards a unified European political, economic, and social space should not detract from agreements reached within the Mediterranean policy process, nor should the importance of the process be considered diminished as a result of developments in Europe. Stability within Europe can only contribute to strengthening trans-Mediterranean stability.

Though EU membership remains an unattainable option for the Maghreb countries – notwithstanding Morocco's 1987 membership application – the need to acknowledge the ongoing linkages between Europe and the Maghreb requires a policy that serves the interests of both parties and contributes to stability and prosperity on a wider scale. The importance of Moroccan application was thus as a symbolic gesture, emphasizing the need for Europe to organize better its relations with the Maghreb countries, and thus not to leave them aside.

8.2.3. Reactive regionalization, Europeanization and globalization

The notion of Europeanization used here refers to the process by which the countries of the AMU undertake structural transformations in order that they may benefit from the economic networks created by the needs of European business interests. Countries such as Morocco have been willing to open their markets to European competition even in such sensitive areas as agriculture (Buchan 1993, p. 113).

The pressure for such adjustments has, however, often gone beyond the economic level. Regional integration as a process of reactive regionalization can play an important role in encouraging democratic transformations through support for democratic political forces. In this way the European Parliament uses "conditionality" principles to set minimum standards for democracy and human rights in the Maghreb countries, which can be an effective way of encouraging the development of democratic forces across the region. The European Parliament has used its power to veto agreements with third countries, over the human rights issue.[4]

---

[3] Financial assistance to the Central and Eastern European countries for the period 1995–1999 amounts to 6,693 million ECUs, while the total allocated to the Mediterranean countries is 4,685 million ECUs. As a further indicator of the disparity, EU aid to the Maghreb has been 2.5 ECU per inhabitant per year, as against 7 ECU for Eastern Central European countries and 4.5 ECU for Lomé countries (Navarro 1993).

[4] An example is the resolution by the European Parliament regarding fourth financial protocols with Syria, Morocco, Algeria, Egypt, Tunisia, Jordan, Lebanon and Israel and their respect for human rights and international agreements, which insisted on refraining from implementing the protocols with Syria and

Attached to the current development programmes for the region are conditions outlining a basic respect of human rights, without which the goal of creating a free trade zone by 2010 will not be achieved. In 1995 the customs union treaty between the EU and Turkey was signed on the condition that Turkey implement political reforms and ensure fair treatment of national minorities (i.e. the Kurds). As these conditions were not met, the EP froze all aid (except that which was aimed at enhancing democracy, human rights and the role of civil society) to Turkey.[5]

Europeanization is often used as a synonym for universalization. Though similarities do exist, such a view is simplistic. Universalization and globalization refer to processes that have deeper implications for the whole reality of social relations, involving the compression of time and space beyond the geographical (Harvey 1989). Europeanization only partially reflects this. Europeanization in the context of the EU's relations with the Southern Mediterranean region refers to the extension of economic and political interdependencies, but also to the attempt by the EU to impregnate the values of the globalized capitalist system that eventually assimilate or override local models of societal development.

Moreover, the processes of Europeanization and globalization impinge equally upon the economic, political, cultural and security realms of social existence. The way in which the power structures, both political and commercial, are transformed in the processes of globalization and Europeanization presupposes a system in which the dividing lines between political and economic power are now harder to distinguish. No longer are sources of authority clear-cut and state-centric; instead they are diffused between economic and political agents and actors in the sphere of globalizing markets (Strange 1996). Even if it is assumed that government decision-making, at least among the major states, remains the major impetus to the determination of the direction of economic and social development, we can assume that such control over the factors influencing this is increasingly limited. If political power is seen as the ability to control the machinery of the state or to influence government policy (Cox 1987, p. 18), this ability is now divided among a larger and a more varied group of actors. Globalization ensures that the power to control economic forces at a national level is increasingly diminishing. Instead, power is displaced across and beyond borders to the level of transnational commercial and political élites.[6]

Politico-economic élites on a global scale can influence the way in which power is distributed. Fragmented sovereignties have, in the Mediterranean region as elsewhere, endowed TNCs with unique opportunities for manoeuvre and manipulation, compromising the effective sovereignty of states in some areas of critical importance

---

Morocco until they conformed with the conditions regarding respect for human rights and resolutions passed by the UN Security Council (OJEC C 39/50, 15 Jan. 1992). In the end the European Parliament decided, based on the assent procedure, to decline the Commission's recommendation to the Council (COM(91) 0814) regarding the protocols on financial and technical cooperation between the European Community and Morocco.

[5] European Parliament: *The Week*. PE 251.453, 16–20 Sept. 1996.

[6] This has profound implications for democratic representation. Democratic systems are neither as mobile nor as flexible as markets: their ability to remodel themselves transnationally is severely questioned (Habermas 1992).

(Jones 1993, p. 105). Robinson theorizes this by highlighting the fact that the traditional realist assumptions regarding the separability of the economic and the political in the field of international relations thus no longer hold:

The increasing separation of classes from territoriality and class power from state power involves a dispersal of global decision-making away from specific core states, even though transnational groups continue to filter policies through existing state apparatuses (Robinson 1996, p. 20).

Under globalization, capitalist production relations are displacing, and the state, as a theoretical abstraction, is becoming separated from the nation-state as a concrete sovereign territorial unit. Production is transnational while the discourses of security and democracy remain state-centred. Globalization can thus be seen as a second generation concept of interdependence – similar in nature, but wider in scope – with implications for the sovereignty and actor capability of states, markets and individuals. As such it is of utmost relevance in a region where interdependencies, their asymmetrical nature and the power structures around which they evolve have been determining factors in the emergence of the highly uneven relations of asymmetrical interdependence. Though Europe and the Maghreb are interdependent in security terms,[7] the dependence of the Maghreb on Europe both in relation to security and economy is of a far greater magnitude. In terms of EU's main trading areas, for example, the Southern and Eastern Mediterranean together account for a proportion of trade similar to that of Eastern Europe (Niblock 1996, p. 118). Yet it is clear that the role of the EU in the region is of critical importance. Since economic aid and investment come with strings attached, with a demand for certain reforms, linkage between the economic and the political is enhanced.

Though we have here tried to clarify the concept of globalization and Europeanization as we understand them, it is important to note that the "global" does not encapture a fixed meaning, but rather it is embedded in the social realities of a given situation, being contingent on the conflicts over the control of political power, resources and cultural identity. Thus the definition of the global for any society is not given, but depends on conflicting interests based on class, gender, ethnicity, religion, employment, or geographic origin (Hadjimichalis 1995, pp. 239–240.) This is evident in the situation of the Maghreb, since the region is in so many ways interlinked through these questions of identity and power.

Community building, identity and social relations are important factors that both shape and are shaped by the constellation of interlinked politico-economic relations. A key element of globalization in this sense is the compression of time and space, as it relates to political spaces and relations between them. As argued by Jan Art Scholte,

globality involves a different kind of location, such that "directly experienced" social relations need no longer be those of proximity in accordance with conven-

---

[7] Niblock (1996) is, however, essentially correct to point out that a situation of asymmetric dependence exists between the EU and the Mediterranean region as a whole. Most studies of the problems of the region, he claims, start from the assumption of symmetrical interdependence and then define security needs to protect such economic interactions as do exist. His approach suggests that the problem is to find adequate security structures where no profound European economic interests are deemed to be at stake.

tional Euclidean measurements. Global relations are not links at a distance across territory but circumstances without distance and relatively disconnected from particular location (Scholte 1996, p. 49).

This description is evident in the pattern of relationships stretching across the Western Mediterranean. The interrelated questions of economy, religion, immigration, and cultural identity are not limited to geographical location, but touch on the very construction of the region in a wider sense. Geographical distance is not the key factor determining regional interests, although the two shores of the Mediterranean divide the region geographically. This is indicative of the globalized geography in which a "progressive sense of place" emerges, referring to the way in which a particular region constitutes itself, not geographically or functionally, but by its links to places beyond (Massey 1993).

8.3. The Concept of "External Relations" and the Development of the EC's Mediterranean Policy – the Historical Legacy

8.3.1. External relations as "civilian power"

The institutionalized nature of Europe's interaction with the Maghreb was, until the TEU, complicated by the enforced differentiation between external relations, dealt with through the supranationalist framework of the EC, and foreign policy, created through the use of the intergovernmental structures of EPC. The economic and political aspects of interaction with third parties were therefore strictly separated. Across this divide, the history of European integration as a process, and the subsequent development of particular institutions and patterns of cooperation, can be traced. The particular character of external relations, often referred to as "civilian power", emerges from such developments. (Duchêne 1973, Bull 1982, Hill 1990, Lodge 1993).

The logic of external relations lay in the development of the customs union and common market devices, which necessitated the adoption of a common external tariff (CET) around the developing community. The nature of the CET created the need for the integration of the trade policies of member states within a Common Commercial Policy (CCP). Member states must act together in the setting of the external customs tariffs and in negotiating agreements on customs duties and trade with non-members. Similarly, action to impede trade, questions of sanctions, dumping, and subsidies all have to be taken in common. For this reason, the Commission has traditionally been given the lead role in the preparation of multilateral trade and aid negotiations. The lack of a common macroeconomic policy, however, restricted the potential for "spillover" from the economic to the political arenas of foreign policy, creating the gap between capabilities and expectations, especially as this was perceived from the developing world (Hill 1993).

The Treaty of Rome gave the Community a number of instruments with which to conduct its external relations (trade, association, and development aid). Strictly speaking, legal personality in the area of external relations post-Maastricht remains with the EC (pillar one of the TEU). Implemented under the terms of the acquis communitaire, the driving force in the policy process is the Commission in DGI.

Eschewing simplicity, the three main areas of responsibility within the framework of external relations are dealt with under different articles of the Treaty of Rome: Articles 110–116 deal with trade agreements with particular reference to the GATT process; Article 228 was used for trade and economic cooperation agreements, such as the agreements struck between the EC and countries with which a privileged or special relationship was sought; and Article 238 arrangements were used for Association agreements spanning a wide variety of economic and financial possibilities. Each article distributes the balance of powers and responsibilities between and across the institutions in different ways, leading to an overall framework which can at best be characterized as rather disjointed.

8.3.2. The EC and the developing world

The basis of EC trade policy is a hierarchical system of trade preferences with different regional groups and individual countries, rather than a firm commitment to the multilateralism of the most favoured nation (MFN) regime. In relation to the developing world, three separate groups of countries can be identified towards which the EC sought to create special or preferential relationships. The first group saw the countries of the northern shore of the Mediterranean offered association agreements leading to promises of eventual accession to the community. Of this group, only Malta, Cyprus and Turkey remain in the ante-chamber.[8] The second group consists of those countries of the eastern and southern Mediterranean – the Maghreb and the Mashreq – which are deemed to be non-European and therefore unsuitable for full membership of the EC under the provisions of Article 237,[9] yet which the EC felt needed to be bound into a wider Mediterranean trade regime initially through the process of bilateral cooperation agreements. The third group of countries, the African, Caribbean and Pacific (ACP) ex-colonies, were dealt with in a more structured fashion initially through the Yaoundé and subsequently through the Lomé agreements.[10]

The colonial legacy of the EC's member states ensured that a close relationship with Africa in particular would be maintained after the emergence of the EEC based on a customs union and a common external tariff. In the 1950s and 1960s, France[11] was the major driving force behind the community's policy towards "the south" (Grilli 1993, p. 1). After British entry, however, and with Dutch and German support, a

---

[8] The fragments of ex-Yugoslavia are in a somewhat anomalous position. Yugoslavia signed a non-preferential trade agreement with the EEC in 1970 (renewed in 1973), and a cooperation agreement under Article 238 to run for an unlimited duration, in 1980. The war across Yugoslavia from 1991 to 1994, however, left all the "successor states" in limbo, with no clear trajectory towards EU membership.

[9] This Article has been superseded by Article O TEU, but without any real change to the significance of the wording.

[10] See for instance Grilli (1993).

[11] For a good introduction to the history of French policy in Africa, see Chipman (1985, 1989).

move away from the paternalistic aid model towards cooperative partnership was instigated (Dinan 1994, p. 457).

However, the residual power of French influence over community policy in this area was illustrated on the completion of the cooperation agreement process with Tunisia, Algeria and Morocco on 27 April 1976 by the EC Commissioner for Development Claude Cheysson, who suggested that the emerging pattern of relationships between the EC, sub-Saharan Africa and the Arab world represented "an interesting picture in which each of the three groups...was endeavouring to develop its cohesion, assert its desire to be independent and reject outside intervention" (Commission of the European Communities 1990a, p. 12).

Agreements had been signed with states across the northern shore of the Mediterranean in the decade between 1962 and 1972, as traditional trading partners of the EEC countries sought to safeguard their trade privileges and their access to European markets. Initially at least, the Maghreb countries were dealt with on a similar basis to the ACP countries. By 1969, however, Tunisia and Morocco had signed preferential trade agreements with the EEC which were geared to the eventual creation of a free trade area, giving free access to the community market for almost all industrial goods and to the setting up of privileged arrangements for some agricultural goods.

8.3.3. Politicizing the EC's Mediterranean Policy

Development of an overtly political arm of EC foreign policy-making can be traced back to the creation of EPC in 1969, and from there through the period of ambiguity, where the informal meeting of foreign ministers on an ad hoc basis was slowly institutionalized into an intergovernmental tool of the European Council for crisis management. It became clear after the creation of the European Political Cooperation (EPC) process in 1969, as the EEC worked towards enlargement in the early 1970s, that a wider political profile was being adopted by the community as a whole. An integral part of this process was a recognition that the piecemeal approach to relations with the states of the southern Mediterranean was no longer acceptable. This led to a new phase of policy development in the region with the implementation of the so-called "global Mediterranean approach". This "global" labelling still underplayed the strong undercurrent of residual bilateralism structuring the relationships. The three parallel "global" agreements signed with Tunisia, Algeria and Morocco in 1976 remained devoid of any fundamental integrative logic. The major question continued to be how to order the relationship between metropole and periphery – thus questions of trade and development aid were the main areas of significance – rather than how to induce intra-regional trade across the Maghreb.

The "oil shocks" of 1973, the general demand by developing countries for a "new international economic order" (NIEO), and the promotion of the Euro-Arab dialogue after 1973, in part as a political response to these events, ensured that the overall cooperation agreements struck with the Maghrebi states in 1976 were extensive (Niblock 1996, p. 122). These agreements included issues beyond trade relations, addressing questions of financial and technical cooperation, joint institutions, and issues of social concern, such as the conditions of Maghrebi workers in Europe (Commission of the European Communities 1990a). The structure of these cooperation agreements was fairly uniform, having the broad objectives of furthering the development of production capacity and developing the infrastructure of the partner countries. Moreover, the Community sought to insert itself in the industrialization process, in the modernization of agricultural production, and in the promotion and marketing of exports. Institutionally, each agreement promoted a Cooperation Council and a Cooperation Committee composed of representatives of the two parties, who were charged with the administration of the agreements (Grilli 1993, p. 194).[12]

Notwithstanding the concessions and preferences granted to the Maghreb countries within the terms of these agreements, it was in the area of technical and financial cooperation that innovative steps were taken. After the creation of the Global Mediterranean Policy in the period 1972–1976, subsequent extensions of these cooperation agreements with the Maghreb countries would be dealt with through renegotiations of the various financial protocols signed in 1976. Contributing to the economic and social development of the Maghreb, the EC sought to finance capital projects in the production and infrastructure fields. Financial assistance was allocated to a specific period and broken down into two major areas, budgetary contributions and European Investment Bank (EIB) loans. The budgetary contributions, in the form of grants, were usually directed towards areas such as health and education (Grilli 1993, p. 195), whereas the EIB loans were reserved for risk capital ventures to encourage the flow of private investment from north to south, increasing the possibility of joint operations or ventures between EU-based and local Maghrebi firms (Commission of the European Communities 1990a, p. 10).

Since 1977, financial protocols for four periods of four years each with Morocco, Algeria and Tunisia have been negotiated. For the period of the first protocol the total in ECUs was 339 million, rising to 1,072 million for the fourth protocol. These figures, however, reflect a basic European neglect of the Maghreb rather than any significant involvement. Indeed, as Garcia and Villaverde note,

> when these figures are compared with those that represent commercial deficits or levels of existing external debt in the region, it can be immediately deduced that the EC has not yet decided to play an important role in the search for solutions to the challenges posed on its most immediate borders (Garcia and Villaverde, 1993, p. 135)

A number of factors detracted from the ability of the community to achieve its goals for the Maghreb under the "global Mediterranean approach" regime, the most important of which were the decline of détente and the subsequent re-emergence of the Cold War in the late 1970s, returning Europe's strategic focus to Central Europe; the undermining of Maghrebi trade advantages as preferences were generalized across the region as a whole; and the accession of Greece, Spain and Portugal to the com-

---

[12] Only for the Maghreb countries was the Cooperation Committee mandated; for the Mashreq countries it was optional.

munity, leading to increasing self-sufficiency in Mediterranean agricultural produce for the EC and thus a loss of market share for non-members of the community. Northern Mediterranean enlargement in the mid-1980s, and the unveiling of the 1992 internal market programme, with its knock-on implications for trade relations with third parties outside the newly emerging Union (Stevens 1990, Davenport 1990, Zallio 1992), created an ever-stronger impetus for EC involvement in the development of the Mediterranean region.

The "renewed Mediterranean policy" was announced on the eve of the Spanish and Portuguese enlargement on 30 March 1985, and was designed to give greater protection to the community's traditional trading partners from the southern shore of the Mediterranean, to increase overall EC involvement in the economic development of the region, and to promote wider regional political cooperation. This was to be achieved by support for domestic food production to combat import dependency, by increasing industrial, scientific and technical cooperation in the hope of attaining greater commercial complementarity between the two shores of the Mediterranean, and by the sponsoring of sub-regional integration among the southern countries themselves.[13]

The European Council made a fundamental political undertaking in defining its priorities for future community action in the region, stating that:

> The Mediterranean policy of the enlarged Community will have to be of an ongoing nature and....in terms of economic development, make for significant and stable results in the medium term. From an overall and long-term point of view, the Community will direct its efforts to pursuing financial and technical cooperation with the Mediterranean partners in order to make an appropriate contribution to their economic and social development (Commission of the European Communities 1990b, p. 15).

It is here that the relationship between economic aid and development cooperation becomes bound up with an insistence on the part of the EC for political arrangements in the Maghreb that more accurately reflected European political and economic choices for free-market capitalism buttressed by multilateral frameworks of interregional cooperation. This process of reactive regionalization, therefore, suggests that the Maghreb countries are, through élite-level interaction, accommodating themselves to the global market philosophy and to the particular European institutional arrangements that have been part cause, part consequence of this process.

Such notions were further enhanced by a Commission communication to the Council on 25 September 1985, which talked of the need to create "a better integrated

---

[13] The Maghreb countries conduct very little trade between themselves. Interregional trade was estimated, in 1991, to be under 3% per annum (Commission of the EC 1991a, p. 7). European help in encouraging interregional trade through the sponsoring of major infrastructure projects, though laudable in one sense, is merely another example of European inscribing or enframing of the Maghreb for its own needs. The reason that interregional trade is so low across the Maghreb relates to the nature of European colonialism, where the economies of these countries were specifically engineered to serve the metropoles with cheap agricultural and textile goods. Current European desires for a more integrated Maghreb, then, reflect European needs as much as they do Maghrebi ones.

common economic area" in a way that suggested that the Commission saw an increasing complementarity between EC interests and those of the Maghrebi states (Commission of the European Communities 1985). Indeed, in 1982 the Commission had already signalled its concerns over the direction of Community policy towards the Mediterranean by reiterating the "special political value" of the area as a whole. As such, it recommended that the wider EC–Mediterranean relationship needed to be recast away from the purely commercial focus of the initial agreements towards a framework that would create the conditions for regional peace and political development (Commission of the European Communities 1982, p. 22). The existing cooperation agreements between the EC and the core Maghreb countries, dating from 1976, were therefore augmented by additional financial protocols, and signed between December 1986 and February 1988. In the interim, in July 1987, Morocco made an application to join the EC which was politely if emphatically declined by the Commission.

By the mid-1980s, with Southern European enlargement becoming a reality, it was accepted that the "Global Mediterranean Policy" model of the 1970s would no longer suffice. In general, the Commission argued that the free access to the Community's industrial market granted to Morocco, Tunisia and Algeria in the period after the inception of the policy had not been enough to delocalize production or attract foreign investment. In reality, protectionism throughout the EC had remained an issue in the areas of textiles and agriculture, something which the economic downturn of the early 1980s across the Western world did little to alleviate. Without implementation of the basic commercial clauses of the agreements, the financial aid packages would have, of themselves, little impact on the overall structural nature of the EC–Maghrebi relationship.

The answer, for the Commission at least, lay in the creation of freer markets, financial stability, and the drive to widen the narrow national market base for industrial goods in the Maghrebi countries. The development model used by the Commission was one in which much had been invested – both intellectually and politically – in the Western world in the 1980s, stressing the need, at the local level, for macroeconomic structural adjustments of the Maghrebi economies.[14]

8.3.4. The AMU – kick-start or false start?

AMU cooperation was ostensibly made possible by the reconciliation of long-

---

[14] The emergence of neo-liberalism as the guiding developmental philosophy of the 1980s undercut the notion that the state could provide "the greatest happiness for the greatest number". Instead, the market mechanism was elevated in status to that of societal regulator; thus efficiency was prized above social justice as the development process became anchored to the aspect of modernity stressing rationality, social control and the manufacturing of "Westernized" self-interested autonomous individuality across the third world. The institutional manifestations of this philosophical/intellectual project were the multilateral economic institutions such as the IMF and the World Bank, whose basic model the EC adopted in the mid-1980s for its Mediterranean trade and aid programmes. In general, such neo-liberal economic development policies went under the label of "structural adjustment" (see e.g. Buchanan 1986).

standing border disputes between Tunisia and Libya in December 1987, and between Morocco and Algeria in May 1988, with the Treaty of Marrakesh signed on 17 February 1989. The pressure of European expectations for regional integration, combined at the practical level with increasing linkage between EC aid and structural reform in the recipient countries, was, however, a significant factor in the encouragement of this regional integration process (Garcia and Villaverde 1993, p. 137; Badini 1995, pp. 106–08).[15]

The AMU process was, however, to be curtailed rather quickly, as the wider issues of Middle Eastern geopolitics, such as the international community's response to the Iraqi invasion of Kuwait, and the differential impact this had on the domestic politics of the separate Maghrebi states, intervened to put thoughts of economic cooperation in limbo (Aliboni 1996, p. 52)

8.3.5. Post-Cold War security in the Mediterranean

The Mediterranean region was profoundly unhinged by the end of the Cold War. Moreover, the conflict's end failed to deliver peace and stability. In its place, a most uncertain period unfolded, as the strategic balance collapsed and the ability of local powers to use the superpowers as external balancers ceased. The bipolar compression of regional conflict, maintained by the threat of superpower intervention, was abruptly released. A number of ad hoc Mediterranean security fora were created in the early 1990s to deal with the emerging problems across the region. However, the failure of regional and sub-regional cooperation initiatives, such as the Conference on Security and Cooperation in the Mediterranean (CSCM) and the 5+5 forum, refocused attention on the overt multilateralism of the Community's traditional approach (Declaration des Neuf sur la Dialogue et la Cooperation en Mediterrannee Occidentale 1990, Bonvicini 1996, p. 102).[16]

The Lisbon European Council of 26–27 June 1992 acknowledged that the Maghreb would be an area where the EU would seek to develop "joint actions" on the basis of its emerging CFSP. In an annex to the final Council statement, the "Declaration by the European Council on Relations Between Europe and the Maghreb", the notions of solidarity, partnership and good neighbourliness were raised, but this was done by establishing a profoundly Eurocentric and capitalistic worldview as the norm. The declaration's view of the Maghreb's future included a call for the buttressing of human rights and political democracy, while also calling for "the introduction of true market economies" and the setting up of a free trade area, all of which, it was hoped, would be overseen by the re-emergence of the sub-regional

---

[15] The European Council statement on the Mediterranean of 30 March 1985 set out four guiding principles for the continuation and development of EC–Maghrebi relations on the basis of then current arrangements. These were: (1) trade advantages maintained, (2) more appropriate, slightly increased trade, (3) creation of structures for a less formal dialogue, and (4) implementation of new forms of regional or multilateral cooperation (Commission of the European Communities 1990a, p. 16).

[16] The desire by France to maintain its own quasi-hegemony across the Maghreb was also a factor in the demise of the CSCM project (Badini 1995, p. 111).

integration strategy centred around the rebirth of the EU–AMU dialogue (Commission of the European Communities 1995, p. 23).

The Corfu European Council of 24–25 June 1994 saw further stress on the themes of globalization, liberalization and regionalization.[17] On the question of Algerian structural adjustment, it was noted that:

> The European Council encourages the rigorous pursuit of the national dialogue and the process of structural reform which is essential for the liberalization of the Algerian economy and its better integration into the world economy (ibid., p. 130).

On the question of intra-regional cooperation, the value of finding solutions to the complex political, economic and social problems besetting the Maghreb within the "context of regional cooperation" was stressed.

Between the Corfu Council and the Essen Council of 9–10 December 1994, the Commission had, at the Council's request, submitted recommendations for the strengthening of the Mediterranean Policy through the establishment of a Euro-Mediterranean Partnership (Commission Communication to the Council, 25 October 1994, COM (94)427 final) which integrated the ideas of trade/aid and security regimes across the Mediterranean under one roof, the suggestion being that the creation of a Euro-Mediterranean economic area was designed to accompany the consolidation of a political area of peace and stability. At Essen, the Euro-Mediterranean Partnership process was accepted and a new budget line was created by the European Parliament.[18]

The European Councils at Cannes on 26–27 June and Barcelona 27–28 November 1995 laid the groundwork for the Euro-Mediterranean Partnership, which focused on three interrelated areas: political and security partnership, economic and financial partnership, and partnership in the social and human field.[19]

The Barcelona Declaration of 25 November 1995 (Conference Euro-Mediterraneenne de Barcelone Declaration Finale, Commission Europeenne, Info-Note No. 52/95), based on the recommendations made at Cannes and negotiated between the fifteen member states of the EU, eleven non-member Mediterranean states, and the Palestinian Authority, was designed to

> create among the participants a comprehensive partnership, through strengthened political dialogue on a regular basis, the development of economic and financial cooperation, and the greater emphasis on the social, cultural and human dimension (Europe Documents No. 1964, 6 Dec. 1995).

Echoing numerous past agreements and proposals, the Barcelona Declaration unveiled the European strategy of promoting "exchange and dialogue" across the

---

[17] The TEU gives this philosophy solid practical application, as Article 130u states that in the field of development cooperation, the Community fosters "the smooth and gradual integration of the developing countries into the world economy". One way to achieve that goal is to promote regional cooperation, which in turn spurs multilateral cooperation.

[18] Budget line: MEDA (B7-410).

[19] Linjakumpu (1995) rightly states that the groundwork plans for Barcelona were laid at the Cannes Summit of June 1995 (Position of the EU. Presidency Conclusions. S/N 211/95, Part B).

region, guarenteeing peace and stability. Three defined aspects of cooperation were proposed in the areas of politics and security, economics and finance, and social and human affairs, though the economic proposals in the declaration were the most developed of the three "baskets" (Linjakumpu 1995, pp. 80–83). The economic highlights of the declaration were the proposal of a free trade area for industrial products by 2010, and the setting aside of 4,685 billon ECUs up to the end of 1999 for aid to the southern Mediterranean states (Lister 1997, pp. 88–89). Such economic and financial inducements were, however, tied to the ethnocentric desire to enframe a Eurocentric discourse of "global riot control" across the Mediterranean which concentrated on the dangers posed by the flow of crime, drugs, terrorism and immigration from an "unstable" South to a "settled" North.[20]

Thus Barcelona once again demonstrated the difficulty that the EU faces in its relations across the Mediterranean. Barred from entry, but integral to the wider development of the European integration process, the southern Mediterranean countries must be integrated, politically and economically, into a stable framework of relations (Lorca and Nuñes 1993, p. 56). The EU's desire to tackle this problem primarily at the political rather than the economic level illustrates most profoundly the strict ordering of the "dual-purpose" motivations for "exchange and dialogue" across the region. The desire to maintain peace and stability (riot control) outweighs the desire to promote economic growth, which, in classical liberal fashion, is expected to flower in an unfettered fashion once the basic elements of "stability" are in place. The alternative approach of vigorously promoting economic growth to create political stability is seen as too costly, and ideologically unacceptable, given the current hegemony of neo-liberal economic doctrines and cultural practices.

Thus, though the EU appeared to have emerged with an integrated multifaceted policy for dealing with the problems of the Mediterranean after Barcelona, the reality is rather different. The Cannes Council had approved major new financial commitments to facilitate the creation of the free-trade area,[21] while in the final Barcelona document the explicit linkage between financial assistance, structural adjustment and regional integration was solidified. Yet notwithstanding these modest developments and potentialities, EU policy remains dictatorial yet indifferent to the countries of the southern Mediterranean region: dictatorial because Barcelona maintains the historical pattern of cultural, political and economic enframement, fuelled now by an emerging neo-colonially inspired identity–difference discourse, and indifferent because of the fundamental lack of attention paid to the region by the EU's major players in northern and central Europe.

---

[20] Linjakumpu is again right to stress the importance of identity/difference discourse in this area which ultimately destabilizes the rhetoric of "exchange and dialogue" proposed at Barcelona. Exchange and dialogue, to be equitable, presuppose an acceptance of, and respect for, "others" as they are, which is fundamentally undermined by the sub-text of Barcelona's "global riot control" agenda in its establishment of a hierarchy of Europe/non-Europe based on the existence of the settled referents of liberal–capitalist ideology. "Democratic" exchange and dialogue cannot take place when one side so patently percieves the other to be inferior (Linjakumpu 1995, pp. 84–90).

[21] 4,685 million ECUs was set aside for this purpose in the form of available Community Budget funds for the period 1995–99, with the possibility of supplementary funds from the EIB in the form of increased loans and bilateral finance contributions from the member states.

8.4. Conclusions: the political economy of EU–Maghrebi relations –
towards hegemony?

8.4.1. Relations of dependence

The relationship between the EU and the Maghreb countries is one of asymmetric dependence. The relationship is based on two key factors: firstly, the dependence of the Maghreb region on the EU for aid and trade, and secondly, the fragility of the political situation in the Maghreb and the possibility of spillover or contamination of the Southern EU countries by low-level but persistent and intractable security problems which are manifested in the first instance by the countries of the Maghreb. Problems such as poverty, debt, population growth, the demonization of Islamism, denial of democracy, violation of human rights, immigration and the re-emergence of virulent anti-foreigner-based racism are ever-present in the debate over regional stability, both in the Southern Mediterranean region itself and in the EU.

Economic indicators testify to the disparity of development in terms of economic growth and trade. As of 1992, the EC conducted only 4 per cent of its external trade with the Maghreb, while the entire non-EC Mediterranean accounted for 8 per cent of such trade (Garcia and Villaverde 1993, p. 136). In contrast, in 1992 the EC took 87.2 per cent of Libyan exports, 75.6 per cent of Tunisian exports, 74.8 per cent of Algerian exports, and 67.0 per cent of Moroccan exports (Niblock 1996, p. 119). Moreover, there is little evidence to suggest that the level of integration in terms of intra-regional trade is on the increase: intra-Maghreb trade actually represents barely 3 per cent of the total trade in the Maghreb (Lorca and Nuñez 1993). Thus it is clear that integration and regional cooperation have a long way to go before they can help to consolidate economic development and political stability.

The nature of the relationship between the two shores of the western Mediterranean has evolved over time at the policy level, yet has remained remarkably constant at the geo-strategic level. The development from a relationship based on a commercial rationale to one emphasizing other policy areas, promoting "partnership" instead of "aid", is simply the latest manifestation of neo-colonialism. The first agreements with Morocco and Tunisia in 1969 were commercial in orientation, and political only to the extent that certain "geo-strategic" priorities were recognized, such as maintenance of the supply of raw materials, energy and mineral supplies from the region. Moreover, at this time, the Community was only beginning to establish the process of European Political Cooperation (EPC). The prevailing "civilian power" image of Community foreign policy relations essentially enforced the strict separation between the external economic relations of the Community and the foreign policies of the individual states. The colonial legacy, the struggle for self-determination, and the bipolar Cold War balance left little room for an expansive European policy in this area. Instead, this was a period of political retrenchment, though in the longer term, the basic precepts of the "civilian power" model were to prove essentially correct, in that economic and commercial power did prove to be an adequate replacement for military predominance.

The 1976 agreements were more varied than those of 1969, including cooperation in the technical, the financial and – to a limited extent – the social field. Though preferential treatment for products from the Maghreb was ensured, this was in reality of no great significance, since the most competitive exports such as textiles were still subject to annual quotas outside the framework of the agreements with Morocco and Tunisia (Commission of the European Communities 1990a, p. 18). Moreover, in the vital area of agricultural produce, the EC granted concessions only to those products which were of direct interest to its members, such as "out of season" produce, which did not threaten their own production.

The adjustments made to the Mediterranean policy in the 1980s in the wake of the Southern enlargement saw a marked politicization of the EC–Maghrebi relationship. Enlargement of the Community to include all of Southern Europe brought directly to the fore the question of purpose in the Community's Mediterranean policy. Moreover, the hardening of the ethno-political border across the Mediterranean, by a restrictive definition of EC Article 237 in relation to the Moroccan application for EC membership in 1987, settled once and for all the possibilities of Community membership. The results of this imposed division, however, were that some of the original core Community's Mediterranean trade partners were inside the now enlarged EC, whereas others, on the Southern shore, were permanently excluded.

As Grilli suggests, on the basis of the geopolitical realities brought up by the southern enlargement process, the Community had to choose between three policy options in the re-orientation of its now failing Mediterranean policy. Firstly, it could make the Maghrebi countries simply absorb the loss of its trade preferences. Secondly, it could compensate them for loss of trade preferences by increasing financial assistance and granting new preferences, especially in the agricultural field, at the expense of other third parties. Thirdly, it could accept that full integration with the Southern Mediterranean was unfeasible, and thus change the whole basis of the Mediterranean policy by trying to reduce the Maghreb's dependence on the EC, providing diversification assistance finance in the short to medium term (Grilli 1993, p. 201). The result of the Community's reassessment of its Mediterranean policy was, however, a somewhat uneasy compromise between the second and third options.

The creation of the Single Market initiative made the Mediterranean a global issue for the Community as a whole. The traditional Northern European policy of delegating responsibility for the Mediterranean to the Southern Europeans, and in particular to the French, became an increasingly unattractive option as the logic of the Single Market reordered the Community's geo-political space, making Germany as theoretically accessible to North African immigration as was Spain.

By the early 1990s, the political consequences of socio-economic decline across the Maghreb began to mobilize the desire for yet another reformulation of the Community's Mediterranean policy. The financial protocols were in any case due for renewal in 1992, prompting the need for a fuller review of the policy as a whole. The Iraqi invasion of Kuwait simply added to the immediacy of the desire for change. Undoubtedly the decline of socio-economic conditions in the Maghreb, and the potential political effect they could have on Europe, through the linkage of immigration, unemployment, access to welfare provision and European neo-fascism, motivated European states to look again at their provisions for the Maghreb, underlining the essentially political rationale for the new policy.

The reform process was begun by the Commission proposals to the Council on "redirecting" the Community's Mediterranean policy (Commission of the European Communities 1989, 1990b) and institutionalized by the outline for a new policy submitted by EC Commissioner Abel Matutes (Commission of the European Communities 1991b). The decisions taken at the Lisbon European Council meeting of 26–27 June 1992, and thereafter up to the Cannes and Barcelona Summits, consolidated the new approach.

At Lisbon the Maghreb was identified as an area where "joint actions" under the EU's CFSP could potentially be applied. Moreover, in an annex to the main set of Presidency conclusions dealing with the likely development of CFSP, the political importance, and indeed the overriding political desire to enframe the Maghreb as a non-threatening reflection of European values, was given its most explicit airing to date.

The Maghreb is the Union's southern frontier. Its stability is of important common interest to the Union. Population growth, recurrent social crises, large scale migration, and the growth of religious fundamentalism and integralism are problems which threaten that stability (Commission of the European Communities 1995).

What was missing from this declaration, of course, was any admission of culpability in the creation of the conditions in the Maghreb that were now deemed to be such a threat to European security.

We can conclude that trade relations between the EU and the Maghreb continue to exhibit fundamental asymmetries. Maghrebi exports to the EU are predominantly in the raw materials sector, such as minerals and agricultural produce. Yet the Maghreb countries remain highly dependent on the EU for their manufactured goods. The ability of the Maghrebi countries to have an impact in the manufactured "value added" sectors remains slim, and indeed with the renewed emphasis on the European Single Market since the mid-1980s, has proved even more impracticable (Stevens 1990). In essence, the EU's dominating market position ensures that the economic relationship with the Maghreb, based on the pattern of asymmetric interdependence, is set to continue. Current trade figures continue to reflect long-established patterns of production and as such reflect the vulnerability and sensitivity of Maghrebi dependence on Europe.[22]

8.4.2. Ties that bind – regionalization and hegemony

Is this relationship hegemonic? It was argued at the outset that the EU encourages other forms of macro-regionalism to emerge. Yet it is obvious from the example of the AMU that the EU, through cajoling and financing, can achieve only so much. The EU has tried to push for further integration in the region by funding a study called "The Cost of Non-Maghreb", a parallel exercise to the "Cost of Non-Europe" study

---

[22] On the historical development of trade relations between the two regions, see e.g. Commission of the European Communities 1984.

undertaken by Paolo Cecchini, which highlighted the inefficiencies and waste of market fragmentation in the EC. This was indeed logical when considered in the light of the establishment of the AMU as a response to the challenges posed to the region by further European integration.[23] Moreover, the AMU has an element of reactivity in the sense that it has been proposed that a larger proportion of EU aid should be in the form of projects linked to regional cooperation (Buchan 1993, p. 110). However, the extent to which the regional integration process can be micro-managed from the outside should not be exaggerated. The acknowledgement of the need to cooperate further must in the last instance come from within the region, and as long as countries participating in the AMU are wrapped up in their domestic problems, questions of regional integration are not likely to dominate their agendas.[24] This is naturally something that the outside actors can influence by supporting peaceful changes and democratic progress within these countries.

8.5. REFERENCES

Aliboni, R. (1993). "Instability South of the Mediterranean: Recommendations for the West". *The International Spectator XXVII*, No. 3, July–Sept.

Aliboni, R. (1996). "Collective Political Cooperation in the Mediterranean". In Aliboni, R. *et al.* (eds) *Security Challenges in the Mediterranean Region.* London: Frank Cass.

Badini, A. (1995). "Efforts at Mediterranean Cooperation". In Holmes, J. (ed.) *Maelstrom: The United States, Southern Europe and the Challenges of the Mediterranean.* Cambridge, MA: World Peace Foundation.

Bonvicini, G. (1996). "Regional Assertion, the Dilemmas of Italy". In Hill, C. (ed.) *The Actors in Europe's Foreign Policy.* London: Routledge.

Buchan, D. (1993). *Europe: The Strange Superpower.* Aldershot: Dartmouth.

Buchanan, J.M. (1986). *Liberty, Market and State: Political Economy in the 1980s.* Brighton: Wheatsheaf Books.

Bull, H. (1982). "Civilian Power Europe: A Contradiction in Terms?" *Journal of Common Market Studies 21*, Nos 2–3.

Chipman, J. (1985). "French Military Policy and African Security". *Adelphi Papers*, No. 201, summer.

Chipman, J. (1989). *French Power in Africa.* Oxford: Blackwell.

Commission européenne 1995. Info-note n° 52/95. Conference euro-mediterraneenne de Barcelone. Declaration Finale.

Commission of the European Communities (1982). "Memorandum on the Community's Development Policy". Supplement 8/82 to the Bulletin of the European Communities.

Commission of the European Communities (1984). *The European Community and the Mediterranean Basin.* Luxembourg: Office for Official Publications of the European Communities.

Commission of the European Communities (1985). Commission Communication to the Council, 25 Sept. "Guidelines for Economic Cooperation". Luxembourg: Office for Official Publications of the European Communities.

Commission of the European Communities (1989). "Redirecting the Community's Mediterranean Policy".

---

[23] The Barcelona Declaration is in itself illustrative of the Europeans' desire to lock the Maghreb into the capitalist socio-economic worldview. Any attempt to see this process as dialogic – based on interaction – must therefore be severely questioned. Dialogue turns to hegemony when one side sets the rules, parameters and possibilities of debate. (Commission européenne 1995, 3.)

[24] This is of course a similar situation to the one faced by the USA after 1945, reflecting the consternation felt by some in the US at the slow pace of European integration.

Communication to the Council, Doc. SEC(89) 1961, Brussels, 23 Nov.

Commission of the European Communities (1990a). "The EC, the Mediterranean, and the Middle East". Doc. X 20/90 EN. Luxembourg: Office for Official Publications of the European Communities.

Commission of the European Communities (1990b). "Redirecting the Community's Mediterranean Policy: Proposals for the Period 1992–96". Communication to the Council, Doc. SEC(90) 812 final, Brussels, 1 June.

Commission of the European Communities (1991a). "Proposal for a Council Regulation concerning Financial Cooperation in Respect of all the Mediterranean Non-member Countries". Com(91) 48, Brussels, 12 Feb.

Commission of the European Communities (1991b). *The Countries of the Greater Arab Maghreb and the European Community*. Luxembourg: Office for Official Publications of the European Communities.

Commission of the European Communities (1994)."Strengthening the Mediterranean policy of the European Union: Establishing a Euro-Mediterranean Partnership". Commission Communication to the Council, 25 Oct. 1994, COM (94)427 final.

Commission of the European Communities (1995). "The European Councils – Conclusions of the Presidency 1992–94". Doc.X196/95, Luxembourg.

Cox, R. (1987). *Production, Power and World Order. Social Forces in the Making of History*. New York: Columbia University Press.

Cox, R. (1992). "Global Perestroika". In Milihand, R and Panitch, L. (eds) *New World Order? The Socialist Register 1992*. London: Merlin.

Cox, R.W. (1996). *Approaches to World Order*. Cambridge: Cambridge University Press.

Davenport, M.W.S. (1990). "The External Policy of the Community and its Effects upon Manufactured Exports of the Developing Countries". *Journal of Common Market Studies 29*, No. 2, Dec.

Declaration des Neuf sur le Dialogue et Cooperation en Mediterrannee Occidentale (1990). Rome.

Dinan, D. (1994). *Ever Closer Union? An Introduction to the European Community*. London: Macmillan.

Drucker, P. (1989). *The New Realities: In Government and Politics, in Economics and Buisness, in Society and World View*. New York: Harper and Row.

Duchêne, F. (1973). "The European Community and the Uncertainties of Interdependence". In Kohnstamm, M. and Hager, W. (eds) *A Nation Writ Large? Foreign Policy Problems Before the EC*. Basingstoke: Macmillan.

Garcia, B.L. and Villaverde, J.N. (1993). "Europe and the Maghreb – Towards a Common Space". In Ludlow, P. (ed.) *Europe and the Mediterranean*. London: Brassey's.

Grilli, E. (1993). *The European Community and the Developing Countries*. Cambridge: Cambridge University Press.

Habermas, J. (1992). "Citizenship and National Identity: Some Reflections on the Future of Europe". *Praxis International* 12, No. 1.

Hadjimichalis, C. (1995). "Global–Local Social Conflicts: Examples of Southern Europe". In Amin, A. and Thrift, N. (eds) *Globalization, Institutions and Regional Development in Europe*. Oxford. Oxford University Press; 239–256.

Harvey, D. (1989). *The Condition of Postmodernity*. Oxford: Blackwell.

Hill, C. (1990). "European Foreign Policy: Power Bloc, Civilian Model – or Flop?". In Rummel, R.J. (ed.) *The Evolution of an International Actor; Western Europe's new assertiveness*. Oxford: Westview Press.

Hill, C. (1993). "The Capability–Expectations Gap, or Conceptualizing Europe's International Role". *Journal of Common Market Studies 31*, No. 3.

Hurrell, A. (1995). "Explaining the Resurgence of Regionalism in World Politics". *Review of International Studies 21*, No. 4, 331–358.

Jones, B.R.J. (1993). "The Economic Agenda". In Rees, G.W. (ed.) *International Politics in Europe: The New Agenda*. London: Routledge; 87–110.

Kerdoun, A. (1994). "The Maghreb and the Problem of Security and Cooperation for Development in the Mediterranean". In Calleja, J. *et al.* (eds) *The Search for Peace in the Mediterranean Region. Problems and Prospects*. Msida, Malta: Minerva; 133–146.

Latter, R. (1991). "Mediterranean Security". *Wilton Park Papers No. 48*. London: HMSO.

Linjakumpu, A. (1995). "Euro-Mediterranean Partnership and the Barcelona Summit 1995" In Melasuo, T.

(ed.) 1995. *Beyond Barcelona – Europe and the Middle East in the Mediterranean International Relations.* TAPRI Research Report No. 66.

Lister, M. (1997). *The EU and the South, Relations with Developing Countries.* UACES/Routledge.

Lodge, J. (1993). "From Civilian Power to Speaking with a Common Voice: The Transition to a Common Foreign and Security Policy". *Paradigms 7*, No. 2.

Lorca, A.V. and J.A. Nuñez (1993). "EC–Maghreb Relations: A Global Policy for Centre–Periphery Interdependence". *The International Spectator 28*, No. 3, 53–66.

Massey, D. (1993). "Power-geometry and progressive sense of place". In Bird, J. *et al.* (eds) *Mapping the Futures: Local Cultures, Global Change.* London: Routledge; 64–69.

Melasuo, T. (ed.) (1994). *The Mediterranean Revisited.* TAPRI Research Report No. 57.

Melasuo, T. (ed.) (1995). *Beyond Barcelona – Europe and the Middle East in the Mediterranean International Relations.* TAPRI Research Report No. 66.

Navarro, A. (1993). *La Communidad Europea, el Maghreb y España.* Madrid: INCIPE.

Niblock, T. (1996). "North–South Socio-Economic Relations in the Mediterranean". In Aliboni, R. *et al.* (eds). *Security Challenges in the Mediterranean: A Southern Viewpoint.* London: Frank Cass; 115–136.

Official Journal of the European Communities (1992). No. 39/50, 15 Jan.

Pettman, R. (1996). *Understanding International Political Economy – With Readings for the Fatigued.* Boulder: Lynne Rienner.

Robinson, W.I. (1996). *Promoting Polyarchy. Globalization, US Intervention, and Hegemony.* Cambridge: Cambridge University Press.

Scholte, J.A. (1996). "Towards a Critical Theory of Globalization". In Kofman, E. and Youngs, G. (eds) *Globalization. Theory and Practice.* London: Pinter; 43–57.

Spencer, C. (1993). "The Maghreb in the 1990s". *Adelphi Paper 274.* London: IISS.

Stevens, C. (1990). "The Impact of Europe 1992 on the Maghreb and Sub-Saharan Africa". *JCMS 29*, No. 2, Dec.

Strange, S. (1996). *The Retreat of the State. The Diffusion of Power in the World Economy.* Cambridge: Cambridge University Press.

Waever, O. *et al.* (eds) (1993). *Identity, Migration and The New Security Agenda in Europe.* London: Pinter.

Zallio, F. (1992). "Regional Integration and Economic Prospects of the Developing Countries to the South of the Mediterranean". *The International Spectator 27*, No. 2, April–June.

PART THREE

ECONOMIC AND MONETARY INTEGRATION AND THE WORLD ECONOMY

CHAPTER 9

The international aspects of the EU's exchange rate policy: European integration and dollar dominance

Amy Verdun[1]

9.1. INTRODUCTION

Foreign policy has traditionally been considered to incorporate security and defence matters as well as the international or intergovernmental relations of nation states. Arguably, as this volume shows, the external aspects of many other policies have an impact on the policies of other states. They are also actively used to regulate the relationships with other states, and can thus be considered a type of foreign policy. Within the European context, economic and monetary policies have become increasingly important for influencing these relationships between countries, as well as for the position of any given country in the world economy.

As the general background to monetary policy cooperation is displayed by Bernhard Winkler in Chapter 10, this chapter deals specifically with the external aspect of monetary policy, i.e. exchange rate policy. It examines to what extent exchange rate policy cooperation has been used as an instrument to ameliorate the position of the European Community (EC) member states in the world economy. Often foreign policy cooperation is analysed by seeking to understand why national governments preferred cooperation to *ad hoc* bilateral arrangements, if either was considered. This chapter will focus not so much on understanding domestic causes of preferences of individual national governments as on studying the importance given by the governments of the member states to achieving a successful exchange rate regime in order to influence the global economy.

This chapter will look at the various European exchange rate arrangements from the Treaty of Rome to the Maastricht Treaty and beyond. Two questions are examined. Firstly, has the decision to create a European exchange rate mechanism been influenced by external (global) factors, such as the dominance of the dollar, the rise of the yen, or the relative decline of Europe? Secondly, have the member states wanted the European Monetary System (EMS) and later the European single currency to influence global exchange rates, to create their own international reserve currency, and/or to have greater influence in the global economy?

The structure of this chapter is as follows. The next section gives a brief history of

[1] The author would like to thank Michael Artis and Bernhard Winkler for useful comments on an earlier version of this chapter. The usual disclaimer applies. This chapter was written during the author's European Forum Fellowship at the European University Institute, Florence.

175

exchange rate cooperation in the European Community, and looks at the main motives and objectives as held by the Member State governments. The third section discusses the institutional structure which has been created for exchange rate cooperation, examines to what extent sovereignty has been transferred from the member states to the European level, and looks at why it was seen as useful (or not) to transfer this sovereignty. The fourth section analyses how exchange rate cooperation in the EU has been a reaction to, and/or a strategy for, global changes. It evaluates the ever-recurring question of what motivates exchange rate cooperation by looking at the importance of global factors. Finally, the fifth section draws some conclusions about whether or not exchange rate cooperation has been a response to global factors and whether or not these developments aimed at influencing the global economy.

9.2. EXCHANGE RATE COOPERATION IN THE EUROPEAN COMMUNITY

9.2.1. The Rome Treaty and Bretton Woods

In the founding treaty of the European Economic Community (EEC), i.e. the Treaty of Rome (1957), there was no explicit mention of exchange rate cooperation. The Treaty of Rome stated that member states should consider economic and monetary policies as a matter of common concern. How member states needed to achieve this was set out in various Articles of the Treaty of Rome (e.g. Arts 103–108).

The fact that exchange rate cooperation was absent from the original Treaty establishing the European Economic Community needs to be placed against the background of a well-functioning international monetary regime, namely the Bretton Woods system (see e.g. Tew 1988). After the Second World War, a system of fixed exchange rates was set up, whereby individual currencies were not supposed to fluctuate more than 1 per cent against a fixed gold-parity, and in practice even less (i.e. 0.75 per cent). The US dollar had a fixed gold–dollar parity and the US monetary authorities had committed themselves to buying and selling gold at a fixed rate ($35 per troy ounce). The European currencies were hence pegged to a gold-parity, which in turn was pegged to a fixed dollar parity. Although towards the end of the 1950s it became increasingly clear that the European currencies were *de facto* pegged to the dollar, this had not been the aim at the outset. Nevertheless, at the time of drafting of the Treaty of Rome, the Bretton Woods system worked satisfactorily for the European governments, in that it provided stable exchange rates in Europe and beyond.

The Bretton Woods System was a reaction to the depression of the 1930s and the Second World War. Its aim was to ensure stability in the international system. The immediate post-War years were characterized by a dollar shortage, and most European countries were occupied with reconstruction. The Marshall Plan added to an asymmetric relationship between the US and the individual European countries. Hence, in the earlier years the European member states were much dominated by the United States, but were grateful for US help.

During the 1960s the international monetary system started to change. Whereas the 1950s had been characterized by dollar shortage, the 1960s was a decade of dollar surplus. The US Balance of Payments (BOP) permanently showed a deficit, and led to a flood of American dollars in the international markets. The dollar surplus started to undermine the gold–dollar parity. This led to a general debate over the stability of the system, first triggered by Robert Triffin's *Gold and the Dollar Crisis* (1961). The European monetary authorities began to feel less comfortable with holding dollars. The French government responded during the 1960s by converting dollars into gold. When devaluations occurred, and the US government continued its expansionary monetary policies towards the end of the 1960s (now further necessitated by the Vietnam war), it was clear that the Bretton Woods system was at the brink of break-down.

9.2.2. European exchange rate cooperation independent of the United States

At the end of the 1960s the European Communities stood at an important crossroads. The customs union had been completed in 1968 ahead of schedule, and various European countries, such as Denmark, Ireland, Norway and the United Kingdom, were lining up to join the European Communities. The original six member states had to decide to "deepen" integration before letting more countries in (Rosenthal 1975) – a decision which would be made again in the early 1990s. Frustrated with the US policies and full of hope of finding a satisfactory European solution to the increasingly distorted international monetary system, the six member states opted for the creation of an Economic and Monetary Union (EMU) (see Krause and Salant 1973, Kruse 1980, Tsoukalis 1977).[2]

In The Hague, in 1969, the Heads of State and Governments of the Six gave a committee of financial experts, representing each of the member states, the task of examining the possible road to Economic and Monetary Union. The path to EMU would imply having fixed exchange rates and eventually a single currency.

The Group, chaired by the Finance Minister and Prime Minister of Luxembourg, Pierre Werner, published its report in 1970 (Werner Report 1970). The EMU plan was accepted by the Council of Ministers in March 1971, after some changes. These changes mainly implied the delay of transfer of sovereignty to the institutions which would be newly created. The EMU plan envisaged the parallel development of economic and monetary union. Economic union would imply the creation of a common market, a certain degree of harmonization of macro-economic policies, and limited communal policies in the area of fiscal policy. A new institution, a Centre for Decision of Economic Policy (CDEP) would be created which would be responsible for coordinating these policies. Monetary union would imply a single monetary policy, a single currency and the creation of a European central bank modelled on the US Federal Reserve system.

The EMU plan did not survive the unexpected challenges of its time. This was

---

[2] It is worth noting that all three countries that joined the EU in 1973, i.e. Denmark, Ireland and the UK, underwrote the principle of creating EMU. Norway did not join the EC when a majority of its population rejected EC membership in a referendum.

partly due to an opportunistic view of how to achieve economic and monetary integration in the EC; difficult decisions regarding how and when sovereignty would be transferred to the new community institutions (the CDEP and the new European central bank) were not addressed. But the EMU plan was also badly constructed because it was full of compromises. Between the member states there existed a severe schism about how EMU ought to be reached, i.e. economic convergence before fixing exchange rates and moving towards monetary union, or vice versa (see Chapter 10). The two camps had irreconcilable differences concerning the road to EMU. Yet, ultimately the plan failed because of unfavourable international conditions.

These conditions included the *de facto* end of the Bretton Woods System, in August 1971, when the US President Richard Nixon announced a unilateral decision to stop converting dollars into gold. A second unfortunate international circumstance in the early 1970s was the oil shock. The result was that the EMU plan was shelved.

Several months after the Bretton Woods System collapsed it was decided to arrange a new system of fixed exchange rates – the Smithsonian agreement. Currencies were allowed to fluctuate not more than 4.5 per cent from a fixed parity. The European governments of the EC member states decided that they wanted even smaller margins, and hence came to the agreement that they would accept 2.25 per cent fluctuation margins. This system became known as the "Snake in the Tunnel". The Snake had only limited success, as few EC member states were able to keep the currencies within the exchange rate bands. Notably, France, Italy, and the UK had been unsuccessful in maintaining their currencies in the system. Moreover, during the 1970s many non-EC countries participated in it. The Snake could hence be characterized as a European but not an EC exchange rate arrangement.

9.2.3. The creation of the EMS – irritation with dollar insecurity

Towards the end of the 1970s the European countries became irritated with the volatility of the dollar and the fact that this frustrated the strive for currency stability between the European currencies. Hence, in the late 1970s a renewed attempt was made to create a new European Community exchange rate system. One of the main reasons to set up a new system, rather than to restructure the Snake, was that the French monetary authorities wanted the French franc to join the European exchange rate once again (Ludlow 1982), which led to the construction of the European Monetary System (EMS), (Commission of the European Communities, 1979a).

The reason that the French were interested in joining the new system was that they believed that their country could participate fully in an increasingly global world only by formulating a European answer to the challenges they were facing. The German government shared this view and negotiated with the French to formulate the set-up of the EMS. Because the Bundesbank, the German central bank, did not share this view, the negotiations about the institutional set-up of the EMS took place in secret Franco-German governmental meetings. When the EMS proposal was put on the table, many European countries agreed that there was a need for a European response to the irritation with the dominance of the dollar; fluctuations of the dollar made the European attempt to stabilize exchange rates extremely difficult. Another important factor which gave rise to the desire to create the EMS was the increasing challenge generated from other centres in the world, in particular the Pacific basin.

Though the EMS was not given much hope at the time by politicians or economists, the plan had remarkable success after its initial start-up period. By 1979 the EMS was set up, and in the first four years there were many revaluations and devaluations (Commission of the European Communities 1979b, 1982). These parity adjustments were foreseen in the construction of the EMS, as it was set out to be a system of "fixed but adjustable" exchange rates. Nevertheless, the period 1983–1987 showed fewer realignments, and the period 1987–1992 was characterized by no realignments at all (Giavazzi *et al.* 1988, Gros and Thygesen 1988, Ungerer *et al.* 1983, 1986, 1990).[3]

Between 1985 and 1987 there was, for the first time since the collapse of the Bretton Woods System, a window of opportunity for international policy cooperation (Funabashi 1988). In September 1985, at the Plaza hotel in New York, the G-5 countries came together to discuss economic policy coordination. In February 1985 the dollar had reached a peak in its value *vis-à-vis* the European currencies and the yen, and was arguably 30 per cent overvalued. The main problem felt by the Japanese and the Europeans was that the US budget deficit was exorbitantly high, and that the Reagan administration was extremely reluctant to take action against it. Moreover, in 1985 the US, for the first time in more than 65 years, became a net borrower (a net debtor nation). In January and February 1985 the Bundesbank also intervened by selling dollars (Henning 1994).

The Plaza agreement did not succeed in addressing the problem of the US budget deficit, but it did succeed in achieving a spirit of cooperation. It reached agreement on a controlled reduction of the value of the dollar ("soft landing" instead of "hard landing"). The European governments' main motive for participating in the Plaza deal was that they had been much concerned that a sudden fall of the dollar would undermine the EMS. In addition, the member state governments had specific domestic reasons for favouring this policy coordination. In retrospect, the Plaza Accord in fact had limited success (Funabashi 1988, p. 214). There was no "hard landing", and US trade balance improved and the protectionist bills in Congress disappeared.

In 1987 the situation had reversed. Interest rates in the US started to rise very strongly, but there were concerns that there was insufficient foreign capital flowing to the US. Hence the US agreed to another attempt at coordinating economic policies. However, the Louvre Accord, which included, among other things, an agreement for expansionary fiscal policies in Japan, was very much an *ad hoc* agreement, and was never seriously implemented in the US or Germany. The stock market crisis of October 1987 only made things worse; the US administration abandoned the Louvre accord, which hence had limited effect (Funabashi 1988).

The lack of clear success of these international arrangements, plus a number of other factors, such as the strong emergence of the Pacific basin and the loss of com-

---

[3] Formally speaking, the Italian lira realigned in 1990 when it went from the larger 6 per cent band to the smaller 2.25 per cent band, as the central parity was relocated at the top of the old band.

petitiveness of European firms, led to a new initiative to strengthen the economic position of the EC; the White Book for the creation of the Internal Market was published (Commission of the European Communities 1985). In the wake of this initiative, mention was made of the need to relaunch the EMU. In this way, EMU came on the agenda as an immediate reaction to the plan to complete the Internal Market by the 31 December 1992. The European Council in Hanover in 1988 suggested that there should be a committee of experts[4] to examine a possible road to EMU (Delors Report 1989).

The Delors Report was incorporated in the Maastricht Treaty with only minor changes (Artis 1992, Italianer 1993). Many analyses have attempted to explain why EMU came on the agenda again in the late 1980s and why it was incorporated so successfully in the Maastricht Treaty (see Verdun 1995). These analyses taken together identify five factors in their explanation of the EMU phenomenon. First, the importance of convergence of ideas over monetary policy-making prior to the 1988 period is pointed to (see, *inter alia*, McNamara 1997). particularly the fact that member states (especially France) had agreed on price stability being a very important objective for monetary policy (Sandholtz 1993). Second, all member states (except the UK) were for various reasons in principle in favour of further integration, as they saw it as a way to achieve various (domestic) objectives in the form of a total package deal (e.g. Martin 1993). Third, as had happened towards the late 1960s, European integration had in the late 1980s again reached a crossroads, as the plan to create the Internal Market gained momentum. Moreover, the existence and proper functioning of the EMS had led to a considerable degree of monetary convergence (e.g. Dyson 1994). Fourth, the EMS worked on an asymmetric basis, whereby German monetary policies operated as the reference policy for most countries (e.g. Gros and Thygesen 1992, Smeets 1990). Fifth, the changes in the balance of power more generally resulting from the fall of the Berlin Wall and the demise of the Soviet empire fuelled the European desire to come up with a significant move to deepen the integration process.[5] Finally, the global situation had made the Europeans eager to find a European solution to global challenges (e.g. Andrews 1994, Pauly 1992, Verdun 1995[6]). This paper will not deal with the first five factors, but will focus on this last factor.

---

[4] The Delors Committee consisted of the twelve central bank presidents, two members of the European Commission (one of whom was the European Commission President, Jacques Delors) and three independent experts. On the way in which the Delors Report came about as a logical consequence of the composition of the committee, see Verdun (1996a).

[5] Arguably, the EMU process had already gained momentum before the peaceful revolutions of 1989 in Central and Eastern Europe. Nevertheless, these changes on the EC's Eastern border and the more general changes in international political economy helped to increase the momentum for deepened European integration.

[6] One of these global challenges was the need to restructure the welfare state. Elsewhere I have argued in detail that European monetary integration was also used by political actors to legitimize the restructuring process of the domestic economy, which was seen as necessary regardless whether or not EMU would be created (Verdun 1995).

9.2.4. The Delors Report and the Maastricht Treaty

The Delors Committee published its report in April 1989. Like the Werner Report, the Delors Report (1989) contained parallel roads to EMU. A European System of Central Banks (ESCB) was to be set up with price stability as its overriding mandate. As regards exchange rate policy the ESCB would have the task of conducting day-to-day matters, but the final decisions on the regime chosen for the future European currency remained the responsibility of Finance Ministers, in particular the Ecofin Council.[7]

The main reasons to create a single currency were to strengthen the Internal Market, support the integration process, institutionalize the commitment to anti-inflationary monetary policies, and reduce transaction costs. The aim was not, formally, to challenge the dollar. Neither the Delors Report nor the Maastricht Treaty mentions that the European single currency should be created in order to rival the dollar as an international trade and reserve currency. But this side-effect of the creation of a single European currency is likely to have been in the back of the minds of some political and economic actors: in particular, the French government and employers' organizations have mentioned the importance of having a single currency to compete with the dollar as a leading currency (Verdun 1995).

In 1990, *One Market, One Money* was published (Commission of the European Communities 1990). This report, commissioned by the Commission of the European Communities, assessed the costs and benefits of EMU. It made clear that the so-called benefits of EMU included the fact that EMU participants would have access to a currency which could potentially challenge the dollar. The Euro could of course become used as an international trade currency or reserve currency by all EU countries, even those that would not be participating in EMU straight away. The use of the European single currency, the Euro, for intra-European trade, as well as for extra-European trade in commodities such as oil, could imply that the Europeans would become less influenced by the changes in the level of the dollar (see Peters 1997).

The countries that will not join EMU from the outset in 1999 are also going to be confronted with this new currency. First, the Euro will be the currency of their main trading partner, and trade could well be denominated in that currency. Second, following recent decisions, an exchange rate mechanism (ERM-2) will be set up.[8] The new exchange rate mechanism will operate around parities denoted in Euros.

---

[7] No arrangement had be made to construct a new institution which would be responsible for coordinating macro-economic and budgetary policies. The Delors Report had in this way led to greater asymmetry between economic and monetary union than the Werner Report had done. For a discussion of this asymmetry see Verdun (1996b).

[8] The Exchange Rate Mechanism 2 (as opposed to the system which functioned in the context of the EMS during the 1980s and 1990s) will operate for those countries that will not immediately participate in EMU. It will have wide bands, similarly to the way the ERM-1 functioned after August 1993, when the bands were extended to 15 per cent from 2.25 per cent.

9.2.5. Problems with ratification and the EMS

After the signing of the Maastricht Treaty, which incorporated EMU in the original EEC Treaty, problems occurred in the EMS. This did not surprise many economists and other commentators, who had warned about the lack of flexibility in the EMS of the late 1980s (Dornbusch 1988, 1991; De Grauwe and Papademos 1990). As we have seen above, the EMS was a fixed but adjustable system of exchange rates. However, in the period 1987–1992 the member states participating in the exchange rate mechanism (ERM) of the EMS had started to treat their stable exchange rates as "symbolic" for successful European integration. Furthermore, there was increasing belief that monetary policies needed to gain credibility – a factor which could mainly be achieved by having a "good record" of exchange rate stability and low inflation.

Hence, most monetary authorities did not want to adjust parities, even when it became clear that underlying economic factors necessitated adjustment. This was very obvious in the case of the Italian lira, where higher than average inflation was resulting in an overvalued lira. When the British pound joined the ERM for the first time in October 1990, the British government insisted on having it participate at the "high" exchange rate of DM 2.95, which soon proved to be unsustainable. The situation escalated when ratification problems occurred in Denmark and France in the spring and summer of 1992; a period which coincided with historically high interest rates differentials with the United States and a weak dollar (European Commission 1993, Portes 1993, Sandholtz 1996, Verdun 1995). The result was a "hot" summer and autumn in which severe speculations led to a withdrawal of the Italian lira and the British pound from the ERM and forced other currencies to devalue.

In August 1993 a stormy year of exchange rate turbulence was ended when the EC monetary committee[9] decided to widen the bands of the ERM from ±2.25 per cent (or ±6 per cent for some countries) to ±15 per cent, with the exception of the Dutch and German currencies which maintained the original narrow band. The period thereafter showed relative tranquillity in the financial markets, with the exception of some currency turmoil in 1995.

From this historical overview of exchange rate cooperation it can be concluded that global factors, among other things, played an important role in the (re)launch of exchange rate mechanism/arrangements in the European Community. The EC has not outwardly promoted these arrangements to improve its position in the world, but there was a tacit assumption that Europe as a whole would gain weight in the international monetary system and the economic situation in general. Moreover, as the EC consists of many small countries, each of the countries decided that European responses were the more effective way to address the challenges of the global economy.

---

[9] The EC Monetary Committee is an advisory body consisting of officials of national central banks and finance ministries of the member states.

9.3. INSTITUTIONS AND TRANSFER OF SOVEREIGNTY

9.3.1. European exchange rate systems

The institutional framework of the European exchange rate systems has been clearly set out in the relevant provisions. The Snake, as mentioned before, was not a purely EC institution. The EMS, on the other hand, did work in this manner. Exchange rate cooperation in the European Community has been based on a system whereby the official responsibility for intervention and the decision to maintain or change the level of exchange rates have remained with national monetary authorities (national central banks and ministries of finance). If any realignment was put on the agenda, the monetary committee would meet and decide (unanimously) whether a change was appropriate.[10] The unanimity clause is important, as illustrated by the fact that in the 1987–1992 period suggestions were made to devalue/revalue some of the EMS currencies, but without any result, as the member states could never reach a unanimous agreement. This unanimity, of course, also prevented countries from making a unilateral decision to devalue their currencies within the EMS.

Under EMU, monetary policy will be transferred to the ESCB. However, as mentioned earlier, exchange rate policy will remain in the hands of the Ecofin Council. Let us turn to what this means in practice.

9.3.2. The dollar–Euro exchange rate relations under EMU

The ECB will be responsible for the day-to-day management of exchange rates, but the regime will be determined by the Ecofin Council – the EU Ministers for Economic and Financial Affairs. What can we expect from them? This is where it becomes interesting to see what role is anticipated for the Euro *vis-à-vis* the dollar. Broadly speaking, one could imagine four scenarios. First, the dollar and the Euro could be left to float freely. Market forces could then determine the exchange rate without any intervention from the side of the European central banks. Second, there could be a "managed float", i.e. a degree of free flotation, but possibly a ceiling or floor to the extent to which the dollar and the Euro could fluctuate *vis-à-vis* one another, chosen unilaterally by either the US or the European authorities. Third, there could be a unilateral decision from the Ecofin Council to link the Euro to the dollar. Fourth, the European authorities and the US authorities together with, perhaps, the Japanese authorities could decide to try, once again, to coordinate international exchange rates.

Not all these four scenarios are equally likely. It is, for example, unlikely that the Euro and the dollar would float freely without any implicit or explicit ceiling or floor, the reason being that a free float could induce strong exchange rate fluctuations as occurred in the mid-1980s. Strong fluctuations between the major currencies at the moment could possibly disrupt the carefully negotiated recent trade agreements achieved under the General Agreement on Tariffs and Trade (GATT) and the World

---

[10] On the role of the monetary committee in these matters, see Kees (1987) and Dyson (1994).

Trade Organization (WTO) (see Chapter 11 of this volume). On the other hand, a unilateral European decision to peg the Euro to the dollar is also very unlikely, if only for (symbolic) political reasons. Hence, this leaves us with two options: a managed float or a unilateral decision to keep the dollar–Euro fluctuation between limits. Reflecting on these four scenarios it is rather interesting to keep in mind that the responsibility over exchange rate policy formally stays at the level of the Ecofin Ministers. Nevertheless, drawing on the lessons from the current situation in Germany (where the Bundesbank as adviser to the government has large influence over exchange rate policies), that *de facto* power of the future European Central Bank as adviser to the Ecofin Council should not be underestimated. The ECB is likely to be very influential in determining exchange rate policies.

9.3.3. Usefulness of the exchange rate instrument

If EMU comes into operation according to plan in 1999, the participating countries will have until the year 2002 to prepare themselves fully for the introduction of the Euro-coins and Euro-banknotes (European Commission 1995). By abolishing their national currencies, and where necessary making their national central banks independent of governmental politics, member states surrender sovereignty over the issuing of their national currency to the ESCB.[11] They thereby also give up the possibility to use the exchange rate of a national currency as an instrument of adjustment. Is this a problem? The experience of the recent ERM crisis with the devaluations of the Italian lira, the British pound, the Irish pound, the Spanish peseta, and the Portuguese escudo raises the question of whether devaluations are still useful policy instruments.

One can wonder whether the loss of the exchange rate instrument poses a real threat to national sovereignty. Let us reflect a moment on the role and usefulness of the devaluation instrument in the European Community. Even though recent devaluations seem to have yielded some positive effects on trade, economic analyses suggest that competitive devaluations in Europe will not generate positive results, for the domestic economy as a whole, for a number of reasons (Gros 1996). First, a competitive devaluation would at best improve the competitiveness of the country. However, devaluation leads to higher import prices, which could force up the domestic price and wage level. Second, in most member states the proportion of trade to total GDP is around 30 per cent. Hence, total output and employment will not be affected as much by trade as by other factors. Third, if, for whatever reason, the competitive devaluation has generated positive results for one country, in the European case, given the large proportion of intra-EU trade as a percentage of total trade, such positive results would have been achieved at the expense one or more other member states. Hence, the negatively affected countries could easily be tempted to follow the same path of competitive devaluations, which would annihilate the original effects of the first

---

[11] The European System of Central Banks (ESCB) will comprise the national central banks and the European Central Bank (ECB). The ECB will be established at the start of the third stage of EMU, in 1999.

country's successful competitive devaluation. Finally, even if devaluations result temporarily in a better trading position, in the long run these devaluations do not pay off; ultimately financial markets will impose a premium on interest rates on accounts denominated in the devalued currency in order to protect capital against the possible risk of future devaluations. These premiums are "costs" on capital which will not be imposed on a currency of European country that is unlikely to devalue (such as the German D-mark). In summary, given the delicacies of the European interdependent economic, monetary, and trade relations, the exchange rate as an instrument for intra-European currency adjustments is unlikely to be an extremely effective instrument, even without EMU.

9.4. ANALYSING EXCHANGE RATE COOPERATION

9.4.1. Institutions resulting from history

As seen from the above, the ERM, ERM-2 and EMU took on their specific institutional structure because of the unique historic circumstances in which they were created; the EMS followed the experience of a failed EMU and a moderately successful Snake against the background of a problematic relationship with the dollar. The EMS started as a system of fixed but adjustable exchange rates but eventually became a system of *de facto* fixed exchange rates because member states wanted to show their commitment to the integration objective (i.e. their commitment to the Internal Market programme as well as to the EMU project). Finally, after heavy financial market speculation, it had to restructure; central banks had to accept that they could not guarantee the exchange rates against full financial market speculation. ERM-2 came about as a reaction to the fact that some countries which will remain outside EMU. ERM-2 had been modelled on the "post-August 1993 ERM", i.e. on wide bands of ±15 per cent.

The institutional set-up of EMU was a result of the desire to move forward towards monetary integration for a variety of domestic and external reasons. Dollar dominance was one of these reasons – the fluctuating dollar frustrated European efforts to coordinate exchange rates. The specific characteristics of EMU were directly related to the fact that consensus had been achieved regarding the aim and objectives of EMU (price stability). Because the system would replace German monetary hegemony, it was closely modelled on the German institutional arrangements. It is also noteworthy that in Germany, which has an independent central bank, the exchange rate regime is determined by the German ministry of finance (Henning 1994).[12]

Let us reflect on what these various institutional set-ups imply for the future of the European Union, and its relations with third countries. As regards exchange rate policies, the Ministers of Economic and Financial Affairs will still have full sover-

---

[12] On the German system see Busch (1994), Kennedy (1991) and Marsh (1992).

eignty over policy-making.[13] Although the day-to-day matters will be conducted by the ECB, these politicians will determine whether the Euro will be a strong or a weak currency. They will determine whether external monetary policies of the EU will be geared towards safeguarding competitiveness, low inflation, or a stable exchange rate with the dollar, or the yen, or, for that matter, any other important trading currency. In the current situation in Europe a debate has been taking place in which the French monetary authorities are arguing in favour of a relatively "weak" Euro which would improve Europe's competitiveness *vis-à-vis* the rest of the world. By contrast, the German monetary authorities want the external monetary policies of the Euro to be primarily decided by market forces, provided that the price stability objective will not be endangered. It will be interesting to see what exchange rate regime will prevail once the Euro is introduced.

9.4.2. Implications for the future of international relations

The fact that the Ministers of Economic and Financial Affairs (Ecofin ministers) will remain responsible for exchange rate policies of the Euro-zone implies that exchange rate policy will remain at the core of external policies of the EU, and will hence influence the course of international relations. If the Ecofin ministers agree to pursue an external exchange rate policy which is detrimental to international trade relations, this could easily lead to trade wars or to protectionism, thereby threatening all that has been achieved within the context of the GATT and the WTO.

For the future of international relations it means that international exchange rate agreements, such as the Plaza and Louvre accords, may perhaps get another boost. The situation in the mid-1980s implied that an agreement needed to be made between too many different countries. If "Europe" will finally speak with one voice – with one currency – then it will be easier, and more necessary, to coordinate policies. If the European national governments can agree on the exchange rate regime for the Euro, they will be more influential in international exchange rate negotiations. It is, however, still not guaranteed that once the Europeans have a single currency they will be able to agree on a single exchange rate policy. It is possible that some countries would favour a relatively "expensive" Euro, whereas others would favour a relatively "inexpensive" Euro. Some might desire a Euro which is free floating from the other major currencies, whereas others might want the Euro not to fluctuate much from the dollar and/or the yen.[14]

---

[13] This is in sharp contrast to what will happen to all other areas of monetary policy, where the ECB will have full sovereignty.

[14] Issing (1996) has recently examined the prospects for the Euro as a real central currency with four functions: a reserve currency, a reference currency, a transaction currency and an anchor currency for the exchange rate mechanism.

9.5. CONCLUSION

This chapter has shown that European exchange rate cooperation has in part been instigated by global forces, and in part been caused by member states' search for a European answer to the global challenge. Other explanations of European exchange rate cooperation are not discounted, but this aspect of exchange rate cooperation in particular has been examined.

The history of European exchange rate cooperation has been strongly influenced by irritation or frustration with dollar dominance, i.e. the adverse effects of a fluctuating dollar on European exchange rate relations. The European member states sought their own exchange rate mechanisms to accomplish autonomy from the United States. The progress from the Bretton Woods System to the first EMU plan, the Snake, the EMS and the recent EMU plan shows an incremental path to further European integration. But it does not show the transfer of sovereignty over exchange rates to a new independent institution, as has happened in other areas of economic and monetary policy-making. Member states will of course lose some sovereignty over exchange rate policy, because under EMU the exchange policy of the Euro will be decided communally by the Ecofin ministers. At the same time, governmental policies will still determine the outcome of exchange rate policies of the European Union.

Exchange rate policies will increasingly be at the heart of the relationship between Europe and the rest of the world, in particular the other dominant economic countries, i.e. the US and Japan. If the Europeans can "get their act together" they may be significantly more influential in any eventual international exchange rate negotiations than they have ever been before. It will all depend on whether the Europeans will be able to stand as a "single" country behind their "single" currency.

9.6. REFERENCES

Andrews, D.M. (1994). "Capital Mobility and State Autonomy: Toward a Structural Theory of International Monetary Relations". *International Studies Quarterly 38*, No. 2, 193–218.

Artis, M.J. (1992) "The Maastricht Road to Monetary Union". *Journal of Common Market Studies 30*, 299–309.

Busch, A. (1994). "Central Bank Independence and the Westminster Model", *West European Politics 17*, No. 1, 53–72.

Commission of the European Communities (1979a). "European Monetary System". *European Economy 3*, July.

Commission of the European Communities (1979b). "European Monetary System: the first six months". *European Economy 4*, Nov., 79–81.

Commission of the European Communities (1982). "Documents relating to the European Monetary System". *European Economy 12*, July.

Commission of the European Communities (1985). *Completing the Internal Market. White Paper from the Commission to the Council.* Luxembourg: Office for Official Publications of the European Communities.

Commission of the European Communities (1990). "One Market, One Money". *European Economy 44*, Oct.

Delors Report (1989). *Report on Economic and Monetary Union in the European Community* (Committee for the Study of Economic and Monetary Union). Luxembourg: Office for Official Publications of the

EC.

Dornbusch, R. (1988). "The EMS, the Dollar and the Yen". In: Giavazzi, F. *et al.* (eds) *The European Monetary System.* Cambridge, MA: MIT Press; 23–41.

Dornbusch, R. (1991). "Problems of European monetary integration". In: Giovannini, A. and C. Mayer (eds) *European Financial Integration.* Cambridge: Cambridge University Press.

Dyson, K. (1994). *Elusive Union. The Process of Economic and Monetary Union in Europe.* London and New York: Longman.

European Commission(1993). "Annual Economic Report", *European Economy 54.*

European Commission(1995). "Green Paper on the Changeover to a Single Currency", Brussels.

Funabashi, Y. (1988). *Managing the Dollar: From the Plaza to the Louvre.* Washington, DC: Institute for International Economics.

Giavazzi, F., S. Micossi and M. Miller (eds) (1988). *The European Monetary System.* Cambridge, MA: MIT Press.

Grauwe, P. de and L. Papademos (eds) (1990). *The European Monetary System in the 1990s.* London: Longman for CEPS and the Bank of Greece.

Gros, D. (1996). "Towards Economic and Monetary Union: Problems and Prospects". CEPS Paper No. 65. Brussels: CEPS.

Gros, D. and N. Thygesen (1988). "The EMS: Achievements, Current Issues and Directions for the Future". Brussels: Centre for European Policy Studies (CEPS), No. 35.

Gros, D. and Thygesen, N. (1992). *European Monetary Integration.* London: Longman.

Henning, C.R. (1994). *Currencies and Politics in the United States, Germany, and Japan.* Washington, DC: Institute for International Economics.

Issing, O. (1996). "Mögliche Auswirkungen der Europäischen Währungsunion auf die internationalen Finanzmärkte", speech given at the 11th International Interest-Forum, printed in *Auszüge aus Pressear-tikeln*, No. 76, 6 Dec.

Italianer, A. (1993). "Mastering Maastricht: EMU Issues and How They Were Settled". In: Greschmann, K. (ed.) *Economic and Monetary Union: Implications for National Policy-makers.* Maastricht: European Institute of Public Administration, 51–115.

Kees, A. (1987). "The Monetary Committee of the European Community", *Kredit und Kapital 20*, No. 2, 258–267.

Kennedy, E. (1991). *The Bundesbank: Germany's Central Bank in the International Monetary System.* Royal Institute of International Affairs. London: Pinter.

Krause, L.B. and W.S. Salant (eds) (1973). *European Monetary Unification and its Meaning for the United States.* Washington, DC: Brookings.

Kruse, D.C. (1980). *Monetary Integration in Western Europe: EMU, EMS and Beyond.* London and Boston: Butterworths.

Ludlow, P. (1982). *The Making of the European Monetary System: A Case Study of the Politics of the European Community.* London: Butterworths.

Marsh, D. (1992). *The Bundesbank. The Bank that Rules Europe.* London: Mandarin.

Martin, L.L. (1993). "International and domestic institutions in the EMU process", *Economics and Politics 5*, No. 2, 125–145.

McNamara, K.R. (1997). *The Currency of Ideas: Monetary Politics in the European Union.* Ithaca: Cornell University Press.

Pauly, L.W. (1992). "The Politics of European Monetary Union: National Strategies, International Implications". *International Journal 47*, winter, 93–111.

Peters, P. (1997). "The Development of the Euro as a Reserve Currency". *European Foreign Affairs Review,* winter.

Portes, R. (1993). "EMS and EMU, after the fall". *The World Economy 16*, No. 1, 1–16.

Rosenthal, G.G (1975). *The Men Behind the Decisions: Cases in European Policy-Making.* Lexington, MA, Toronto and London: Lexington Books, D.C. Heath.

Sandholtz, W. (1993). "Choosing Union: Monetary Politics and Maastricht", *International Organization 47*, No. 1, 1–39.

Sandholtz, W. (1996). "Money Troubles: Europe's Rough Road to Monetary Union", *Journal of European Public Policy 3*, No. 1, 84–101.

Smeets, H.-D. (1990). "Does Germany Dominate the EMS?". *Journal of Common Market Studies 29*, No. 1, 37–52.

Strange, S. (1976). *International Monetary Relations*. Vol. II In: Shonfield, A. (ed.), *International Economic Relations of the Western World 1959–1971*. London, New York and Toronto: OUP for RIIA.

Strange, S. (1985). "Interpretations of a Decade". In: Tsoukalis, L. (ed.) *The Political Economy of International Money. In Search of a New Order*. London: Royal Institute of International Affairs and Sage.

Tew, B. (1988). *The Evolution of the International Monetary System 1945–1987*, 4th revised edn, Hutchinson.

Thygesen, N. (1994). "Towards Monetary Union in Europe – Reforms of the EMS in the Perspective of Monetary Union". *Journal of Common Market Studies 31*, No. 4, 447–72.

Treaty on European Union (1992). Council of the European Communities/Commission of the European Communities. Luxembourg: Office for Official Publications of the European Communities.

Triffin, R. (1961). *Gold and the Dollar Crisis. The Future of Convertibility*. Revised edn, New Haven and London: Yale University Press.

Tsoukalis, L. (1977). *The Politics and Economics of European Monetary Integration*. London: Allen and Unwin.

Ungerer, H. (1989). "The European Monetary System and the International Monetary System". *Journal of Common Market Studies 26*, No. 3, March, pp. 231–248.

Ungerer, H., O. Evans and P. Nyberg (1983). "The European Monetary System: the experience, 1979–1982", *Occasional Paper 19*. Washington, DC, International Monetary Fund.

Ungerer, H., O. Evans, T. Mayer and P. Young (1986). "The European Monetary System: Recent Developments". *Occasional Paper 48*, International Monetary Fund, Washington, DC.

Ungerer, H., J. Houvonen, A. Lopez-Claros and T. Mayer (1990). "The European Monetary System: developments and perspectives", *Occasional Paper 73*, International Monetary Fund, Washington, DC.

Verdun, A. (1995). *Europe's Struggle with the Global Political Economy. A Study of How EMU is Perceived by Actors in the Policy-making Process in Britain, France and Germany*. PhD dissertation, European University Institute, Florence.

Verdun, A. (1996a). "EMU – The Product of Policy Learning and Consensus Among Monetary Experts". *Human Capital and Mobility Occasional Paper Series*, No 7.

Verdun, A. (1996b). "An 'Asymmetrical' Economic and Monetary Union in the EU: Perceptions of monetary authorities and social partners". *Journal of European Integration/Revue d'Integration Européenne 20*, No. 1, Autumn, 59–81.

Werner Report (1970) "Report to the Council and the Commission on the Realization by Stages of Economic and Monetary Union in the Community". Council and Commission of the EC, *Bulletin of the EC*, Supplement 11, October.

Winkler, B. (1996). "Towards a Strategic View on EMU: A Critical Survey". *Journal of Public Policy 16*, No. 1.

CHAPTER 10

The political economy of European Monetary Union: between economic logic and political imperatives

Bernhard Winkler

10.1. INTRODUCTION

Economic and Monetary Union (EMU), as agreed in the Treaty of Maastricht adopted on 10 December 1991, arguably represents the most ambitious and risky project of European integration to date. The creation of a European Central Bank (ECB) to take control of European monetary policy from January 1999, at least for the countries that by then will qualify for participation, will alter both the internal policy framework within the European Union and its external relations with the rest of the world. The role that Europe and its new currency, the Euro, can expect to play in the global political economy is studied in greater detail by Amy Verdun's contribution to this volume (Chapter 9). Fundamentally, however, the international standing of the Euro will depend on Europe's economic strength and political cohesion. To assess EMU's chances of success, this chapter briefly reviews the history of European monetary integration (section 2), explores the economic and political motivations for EMU (section 3), and examines the methods chosen in the Maastricht Treaty to achieve these objectives (section 4), before drawing some tentative conclusions in section 5. The main questions addressed, therefore, are *why* Europe chose to pursue EMU and *how* it set about achieving it.

At the risk of oversimplification, it is useful to relate both issues to the principal rival theoretical accounts of European integration. Three main *triggers of change* can be distinguished at the origin of the EMU project, at the national, the European, and the global level. "Intergovernmentalists" tend to view European integration as driven by national interests articulated in inter-state bargaining (Moravcsik 1991, 1993). "Neo-functionalists" and "supranationalists" emphasize the inner logic of European integration progressing from one interdependent policy area to the next when supra-national institutions become more effective than national ones (Haas 1958, Schmitter 1970). "Global structuralists" interpret European integration as prompted by changes in the global political economy (Keohane and Nye 1977, Strange 1988), i.e. external challenges confronting European countries (individually and as a group). All three sets of factors – domestic, inner-European and external – are important for understanding the drive for EMU.

On the *method of integration*, bottom-up and top down approaches can be distin-

A. Cafruny and P. Peters (eds.), The Union and the World, 191–208
© 1998 *Kluwer Academic Publishers. Printed in Great Britain.*

guished. Under the first, common policies are the natural outcome of individual national efforts pursuing similar objectives. This can come about by free choice, perhaps coordinated, and/or via pressure from market forces. The bottom-up approach, termed "behaviouralist" by Bini-Smaghi *et al.* (1994), corresponds most closely to the intergovernmentalist view of integration, where the nation state is seen as the *agent of change*. By contrast, a top-down ("institutionalist") design uses supranational institutions as an (autonomous) instrument of integration and is closer to neofunctionalist thinking. The main difference between the approaches concerns the locus of sovereignty, wedded entirely to the nation state at the one extreme and transferred and pooled at the European level at the other. Obviously there is a continuum of intermediate cases where national sovereignty is constrained by supranational rules and institutions to varying degrees. However, it is important to distinguish *de jure* sovereignty, i.e. the location of decision-making authority, from *de facto* sovereignty, i.e. the power and ability to implement objectives.

The question of the method of integration is important in order to understand the institutional framework of EMU once it becomes fully operational, as well as in the transition period leading up to it. For example, arrangements differ starkly between monetary policy and other economic policy areas. Therefore the logic of integration across different policy areas must be scrutinized just as the integration strategy within each policy area over time. In particular, while monetary policy will be delegated to an independent central bank at the European level, economic policy will essentially remain national, with some constraints and coordination mechanisms put in place at the European level. The fate of EMU in terms of promoting Europe's prosperity and cohesion hinges on a delicate triangular construction, with Frankfurt, the future seat of the ECB, complicating the existing political economy between Brussels and national capitals.

10.2. THE ROAD TO MAASTRICHT

The first attempt at Monetary Union in Europe[1] was initiated at the The Hague summit meeting of 1968, when the Bretton Woods System of fixed but adjustable exchange rates centred on the US dollar was still in place. The Community of six enjoyed a favourable economic climate and had just completed the implementation of the Common Market. A monetary union was seen as a means to eliminate residual exchange rate uncertainty within the integrated trade area and to avoid the difficulties periodic realignments caused in the functioning of the Common Agricultural Policy. The Werner Report in 1970 envisaged progressive stages of closer integration, with full monetary union to be achieved by 1980. The report was a compromise between two views about the sequencing of economic convergence and monetary integration. The so-called "economists" (mainly represented by Germany and the Netherlands) held the bottom-up view that convergence should precede monetary integration, whereas the "monetarists" (France, Italy) argued the opposite. The report, while

---

[1] For more on the history see Gros and Thygesen (1992) and Chapter 9.

endorsed by European leaders, was never implemented, as the early 1970s saw national policy-makers respond very differently to the first oil crisis and the break-up of the Bretton Woods System. The "currency snake" put into place in 1972 to preserve exchange rate stability in Europe quickly reduced to a DM zone, where only the smaller neighbours (Netherlands, Belgium and sometimes Denmark) managed to maintain parities against the DM, while the UK, Italy and Ireland quickly left and France, having returned once, finally quit in 1974.

The Bremen summit of 1978 resumed the effort to create a zone of monetary stability in Europe. One important motive, especially for Germany, was the weakening of US leadership in the international monetary system and the concurrent decline in the US dollar, which pushed up the DM and disrupted European currency relations. The European Monetary System (EMS), starting operations in 1979, was seen as a way to stabilize European exchange rates, and also to give a new impulse to European integration after a period of stagnation. Formally the Exchange Rate Mechanism (ERM) of the EMS was centred on the new European currency unit (ECU), which was designed as a basket of national currencies. Intervention obligations in defence of the currency bands were to be symmetric, i.e. undertaken by both the weak and the strong currencies. In practice the Bundesbank, hostile to external constraints on its monetary autonomy, had obtained assurance that it could suspend intervention if it was seriously to threaten domestic price stability in Germany. The UK remained outside the ERM until 1990.

In the early years of the EMS currency realignments were frequent and domestic policy choices seemed little constrained. The original plan of creating a common institution, the European Monetary Fund, two years on, was quietly dropped. After France abandoned the early socialist experiments of the first Mitterand government in favour of a *franc fort* policy in 1983, however, the EMS experienced a convergence of policies towards disinflation and the German stability standard. Consequently the frequency and size of realignments was reduced and from 1987 onwards the EMS operated as a quasi-fixed exchange rate regime, without parity changes until the crisis of 1992. Greater exchange rate stability was conducive to the leap of integration that the community took in the form of the single market programme to remove remaining barriers to trade and factor mobility by 1 January 1993.

After the "Eurosclerosis" of the early 1980s, the renewed integration momentum, the single market programme itself and the positive experience of the EMS provided the climate that led European leaders at the Hannover summit in 1988 to solicit a report on economic and monetary union. Similarly to the Werner Report, the report of the Delors Committe proposed to move to monetary union in three different stages. However, the dates and conditions of moving from one stage to the next were left open. Progress on monetary and economic convergence would have to move in parallel and a new institution, the European Central Bank, was to be installed in stage two but to take control over monetary policy only in stage three.

10.3. THE CASE FOR EMU

A fundamental condition for a successful EMU is that there must be a valid case for it, be it economic or political. This requires an examination of the main theoretical arguments as well as the motivations and objectives that policy-makers actually pronounce in support of the project. A separate issue is then whether the particular integration strategies chosen at Maastricht are appropriate in order to achieve the declared goals. We return to the earlier classification into domestic, European and external factors, each divided into economic and political considerations.

The Maastricht Treaty was the outcome of an intergovernmental conference, and it required ratification by each member state in order to come into force. It therefore seems sensible to assume, in line with the intergovernmental theorists, that the outcome must be in the (perceived) national self-interest of each individual country (or at least the respective governments). This, of course, follows from the assumption that actors (here the national goverments) are rational. However, the individual rationality assumption need not necessarily be applied to one issue in isolation, here with respect to monetary integration. The picture becomes more complex, and individual national "participation constraints" on EMU can be relaxed, once it is realized that EMU is part of a process of bargaining and cooperation across many issue areas and over time. Issue linkage means that sacrifices in one area can be compensated by concessions elsewhere and agreement to EMU be "bought" by side-payments, inside or outside the Maastricht Treaty. Repeated or continous interaction over time means that deviations from the short-term national self-interest could be compensated by future rewards and by the benefits of ongoing cooperation. This is where the logic of European integration as an institutionalized framework of cooperation could become important in its own right.

Moreover, the rational response of each individual country to the EMU project is not independent of the strategies of the partner countries. For example, a country that has no intrinsic interest or would even like to prevent EMU might nevertheless want to join EMU if the latter would go ahead regardless. This also points to the importance of the appropriate reference scenario in evaluting national (or European) costs and benefits of EMU, which in turn depends on countries' (individual and collective) strategies in the absence of EMU, and might look quite different from the *status quo*. For example, non-EMU might lead to an extended DM-zone and/or to the unravelling of the single market. Finally, external developments will impact on both the national and the European levels.

10.3.1. THE NATIONAL CASE FOR EMU

With the above qualifications in mind, the theory of optimum currency areas (OCAs) identifies the economic costs and benefits of forming a monetary union between two countries.[2] The benefits come in the form of reduced transaction costs and the elimi-

---

[2] See Tavlas (1993) or De Grauwe (1994a) for an overview of the OCA literature.

nation of exchange rate uncertainty, which is expected to facilitate trade, even though the evidence for this is mixed (Eichengreen 1993, p. 1327). The costs arise from the loss of the exchange rate (and national monetary policy) as a policy instrument. The size of this loss depends on how important this policy instrument was in the first place. This in turn is a function of: (1) the extent of country-specific shocks that call for an autonomous policy response; (2) the extent to which price-wage rigidities or limited factor mobility inhibit a swift market response to any such shocks and therefore may require policy intervention; (3) the extent to which national monetary or exchange rate policies are more effective than alternative policy instruments still available under monetary union, namely stabilization via national fiscal policies.

Most empirical studies have found the European Union an unlikely OCA, except perhaps for an inner core of countries (e.g. Bayoumi and Eichengreen, 1993). If shocks and national economic conditions continue to differ significantly within EMU, transferring monetary sovereignty to the European level will be costly to individual countries. Economists have therefore often concluded that EMU must be driven by political and not economic forces (Frieden and Eichengreen 1994), and/or that further economic convergence is required. However, there is a second strand of literature in economics which turns the OCA argument on its head: the loss, or rather the delegation, of monetary sovereignty can be beneficial, if politicians are prone to abuse it for short-term (employment, electoral) advantages to the detriment of price stabilility.[3] An independent central bank, such as the Bundesbank in Germany, free from political control, would be better placed to achieve low inflation. Therefore, the transfer of national sovereignty to the ECB could be a benefit to the extent that the quality and credibility of monetary policy, and price stability in particular, is improved with respect to national or alternative European arrangements, such as the EMS. However, if credibility is the sole or decisive national motivation, two puzzles remain. First, countries were quite reluctant to grant independence to their national central banks ahead of EMU. This underlines that building credible institutions may be perceived as a costly or risky process. This in turn raises the second question of why the same countries were quite happy to replace a credible existing and proven central bank, the Bundesbank, with an untested new European institution at the helm of European monetary policy.

The arguments from OCA theory and the credibility literature do not appear to be convincing explanations for EMU, at least if each is taken by itself. However, the two together make more sense, once *de facto* and *de jure* sovereignty are distinguished and the *status quo ante* of the latter-day EMS is recalled. At the time of the inception of the Maastricht Treaty, national monetary autonomy had already been drastically reduced in practice by the commitment to maintain stable exchange rates against the D-mark, both as desirable in its own right and as a means to reduce inflation in the domestic economies. In essence the Bundesbank determined monetary policy conditions throughout the EMS. From this perspective the move to EMU would not repre-

---

[3] See Persson and Tabellini (1990) or Cukierman (1992) for comprehensive overviews of the "credibility" literature. Alesina and Summers (1993) present empirical evidence that central bank independence is associated with low inflation.

sent a further loss, but a partial recovery of *de facto* sovereignty to be shared more equally at the European level. In fact at the origin of the EMU project were complaints by the French and Italian governments about the asymmetry of the EMS. The task of EMU was therefore to restore symmetry to European monetary relations, without compromising credibility. Consequently the statutes of the European Central Bank were modelled closely on the Bundesbank's. This was also a condition for the participation of Germany, as the only country unambiguously ceding *de facto* monetary sovereignty in the process. The fundamental reason why a "European Bundesbank" was acceptable to Germany, and a "German-style independent ECB" not resisted by its European partners, was the convergence of policy-makers' preferences towards stability orientation during the course of the 1980s (Sandholtz 1993). Only sufficient and durable convergence of European policy preferences alongside economic convergence could provide solid foundations for a stable monetary union. Only if both conditions are fulfilled will the results of centralized European policy render the transfer of sovereignty acceptable in the absence of overriding political concerns.

Already the economic arguments point to sovereignty as the central issue at the heart of EMU, and of course money – the right to issue currency – is itself an important element and a potent symbol of national sovereignty. However, the puzzle of German motivation for EMU remains, at least as long as the latter-day EMS is accepted as a valid benchmark. The EMS provided exchange rate stability without seriously constraining the Bundesbank's monetary autonomy and it had promoted economic convergence across Europe. To explain German support for EMU, therefore, either the EMS had to be perceived as not viable in the long run and/or additional political motives had to play a role. In fact the principal political argument in favour of EMU comes from the long-standing German commitment to European integration as the post-War response to its history. From this perspective the loss of monetary sovereignty is seen as in Germany's own long-term interest, since in the absence of EMU Germany would become too powerful financially and economically and thereby provoke concerns and counter-alliances among its partners, a constant preoccupation of German diplomacy since the days of Bismarck, as stressed by former Chancellor Helmut Schmidt (1995). Therefore it is no coincidence that the German foreign minister reacted positively to the French and Italian concerns over German dominance within the EMS, by launching the idea of monetary union in the Genscher memorandum in February of 1988, to the dismay of the more sceptical finance ministry and the Bundesbank, which had not been consulted (see Gros and Thygesen 1992).

For the French government, EMU seemed the only viable strategy in order to break the Bundesbank's dominance and reach its long-standing strategic objective of economic parity with Germany as a necessary condition for sustaining France's political leadership. For all countries, external European commitment via EMU, via the latter-day EMS and via the single market project (Moravcsik 1991), also provided a useful device to pursue and legitimize domestic policy agendas, such as liberalization and reforms of the welfare state (Verdun 1995). This is the political equivalent of the economic credibility mechanism, where delegation of sovereignty can enhance discipline. A favourable economic climate at the end of the 1980s and strong domestic political positions of the major governments also contributed to the remarkable momentum that built up for EMU from the Hannover summit in 1988 until the Maastricht conference in 1991.

10.3.2. The European case for EMU

The European case for EMU, in line with neo-functionalist theories, interprets EMU as the implication of prior steps in the process of European integration. In particular, EMU is seen as the logical continuation of the EMS in securing exchange rate stability and promoting economic convergence. Moreover, as argued in the Commission's report "One Market, One Money" (Emerson *et al.* 1992), EMU is regarded as necessary to secure the full benefits of the Internal Market. The emphasis is on the incremental logic of the EMU project within the dynamics of European integration and on the spillovers from one policy area to the next, which pushes integration ahead almost automatically. The classical economic argument here is that the single market required a reasonable degree of exchange rate stability, but that the liberalization of capital flows, as part of the single market programme, would undermine the stability of the EMS. Therefore EMU, the centralization of monetary policy and permanent locking of exchange rates, would be the only way to secure three out of four policy objectives of the "inconsistent quartet" (Padoa-Schioppa 1988), i.e. the single market, capital mobility, exchange rate stability and autonomous monetary policy.

The argument that monetary union *per se* is necessary for the single market is not shared by most economists, but this may be partly due to the fact that the role of money in the economy still is not understood very well by economic theorists (Krugman 1992). On the other hand, widely fluctuating exchange rate are seen as a threat to the single market, if not for efficiency reasons then for their redistributive effects, which would threaten political support for it (Eichengreen and Ghironi 1995). This last concern has been borne out by calls for retaliatory measures in some countries as a response to "unfair competition" as a result of the undervalued Italian lira in the wake of the 1992–1993 EMS crises.

To understand the internal logic of the EMS, recall that, while designed as a symmetric system, it had evolved into an asymmetric system. This happened for two reasons: Germany provided the performance standard and partner countries willingly subordinated domestic monetary policy to German leadership in order to reduce domestic inflation by "importing credibility" via the exchange rate link (Giavazzi and Pagano 1988). Once disinflation was achieved and policies became more similar, German leadership would become both more difficult to sustain in terms of monetary control[4] and less acceptable economically and politically to partner countries. Since Germany lacked the economic size and political strength (and will) to function as a natural hegemon in the EMS in the way the US dominated the Bretton Woods System, systemic stability would therefore require European monetary policy to be

---

[4] Domestic monetary control becomes more difficult as currencies become closer substitutes in the presence of capital mobility.

managed jointly in the longer run. Germany's *de facto* dominant position in European monetary affairs, moreover, was in line neither with the logic of European integration as a community of equals nor with Germany's long-term foreign policy goals, despite its economic usefulness during the 1980s. Thus EMU represents the attempt to recover the political ambition of symmetry in European monetary affairs, by replacing the Bundesbank with a European Central Bank at the heart of the system.

The second argument for EMU as a logical, incremental extension of the EMS is that since 1987 the EMS had already operated as a "quasi-EMU". Policy-makers, perhaps prematurely, no longer made use of the instrument of exchange rate adjustments, but they were still paying a price in the form of interest rate differentials with respect to the D-mark, for an option that they no longer wanted to exercise anyway. In this perspective EMU would simply make the existing *de facto* exchange rate commitment fully credible, in what appeared to be an innocuous final, primarily technical, step at the end of the convergence process of the 1980s.

The regained momentum of European integration in the wake of the single market programme, together with the success of the EMS and a favourable economic climate, provided a fertile ground for the idea of European Monetary Union. For the political dynamics of EMU the active role of the European Commission and the European commitment of national leaders, Kohl and Mitterand in particular, was important. External developments, to which we turn next, reinforced the integrationist momentum of the late 1980s.

10.3.3. EMU as a response to global change

Whether EMU was born primarily out of domestic exigencies or out of the inner logic of European integration, policy-makers' choices were also shaped by external factors. These mainly regarded international monetary relations, increased competition in the global economy, and the new geopolitical situation after the end of the Cold War.

As stressed in section 10.2, the inception of the EMS had been in large part a response to instability in the international monetary system exacerbated by the demise of Bretton Woods and the weakness of the US dollar. Intra-European currency stability, however, continued to be affected by the substantial variations of the value of the dollar throughout the 1980s and 1990s. In particular, a weakening dollar, translating into an appreciation of the D-mark, repeatedly threatened exchange rate stability inside the EMS and also contributed to the near-lethal crises of 1992–1993. Efforts to stabilize the dollar, e.g. via the Louvre and Plaza accords in the 1980s, had proved short-lived. Therefore EMU was perceived as the only durable instrument to coordinate monetary policy and secure exchange rate stability within Europe and at the same time to increase Europe's weight and thereby the symmetry and stability of the international monetary system. This would entail sharing the burden and the privileges of the status of the D-mark as the world's second most important reserve currency. However, the Euro will not inherit the D-mark's reputation and status automatically and the ambition to rival the dollar on the international scene over the longer term will depend on the internal strength and stability of EMU.

The second important international development affecting the dynamics of EMU was the end of the Cold War. At the time of the fall of the Berlin wall in November 1989 discussion of EMU was already under way, but the ensuing reunification of Germany in particular helped to accelerate the drive to EMU. Monetary union was seen by Germany itself, as well as by its European partners, as desirable in order to lock the larger Germany firmly into the European construction. German unification presented a "window of opportunity" (Andrews 1993), where Germany was particularly susceptible to deeper European integration and more willing to make concessions, both *per se* and/or as an implicit *quid pro quo* for European support for reunification. In terms of the changed geopolitical situation, the end of bipolarism also led to calls for a stronger European political and defence identity. The main external challenge, however, arose from the prospective Eastern enlargement of the Union. Here, the effect on the momentum for EMU was ambiguous. On the one hand, keeping the integration momentum by further deepening the Union was seen as a precondition for meeting future challenges. On the other, such deepening, and EMU in particular, was perceived as a potential obstacle to widening and an early Eastern enlargement, which called for a looser and more flexible form of integration. Negative effects were also to arise from the fallout of German monetary union in 1990, which proved a heavy and persistent financial burden, threatened German economic stability and contributed to policy conflicts within the EMS culminating in the currency crises of 1992–1993.

The third external stimulus for EMU can be attributed to globalization and intensified competition in the global economy. This favoured (or necessitated) an increasing market orientation of policies from the 1980s onwards, as evidenced also in the wave of deregulation and liberalization effected by the Single Market programme. Europe's relatively poor growth and employment record nurtured the conviction that reforms were necessary and that the new external competitive challenges would require a response at the European level, rather than merely the national level, as increasing economic interdependence undermined the effectiveness of national policymaking (Frieden 1991). The increased mobility of capital and the greater power of international financial markets were seen to render capital controls, which had been in place in a number of EMS countries until the late 1980s, both anachronistic and ineffective. Moreover, the discipline imposed by financial markets was perceived to limit the room for manouvre of national policies, in particular by punishing deviations from sound budget policy and price stability. EMU in this perspective was seen as a mechanism to achieve the required macroeconomic stability, based on what was regarded as a successful German model. Secondly, monetary unification was seen as a device to regain some of the *de facto* sovereignty that had been eroded by financial markets. Again, as for the national and European motivation for EMU, the issue of sovereignty, both economic and political, emerges as the central theme.

10.4. THE METHODS OF INTEGRATION IN THE MAASTRICHT TREATY

After the overview of the principal motives behind Europe's drive for EMU, this section examines the strategies that the Maastricht Treaty employs in order to realize those objectives.[5] The distinction made in section 10.1 between bottom-up and top-down approaches to integration has two dimensions. One regards who is the *agent of change*, i.e. whether national policies and market forces or whether common institutions are the driving force of integration and the decisive locus of sovereignty. The second aspect concerns the time dimension, i.e. the choice between gradualism and "cold turkey", an evolutionary approach versus a sudden shift in regime. Each transition strategy carries costs and benefits. Decentralized policy-making, in line with the subsidiarity principle, will tend to be more responsive to local information, conditions and preferences. Competition between policy systems should be more likely to produce efficient outcomes. Centralized policy, on the other hand, could solve coordination problems more effectively, i.e. achieve and enforce common interests that could be lost if decisions were left to national governments or market forces. As regards the time dimension, in general any required adjustment is likely to be costly (but so is non-adjustment in a changing world). Gradual change spreads these costs more evenly over time and allows for a learning period, which should help minimize uncertainty and the risks of mistakes. "Cold turkey", on the other hand, avoids the credibility problems of a drawn-out transition period, which could lead agents to doubt whether announced plans will actually be carried out and therefore postpone adjustment. Coordination and credibility issues are essential to understand the Maastricht transition strategy, for each policy area in isolation as well as across policy areas. Both problems are again intimately linked to the question of sovereignty, i.e. the extent to which decision-making can be pooled and enforced.

10.4.1. Monetary union

With respect to the final framework of monetary policy within EMU, a clearly supranational top-down set-up, as already proposed by the Delors committee, prevailed over bottom-up alternatives. Thus the Maastricht Treaty chose to create a new integrated monetary system rather than merely linking existing national systems via fixed exchange rates or having national currencies, or a hardened ECU alongside national currencies, compete, as advocated by the UK. However, the Treaty prescribes a twofold transfer of monetary sovereignty, from the national to the European level and from governments to an independent central bank.

The double transfer of sovereignty is more ambiguous with regard to the external dimension of monetary policy, i.e. exchange rate policy. According to Article 109 of the Treaty any participation of the Euro in any international exchange rate system requires the unanimous decision of the Council, while general orientations for exchange rate policies can be passed by qualified majority, but must not compromise the ECB's commitment to price stability. Consultation with the Commission and/or the ECB is also foreseen for any international agreements on monetary or exchange rate matters, where again the final decision is taken by qualified majority in the Council. Article 109c creates the Economic and Finance Committee composed of representa-

---

[5]   See Kenen (1995) and Bini-Smaghi *et al.* (1994) for more details.

tives from the ECB, the Commission and national governments, as an advisory body to the Council of Ministers. It is not clear from the Treaty how countries in the Euro area will be represented in the international arena, e.g. the G-7 meetings, and how a unified policy could be achieved. Therefore exchange rate policy and the Euro's role in the world monetary system are likely to become a testing ground for *de facto* ECB independence and the balance of power in the new institutional triangle formed between Frankfurt, Brussels and national capitals.

With respect to the transition strategy in the monetary field the Treaty envisages the realization of EMU in three stages, characterized by increased policy convergence and coordination in the framework of the EMS. Stage 1 of EMU was in effect from 1 July 1990 after the lifting of remaining capital controls; stage 2 started on 1 January 1994 with the creation of the European Monetary Institute (EMI). The existence of several transitional stages points to a gradualist strategy. However, the fact that the passage to all three stages, including the final 1999 deadline for stage 3, was fixed as political and institutional decisions is a clear indication of a top-down strategy. Moreover, the decisive transfer of sovereignty to the ECB only happens at the beginning of stage 3, so that the *de jure* regime change is sudden and not evolutionary. In contrast with the recommendations of the Delors Committee, the ECB as a supranational agent of change was not already put in place in stage 2. The compromise found between the institutionalist and the behaviouralist camps in the Maastricht negotiations consisted in the creation of the EMI, which however was endowed with only weak advisory functions and the technical preparations for EMU. Institutionally, therefore, the EMI represents little more than an upgraded committee of national central bank governors.

The decisive argument against gradualism, advanced in particular by the Bundesbank, was the "indivisibility of monetary policy", i.e. the notion that the responsibility for monetary policy had to be assigned clearly to avoid confusion and grey areas. This was seen to preclude an evolutionary approach to monetary integration, where the ECB would have gradually taken over monetary coordination and control in stage 2. Therefore the locus of sovereignty remains national throughout the transition, with the important constraint of the Treaty deadlines, in particular the setting of 1999 as the latest possible date for the transition to stage 3. This automaticity in the Treaty is a crucial supranational element, since countries qualifying for stage 3 are obliged to join (except in the cases of the Danish and UK opt-outs) and the assessment of who qualifies is taken by qualified majority by the Council. This precludes national vetos and, at least on paper, could force countries to join against their will. During the Maastricht negotiations the UK and Germany were against setting firm deadlines and in particular advocated unanimity for the decision to proceed to stage 3. In fact the early Dutch draft of the Treaty (the "Maas proposal", later withdrawn) had contained a "generalized opt-out", i.e. it left the decision to join EMU to the individual countries. The automaticity of EMU in 1999 was a last-minute concession by German Chancellor Kohl to his French and Italian counterparts, Mitterrand and Andreotti, and a cause of surprise and dismay to the German delegation (Bini-Smaghi *et al.* 1994). However, the Maastricht ruling of the German constitutional court of 12 October 1993 argued that the automaticity of the Treaty was not legally binding in the case of violations of a strict interpretation of the entry conditions.

10.4.2. Economic and Monetary Union

The Hannover summit in 1988, which instituted the Delors Committee, described its objective as "Economic and Monetary Union", reflecting the principle of "parallelism" between monetary and economic integration. The term "Economic Union" is not very precise and is usually seen to comprise a customs union, a common internal market and, perhaps, the integration or coordination of further areas of economic policy-making. Again, one can distinguish *de facto* convergence and integration of economies as opposed to common institutional arrangements. The European Internal Market, formally in effect since 1993, represents a supranational market order in important respects, in particular via the expansion of majority voting in a number of policy areas. Its integration strategy, however, is largely inspired by a bottom-up philosophy. Unlike the earlier top-down approach of harmonizing rules and standards, the internal market programme was based on the principle of mutual recognition of existing national regulation, thereby encouraging competition between national regulatory systems and the operation of market forces, supplemented by successive top-down moves towards liberalization and deregulation in specific areas.

The intellectual climate that favoured a more market-based approach to economic integration, in particular reduced confidence in the role of the state in the economy, helps explain why economic policy is much less centralized in the Maastricht design than under the Werner plan. In the 1960s and 1970s it was believed that monetary union required a fairly comprehensive centralization of economic governance, in particular of fiscal policy, which is also one suggestion of the theory of optimal currency areas mentioned in section 10.3. In the Maastricht design (arts 102-104c), by contrast, responsibility for economic policy remains firmly with national governments and the EU budget will remain much too small for any macroeconomic stabilization function.

In contrast to monetary policy, a substantial transfer of sovereignty in other areas of economic policy was seen as a politically unacceptable erosion of the nation state. It was regarded as undesirable by those concerned that anything like a "European economic government" could threaten the position and independence of the ECB or lead to a transfer union with substantial financial redistribution. It was regarded as unnecessary, in the behaviouralist thinking, to the extent that the decentralized pursuit of similar policy objectives combined with market pressures and a strong ECB would lead to similar results in any event. Rather than being concerned about building an effective common economic policy capacity at the European level, the Treaty puts restrictions on national fiscal policies, recently strengthened by the "pact for stability and growth" agreed at the Dublin summit[6] in December 1996. In the domain of fiscal policy, "negative" integration, in the form of constraints and sanctions for undisciplined national budget policies (the "excessive deficit procedure" of art 104c, the

---

[6]   See *Financial Times*, "Germany Pushes EU into Tough Pact over Euro", 14–15 Dec. 1996, p. 1.

prohibition of monetary financing in art 104a and the "no bail-out clause" of art 104b), takes precedence over "positive integration", i.e. the effective pooling and joint exercise of sovereignty at the European level. While Article 103 of the Treaty calls for the coordination of economic policies to be regarded as a matter of common interest, Council decisions in this area will not be legally binding on national governments.

The unbalanced institutional structure of EMU, which centralizes policy only in the monetary field, not in other areas of economic policies, could lead to potential coordination problems both within these other policy areas, e.g. national fiscal policies, and between supranational monetary policy and (national) economic policies. While the notion of central bank independence implies that monetary policy should be set autonomously and therefore not be explicitly coordinated with other policy, in practice the success of central bank independence in achieving low inflation depends on the degree of *implicit* coordination in the economy, i.e. the degree to which economic actors, fiscal authorities and wage-setters in particular, accept the central bank's policy leadership and adapt their behaviour accordingly. The risk of insufficient implicit coordination, i.e. an ECB independent but left "alone" in promoting price stability, may lead to conflicts and economic instability in EMU (Jones and McNamara 1996).

The classic methodological debate over EMU concerns the transition strategy, i.e. the sequencing of economic convergence and monetary union. Going back to the discussions surrounding the Werner Report, the bottom-up camp ("economists") held that economic convergence must precede monetary integration in order for the latter to be stable and sustainable. Therefore moves towards EMU had to be made conditional on economic performance. The top-down ("monetarist") argument, on the contrary, saw monetary union as the institutional instrument in order to induce economic convergence, which would not be (easily, or at all) achievable otherwise. Therefore, definite deadlines and institutional reforms should drive the integration process. The two views on the preferable approach to monetary union also correspond to conflicting national economic interests in the EMU process. Countries with high domestic monetary credibility fear that premature unification risks economic instability and higher inflation, while low-credibility countries prefer early and unconditional EMU because it would make convergence easier to achieve.[7]

With respect to the crucial transition to stage 3 of EMU, the Maastricht provisions (arts 109l–109m) represent a compromise between the two positions. There is a definite deadline by which EMU will take off, but participation of individual countries depends on the fulfilment of quantified "convergence criteria" (art 109j) concerning price stability, interest and exchange rates as well as government debt and deficits, which are specified in a separate protocol to the Treaty. This peculiar construction presents a dilemma in the event that too few countries should satisfy the entry conditions to form an economically meaningful monetary union in 1999. In this case a

---

[7] Garrett (1993) confirms that Germany, supported by Benelux and Denmark, pushed for "convergence first" to ensure a "hard" EMU, whereas for other countries the primary objective was to soften and transform the EMS into a cooperative EMU sooner rather than later (Sandholtz 1993).

conflict between the state-contingency (i.e. satisfying the criteria) and the time-contingency (i.e. the deadline) in the Treaty arises. The criteria have attracted criticism by economists because of the arbitrary nature of the numerical values chosen for the fiscal criteria (Buiter *et al.* 1993) and because the other (nominal) criteria would be automatically satisfied after the regime shift of EMU, but hard and costly to fulfil in advance for countries with low domestic credibility (De Grauwe 1994b). Moreover, the criteria had little to do with the conditions identified by the theory of optimum currency areas, such as factor mobility, price/wage flexibility and trade integration.

As argued in Winkler (1995, 1996a), all the criteria can be interpreted as indicators of "stability culture", and by abiding by the criteria ahead of EMU countries are asked to demonstrate their willingness and ability to sustain stability-oriented policies, which will also be required for a successful EMU. Moreover, by making entry conditional on satisfying the criteria, the Maastricht Treaty also provides an extra incentive for domestic policy-makers to direct their efforts in the desired direction (Winkler 1996b, 1997). Finally, the criteria are best understood as an "incomplete contract", i.e. as imperfect proxies for stability orientation, which are not to be applied mechanistically, but allow room for interpretation by the Council, which decides by qualified majority on the basis of convergence reports prepared by the Commission and the EMI. Nevertheless, the criteria and their interpretation remain the most contentious element of the Maastricht Treaty (De Grauwe 1996, Artis 1996). In the controversy on the application of the criteria and their implication for size, starting date and initial conditions of EMU, the deeper conflicts between countries that fear to lose and those that stand to gain most from the transfer of monetary sovereignty resurface (Alesina and Grilli 1993).

10.4.3. EMU and Political Union

The concept of Political Union is even more vague than that of economic union (Gros 1996). It is, however, relevant for EMU for a number of reasons. First, the original German position ahead of Maastricht posited a *junctim*, i.e. "no Monetary Union without Political Union" (Woolley 1994). The link between the two has repeatedly been stressed also by the Bundesbank. Second, at Maastricht there were two separate intergovernmental conferences, one on EMU and one on Political Union. Third, the economic benefits of EMU are often regarded as small (if not negative) and therefore monetary union is regarded as a primarily political objective. Fourth, European integration, from its very beginnings in the European Coal and Steel Community, has always been a dialectic process between wider political ambitions and concrete economic progress.

Two principal aspects of Political Union can be distinguished. First, the material aspect, i.e. the extension of European integration to classical prerogatives of the nation state, such as foreign policy, defence and internal security. Second, the development of the Union's institutions in terms of their democratic legitimacy, accountability and effectiveness. Progress on both counts has been very limited both at Maastricht and at the subsequent intergovernmental review conference concluded at

Amsterdam ("Maastricht II") despite considerable pressure for reforms in order to begin enlargement negotiations with Eastern European countries. In fact the Maastricht Treaty introduced a "three pillar" structure, in which foreign and security policy as well as internal policies are kept outside the existing legal Community framework that comprises the Single Market and also the provisions for EMU. Thus the policy areas most pertinent to Political Union are explicitly based on intergovernmental cooperation rather than common institutions or qualified majority voting. In these areas national governments were not willing to let common purposes override national interests.

Therefore the Maastricht construction is characterized by two imbalances: between Political Union and EMU, and between Economic and Monetary Union. However, a stable EMU requires a broad consensus among economic and political actors on economic policy objectives, especially price stability. It also requires legitimacy and public support for its institutions, the ECB in particular, in enforcing a common policy. The latter is particularly important because of the double transfer of monetary sovereignty to an independent and European central bank, removed from political control at both the national and European level. Progress on Political Union would therefore be important to the extent that it enhances the legitimacy of European decision-making. Moreover, it would increase the stock of shared interests and the effectiveness of common institutions in enforcing common policies and in managing policy conflict. This is of *economic* importance if inflation depends on the degree of (political, distributional, regional, social) conflict in a society as well as on the degree of overall institutional instability (Grilli *et al.* 1991). It may be *politically* necessary in order to strengthen commitment to the irreversibility of EMU and therefore the latter's ability to withstand policy conflicts in the future. Historical experience suggests that monetary unions have survived only in the presence of strong political commitment (Cohen 1993, Theurl 1992), and the fact that currency areas and political jurisdictions tend to coincide confirms the view that money indeed is at the core of national sovereignty.

10.5. CONCLUSIONS AND OUTLOOK

This chapter has examined the logic of the Maastricht design for European Monetary Union. The motivation for EMU was driven by a combination of domestic objectives, the internal logic of the European integration process and external factors. The crucial precondition for EMU was the convergence of national objectives. The decisive momentum that built up during 1988–1991 was primarily a response to the internal dynamics of integration, the success of the EMS and the implications of the Internal Market programme in particular, and to external challenges from crumbling "walls" shaking up both global geopolitics and the global economy. Most of the arguments for EMU, whether domestic, European or external, whether economic or political, boil down to the issue of sovereignty, i.e. the delegation and sharing of decision rights and *de facto* power to implement policy objectives in the global economy.

The integration strategy of the Maastricht Treaty on EMU adopts a clear top-down approach, i.e. a genuine supranational institutional set-up, for monetary policy in stage 3 of EMU. This contrasts with a prevalence of bottom-up, intergovernmental elements with respect to Economic and Political Union as well as with respect to the transition period in stage 2. These asymmetries of integration reflect conflicting interests with respect to the *locus* of sovereignty. In particular, countries other than Germany had little *de facto* sovereignty to lose by signing up for EMU: on the contrary. For Germany, the transfer of sovereignty was acceptable, perhaps even desirable, in the larger (political) context of European integration, provided that the European Central Bank was independent from political interference and that the Bundesbank retained control of monetary policy in the transition process.

Monetary unification, far from being a purely technical step, represents a qualitative leap in European integration. By transferring a core element of national sovereignty to a new European institution, the Maastricht Treaty may turn out to be "a treaty too far". By not achieving a more balanced and comprehensive European polity, it may at the same time be "a treaty not far enough". The key question regarding the stability of EMU and its impact on European integration is whether the isolated double transfer of monetary sovereignty will be acceptable and sufficient in the long run. There are three basic possible scenarios for the internal (and therefore external) stability of EMU in the light of the integration strategy analysed in this chapter.

Under the first scenario, different national economic priorities and policy conflicts quickly emerge within EMU and the ECB runs into a crisis of legitimacy. From the point of view of national policy-makers the independent European Central Bank makes for an almost ideal scapegoat. Rather than promoting European unity, EMU becomes a recipe for conflict, with negative consequences for the stability of its currency and the process of European integration in general. In this respect the lack of public support for EMU bodes ill for the future, signalling that Europe may not be ready for Maastricht politically. European integration may have peaked, and Europe may recede to looser and more flexible forms of cooperation in the future.

In the second scenario Maastricht represents a stable arrangement with the management of the currency supranational and "depoliticized", while the locus of remaining economic and political sovereignty remains essentially national. The single currency binds European economies and polities closer together. Market pressures, "peer pressure" and competition among national governments as well as common external challenges discipline and unify national responses. In the third scenario Maastricht represents an incomplete step in the ongoing process of European integration. The imbalances identified above come to the fore sooner or later and will lead to further steps of integration over time. In line with economic pressures, the need for coordination and decision-making at the European level increases in order to support and balance the role of the ECB. Likewise, the need for democratic legitimacy of European policy induces institutional steps towards greater Political Union over time.

The above presupposes that EMU will happen, that the Maastricht transition strategy will be effective, that it will employ the right mixture of top-down and bottom-up elements in balancing national interests and common purpose. The mix of integration strategies and the corresponding institutional set-up also determines the long-run stability of EMU and therefore its role in the world political economy. The main concerns emphasized in this chapter are, first, that the isolated double transfer of monetary sovereignty may not be a sufficient condition for producing economic stability. Just as in the German context, price stability in Europe will be the product of institutional cohesion, national solidarity and social harmony (Jones and McNamara 1996). Second, the required political legitimacy, responsibility and support for stability may be lost in the institutional "Bermuda triangle" between Brussels, Frankfurt and national capitals. The single European currency will be managed by a European institution but will reflect and interact primarily with national polities, national economic and political cultures and aspirations. The pooling of monetary sovereignty under EMU puts the theories of European integration, and the European construction itself, to the test. In the final analysis Europe's currency will be as strong as her people are united. Whether such unity would come as the result of common institutions, or whether common institutions should be the result of such unity, will continue to be debated whatever happens to EMU.

10.6. REFERENCES

Alesina, A. and V. Grilli (1993). "On the Feasibility of a One- or Multi-speed European Monetary Union". *Economics and Politics 5*, 145–159.

Alesina, A. and L. Summers (1993). "Central Bank Independence and Macroeconomic Performance: Some Comparative Evidence". *Journal of Money, Credit, and Banking 25*, 151–162.

Andrews, D. (1993). "The Global Origins of the Maastricht Treaty on EMU: Closing the Window of Opportunity". In: Cafruny, A. and G. Rosenthal (eds) *The State of the European Community: The Maastricht Debate and Beyond*. Boulder: Lynne Rienner Publishers.

Artis, M. (1996). "Alternative Transitions to EMU". *Economic Journal 106*, 1005–1015.

Bayoumi, T.A. and B. Eichengreen (1993). "Shocking Aspects of European Monetary Unification". In: Torres, F. and F. Giavazzi (eds) *Adjustment and Growth in the European Monetary Union*. Cambridge: Cambridge University Press.

Bini-Smaghi, L., T. Padoa-Schioppa and F. Papadia (1994). "The Transition to EMU in the Maastricht Treaty". *Essays in International Finance No. 194*, Princeton University.

Buiter, W.H., G. Corsetti and N. Roubini (1993). "Excessive Deficits: Sense and Nonsense in the Treaty of Maastricht". *Economic Policy 16*, April, 57–100

Cohen, B. (1993). "Beyond EMU: The Problem of Sustainability". *Economics and Politics 5*, 181–202.

Cukierman, A. (1992). *Central Bank Strategy, Credibility, and Independence: Theory and Evidence*. Cambridge, MA: MIT Press.

De Grauwe, P. (1994a). *The Economics of Monetary Integration*. Second revised edition, Oxford: Oxford University Press.

De Grauwe, P. (1994b). "Towards European Monetary Union without the EMS". *Economic Policy 18*, 149–174.

De Grauwe, P. (1996). "The Economics of Convergence: Towards Monetary Union in Europe". *Weltwirtschaftliches Archiv 132*, 1–27.

Eichengreen, B. (1993). "European Monetary Unification". *Journal of Economic Literature 31*, 1321–1357.

Eichengreen, B. and F. Ghironi (1995). "European Monetary Unification: the Challenges Ahead". *CEPR Working Paper 1217*.

Emerson, M. *et al.* (1992). *One Market, One Money*. Oxford: Oxford University Press.

Frieden, J. (1991). "Invested Interests: The Politics of National Economic Policies in a World of Global Finance". *International Organization 45*, 465–487.

Frieden, J. and B. Eichengreen (1994). "The Political Economy of European Monetary Unification: An Analytical Introduction". In: Frieden, J. and B. Eichengreen (eds) *The Political Economy of European*

Monetary Unification. Boulder: Westview Press; 1–23.

Garrett, G. (1993). "The Politics of Maastricht". *Economics and Politics 5*, 105–123.

Giavazzi, F. and M. Pagano (1988). "The Advantage of Tying One's Hands. EMS Discipline and Central Bank Credibility". *European Economic Review 32*, 1055–1075.

Grilli, V., D. Masciandro and G. Tabellini (1991). "Political and Monetary Institutions and Public Financial Policies in the Industrial Countries". *Economic Policy 14*, Oct., 341–392.

Gros, D. (1996). "Towards Economic and Monetary Union: Problems and Prospects". *CEPS Paper No. 65.*

Gros, D. and N. Thygesen (1992). *European Monetary Integration.* London: Longman.

Haas, E. (1958). *The Uniting of Europe: Political, Social and Economic Forces.* Stanford: Stanford University Press.

Jones, E. and K. McNamara (1996). "Germany's Monetary Role in Europe". *Occasional Paper European Studies Seminar Series No. 2*, The Johns Hopkins University Bologna Center.

Kenen, P. (1995). *Economic and Monetary Union in Europe: Moving beyond Maastricht.* Cambridge: Cambridge University Press.

Keohane, R. and J. Nye (1977). *Power and Interdependence.* Boston: Little Brown.

Krugman, P.R. (1992). "Policy Problems of a Monetary Union". In: *Currencies and Crises.* Cambridge, MA: MIT Press; 185–203.

Moravcsik, A. (1991). "Negotiating the Single European Act: National Interests and Conventional Statecraft in the European Community". *International Organization 45*, 19–45.

Moravcsik, A. (1993). "Preferences and Power in the European Community: A Liberal Intergovernmentalist Approach". *Journal of Common Market Studies 31*, 473–524.

Padoa-Schioppa, T. (1988). "The EMS: a Long Term View". In: Giavazzi, F., S. Micossi and M. Miller, (eds) *The European Monetary System.* Cambridge and New York: Cambridge University Press; 369–384.

Persson, T. and G. Tabellini (1990). *Macroeconomic Policy, Credibility and Politics.* Chur: Harwood Academic Publishers.

Sandholtz, W. (1993). "Choosing Union: Monetary Politics and Maastricht". *International Organization 47*, 1–39.

Schmidt, H. (1995). "Deutsches Störfeuer gegen Europa". *Die Zeit No. 40*, 6 October 1995, p. 1.

Schmitter, P. (1970). "A Revised Theory of Regional Integration". *International Organization 24*, 836–868.

Strange, S. (1988). *States and Markets: An Introduction to International Political Economy.* London: Francis Pinter.

Tavlas, G.S. (1993). "The 'New' Theory of Optimum Currency Areas". *The World Economy 16*, 663–685.

Theurl, T. (1992). *Eine Gemeinsame Währung für Europa.* Innsbruck: Österreichischer Studien Verlag.

Verdun, A. (1995). *Europe's Struggle with the Global Political Economy. A Study of How EMU is Perceived by Actors in the Policy-Making Process in Britain, France and Germany.* PhD dissertation, European University Institute: Florence.

Winkler, B. (1995). "Reputation for EMU – An Economic Defence of the Maastricht Criteria". *European University Institute Working Paper ECO 95/18.*

Winkler, B. (1996a). "Towards a Strategic View on EMU: A Critical Survey". *Journal of Public Policy 16*, 1–28.

Winkler, B. (1996b). "Is Maastricht a Good Contract?". *EIB Papers 1, Special Issue on EMU*, European Investment Bank, Luxembourg, 79–96.

Winkler, B. (1997). "Of Sticks and Carrots. Incentives and the Maastricht Road to EMU". *European University Institute Working Paper ECO 97/2.*

Woolley, J. (1994). "Linking Political and Monetary Union: The Maastricht Agenda and German Domestic Politics". In: Frieden, J. and B. Eichengreen (eds) *The Political Economy of European Monetary Unification.* Boulder: Westview Press; 67–86.

PART FOUR

INTERNATIONAL TRADE AND INDUSTRIAL POLICY

CHAPTER 11

The institutional challenges and paradoxes of EU governance in external trade: coping with the post-hegemonic trading system and the global economy[1]

Jens L. Mortensen

11.1. THE TROUBLESOME TRANSITION TOWARDS AN EU FOREIGN ECONOMIC POLICY

The EU is the most important market in the world economy. In 1996, Western Europe accounted for roughly 40 per cent of total world merchandise trade, and about 50 per cent of world trade in services (*WTO Focus* No. 18, 1997). External trade is of paramount importance to the health of the European economy and, by extension, the future of the European integration process. While the extra-EU trade balance has been positive for more than two years, intra-EU trade has slowed down significantly. Thus it has primarily been the external demand for EU products and services that has helped to sustain economic growth, output and employment in the EU in the mid-1990s. Europe is a *trading* bloc – not so much in the sense that it excludes foreign producers to a larger extent than other major markets as in the sense that it is, for better or worse, deeply interwoven into the global economy.

The EU faces a number of challenges with respect to its new role in the international political economy. The five chapters in Part IV of this book shed light on some of the institutional challenges that Brussels has come to encounter in the realm of its external trade policy, industrial policy, telecommunication policy, agricultural policy and energy policy. Some of these challenges stem in one way or another from wider contextual changes in the international political economy, such as "the decline of US hegemony", "the end of the Cold War" and "the process of globalization". Other challenges stem primarily from the European integration process itself. None the less, the common theme presented in this section on trade is the troublesome transition which the EU has come to experience as its external economic relations have shifted from traditional "trade policy" towards "foreign economic policy". The presence of third-country lobbyists and multinational corporations in the EU policy-making process has made globalization more visible (see Chapter 4). Severe tensions have been induced into EU trade politics by the creation of the World Trade Organization (WTO), and thus indirectly from the process of globalization itself (this chapter). Globalization has furthermore shaped the course of the internal liberalization process

---

[1] Some of the information in this paper is based on a series of interviews conducted in Brussels with DG I officials in mid-October 1996.

A. Cafruny and P. Peters (eds.), The Union and the World, 211–232

of the telecommunication sector (Chapter 15) and the restructuring of the Common Agricultural Policy (Chapter 14). It has meant that former internal policies have become integrated into the external agenda of the EU. Moreover, globalization has made the predominant mode of production in the European car industry outdated, and made a common EU policy a less obvious solution (Chapter 12). In their most abstract sense, these developments reflects the increasingly artificial distinction between the domestic and international spheres of economic relations: that is, how national authorities have lost control with the global flows of trade and investment (see e.g. Cerny 1996, Strange 1996), and how international trade issues have been integrated into the domestic political agenda (see Ruggie 1995). Moreover, as recently pointed out by numerous scholars, this also reflects the eroding distinction between traditional foreign policy, security policy and commercial policy (Smith 1994, Tooze 1994). The 1994 Energy Charter Treaty is an excellent illustration of the intertwined relationship between security and economic issues in the larger external agenda of the EU (Chapter 13). Trade policy has consequently grown into one of the most important foreign policy instruments in the 1990s. But these changes have also implied that the EU trade policy has come to reflect concerns other than those of purely commercial interests.

11.2. THE INSTITUTIONAL CAPACITY TO GOVERN EXTERNAL TRADE RELATIONS

The increasingly intangible web of "unchecked" economic cross-border activities has given rise to "the competitive state": the nation state as an active promoter of its favourable domestic investment climate at the expense of those of other states (Cerny 1995, p. 611). Consequently, neither international trade politics nor domestic economic policies can be separated from this global game of competition for valuable FDI. This fundamental political conflict has surfaced in the discourse of the international trade policy agenda as "unfair trade practices" and "social and environmental dumping". Within the EU, the institutional consequence of global liberalization process has been an "unchecked" expansion of the exclusive competence of the Commission in the trade policy area without the consent of the member states. The vast potential scope of the future WTO agenda necessitates a clarification of the Commission's exclusive competence to govern EU's external trade relations. The European Court of Justice's (ECJ) so-called WTO opinion in December 1996 attempted to solve the problem, yet its ruling was somewhat indecisive. This chapter will argue that the EU may lose its capacity to govern external trade matters altogether if no institutional solution to this problem is found. Moreover, as the very fate of the multilateral trade system depends on an active EU foreign economic policy, this problem is no longer an internal one. However, the transformation toward a more active foreign economic policy actor in Brussels is difficult. The paradox is that the establishment of stronger and more effective EU institutions may undermine the domestic support and political acceptance of a common EU trade policy altogether. A study of the Uruguay Round found that EU trade diplomacy proved to be most effective when the process was characterized by technocracy and non-transparency. It also found that the EU has great difficulties in dealing with politicized issues (Woolcock and Hodges 1996, pp. 24–25). The institutional capacity to act effectively in the international domain is inevitably linked to the capacity to solve internal struggles, as emphasized by the two-level game approach (Putnam 1988). The process offers a range of strategic opportunities to "the chief negotiator" to manipulate domestic settings, solve deadlocks, and promote particular substantial or institutional interests at home and abroad. Can the Commission be said to be "the chief negotiator" in Europe? How much room is allowed for the Commission to act as a self-interested actor and political entrepreneur? Has it grown into a cautious policy-innovator acting according to its own interests, values and norms? This chapter will argue that there are some difficulties in identifying "a chief negotiator" in Europe. Yet the metaphor of the two-level game is nevertheless of some use due to the complex and multilayered structure of the EU policy-making process.[2]

   This chapter will focus on the tensions and changes in the governance of the EU's external trade relations by the WTO, and attempt to generate insights into the broader institutional problems which the EU has come to encounter in this process. Specifically, it will address the question of what institutional challenges lie ahead for the development of a fully-fledged foreign economic policy actor in Brussels, outline the key features of the existing institutional framework of the EU external trade policy in terms of a "governance regime", and focus on some of the changes that occurred after the Maastricht treaty and the conclusion of the Uruguay Round. Finally, some observation of recent events in the multilateral trade diplomacy of the EU will set the stage for concluding remarks on what institutional improvements would be necessary for the development of an foreign economic policy, and why the transition will remain so troublesome.

11.3. THE DUAL CHALLENGE

The fundamental institutional challenge posed by the transition towards an EU foreign economic policy is *to acquire an internal structure which can minimize the risk of defection of the individual member states while maximizing its capacity to negotiate externally.* Yet it also implies that formerly distinct elements of national foreign policies must be coordinated in Brussels to a much larger extent than before, and that formerly distinct common policies have to be coordinated under the auspices of the external trade actors within the Commission itself. The transition concerns not only the mechanisms of effective governance in terms of negotiation capacity, but also the mechanisms of legitimate governance. Although the question of the democratic deficit in the realm of EU external relations cannot be omitted, it is not the primary concern of this chapter. Rather, the issue of effectiveness will mainly be addressed. The

---

[2] Some prefer to conceptualize the EU as a three-level game (Conybeam 1992, Moyer 1993). Others reject the notion of separated games altogether, and argue that the EU external trade policy is characterized by "continuous negotiations at Community level where policy determination and output constitute a most a seamless web and where the feedback between processes of internal bargaining and international interaction can be extremely difficult to disentangle" (Smith 1994, p. 463).

institutional dilemma stems in this respect from the simultaneous nature of external trade diplomacy and internal trade policy-making. Internal battles have external implications, and vice versa. Although the two dimensions of EU external trade governance are difficult to distinguish *empirically*, it is helpful to distinguish between them *analytically*, as follows.

- *Internal governance capacity* refers to the institutional structures of the internal EU governance regime. In this respect, the internal challenge is to develop an institutional structure which would be able to aggregate individual preferences effectively, strike internal bargains in a manner whereby its external negotiation capacity remained flexible and intact, and prevent violations of agreements concluded by the EU.

- *External governance capacity* refers to the institutional structures which would enable the EU to speak with a louder and more credible voice in international matters. It does not refer solely to the organizational capacity to conduct international negotiations. Post-hegemonic trade relations also require an institutional framework which could enhance "global leadership capacity" of the EU. In this respect, it asks whether there are possible institutional barriers which prevent the transformation from a *reactive* toward a *proactive* external trade policy in terms of visionary policy-innovation.

11.4. INSTITUTIONAL FRAMEWORK OF EU GOVERNANCE IN EXTERNAL TRADE

What are the instruments and institutions of EU governance in external trade relations? The usage of "EU governance" in this chapter suggests that institutions matter in their own right. Institutions not only provide a forum for negotiation, but in time they also shape the preferences and goals of the actors themselves. But there is little consensus in the literature as to exactly how institutions matter. One way of capturing the institutional dynamics of the EU process is to identify the different EU sub-systems of "governance regimes" (Bulmer 1995, p. 351). Each of those "governance regimes" is characterized by various institutions of governance (either supranational or intergovernmental), empowered with different sets of "governance instruments" (such as treaties, secondary EU legislation, jurisprudence or soft law), and endowed with a distinct organizational history and culture. These three distinct, yet interlinked, modes of EU governance will here serve as a conceptual framework for a description of the institutional characteristics of the EU's external trade policy.

- *Governance as provided by the Treaties:* The legislative framework of EU governance is laid down by the Treaties in which the formal decision-making arrangements and policy responsibilities are established. The Treaties provide the basic order of inter-institutional relations wherein the internal power balance between the intergovernmental and supranational institutions is clarified. In special circumstances, though, this balance may derive from other types of governance instruments such as the rulings of the ECJ.[3]

- *Governance as intra-institutional procedures and internal organization:* The operational and procedural set-up of the process as established by instruments of governance other than the treaties. Examples are the organizational set-up of the Commission and the decision-making practice in the Council of Ministers.
- *Governance as institutional norms:* Cross-cutting norms which affect inter- and intra-institutional relations in ways not provided for in the treaties or elsewhere. In particular, these could include organizational DG-specific norms, the ideas underpinning the work of the ECJ, or what has been termed the "EU policy style" – that is, the particular set of norms which shape the mode of interest mediation in the EU system.

11.5. THE PROVISIONS OF THE TREATIES FOR THE EC COMMON COMMERCIAL POLICY

The common commercial policy dates back to the original Treaty of Rome of 1957. But it was especially after a Court ruling in 1971, which affirmed the complete transfer of the rights and obligations of the member states in the GATT regime to the European level, that the external trade policy took the shape it has today. The basic provisions of the treaties which govern the EC common commercial policy are set out in arts 110–115 and 228.

Article 110 states that the objective of the EC common commercial policy is "*to contribute, in the common interest, to the harmonious development of world trade, the progressive abolition of restrictions on world trade and the lowering of customs barriers*". The legal basis for an EU external trade policy lies art 113 – probably the most frequently used article in the exercise of EU external relations (Macleod *et al.* 1996, p. 266). Firstly, it defines the principal policy instruments: the common customs tariff, export promotion measures, and trade protection policy instruments. Article 113 (1) states that the common commercial policy is to be based on "*uniform principles particularly in regard to tariff rates, the conclusion of tariff and trade agreements, the achievement of uniformity in measures of liberalization, export policies and measures to protect trade such as anti-dumping or subsidies*". Hence, the external tariff barriers surrounding the entire EU are to be fixed at one level, and the investigation and implementation of any trade protection measures against dumping practices and subsidized imports are to be carried out by the Commission – and not by individual member states – within the directives issued by the Council. Secondly, art 113 (3) set outs the procedures for the conduct of trade negotiations between the EU and third countries. The process of EU external trade policy-making is primarily a matter between the member states, which legitimize the policy through the decision-making processes in the Council, through the COREPER or in the article 113

---

[3] In the words of the ECJ in the ILO case (Opinion 2/91): "The exclusive or non-exclusive nature of the Community's competence does not solely flow from the Treaty but may also depend upon the scope of the measures which have been adopted by the Community institutions for the application of those provisions and which are of such a kind as to deprive the Member states of an area of competence which they were able to exercise previously on a transnational basis".

committee on one hand, and the Commission, which formulates, negotiates and oversees the implementation of the policy, on the other. It is possible to distinguish between four phases in the EU process: the policy formulation phase, the issuing of the mandate, the negotiation phase, and the ratification phase.

- *Policy formulation phase:* Whenever international agreements are to be negotiated, the Commission makes recommendations to the Council which will authorize the Commission to open the negotiations by issuing a mandate under the approval of the Council by qualified majority voting (QMV). The Commission alone has the right to initiate proposals and make recommendations as to whether the EU should enter into a particular negotiation. Some discretionary power is thus granted the Commission in the initial phase.

- *Issuing the mandate:* The ultimate responsibility lies with the Council of Ministers – usually the Council of Foreign Ministers, with the notable exception of the Council of Agricultural Ministers – which decides whether the EU will follow the recommendations of the Commission. The Council may decide to change, or even reject, the recommendations of the Commission.

- *Negotiation phase:* After the Council has issued the necessary mandate, the Commission becomes the sole negotiator, a uniquely strong supranational feature compared to other areas of EU external relations. None the less, art 113 requires that the conduct of these negotiations be monitored closely by a special committee appointed by the Council ("the article 113 committee"). Furthermore, the external activities of the Commission are to be conducted within the directives issued by the Council. The negotiation mandate may thus be modified by the article 113 committee if the matter is considered to be a minor technical one. If issues of greater political sensitivity are touched upon, the matter is instead referred to the Committee of Permanent Representatives (COREPER). Article 113 makes no provision for the Parliament to be involved in the implementation of an EC common commercial policy, nor are there any formal requirements for consultations with outside interest-groups or experts. The activities of the EU are thus governed primarily by institutional practices evolved from past experience (see below).

- *Endorsement and ratification:* Article 113 mandates the agreements to be endorsed by the General Affairs Council on behalf of the Member States by QMV. Agreements like GATT 1994 are subject to domestic ratification procedures if required by the respective national constitutions. Though usually a rubber stamping exercise, the ratification of the Uruguay Agreement was fiercely debated in some national parliaments just as it was the case in the US Congress.

11.6. PROBLEMS WITH ARTICLE 113: THE CONCEPT OF "MIXED AGREEMENTS"

One fundamental problem with art 113 is the non-exhaustive definition of "the EC common commercial policy" (MacLeod *et al.* 1996, p. 268; Devuyst 1995, p. 462). According to art 113 (6), such disagreements must be referred to the ECJ. However, the ECJ has left the precise scope of the common commercial policy deliberately open-ended in acknowledgement of the dynamic nature of international trade

(Opinion 1/94). The treaties are therefore not in themselves sufficient instruments of governance. Instead, it would probably be more correct to say that the precise scope of the EC common commercial policy has largely been defined at the international level, and then imported into EU legislation. The exclusive competence of the Commission has almost automatically broadened since the EC completed its first GATT agreement (the Dillion Round in 1960–1961) The international trade regime has throughout its existence continuously redefined the concept of international trade. The agenda has witnessed a shift from dealing solely with quantitative tariff barriers to the inclusion of non-tariff barriers such as subsidies, antidumping measures, preferential government purchasing policies following the Tokyo Round, and the inclusion of regulatory barriers to trade in services and structural barriers to market access in the Uruguay Round. The potential scope of the future WTO agenda is enormous. The possible inclusion of investment issues, competition, labour market relations and environmental policies into the sphere of exclusive Commission competence would in effect mean that increasingly important issues may bypass the intergovernmental level of decision-making in the EU, in effect rendering the art 228 limitations on exclusive EU competence obsolete. If a trade agreement includes non-commercial aspects, it is a "mixed agreement", arguably one of the most difficult features to grasp in EU external relations (MacLeod 1996, p. 142). It is a legal term intended to describe an agreement to which both the EU and the member states are parties, and whose subject matter is beyond the exclusive competence of either the EU or the member states. "Mixed agreements" require a number of different procedures, including consultation procedures with the European Parliament (EP) and unanimous decision-making in the Council. Equally importantly, the Commission cannot act as the sole negotiator. The Court has established a practice of emphasizing "the duty of close cooperation" in order to ensure consistency of the external activities of the EU as a whole. This "duty of close cooperation" is a fundamental feature of the legal basis of EU external relations. It is intended to ensure some degree of democratic legitimization in the external trade policy process. But it is also an extremely vague foundation to the development of an EU foreign economic policy – a policy area which by definition entails more than purely commercial matters.

11.7. INTRA-INSTITUTIONAL PROCEDURES AND INTERNAL ORGANIZATION OF THE EXTERNAL TRADE AREA: THE FRAGMENTED COMMISSION, AND VETO-POINTS IN THE COUNCIL

The internal and external governance capacity of the EU is derived from the treaties, but the organizational set-up of EU external trade relations has slowly evolved from past practices and experiences. Institutions learn – but institutions tend to reflect political battles of the past and project them into the future to the extent that some parts are "captured" by particular interests.

A number of anomalies in the operational set-up make the EU even more distinct from other international actors. The first concerns the fragmented organization of the Commission. The second concerns the decision-making procedures in the Council.

These two organizational anomalies have put severe constraints on the EU's crisis management capacity.

11.7.1. The fragmented Commission

The EU's external trade policy is coordinated and carried out by DG I in the Commission. Its organizational tasks include (1) *multilateral trade policy* (the WTO, ILO and OECD, among others); (2) *sectoral trade policies* in cooperation with other DGs (primarily textiles, steel, automobiles and high technology); (3) *support to European business* concerning access to foreign markets; and (4) *implementation of trade policy instruments* (such as anti-dumping and anti-subsidy measures). The DG I is the coordinating unit in the Commission, and thus not directly linked to specific issue areas. It is, however, in close contact with other DGs – especially DG III (industrial policy), DG IV (competetion policy), and DG VI (agriculture).

The policy formulation phase involves four stages:

(1) The preparation of specific draft recommendations by avarious DGs. This is when outside interests seek to influence EU policy through the notoriously complex network of formal and informal contacts between the DG officials and various lobbyists, experts or national representatives (see Mazey and Richardson 1993, Van Schendelen 1993)

(2) The specific draft recommendations are then coordinated in the DG I's inter-service working group.

(3) The DG I then formulates a common recommendation which circulates for comments throughout the entire Commission.

(4) The final recommendation returns to the inter-service working group for approval by simple majority before it finally is submitted to the Council.

The EU system is plagued by an institutional bias towards DGs acting on behalf of issue-specific interests *vis-à-vis* DG I which acts on behalf of the "Community" interest. One analysis of the Uruguay Round concluded that it was indeed very easy for the powerful DG VI (agriculture) to concentrate its resources on defending the CAP in the inter-service working group, and thereby influence the EU negotiating position from the very outset of the GATT negotiations (Moyer 1993, p. 99). DG I is at this stage preoccupied with coordinating the recommendations across a vast number of issue areas, and is not in the position to devote sufficient resources to fighting special interests in the policy formulation stage. Sectoral DGs may easily be captured by special interests that have managed to extend domestic "iron triangles" to the EU in this manner. DG officials are said to be in close – or even daily – contact with the representatives from the national ministries (Haynes 1993, p. 124). Much of the recent literature on EU policy-making has suggested that the distinction between supranational and intergovernmental levels of EU policy-making is blurred in reality. Firms and organized interests pursue a two-tier strategy designed to obtain influence simultaneously in Brussels and at home (Mazey and Richardson 1995, p. 354). Yet the almost symbiotic relationship between the national policy actors and EU officials, which has increasingly come to characterize many other areas of EU policy-making, seems not to have been fully extended to the external trade policy, as evident in its new market access strategy (Commission 1996b). Another study similarly observed that European firms prefer to lobby the national governments rather than at the EU level directly when it comes to trade policy (Murphy 1990, p. 127).

The negotiation phase starts after the mandate has been issued by the Council. It is the DG I that coordinates and conducts the actual negotiations. There is one notably exception to this: it has been the DG VI (agriculture) that has conducted negotiations in the agricultural sector. One study even concluded that "the organization with the strongest interests in maintaining the CAP is placed in the driver's seat of the actual conduct of the negotiations" (Moyer 1993, p. 103). Agriculture has enjoyed *de facto* veto power as the only sectoral interest in the EU. DG I's flexibility has furthermore been constrained by the direct presence of the GATT national delegations in Geneva. Moyer's study also pointed out that DG IV officials were able to work closely with national GATT delegations (i.e. representatives from national agricultural ministries). The DG I therefore had little knowledge of the actual negotiations on this crucial trade issue. Another problem has been that the successful EU trade diplomacy has undermined itself. The secrecy of high-level trade diplomacy has tended to leave the national GATT delegations in isolation, to the point when the working climate has deteriorated drastically. In the words of the former Italian Trade minister – and now General Secretary of the WTO – Renato Ruggiero: "The Commission was practically conducting the negotiations alone.... [The ministers'] only actual impact was to keep a rigorous watch on the Commission's respect for the negotiations' mandate. The Commission thought that...being alone would provide it with greater flexibility. But the result was quite the opposite" (Haynes 1993, pp. 124–125).

In fact, the institutional dilemma of the EU is precisely related to this observation. Effective trade diplomacy seems by its very nature to necessitate that negotiations are conducted in a non transparent manner. Yet the good diplomat will never obtain an outcome that is unacceptable to his own constituency. Moreover, it is crucial that the opposite party does not know exactly what is acceptable at home. The institutional anomalies of EU trade diplomacy tend to be prone to exactly such a situation: it is impossible to know what will be acceptable at home without opening up and putting possible gains in jeopardy.

11.7.2. The decision-making structure in the Council

The final recommendations of the Commission are discussed in the article 113 committee, where national civil servants evaluate the proposals together with the DG I, who represents the Commission. It reaches its conclusion by consensus. The recommendation is then sent to the COREPER, which screens the political aspects of the proposal before the recommendation is eventually subject to be decided upon in the Council. Here, one encounters another peculiarity of the EU external trade policy process: there is no separate Council for Trade Ministers. The different proposals are dealt with in the Council of Foreign Ministers, where the DG I represents the Commission. Again, there is one notable exception to this. It has been the Council of Agricultural Ministers that decides on matters in agricultural trade. Here, the Commission has been represented by DG VI. Whereas the DG VI can defend its institutional interests among like-minded agricultural ministers, the DG I has to defend its position all other areas of international trade in front of the EU foreign ministers who have several other – and perhaps more immediate – issues on their agenda. One could argue that Council must provide such veto-points as it is the only democratic institution in the EU trade policy process. But one could question whether these veto-points should be understood in terms of democratic legitimization. Some of these built-in veto-points have in the past served as institutional strongholds of defensive producer interests which were able to paralyse the entire EU system in a highly effective manner at the expense of broader commercial and consumer interests.

11.8. BY-PASSING INSTITUTIONAL DEADLOCKS: FAST-TRACK COUNCILS, STRATEGIC DIPLOMACY AND INSTITUTIONAL NORMS

After the above gloomy picture of the EU as a fragmented actor plagued by institutional inertia, it may strike one as a paradox that the EU is able to function at all. How are diverse interests like these reconciled in such a biased multilayered governance system ? There are three possible answers to this question.

11.8.1. Crisis-management and fast tracks

It must be remembered that the Council has managed to by-pass special interests and solved such deadlock situations in the past with the so-called "Jumbo Councils".[4] These meetings function as institutional mechanisms of crisis management in the EU. They enable substantial side-payments and issue linkages to be made in short time, and they break domestic deadlocks by putting special interests under intense pressure. Scholars have long argued that the EU needs something similar to a "fast-track process" in order to avoid too much political interference (Devuyst 1995, p. 452). The Jumbo Councils and the intensified Council monitoring of the final months of the GATT negotiations proved to be such a mechanism, even if they constrained the EU negotiators in Geneva even further (Devuyst 1995, p. 454). The formal requirement of QMV in matters of exclusive Commission competence has long been subject to a *de facto* consensus norm in the Council,[5] which can be traced back to the Luxembourg

---

[4] The consensus norm has rarely been broken in the Council. Prior to the Montreal meeting in 1988, Italy and Portugal decided to vote against the recommended EC negotiation position in the textiles sector – but the recommendations of the Commission were eventually approved by the qualified majority of the Council (Murphy 1990, p. 112). Portugal later received some concessions in the form of a trade adjustment assistance (Woolcock and Hodges 1996, p. 23).

[5] The Jumbo Council of 20 September 1993 was a dramatic meeting where the EU foreign ministers, trade ministers and agricultural ministers overcame the French resistance to the Blair House agreement by altering the Council's decision-making procedures regarding the use of safeguard and anti-dumping

Compromise of 1966. Yet, the negative impact of the consensus norm on the external governance capacity can be by-passed by Jumbo Councils – even if such meetings are ideal platforms for tactical "black-mail" between the Member States.

11.8.2. Tied hands as bargaining chips

From a two-level game perspective, it may even be advantageous for the EU to claim that its hands are tied at home in international negotiations. The DG I negotiators may not be entirely dissatisfied after all with the prominent position of agricultural interests within the system – even if it diminishes their control within the actual negotiations. It is obvious to the rest of the world that the EU is internally fragmented, and thus if a particular proposal would be rejected immediately, the bargaining power of the EU would consequently increase. The EU negotiator would be in a position to demand concessions on other issues in exchange for acceptance. This tactic may easily back-fire, however. It is just as plausible that the counterpart would also demand concessions in return for an improved offer to solve the deadlock. Some evidence indicates that the EU may easily be exploited as the scapegoat in international negotiations because of the complexity of the EU external trade policy. Studies of the Uruguay Round observed that the American negotiators took advantage of the EU's weaknesses in the early stages of the GATT agricultural negotiations in order to take the heat off the US in those areas in which it was under attack (see Moyer 1993, Paaul berg 1993 among others).

11.8.3. The existence of an "EU policy style"

The differences between various DGs, the EU and the national representatives may not be that significant after all. The EU machinery might work sufficiently fast due to the existence of a common set of values, shared world views, and institutional norms at the élite level. A growing body of literature has recently argued that EU governance is better characterized by an incremental "policy style" where conflicting interests throughout extensive and cross-cutting policy networks negotiate and solve problems prior to the formal decision-making process (Mazey and Richardson 1995, p. 342; see also Kassim 1994, Peterson 1995). Policy actors may have come to dominate particular policy arenas which may link formerly distinct issue-areas in a manner not entailed by any formal procedures or agreements. In daily routine matters, the relationship between the DG I and the article 113 Committee is more harmonious than formal institutional analysis suggests. The existence of shared norms and institutionalized ideas has made the EU governance capacity in trade matters more flexible and effective than one would otherwise expect. Although the Commission has been known for

---

measures. This change makes it impossible for the traditional free traders (UK, Germany, Netherlands and Denmark) to block decisions in the Council on retaliations against "unfair" trade practices: a reform which had been blocked by these countries for more than a year. French opposition was also softened by the fact that the French farmers had received an extra share of the CAP budget (Devuyst 1995, p. 457).

its self-assessment as "the conscience of the EC" (Bulmer 1995, p. 363), there are also vast differences in the ideas underpinning various sections of the Commission. For instance, DG I is usually seen as the diplomatic corps of the EU. Its role as coordinator has made DG I less associated with outside actors to the point where EU officials in DG I express concern about the lack of active participation from outside interests (see below). It is known for its pro-liberal stand on trade issues *vis-à-vis* particular interests, under the strong personal guidance of current Vice-President of the Commission, Sir Leon Brittan. DG VI, on the other hand, is directly linked to agricultural interests (see Chapter 14). DG VI owes its very existence to the CAP, and it is in its institutional interest to defend the CAP's viability. Nevertheless, the existence of an EU policy style suggests that underlying these differences is a shared value which could be termed "negotiated pragmatism"; a built-in preference for incremental policy solutions. Although these networks are primarily at work in "low politics", a similar pattern has expressed itself in the "high politics" of external trade negotiations. For instance, during the GATS negotiation, the EU managed to force the US into acceptance of a "managed approach" to market liberalization with a special committee appointed to consider the political implications of the process. This was in contrast to the US preference for unconditional and rapid liberalization of trade in services (Drake and Nicolaïdis 1992: 77). This has been interpreted as a less liberal position of the EU on the GATS issue (e.g. by Arnhild 1995). Yet liberalization of the service industry was nevertheless a top priority of the EU. It could equally be understood as the typical incrementalist policy response of the Commission in the face of the uncertainties and novelty of the GATS issue.

11.9. INTERNAL GOVERNANCE CAPACITY: POST-MAASTRICHT AND POST-URUGUAY CHANGES

The internal dimension of EU trade governance concerns the capacity of the EU to solve internal deadlocks and comply with its international obligations. What changes has the EC Common Commercial policy undergone in the 1990s? There have been externally induced changes following the Uruguay Agreement, and internally generated changes as a result of the Maastricht Treaty, the ECJ's WTO opinion.

11.9.1. The Maastricht Treaty

The common commercial policy has not been significantly affected by the Maastricht Treaty (TEU). It remains within the first pillar of the EU: the European Communities. The TEU brought about two changes. Firstly, article 113 used to allow the Member States the right to implement certain temporary safeguard measures themselves against alleged dumped or subsidized imports in cases of urgency. They then had to inform the Commission, which would subsequently carry out investigations on whether or not it could be established that European interests had suffered from third country protectionist trade practices. After the Maastricht Treaty, it is now solely the

Commission that may authorize the implementation of otherwise GATT-legitimate safeguard measures for a limited period (Macleod *et al.* 1996, p. 268). The Commission is now in a better position to coordinate the external trade activities of the entire EU. Secondly, the Maastricht Treaty clarified procedural requirements. Whereas the legal basis for external negotiations prior to the Maastricht Treaty could be found in article 113 or article 238, the TEU now sets out several possible procedures in article 228. The amendments do not affect the external trade policy, however. Yet, as argued above, it remains unclear from a legal perspective whether an agreement is subject to exclusive or shared competence. It depends largely on the subject matter (Macleod *et al.* 1996, p. 84). It is not difficult to imagine how complicated negotiations would be if the Commission had to ask the Court for an opinion on whether or not a particular matter could be considered "pure trade" or "mixed" prior to the opening of negotiations themselves. However, the problem has thus far been rather academic. The Commission has developed a sophisticated awareness of political sensitivities. The *de facto* consensus norm in the Council also minimizes the problem. Moreover, the Commission has developed a practice of consultations with the EP in external matters – including trade relations.[6]

11.9.2. The Uruguay Round Agreement

Firstly, the EC was never a "contracting party" in the old GATT regime, it only acted on behalf of its member states. The EU is now recognized as one of the original members of the WTO. The practical implications of this are limited, because it is the individual member state alone that has the right to vote in the WTO. Still, this provides the EU with 15 votes in the WTO instead of one. However, as the WTO prefers to make its decisions on a consensus basis – even though QMV decisions are possible in certain cases – the new formal status of the EU will probably have little effect on the EU trade policy or WTO rules. Secondly, the EU has started to bring its legislation into accordance with its new international obligations per the GATT 1994, GATS, TRIPS and other annexed agreements. Firstly, by January 1995, two regulations came into force with new guidelines for the use of anti-dumping and anti-subsidy measures (Regulations 382/96 and 3298/94). This meant that the use of safeguards in a number of situations was prohibited (export promotion, credit programmes and tax exemptions, among others) and a stricter set of time limits for investigations were established within the EU. However, such trade policy instruments are still legitimate in connection with pre-competitive R&D or environmental policies. Secondly, in 1994, the EU replaced a 1984 directive which had created the "New Community Policy Instrument" with the new "Trade Barrier Regulation" on the exercise of the Community rights under international trade law (Regulation 3286/94). It was the trade

---

[6] A code of conduct was formalized between the Commission and the EP regarding their institutional relationship in international negotiations in April 1995. It was agreed that the Commission would inform the relevant EP committees on draft recommendations and on progress in the negotiations and that EP members could be included as observers – although not as participants – in the EU negotiation delegations in the WTO (Macleod *et al.* 1996, p. 100).

policy reform that the French had demanded in return for their support for the Uruguay Round agreement (see footnote 4). It instituted a number of procedural changes regarding the investigations of complaints of unfair trade practices. The regulation intended to streamline and harmonize the procedures required to use trade defensive measures, and thus to make the EU a more effective actor in combating illegitimate trade practices. This more aggressive stance should be understood in the context of the overall EU response to the growth of aggressive unilateralism in American trade politics. But whereas the US has been criticized for ascribing to itself the role of both judge and jury (Bhagwati and Patrick 1990), the EU directives of 1984 and 1994 make clear that the EU will comply with its international obligations before acting unilaterally (Macleod 1996, p. 282). Thirdly, the new regulation gave – for the first time – rights for individual companies to take action through the Commission directly if they have reason to believe that their business activities in a non-member country are damaged or threatened by trade barriers. This could be the institutional response to a problem for which EU officials have expressed concern – the lack of information on the actual market conditions for European firms abroad. By asking the firms directly, it seems as though the Commission has tried to eliminate some of its dependence on national authorities.[7] The Commission has called for better working relations with national authorities – a possible indication of a lack of necessary resources within the Commission to keep itself up to date with the rapidly changing market conditions of a global economy. The increased coverage of international trade law has made this resource problem more apparent. This action could also be an indication of the bad working relations between the Commission and national trade authorities. Yet the Commission has been eager to stress that its new strategy would "not imply a transfer of responsibility from the Member States to the Community or vice versa in institutional terms ... [as] experience has shown that, in most cases, it is possible, through a pragmatic approach, to reach agreement with Member States about the common defence of their interest" (Commission 1996a, p. 9).

11.9.3. The WTO opinion

The third change concerns the internal power balance after the so-called WTO opinion, in which the ECJ attempted to solve the dispute over the scope of the Commission's exclusive competence to conclude the TRIPs and GATS agreement. The ECJ confirmed exclusive EC competence in connection with multilateral agreements on trade in goods, including agriculture, which had been contested by some member states during the negotiations. But perhaps more importantly, the ECJ stated that the EU and the member states had "joint competences" to negotiate and conclude the GATS and TRIPS agreements. It consequently called upon "the duty to cooperate" according to "the need for international unitary representation". It came as a genuine

---

[7] For instance, the Commission launched in connection with its "Market Access Strategy" an online market access database for European firms on the Internet, urging firms to inform the Commission directly about any difficulties they experienced abroad (Commission 1996a, p. 7).

surprise that the ECJ ruled against the Commission. The ECJ has long had the reputation of taking an pro-integration and expansionary – and thus supportive to the Commission – interpretation of the treaties (Weiler 1993, p. 419).[8] The Commission had argued that the coherence of the internal market was linked to the GATS, and that it could not remain inactive at the international stage in order to pursue that goal. But the ECJ ruled in its WTO opinion that it did not follow from the treaty provisions or from case law that the Commission had exclusive competence to conclude negotiations in areas other than trade in goods – regardless of whether this would have a negative impact on the Commission's capacity to conduct multilateral negotiations in the future.[9] The opinion has generated some uncertainty regarding the Commission's future role in the WTO. The risk of defection is more credible, and negotiations thus more difficult, when it is uncertain who has the mandate to negotiate. The EJC merely emphasized "the duty to cooperate". The significance of the WTO opinion goes far beyond trade policy. It may indicate a more cautious ECJ which will take the political climate into consideration to a much larger extent than it did in the early 1980s.

Hence, the WTO opinion raised serious doubts as to the capacity of the EU to act in a unified manner. The Commission has often referred to the disastrous working conditions in FAO, urging the Court to consider the importance of the WTO and emphasizing the compatibility between the goals of the WTO and the internal market. Prior to the ECJ opinion, the Commission attempted to establish an intergovernmental code of conduct whereby the dispute was to be solved at the Intergovernmental Conference (IGC) instead. This proved to be impossible. The Commission is currently trying to negotiate a new code of conduct with the Council. While a more pragmatic solution has been found in the day-to-day business in the WTO, the institutional issue remains open. Prior to the ISC meeting in Dublin in September 1996, the Irish Presidency presented four proposals[10] designed to enhance the EU's capacity to pursue "a coherent and effective external economic policy noting that the ever closer interlinkages between different aspects of trade have made this essential" (*Agence Europe* 29–30 July 1996, p. 5). These suggestions were later discussed at an informal Council meeting, yet the conclusion was quite negative (*Agence Europe* 7 Sept. 1996, p. 5). Some member states stated openly that they preferred to issue the Commission with detailed directives rather than expanding its exclusive competence a severe constraint on the Commission's negotiation capacity. The Commission, not surprisingly,

---

[8] The ECJ thus confirmed in 1975 the exclusive competence of the Commission to negotiate international agreements (Opinion 1/75 on an OECD agreement). It has taken an expansionary view on how external powers and exclusive competence can be derived from internal powers (Opinion 1/76 on navigation on the Rhine).

[9] In the words of the EC, the problems which "might arise...as regards to the coordination necessary to ensure unity of action...are of no relevance to the question of the division of powers" (Opinion 1/94, section 18).

[10] The four proposals were: (1) granting the Commission exclusive competence in the service and intellectual property area; (2) the Commission alone should speak on behalf of the member states in matters of shared competence but the positions adopted by the Commission should be subject to unanimous voting in the Council; (3) a better legal basis for the negotiation and conclusion of "horizontal agreements" with developing countries; (4) better capacity to act rapidly under particular circumstances when events require a "provisional" application of an agreement.

objected to this: it would in their own words be "very difficult...to negotiate without a certain margin of manoeuvre" (ibid.). A more permanent solution to the internal governance dispute is most likely to be found in connection with the conclusion of the ICG in 1997. Meanwhile, it seems as though the Commission has to manage its WTO affairs on an *ad hoc* basis instead of dedicating its resources toward pursuing a more coherent foreign economic policy of the EU as a whole.

11.10. EXTERNAL GOVERNANCE CAPACITY: COPING WITH THE WTO

Even if important procedural improvements have been undertaken in terms of strengthening the internal governance capacity of the EU in external trade matters, these improvements are limited to "old" trade issues. The uncertainty surrounding the future role of the Commission persists after the somewhat inconclusive WTO opinion. Has this uncertainty had an impact on the institutional capacity of the EU to function as an international actor? In other words, has it affected the EU's capacity to conduct WTO negotiations, pursue long-term objectives, and exert global leadership? The institutional abnormalities of the EU are no longer an internal problem. The EU policy statements and the conduct of its trade diplomacy affect the pace of global trade liberalization to a much larger extent than before. What consequences have the internal changes had on the external activities of the EU so far? The examples below indicate how the EU remains plagued by uncertainty about its new role, despite its far more aggressive-cum-proactive stance than earlier.

The EU has long resisted the development of a legalistic approach to international trade liberalization (Haynes 1993, p. 32). In 1993, however, the EU changed its position and openly accepted a more judicial dispute settlement system. It is not clear what caused this shift. It could indicate a more liberal-minded EU that prefers a strengthened WTO. It could also have been a mere instrumental shift in the overall EU strategy of containment of US aggressive unilateralism. Nevertheless, the EU has on numerous occasions emphasized how essential the strengthened enforcement mechanisms of the WTO are to world trade and European interests (*Europa Document* no. 1971, Commission 1996b, pp. 4–6). Thus far, the EU has made good use of the WTO dispute settlement system, and is currently involved in no fewer than 27 disputes out of a total of 83 cases in the WTO dispute settlement system – a figure surpassed only by the US. The EU received 11 complaints about alleged violations of its WTO commitments, and has put forward 16 complaints about possible unlawful discrimination against EU exports. The EU was initially encouraged by the rulings of the WTO. In one of its first rulings ever, the WTO Appeal body ruled in favour of the EU in a dispute regarding the trade-distorting domestic Japanese tax-system on imported alcoholic beverages from Europe: a recasting of an identical GATT dispute which remained unsolved for more than a decade. Another success story was the change in Japanese intellectual property law on sound recordings which enabled the European music industry to claim royalties for recordings made before 1971. Such lost royalties are estimated to amount to more than $500 million a year (*Economist*, 17 Feb. 1996). However, not all WTO disputes are likely to turn out favourably.

Three of the most controversial WTO cases are briefly summarized below.

11.10.1. The WTO case of the EU import banana regime

The preferential trade arrangement between the EU and former European colonies caused the US, Ecuador, Honduras and Guatemala to issue a complaint alleging that the EU's regime for importation, sale and distribution of bananas was inconsistent with its WTO obligations. A panel, established on 8 May 1996, issued its first report on 22 May 1997. It found that the EU's banana import regime was inconsistent with the GATT, GATS and TRIM agreements. The case will properly be referred to the Appellate Body, and thus postponed for another six months. Yet, if the findings of the panel are considered correct by the Appellate Body, the EU will have no more than 15 months to comply with the ruling. Otherwise, it will face penalties and retaliations in similar or related areas.

The case is controversial in Europe. The banana import regime has not been particularly popular among European banana-importing countries due to price increases. But France in particular sees the Lomé Convention as a crucial element in its relationship with its former colonies. It has also been justified in terms of "trade not aid" development policies. Thus, the EU banana regime will most likely not be dismantled without protests. This is especially true as its demolition is sought by "the Big Three' – the American multinationals Chiquita, Del Monte and Dole – which control more than two-thirds of the world market. Their share of the European market amounts to "only" 42 per cent. The great irony is that the tariff preferences in question were to be dismantled in 2002 in any case.

11.10.2. The WTO case of the EU import ban on meat and meat products treated with hormones

The US and Canada requested the establishment of this WTO panel on 24 April 1996, claiming that the EU import ban restricting or prohibiting imports of meat or meat products of hormone-treated cattle was inconsistent with the GATT. This case dates back to 1989 when the EC banned the import of hormone-enhanced meat. This excluded virtually all US meat exports. The US responded with 100 per cent tariffs on a number of European products. The 1989 trade war was put to an end by an interim agreement which allowed the US to resume export of hormone-free beef. A preliminary report leaked to the public in late May 1997 indicates that the WTO panel will support the American and Canadian claim, and go against the EU. It found that the EU ban cannot be justified on scientific grounds. This may turn out to be just as controversial as the infamous tuna–dolphin GATT ruling from 1987, which sparked off widespread anti-GATT protests in the US. The WTO may experience a similar loss in popular support within Europe, as European consumers are generally known for their dislike of such "unnatural" products and "unethical" production methods. The provisional WTO ruling may create a precedent in other WTO cases, which may paradoxically go against the US in the case of an alleged illegal US import ban on Southeast Asian shrimp which are not harvested according to sound conservation principles.

11.10.3. The case of the Cuban Liberty and Democratic Solidarity Act (the Helms–Burton Act)

On 3 May 1996 the EU requested consultations with the United States concerning the Cuban Liberty and Democratic Solidarity Act of 1996, and other legislation enacted by the US Congress regarding trade sanctions against Cuba. The issue concerned the extraterritorial nature of these laws. Although President Clinton suspended the controversial Title III (which allows US citizens to sue foreign companies "trafficking" in expropriated property for damages in US courts) and Title IV (under which it is possible to deny US visas to foreign business people and their families associated with firms investing in Cuba) for six mouths in July 1996, and again in January 1997, the bilateral talks between Brussels and Washington failed. In October 1996, the EU requested that a WTO panel should investigate the matter. Although the US vetoed this request, the EU decided to re-issue its request for a panel in November 1996 – a request which could not be blocked by the US according to WTO rules. The re-issue of the request came as a genuine surprise. It also came as a surprise that the Americans decided to justify their actions formally in terms of "national interests". The US is allowed to do so according to GATT laws – but the question is whether European investments in the Cuban tourist industry can be said to be a threat to US security.

The case is extremely dangerous for the WTO. Either the WTO will be forced to establish a *de facto* precedent which would justify the use of protectionist trade policies in the future whenever "national interest" is invoked, or the WTO will have to rule against the US on a highly sensitive issue, which might provoke a strong reaction from the US Congress. It should be noted that Congress has retained the right to subject US membership of the WTO to a congressional vote if more than three WTO panel rulings in a five-year period go against the US. The no-turning-back strategy of the Commission also caused some disagreements within the EU. The US and EU managed to postpone the investigations of the panel in May 1997. Yet the EU has reserved its right to take up the case at any time. It may be tempted to do so if the EU trade policy continues to be deemed WTO-inconsistent.

The WTO has emerged as a new actor in EU trade politics. It now remains to be seen whether the Commission and the member states will continue to support the WTO unconditionally. The Commission seems content to have fortified its central position in the external realm of economic policies. However, the WTO offers opportunities for the member states themselves to regain some control over the global liberalization process. Recently, several EU member states have been directly involved in WTO disputes in matters considering "mixed" agreements and national trade policy practices. These include computer customs classification systems (UK and Ireland), legal procedures in national intellectual property laws (Denmark and Sweden) and patent laws (Portugal). Have the EU member states hereby regained some control over external trade policy? In the case of US complaints about computer customs classification systems, the EU has responded that it would "act on behalf of" the UK and Ireland – regardless of whether the matter concerns the failure of national authorities to comply with EU's international obligations under the GATT. In fact, the WTO has implied that it is no longer possible for the Commission to govern the EU external trade policy domain exclusively. Not only has EU trade policy been challenged by the member states, but the WTO has put EU trade policy under stricter surveillance and tighter legal constrains. It is less inclined to tolerate violating practices than its predecessor.

11.11. THE NEW WTO AGENDA: THE ISSUE OF TRADE AND SOCIAL RIGHTS

The EU has also been highly active as an agenda-setter in the WTO – in particular concerning the new issues on the relationships between trade and anti-trust laws, labour standards, and environment (see e.g. Commission 1996b, pp. 5–8). Yet none of these issues have so far been particularly successful examples of EU trade diplomacy. For instance, the issue of "trade and social standards" at the WTO ministerial meeting in Singapore illustrated only too well the inability of the EU to act internationally when it is internally divided. The Commission had prepared a communiqué on the issue in July 1996, wherein it concluded that "the incorporation of social issues within the WTO work programme should be a settled objective for the EU" (Commission 1996c, p. 15). This recommendation, which the member states on the article 113 committee had deemed "worth considering", had been approved by the Council in May 1996. But business circles within the EU were not in favour of this. In a meeting with Sir Leon Brittan in October 1996, the Foreign Trade Association declared that a WTO committee on labour standards "risks opening up Pandora's box" (*Agence Europe*, 19 Oct. 1996). In November 1996, however, the majority of the Council agreed that "the promotion, better definition and universal respect of fundamental social norms" should be included in the WTO 1997–98 work programme. But the UK voted against this version, and a separate declaration had to be issued (*Agence Europe*, 22 Nov. 1996). The Commission's ambitions became significantly more modest after this incident. Rather than pushing for concrete results in Singapore, the Commission suggested that it would seek to initiate "a discussion...at the global level in order to reduce tensions and promote understanding" (Commission 1996b, p. 7). In the Singapore meeting, the WTO decided to refer the issue for consideration in the International Labour Organization (ILO) rather than to establish a WTO committee. This was an acceptable outcome to those developing countries that had threatened to veto the final Ministerial declaration. The ILO has no effective enforcement mechanisms compared to the WTO, and it is therefore considered much weaker.

This "demotion" of the issue came as no great surprise. Many developing countries have expressed fears as to how international rules in this area would legitimize protectionist trade practices in the industrialized world, and deprive them their legitimate comparative advantage of cheap labour. But it came as a surprise when the UK and Germany made it clear that they intended to vote against it too – regardless of whether the issue had been formally approved throughout the various levels within the Commission and by the Council prior to the Singapore meeting. Paradoxically, the EU was among the first to put the issue on the Marrakesh declaration in the first place.

This is a classic example of the limitations of the EU's capacity as a foreign economic actor – of how easily the EU's external position may be undermined at the very last minute. Moreover, and perhaps more significantly, it illustrates only too well how difficult it is for the EU to act in a coherent manner when non-trade and trade issues are linked in reality.

11.12. CONCLUSIONS

The external trade area of the EU has reached an important impasse. The basic framework of EU governance is based on a vague distinction between "pure trade" and "mixed agreements", which in the light of the globalization of world trade and investment has become increasingly difficult to establish in any meaningful sense. As global commercial relations are changing rapidly, it is paramount for the EU to shape the governing rules and institutions of international trade according to its own fundamental goals. It is no longer possible to act defensively in the multilateral trade system; instead it requires a visionary and innovative trade policy, and an institutional capacity to act accordingly on a long-term basis. It also requires the capacity to deal with more immediate matters without causing an international trade conflict or internal deadlocks. It needs to develop a better crisis management capacity that can prevent powerful sectoral interests from paralysing the international activities of the EU. How could this be done? For instance, all EU external trade activities should be conducted by one DG alone. Moreover, a permanent Council of Trade Ministers or something similar to the "Jumbo Council" and a "fast-track authority" should be institutionalized. Furthermore, the "shared competence" is an unacceptable solution as it only creates greater uncertainty – and thus vulnerability – at the international negotiation table. The EU must reflect the present economic realities of the global economy in its institutional design. But there has thus far been little political willingness to reform the system. The lack of transparency and democratic accountability of the present framework rightly gives rise to some concern, and the political unwillingness to strengthen the role of the Commission is thus to some extent understandable. Still, one should not underestimate the ability of EU diplomacy to function effectively regardless of the political climate. The new multilateral trading system has induced severe tensions into the delicate institutional structures which have maintained a fragile balance between successful internal governance and international trade diplomacy throughout the years, yet these structures have produced a highly reactive and defensive EC trade policy in the past. Such a trade policy is no longer possible after the decline of US hegemony. Nor is it a wise strategy in an era of globalization. The EU trade policy in a post-hegemonic era must accept global responsibilities for the management of a stable trading system. The question is whether the existing institutional structures of the EU external trade policy can meet the challenge of reforming themselves.

11.13. REFERENCES

Arnhild, A. (1995). "Comparing GATT and GATS: regime creation under and after hegemony". *Review of International Political Economy 3*, No. 1, 65–94.

Bhagwati, J. and H.T. Patrick (1990). *Aggressive Unilateralism – America's 301 trade policy and the world trading system*. Hemel Hempstead: Harvester Wheatsheaf.

Bulmer, S.J. (1995). "The Governance of the European Union: A New Institutional Approach". *Journal of Public Policy 13*, No. 4, 351–380.

Cerny, P.G. (1995): "Globalization and the Changing Logic of Collective Action". *International Organization 49*, No. 4, 595–625.

Commission (1994). "Growth, Competitiveness and Employment". White Paper, Brussels.

Commission (1996a). "The Global Challenge of International Trade: A Market Access Strategy of the European Union". *Communication Com* (96) 53.

Commission (1996b). "Reinforcing the Open Trading System: The EU's Priorities for World Trade in View of the First WTO Ministerial Meeting". Document downloaded from www.eu.int.

Commission (1996c). "The Trading System and Internationally Recognized Labour Standards". *Communication Com* (96) 402.

Conybearn, J.A.C. (1992). "1992, the Community, and the World". In: Smith, D. and J.L. Ray (eds) *The 1992 Project and the Future of Integration in Europe*. New York: M.E. Sharpe.

Devuyst, Y. (1995). "The European Community and the Conclusion of the Uruguay Round". In: Rhodes, C. and S. Mazey (eds) *The State of the European Union – Building a European Polity?* London: Lynne Rienner.

Drake, W.J. and K. Nicolaïdis (1992). "Ideas, interests and institutionalization: Trade in Services and the Uruguay Round". *International Organization 46*, No. 1, 37–100.

Europa Document No. 1971: "Documents signed at the last Transatlantic Summit between European Union and the United States", p. 7.

Evans, P. and J. Walsh (1994). "The EUI guide to the new GATT". Research report, Economist Intelligence Unit, London.

Haynes, J.P. (1993). *Making Trade Policy in the European Community*. London: St Martin's Press.

Kassim, H. (1994). "Policy Networks, Networks and European Policy Making: A Sceptical View". In special issue of *West European Politics*: "The State in Western Europe: Retreat or Redefinition?". Vol.17, No. 3, 15–27.

Macleod, I., I.D. Hendy and S. Hyett (1996). *The External Relations of the European Communities*. Oxford European Community Law Series.

March, J.A. and J.P. Olson (1989). *Rediscovering Institutions*. New York: Free Press.

Mazey. S. and J. Richardson (1993). *Lobbying in the European Community*. Cambridge: Cambridge University Press.

Mazey, S. and J. Richardson (1995). "Promiscuous Policy making: The European Policy Style?". In: Rhodes, C. and S. Mazey (eds) *The State of the European Union – Building a European Polity?*. London: Lynne Rienner.

Moyer, H.W. (1993). "The European Community and the GATT Uruguay Round: Preserving the Common Agricultural Policy at All Cost". In: Avery, W. (ed.) *World Agriculture and the GATT, International Political Economy Yearbook*, Vol. 7. London: Lynne Reinner.

Murphy, A. (1990). *The European Community and the International Trading System*. 2 vols, Nos 43 and 48. Brussels: Centre of European Policy Studies.

Paarlberg, R.L. (1993). "Why Agriculture Blocked the Uruguay Round: Evolving Strategies in a Two-level Game". In: Avery, W. (ed.) *World Agriculture and the GATT, International Political Economy Yearbook*, Vol. 7. London: Lynne Reinner.

Peterson, J. (1995). "Policy Networks and the European Union: A Reply to Kassim". *West European Politics 18*, No. 2, 389–407.

Powell, W.W. and P.J. DiMaggio (1991). *The New Institutionalism in Organizational Analysis*. The University of Chicago Press.

Putnam, R.D. (1988). "Diplomacy and Domestic Politics: the Logic of Two-level Games" *International Organization 42*, No. 3.

Ruggie, J.G. (1995). "At Home Abroad, Abroad at Home: International Liberalization and Domestic Stability in the New World Economy". *Millennium 24*, No. 3.

Smith, M. (1994). "The European Community: Testing the Boundaries of Foreign Economic Policy". In Stubbs, R. and G.R.D. Underhill (eds) *Political Economy and the Changing Global Order*. Macmillan Press.

Strange, S. (1996). *The Retreat of the State – the Diffusion of Power in the World Economy*. Cambridge University Press.

Tooze, R. (1994). "Foreign Economic Policy in a New Europe: a Theoretical Audit of a Questionable Category". In: Carlsneas, W. and S. Smith (eds) *European Foreign Policy – The EC and Changing Perspectives in Europe*. London: Sage.

Van Schendelen, M.P.C.M. (1993). "Introduction: The Relevance of National Public and Private EC Lobbying". In Van Schendelen, M.P.C.M. (ed) *National and Private EC Lobbying*. Aldershot: Dartmouth.

Wieler, J.H.H. (1993). "Journey to an Unknown Destination: A Retrospective and Prospective of the European Court of Justice in the Arena of Political Integration". *Journal of Common Market Studies*, Vol. 13, No. 4, pp. 417–446.

Woolcock, S. and M. Hodges (1996). "The European Union and the Uruguay Round: The Story behind the Headlines". Paper presented at the BIZA conference 1995. (Also published in Wallace, H. and W. Wallace (eds) *Policy-making in the EU* (3rd edn).) Oxford University Press.

WTO (1997). Various issues of *WTO Focus* and other WTO documents downloaded from www.wto.org.

CHAPTER 12

The EU car industry: structural changes and challenges for foreign and domestic producers

Sandrine Labory

12.1. INTRODUCTION

The issues discussed in this chapter are the consequences of the structural changes occurring in the car industry world-wide, the performance of European producers relative to foreign producers, and the role for a European industrial and trade policy. The major structural change is a technological revolution in the industry. A new technology was introduced by Japanese automakers in the 1970s, providing them with a competitive advantage (absolute cost advantage), so that Western producers had to adopt this technology in order to remain competitive. Moreover, the continued Japanese advantage up to now, despite the adaptation of Western producers, points to factors of performance other than demand or technology conditions or amount of R&D, revealing important dimensions of innovation which were not focused on in the past. Innovation is not only technological, concerning processes and products, but also organizational, because different forms of organization of production, decisions, distribution, and so on lead to different capacities to transform ideas into commercial successes.

The aim of this chapter is to analyse the position of the European industry in the light of this reasoning, and to outline the position of European producers relative to their competitors, in order to point to some advantages and disadvantages, and the role of policies to improve the situation. It will be shown that European producers lack adaptation and preparation for the challenges of the 1990s, probably because of the high protection of the European car market, impeding the necessary adjustments. The role of a European policy will then be explained.

12.2. MAIN CHARACTERISTICS OF THE CAR INDUSTRY

Motor vehicle production is one of the fundamental economic activities in industrialized countries, in terms of both balance of payments contribution and employment. It represents 10 per cent of total industrial employment in France and 11 per cent in Germany, 9 per cent in Japan and about 5 per cent in the United States, and accounts for 15 per cent of trade in these countries. In addition, the automobile industry is a model industry for the rest of the economy. It sets the pace for the diffusion of new

233

A. Cafruny and P. Peters (eds.), The Union and the World, 233–246

management and organization techniques, for industrial relations, trade policy, competitiveness and inter-sectoral diffusion of innovation.

Internationalization in the automobile industry (in the sense of sales to international markets) has a long history: American companies such as Ford established in Europe and Japan well before the Second World War. The world market has developed from roughly the beginning of this century to the 1970s, a decade in which markets became replacement markets rather than expanding markets, especially in the industrialized countries. Nowadays automakers world-wide agree to define three main markets in the world: North America, Europe and Japan.[1] All these markets are characterized by saturation, in that the size of the market is not growing. Hence competition among producers is intensifying as each tries to increase its market share at the expense of rivals.

The automobile market is oligopolistic.[2] The number of producers fell in the early 1980s through the absorption of the smallest specialist producers. Thus for instance Fiat in Italy acquired a number of Italian specialist firms such as Innocenti, Ferrari and Alfa Romeo. Nowadays the number of car manufacturers is relatively stable, with six main European producers, including the VAG group in Germany, PSA and Renault in France and Fiat in Italy, eleven producers in Japan (the most important being Toyota and Nissan, which together hold about 55 per cent of the Japanese market[3]), and three main producers in the USA, namely GM, Ford and Chrysler. All three markets are concentrated, with a few firms (like Toyota and Nissan in Japan) holding a large fraction of the market. The European market is less concentrated. Each of the six major producers in Europe holds 10 to 15 per cent of the market. This market, however, is fragmented, and national markets are characterized by a domination of national champions. Thus Renault and PSA together hold 60 per cent of the French market, while Fiat holds 57 per cent of the Italian market.

The automobile oligopoly has been experiencing big changes since the 1970s. The major change is the shift from the mass production system to the flexible production system. This change in technology has induced an intensification of competition, by allowing new entrants into markets. These new entrants are Japanese automakers which introduced the new technology, especially Toyota. As a result, automakers have to adopt the strategy of globalization, i.e. being present in all markets in the world and in all market segments. Furthermore, foreign direct investments are necessary in order to be closer to each market. Consequently, all major car manufacturers, especially American and Japanese ones, are expanding world-wide, as a key factor in long-term survival in the industry is to be present in all markets.

---

[1] North America represents 24.2 per cent of the world production of vehicles and 30.1 per cent of world sales; for Western Europe these figures are 32.1 and 35.7 per cent respectively, and for Japan 25.2 and 13.1 per cent (Source: Commité des Constructeurs Français d'Automobile (CCFA), 1995).

[2] Oligopolies are markets where few but large firms compete.

[3] *Japan Automotive Yearbook*, Japanese Automotive Manufacturers' Association, 1995.

12.3. WORLD EVOLUTION SINCE 1945

12.3.1. From 1945 to the first oil crisis:
three main automobile oligopolies in the world

Car manufacturers were in very diverse situations at the end of the Second World War. American firms switched rapidly from military vehicle production to commercial vehicles and passenger cars. As early as 1947, car production in the USA reached the level of 1940. The American automobile market was diversified and large in size: sales varied between 5 and 7 million cars per year. The production and variety offered by GM and Chrysler increased rapidly, while Ford started to extend its range of models significantly only in 1960 (Freyssenet 1995).

In Europe, car production reached its pre-War level only in 1950, from which time mass production really began. Markets expanded rapidly since they were at the early stages of the product life cycle, where consumers buy the product for the first time. Between 1950 and 1959, car production increased from 0.26 to 1.13 million in France, 0.52 to 1.19 million in the UK, 0.22 to 1.5 million in West Germany, and 0.10 to 0.47 million in Italy,[4] and a large part of this production was exported (mainly to the USA). The Common Market agreement in 1958 induced a large increase in trade between European countries. Between 1958 and 1973, the share of imports to domestic production rose from 9.2 to 25.9 per cent in West Germany, 2.5 to 26.8 per cent in Italy, 10 to 17.3 per cent in France. However, the Common Market did not establish a unified European car oligopoly, because firms remained focused on their domestic market, a strategy favoured by the policy of "national champions" of national governments. Thus, although experience proved that firms producing the full model range, from small to luxury cars, earned higher profits, some producers concentrated on some model ranges, because the limited demand in their market might have prevented economies of scale. Thus Citroën produced only in the small model range, with the "2CV", and the large model range, with the "DS". In the same conditions, Japanese producers chose the most profitable policy in the long term by producing a complete model range, and compensating small home demand by exports.

Japanese automakers continued to produce trucks and commercial vehicles in only small volumes until the mid-1950s. Both Toyota and Nissan launched their first passenger car in 1954–55. But the Japanese market remained small and production in large volumes, as in the USA, was impossible. Hence firms had to find ways to combine line production (which enables economies of scale) and small volumes. The strategy of Toyota was based on both waste minimization and an incentive system that rewarded gains in productivity and reduction in production time, initiated by the engineer Ohno (1978). Japanese producers had to adapt to problems very specific to their country: low demand, lack of financial funds after the War and the reorganization of the financial sector brought about by the dissolution of *zaibatsu* (big groups) by the American authorities. *Keiretsu* links with suppliers based on trust and cost minimization were established. Also, the social conflicts of the early 1950s led to new

---

[4] Source: CCFA.

agreements between employers and trade unions, which Cusumano (1988) claimed favoured employers rather than workers. The strategy of cost minimization by the reduction of waste and of labour and other variable costs continued afterwards even when the demand in Japan improved. Sales of new cars in Japan first surpassed sales in France only in 1969. The boom of Japanese production took place in the second half of the 1960s. As shown in Fig. 12.1, in 10 years, from 1964 to 1973, the domestic market expanded from 0.5 to 3 million vehicles, while Japanese car makers' production rose from 0.58 to 4.5 million cars, the difference being exported to mainly East Asian markets.

Figure 12.1. Production of passenger cars of Toyota and Nissan, 1960–90 (units per year)

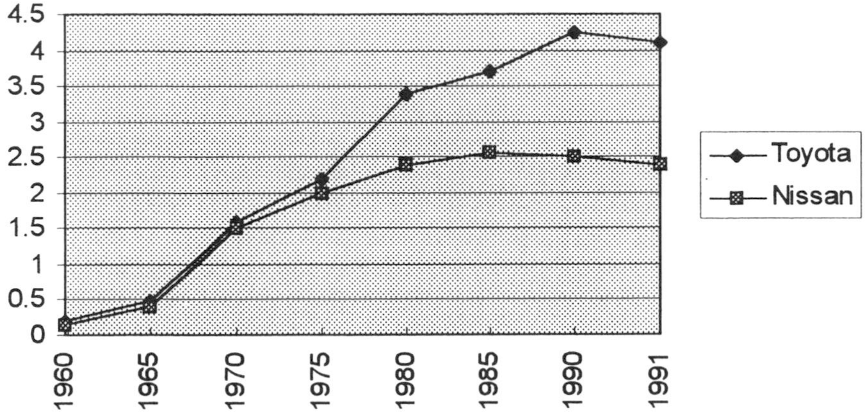

Source: Annual reports.

Parallel to this boom in production, Japanese automakers diversified their models. As shown in Figs 12.2 and 12.3, the range of models of each of the two major producers, Toyota and Nissan, increased from two or three models in 1964 to nine in 1970, thereby surpassing French producers in terms of variety, the latter producing only five (Renault) and four (Peugeot) models at that time. However, other European producers such as Volkswagen and Fiat reached a higher range thanks to a policy of external growth, and produced 14 and 19 different models respectively in 1970. It should be noted that the standardization of platforms[5] was carried out at Toyota as early as 1970. De Banville and Chanaron (1991) explain this in greater detail.

---

[5] The standardization of platforms consists of producing different final models from the same platform, in order to reduce costs and time to produce.

Figure 12.2. Differentiation of Toyota, 1960–90

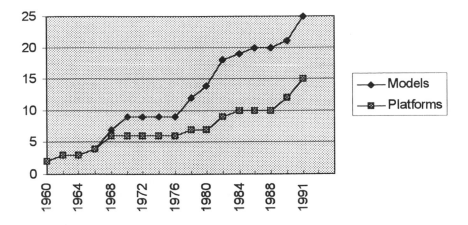

Source: JAMA.

Figure 12.3. Differentiation of Nissan, 1960–90

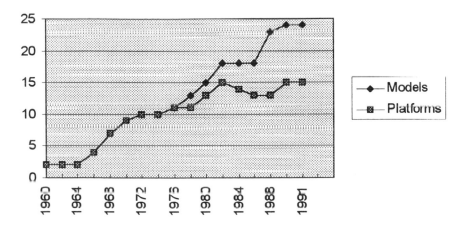

Source: JAMA report 1995.

The structure of the world automobile industry in the early 1970s was therefore fragmented. Few exchanges took place between regions, so that one can characterize the automobile industry of that time as comprising several regional oligopolies. The European oligopoly was itself fragmented, integration and strategies at European level being prevented by differences in regulations and standards and the governments' policies favouring their own domestic champions. Governments in many cases, in Europe and Japan in particular, regarded the car industry as an important engine of industrialization.

12.3.2. From the first oil crisis to 1995: the emergence of one world-wide automobile oligopoly

As pointed out by Boyer and Freyssenet (1995), during this period all car manufacturers were hit by an increasing number of events simultaneously, e.g. the oil crises of 1973 and 1979, fluctuating exchange rates in the early 1970s and financial deregulation in the 1980s. Trade and foreign direct investments increased among the three main markets, so that the industry is now basically globalized, in that all producers compete in different regions and different segments of the markets. A segment is defined as a market for a specific set of characteristics of the generic product. An example is the segment of the monospace, which is a variety of the generic product "car".

Problems specific to some firms or some countries are numerous. In the USA, the 1970s was the decade in which the structure of automotive market experienced an upheaval. The traditional leaders, the "Big Three" (Ford, General Motors and Chrysler), averaged about 88 per cent share of the US passenger car market in the 1960s, falling to 80 per cent after 1970 and under 75 per cent in 1979 (Flynn 1995). Imports were about 15 per cent in 1970, and 22 per cent in 1979. The mix of importers changed dramatically over the decade. In 1970, eight of the top ten importers were European, while at the end of the decade six of the top ten importers were Japanese. Japanese companies expanded their dealership network typically by signing agreements with the Big Three. MMC (Mitsubishi Motors Corporation) and Chrysler; Isuzu and Ford; Mazda and GM signed such agreements. This enabled American producers to complete the range of models offered, since the smaller and more fuel-efficient Japanese cars were sold through the Big Three's outlets. This was an easy access to the American market for Japanese automakers, an initial entry on the small car segment which was to be followed in the 1980s by entry on other car segments, thanks to their cost advantage. American producers did not expect such subsequent aggressive competition of Japanese entrants on their own segments, i.e. large and luxury cars. The 1980s therefore was a tumultuous decade for American car makers, since their share of the market fell by 9 per cent to the benefit of Japanese automakers.

Honda started production in the USA in 1982, and was followed by Nissan in 1985, Toyota (with GM in the joint venture NUMMI) in 1986, Mazda in 1987 and MMC in the joint venture with Chrysler in 1989. This was accompanied by the setting up of about 300 Japanese automotive suppliers on the American market. Japanese cars represented a challenge since they were cheaper, of higher quality, and with a better style, due to more efficient manufacturing processes in terms of lower costs and higher productivity. The profits of the Big Three were under pressure, and access to finance became difficult for them (see Flynn 1995). They reacted to this challenge by taking drastic measures to reduce cost and increase productivity, by introducing new elements in their organization, negotiating new agreements with unions and establishing new relationships with suppliers in order to follow the Japanese "Just in Time" (JIT) system. Ford increased productivity by 50 per cent over the 1980s. GM was much slower to react.

European producers were also challenged by Japanese producers, but to a much lesser extent than their American rivals, because of the protection of the European market from Japanese competition. Until the early 1990s this trade policy of protection was decided by individual governments, without a common position at European level. Thus France and Italy were the most protective, while Germany and the UK were the most liberal. Only in 1991 was the trade policy concerning the automobile industry decided at European level. As a result, European producers have reacted very slowly to the challenge offered by Japanese producers, i.e. low cost, high rate of product renewal, short time to market, high quality. The problems caused by this lack of adaptation will be discussed below.

Thus the period 1973–95 is marked by an integration of the automobile industry into a single world-wide oligopoly. The increasing trade and communication between regions, as well as the increasing number of problems faced by all firms simultaneously, are evidence of this evolution. However, each regional market keeps its specificity, and the standardization of products and strategies is impossible, as shown by the failure of the "world car" concept of Ford. Over the years and especially in the 1990s a contradiction appears: the automobile oligopoly becomes global, and players have to define strategies on a world basis (for example by selling in every possible region in the world), while regions keep their specificity, resulting from different cultures and mentalities, and translating into different consumers' tastes, different governmental regulations, different labour markets, etc. All car manufacturers worldwide have to face this contradiction, notably by adapting their organizational forms.

12.3.3. Technological change: a revolution

The automobile industry is characterized by incremental, progressive innovation. The product is never changed fundamentally but producers innovate to improve incrementally both the production process (e.g. a new machine to produce bodies) and the car itself (e.g. four-wheel drive, ABS braking system, airbags). Until the 1970s, the technology in the car industry was stable, as was the structure of the industry and the organization of firms. However, in the 1970s the internationalization of the industry and the increased competition of Japanese producers induced a drastic change in technology, resulting in a large restructuring of Western firms. Japanese producers introduced a new production system which turned out to be a competitive advantage and all other producers had to adopt that technology. After the generalization of this production system during the 1970s, the focus was again on product innovation and generally incremental innovations from the 1980s onwards.

The innovative technology used by Japanese producers enables the production of variety at low cost. Western competitors had therefore to follow the Japanese and adopt/adapt their system. In other words, the Japanese technological innovation (structural change) brought about a change in market structure (change in the relative market positions of world automakers to the benefit of Japanese producers), implying the need for Western producers to change their internal organization in order to adopt the new technology, which they did over the period 1970 to mid-1980s. Two main measures were taken. First, there was a large increase in automation. Massive investments in machinery were realized in order to match Japanese producers' flexibility. Thus, for instance Fiat constructed "highly automated factories" (Volpato 1995). Second, the technological change translated into large falls in the numbers employed. Table 12.1 shows that Ford reduced its work force by 21.6 per cent in the 1980s.

Table 12.1. Numbers employed (percentage change on previous two years)

	1980	1982	1984	1986	1988	1990	1992
Ford	−13.7	−11.4	−1.3	−2.5	−7.8	+1.4	−9.7
PSA		−3.5*	−10.1	−11.3	−3.4	−0.1	−5.7

*Percentage change on previous year.
Source: Bordenave (1995) for Ford; annual reports of PSA.

It is important to notice that the reduction of the work force was accompanied by a change in its quality. Thus unskilled workers were massively laid off, but the proportion of skilled workers and technicians increased. For example at Renault, the proportion of unskilled workers reduced from 69 to 48 per cent from 1978 to 1993, while that of skilled workers and technicians increased from 27 to 42 per cent over the same period.[6]

This drastic change of technology from the Fordist system (mass production of one model on one assembly line) to the Toyotist system (flexible production of several models on the same assembly line) implied large changes in organizational structures, both inside and outside the firms. Firstly, work organization changed, towards a larger participation of workers. Training was developed to increase workers' skills, in order for them to be able to perform multiple tasks and also make suggestions for improvements. Quality circles, team work, and changes of incentives (whereby wages were no longer based on productivity but, for instance, on the number of skills acquired, or the performance of the whole team (Bordenave 1995, De Banville and Chanaron 1991)), were established. Secondly, parts procurement policies were rethought. Thus most Western automakers experienced a vertical disintegration, and established partnership relationships with suppliers. These relationships involve some shifting of cost and R&D to suppliers, and quality and low price are ensured by comparing suppliers' performance, thereby inducing competition between them. Thirdly, the organization of distribution also changed, towards an involvement of dealers in cost control. Lastly, the internal organization changed towards a reduction of the number of hierarchical levels (for better information flows) and an interaction between functions (marketing, R&D, finance, etc.) for more rapid and more efficient (in terms of meeting customers' requirements of quality and features) product development. This interaction is carried out in the matrix form of organization, where functions at different levels of product development are not separated but integrated. It creates horizontal in addition to vertical communication, and therefore improves the coherence of strategies within firms. Therefore product development in the flexible production system is realized simultaneously by all functions, rather than sequentially as in the Fordist system. In

---

[6] Source: Renault annual report 1994, and Comité des Constructeurs Français d'Automobile (CCFA).

the latter system, the project is passed sequentially from one function to the next, thereby wasting time: if manufacturing specialists realize after engineers pass a project on to them that the project is unfeasible, in the sense that the proposed product is not manufactured easily or at low cost, then the project goes back to the engineers who have to think about another solution. In contrast, the simultaneous project development constantly checks feasibility and saves time and money, thanks to the interactions between functions. This is a key factor for performance nowadays.

These technological and organizational changes induced new structural changes in the market, whereby Western competitors returned to a better position, increasing their market shares, although remaining behind major Japanese producers.[7]

Two conclusions can be drawn. First, structural changes in the car industry show that innovation has different dimensions. Japanese producers first gained a competitive advantage by innovation on the production process, but then maintained their advantage thanks to another innovation: an organizational innovation, whereby information and formation within the firm are optimized. Second, these structural changes represent a true revolution of the industry, which has consequences on policies. The old paradigms on which industrial policies were based no longer hold, and principles of policies have to change, as shown below.

12.4. ROLE OF A EUROPEAN INDUSTRIAL AND TRADE POLICY

The fundamental structural changes in the car industry world-wide have important implications for the role of governments in regulating markets and trade. Two fields of policy-making are particularly affected, industrial policy and trade policy, although actions in these fields affect other fields: for instance, a coherent industrial policy implies macro-economic and environmental actions as well.

The first question that is raised concerns trade policy. The problem is more precisely formulated as follows. Is the protection of the European market efficient? Protection through voluntary exports restraints by Japanese producers, together with negotiated auto-limitations of shares of the European market, is supposed to be put in place temporarily in order to let European producers restructure and therefore equip themselves to compete fairly against foreign producers.[8] However, protection has existed for a very long time,[9] and it does not seem that European producers have completely adjusted yet, since they still lag behind in terms of certain performance parameters.[10] Therefore, the question arises whether protection is not just delaying necessary changes on the supply side of the European car market. Furthermore,

---

[7] In the USA, the Big Three have lost market share to Japanese producers. In Europe, Japanese producers' market shares are limited by a Europe–Japan agreement that protects European car makers until 1999, while they restructure.

[8] The latest agreement is that of 31 July 1991, aiming at giving European producers a transition period in which to adapt to the competition from Japanese producers, by the control of Japanese exports to Europe.

[9] The 1981 Voluntary Export Restraint between Japan and the USA was the starting point of such bilateral agreement, accommodating the Japanese with other major OECD producers.

[10] See Clark and Fujimoto (1991, 1992) for comparisons of performance.

protection bears a high cost for customers, who have to pay a higher price for their cars. Many studies have been carried out in the USA and in Japan to assess the impact of protection on consumer welfare, and identify significant price differentials due to protection.[11] The United States has also negotiated agreements with the Japanese authorities, but with a greater focus on inducing Japan to open its market to American producers, rather than protecting them directly. As a result, the American market has been more open to foreign producers, and American producers have been obliged to make the necessary adjustments. The result is that the Big Three are now much more competitive in terms of quality, cost, time to market and innovation than their European counterparts. They cope with the challenge of globalization and are indeed expanding to all regions and all market segments, which is the strategy most likely to ensure profitability in the long run. Thus, Toyota realizes about 50 per cent of its total sales outside Japan. In contrast, French automakers are very centralized on Europe and not sufficiently present in other world markets: in 1994, 86 per cent of exports from French producers were within Europe, and only 5.9 per cent went to the USA and 3.3 per cent to Asia, including 0.4 per cent to Japan.

However, the negotiations between governments aiming at protection involve more than economic considerations, in that the issue is also highly political, with economic power at stake. In this respect, a common European approach to policy-making and negotiations is required to have a sufficient bargaining power relative to the USA and Japan.

The second question concerns industrial policy. The role of either national or regional governments as favouring national or regional champions is outdated, for several reasons. First, as shown above, protection is an obstacle to efficiency. Second, the new production system leads to new challenges for automakers which question the idea of national champions. In particular, globalization, and the need to be present in all markets and all segments, induces changes in producers' strategies. The aim is now to standardize models as much as possible, by making several final models share the same platforms, parts, engines, etc., and differentiating at the latest stages of the production cycle. Thus 80 per cent of cars are now "commonized". In order to be able to produce all model ranges, for as many markets as possible, producers ally with each other. Such "strategic alliances" aim at sharing development costs, either on common parts of models (e.g. the Renault Safrane, Peugeot 605 and Citroën ZX share the same engine, produced in a common engine factory) or on new products (Volkswagen and Ford have cooperated to produce monospace cars). Therefore some networks of relationships develop between producers, resulting in a complex situation, where some manufacturers cooperate on some market segments or some stages of the production cycle, but compete vigorously elsewhere. A policy favouring one national champion therefore indirectly helps other automakers, even from foreign countries. In short, globalization stands in contrast to nationally focused interests. This is a point that has to be carefully considered.

Since firms in the European car industry have a strategy at European level, the relevant level for policy is undoubtedly the European one, especially since the Euro-

---

[11] Hunker (1984) addresses the situation in the USA; Ginsburgh and Vanhamme (1989) deal with Europe.

pean market is bound to integrate further with the advent of the single currency. Given the conditions of industries nowadays, European policy should consist of two domains of action: competition policy and innovation policy. Competition policy is necessary to guarantee fair competition between players of an industry. For this purpose, the legislative framework provided by EU treaties is appropriate to guarantee that there are no temptations for countries to favour their domestic producers or consumers. The "uneasy triangle" of competition policy that was argued to exist until the 1980s (Berg 1973) does not hold anymore. The claimed dilemma was that scale economies were in contradiction to increasing variety (no longer true in the flexible production system), and that technology conditions were such that there was room in the industry for only a limited number of players. The latter point does not hold either, because the flexible production system reduces the optimal size threshold, and enables monopoly power to be reduced to some extent. Thus the number of producers in the car oligopoly has stabilized since the 1980s. As a consequence, the triangle is now rather "easy", since competition between car manufacturers is very intense.

Innovation policy is a very important field of action, where authorities can play a useful role of catalyst by defining new priorities and helping to focus resources on those priorities. The structural changes in the car industry reveal some new stakes for European competitivity, and new dimensions of innovation policies. Competitivity is here defined as the ability to maintain and gain market shares. The advent of the flexible production system sheds new light on important factors of productivity: not only costs, but also quality, time to market,[12] variety of products, and efficiency of distribution networks. Tables 12.2 and 12.3 illustrate the growing importance of two of these factors: variety (Table 12.2) and time to market (Table 12.3).

Table 12.2. Range of models produced by the main Japanese car makers.

	1984	1985	1986	1987	1988	1989	1990	1991	1992
Honda	12	13	13	14	14	16	16	16	18
Toyota	19	21	21	21	21	23	24	28	28
Nissan	21	20	21	22	23	26	26	23	23

Source: JAMA report, 1995.

The consequence is that innovation is not only technological, i.e. concerning products and processes, but also organizational or financial. A successful R&D policy requires that innovation be treated in all its dimensions. Thus European scientific publications are more numerous than American and Japanese ones, but lead to fewer commercial applications. The problem is that European firms lack a coherent innovation strategy that would involve all the competence existing within the firm, and would enable ideas to be transformed into commercial success. In other words, technological innovation should be accompanied by organizational innovation.

---

[12] Time between conception and commercialization of a product.

Table 12.3. Model changes of Japanese car makers, 1970–89*

	Number of new models		Number of model changes	
	1970–79	1980–89	1970–79	1980–89
Toyota	3	5	15	22
Nissan	3	4	18	19
Mazda	2	1	7	6
Honda	3	4	1	11
Mitsubishi	4	3	6	7
Isuzu	0	0	1	3
Fuji	0	2	4	3
Daihatsu	2	1	0	5

*Excluding very small cars, jeep-type models and cab-over vans.
Source: Clark and Fujimoto (1991, 1992), who point out that although Japanese automakers did not spend more on R&D, they introduced many more models (over the period 1982–87 they introduced 70 new models, against 20 by American manufacturers and 40 by European ones).

A European innovation policy has a role to play in this respect. It can be a catalyst, i.e. something that "helps to do" rather than "does" itself. This is the tendency of recent measures.

The Common Industrial Policy (CIP) now integrates competitivity as a fundamental objective of European construction, in the Treaty of the EU. Titles 13 (article 130) and 15 (concerning R&D) indicate this objective, while Title 8 on social policy commits to facilitating adaptation to industrial changes. Three principles aim at guaranteeing efficiency of the CIP. The first principle is that an efficient industrial policy requires a synergy of all factors influencing industrial activity, even if these factors are elements of other policies: environmental, trade, competition, etc. The second principle is to guarantee competition on markets. The third principle is to adopt a multisectoral approach, in contrast to past policies which were focused on particular sectors, ignoring spillovers between sectors. This new approach has been adopted in a variety of measures. One interesting example is that of Task Forces focused on different projects. One such project is "the car of the future". Given that

- increasing road traffic is causing serious pollution in European cities
- the automobile industry is a key sector in terms of employment and contribution to GNP
- R&D expenditures in the sector are enormous and generally spread among different automakers, but lagging behind R&D effort of major competitors in Japan and the USA
- a programme has been established which pools and multiplies research efforts on the car of the future (clean, consuming little energy, and so on) that automakers would not have managed on their own. The approach is that of a synergy, the project being developed in partnership with industrialists.

12.5. CONCLUSIONS

The change from mass and rigid production to flexible production has changed the concept of efficiency in production: economies of scale are measured by the ability to produce different models in small volumes and at low cost, and no longer by the reduction in cost resulting from the increase in production volumes. The change in production system also implies a change in the internal structure of firms. More interactions have been introduced between functional departments such as R&D, engineering, manufacturing and marketing, new relationships have been developed between producers and part suppliers, and between producers and dealers. In other words, in order to optimize information flows and therefore meet the new performance requirements in terms of cost, quality, variety and time to market, horizontal relationships are created within firms, and between firms, by strategic alliances among producers.

These changes have important implications in terms of policy-making. The main point in this respect is that horizontal relationships creating synergies are also required for policies to be efficient. Concerning foreign policy, the European level is where such synergies are maximum, hence the rationale for Common European policies.

12.6. REFERENCES

Annual reports and company brochures, Ford, Honda and Toyota.

Berg, H. (1973). *Zur Funktionsfähigkeit der Europäischen Wirtschaftsgemeinschaft*. Göttingen: Vandenhoeck & Ruprecht.

Bordenave, P. (1995). "Les voies multiformes du redressement de Ford Motor Company", Troisièmes Rencontres Internationales du Gerpiza, réseau international, 15–17 June.

Boyer, R. and Freyssenet (1995). "The Emergence of New Industrial Models". Troisièmes Rencontres Internationales du Gerpiza, réseau international, 15–17 June.

Campbell, D. (1993). "The Globalising Firms and Labour Institutions". In: P. Bailey *et al.* (eds) *Multinationals and Employment*. Geneva: ILO.

Clark, K.B. and T. Fujimoto (1991). *Product Development Performance*. Boston: Harvard Business School Press.

Clark, K.B. and T. Fujimoto (1992). "Product development and competitiveness". *Journal of the Japanese and International Economies 6*, 101–143.

Cusumano, M.A. (1988). "Manufacturing Innovation: Lessons from the Japanese Automobile Industry". *Sloan Management Review*, 29–39.

De Banville, E. and J.-J. Chanaron (1991). *Vers un Système Automobile Européen*. Paris: Economica.

Flynn, M.S. (1995). "The Strategic Challenges and Business Trajectory of GM: 1974 to 1994". Troisièmes Rencontres Internationales du Gerpiza, réseau international, 15–17 June.

Freyssenet, M. (1995). "Des trajectoires aux modèles. Convergences et divergences". Troisièmes Rencontres Internationales du Gerpiza, réseau international, 15–17 June.

Fujimoto, T. (1995). "Reinterpretation of the Resource-based Theory of the Firm from an Information System Point of View". Tokyo University, Working Paper 94F20.

Ginsburgh, V. and G. Vanhamme (1989). "Price Differences in the EC Car Market: Some Further Results". *Annales d'Economie et de Statistiques 15/16*, 137–149.

Hunker, J.A. (1984). *Structural Changes in the The US Automobile Industry*. Massachusetts: Lexington Books.

Ohno, K. (1978). *Toyota Seizan Hoshiki*. Tokyo: Diammond.

Toyoda E. (1987). *Toyota: Fifty Years in Motion. An Autobiography by the Chairman*. Tokyo: Toyota

Toyota Motor Corporation (1995). *The Automotive Industry; Toyota and Japan*. Tokyo.

Volpato, G. (1995). "The New Trajectory of Fiat". Troisièmes Rencontres Internationales du Gerpiza, réseau international, 15–17 June.

CHAPTER 13

The 1994 Energy Charter Treaty: EU foreign policy in the field of energy?[1]

Anthony Smith

13.1. INTRODUCTION

The Energy Charter Treaty (ECT) was conceived as a programme aimed at creating an Energy Community (EnCom) embracing both halves of a previously divided Europe. Its purpose was to aid the processes of transition within the formerly centrally-planned political economies of East–Central Europe (ECE) and the former Soviet Union (FSU) by stimulating East–West energy trade and investment. This would take place under conditions of non-discrimination (towards foreigners) and market-determined pricing mechanisms, conforming to the neo-liberal, politico-economic agenda of the 1980s and early 1990s. The capital-deficient, but natural resource-rich, producing regions of the FSU were seen as complementary partners for Western companies eager to augment existing oil and natural gas reserves with fresh holdings and new discoveries in non-OPEC (Organization of Petroleum Exporting Countries) regions. Western investments, the focal element emphasized in most of Western policy towards the ex Soviet Bloc, would support socio-economic transition by triggering export-led growth, ensuring the consolidation of political reforms in the East and alleviating security concerns about the fragility of post-Soviet society.

The suggestion for the creation of a Pan-European EnCom was first made by then Dutch Prime Minister Ruud Lubbers at a June 1990 gathering of the EU heads of state in Dublin, which, on the advice of the European Council, was followed up with a set of concrete proposals for its implementation by the European Commission. The EU not only was instrumental in the initiation of negotiations for the European Energy Charter, the non-binding statement of participating states' objectives, but also provided the impetus to the development of the subsequent treaty. The basis for such heavy EU involvement seems obvious, as realization of the proposals would: necessarily involve the participation of most if not all the EU member states and many prominent national and multinational enterprises based in the EU; be of enormous potential significance to the single market program (SMP); provide another opportunity for the EU to demonstrate its "compound abilities" as a negotiator in the media-

[1] I would like to acknowledge a debt to Patrick F.H. Peters for his contribution to a joint paper, "The Energy Charter Treaty: European Governance in the Field of Energy", presented at the European University Institute/Robert Schuman Center conference "Governing Europe into the 21st Century", May 1996. Elements of that paper have been incorporated into this chapter.

A. Cafruny and P. Peters (eds.), The Union and the World, 247–270
© 1998 Kluwer Academic Publishers. Printed in Great Britain.

tion of important international agreements. Most significantly, however, the further development of the Lubbers Plan would help support and/or resolve two unrelated but vital EU policy priorities. First, an instituitonal motive, it would put further pressure on EU member states to press ahead with the conclusion of an energy chapter for the revised Treaty on European Union (TEU2 or Maastricht 2). Second, the construction of an EU-driven EnCom would support the EU's pivotal role in guiding the transition process in Eastern Europe, conforming with general Western policy where the civilian EU was chosen as the natural vehicle, through geographic proximity and political and economic expediency, for channeling Western assistance to the East.

The ECT's impact on the IPE of energy markets should not be underestimated. Prior to the ECT no multilateral treaties in the GATT mould existed solely concerning the energy sector, and covering such contentious issues as property and investment rights, trading restrictions and transit guarantees.

Consequently, this chapter explores both the institutional background to the ECT, i.e. internal and external imperatives which help characterize it as a real foreign policy process of the EU, and the implications the ECT could have on the existing IPE of energy markets. I intend to provide brief accounts of the following three key background issues: (a) present characteristics of global and European energy markets (sections 13.2 and 13.3); (b) the context and policy provisions of the debate surrounding the need for an integrated EU energy policy and energy market (section 13.4); and (c) the general direction of Western policy towards ECE and the FSU (section 13.5). Section 13.6 will provide clarification of the main provisions of the ECT itself.

13.2. GLOBAL ENERGY TRENDS

The ECT could be of major political and economic significance for global and regional investment patterns, production and producer–consumer linkages within the IPE of energy. Its potential impact should be considered in light of the changes that have taken place within global energy structures during the recent past and in anticipation of future energy trends. Previously, major consuming countries, mainly in Western Europe and Japan, were heavily dependent on a single external source of energy supplies, i.e. Middle Eastern/OPEC oil, circumstances which, aided by high oil prices and consumer governments' promotion of energy conservation, diversity of supply and R&D support of new technologies, no longer apply to most of the developed world. However, even with the maintenance of present price levels, OECD oil import dependency is expected to rise from 50 per cent in 1995 to around 58–62 per cent by 2010 in light of falling production in the USA and the predicted peak in North Sea output by the middle of the next decade (IEA 1996b, p. 33)

Additionally, with high demographic growth and protracted economic expansion, in part through energy-intensive industrialization but also through the urbanization of large third world populations, the developing world will affect a fundamental structural shift in global energy consumption and trading patterns. The IEA estimates that consumption in OECD countries will fall from the present 55 per cent of total global energy consumption to less than 50 per cent by 2010 while more than doubling, rising from 28 per cent to 40 per cent of the total, in countries outside the OECD, ECE and the FSU, where demand will remain sluggish. (IEA 1996a, p. 14) The developing world's draw on global energy supplies, particularly oil, will test the ability of the market to provide enough investment in capacity to meet the necessary expansion in production, keeping oil prices stable and supportive of non-Gulf, i.e. more expensive, investments.

Table 13.1. World proven reserves* of oil and natural gas with R/P ratios,** end 1995

Location	Oil (BT†)	% Total	R/P ratio (years)	N. gas (TCM‡)	% Total	R/P ratio (years)
Europe	2.3	1.7	6.9	5.5	4.0	21.5
N. America	11.7	8.5	18.8	8.4	6.1	12.0
OECD	14.0	10.2	14.7	13.9	10.0	14.4
Russia	6.7	4.8	21.9	48.1	34.5	82.1
Total FSU	7.8	5.5	22.0	56.0	40.0	80.4
Mid East	89.2	64.9	92.3	45.2	32.4	100+
OPEC	105.8	76.5	79.5	59.2	42.4	100+
ROW	24.6	17.9	15.9	10.6	7.6	na
Total	138.3	100	42.8	139.7	100	64.7

Source: BP Statistical Review of World Energy, June 1996.

*"Proven reserves of oil/natural gas are generally taken to be those quantities which geological and engineering information indicate with reasonable certainty can be recovered in the future from known reservoirs under existing economic and operating conditions" (BP 1995).

**Reserves/production (R/P) ratio: "If the reserves remaining at the end of any year are divided by the production in that year, the result is the length of time that those remaining reserves would last if production were to continue at the current level" (BP 1995).

†BT: billion (1,000 million) tonnes

‡TCM: trillion (one million million) cubic metres.

An overriding constraint on the use of fossil fuels should be fears for concomitant growth in emissions of CO_2, the main cause of global warming, expected to double in developing countries and rise by up to 30 per cent in OECD areas by 2010, and reinforcing calls for renewed discussion on international climate controls. It remains to be seen if the political will to negotiate can be mustered, given strong disparities in North–South per capita consumption, i.e. the developed world will continue to consume far more primary energy resources on a per capita basis than the developing world (IEA 1996a, p. 16).

13.2.1 Non-OPEC production

Since the late 1970s OECD attempts to escape disproportionate reliance on OPEC oil have led to substantial increases in indigenous OECD oil production despite a much smaller, 10.2 per cent share of proven world reserves and comparatively weak (in comparison to other producing regions) R/P ratios, now estimated at 14.7 years (see Table 13.1). In 1994 OECD production reached 25 per cent of the world total, consuming some three-quarters of oil and gas investment (Tempest 1995, p. 1) climbing to 29 per cent in 1995 (BP 1996, p. 6) Even considering recent examples of scale economies in the oil sector, i.e. through matured long-term investment in infrastructure, and the increasingly prolific techniques and technologies employed by oil and gas operators in the North Sea and elsewhere, worries over growing oil import dependency may be exaggerated in the short term, but beyond the first decade of the next century will become an increasingly prominent issue in the minds of Western energy/security policy-makers, presuming oil in particular remains the mainstay of OECD total primary energy requirement (TPER). The continued development of greater reserve and production portfolios in non-OPEC countries is seen as essential, hence the interest in what can only be described as high-risk, because of domestic instability, though potentially lucrative long-term investments in the FSU.

If recent estimates of probable reserves in and around the Caspian Sea region prove even remotely correct[2] then total FSU oil reserves could be twice or three times the 7.8 BT already confirmed. Kazakhstan and Azerbaijan alone could be producing 272 MT/day by 2010, or 40 per cent of the FSU total (P. Thomas 1996, p. 7), i.e. 8.3 per cent of total world production in 1995 or roughly the amount produced by the UK and Norway. With only marginal increases in FSU demand predicted, the larger part of such production would be destined for export markets which, for reasons of geographic proximity, infrastructure and demand, will mainly be in Europe.

Russian gas reserves at 48 TCM are the largest within the territory of a single state in the world. Overall domestic energy requirements are still falling and with efficiency gains and expanded production there is certainly room for larger volumes of exports to Europe. During 1994 excess Russian capacity of 30 BCM, equal to 35 per cent of Western Europe's net imports, remained shut-in for lack of markets. Stern (1995, p. xvi) has estimated that even with exports to Europe likely to increase by up to 40 per cent over the next five years, the gas "bubble" will increase to 40 BCM by 2000.

Exports and trade links between the FSU and global and regional energy markets are certainly set to grow. However, it is the course such integration will take and the new structures created that could most influence future market conditions and international political developments. Table 1 shows how combined Gulf–FSU oil and natural gas reserves are substantial, with 70.4 per cent of the former and 72.4 per cent of the latter. Western interest in the FSU's oil and natural gas reserves needs to be seen in this global context to be fully appreciated. Energy–producer linkages between the two regions would be seen in the West, still by far the major consuming and importing regions of the world, as a serious threat to economic security, considering past examples of producer muscle-flexing in international energy markets. Though at present it is unlikely with competition for markets/revenues and inward investment and technol-

---

[2] The Kazakhstan government recently published the results of a seismic survey of its portion of the Caspian Sea which gave estimated off-shore oil reserves of some 10 billion tonnes (*Hart's Euroil 7*, Issue 8, Aug. 1996, p. 8).

ogy so acute, there is none the less considerable scope for a convergence of interests and cooperation in the future if demand outpaces the rise in supply, giving suppliers greater leverage than at present. The potential for disruption of the energy supply to OECD countries is already immense because of the considerable and innate social, economic and political instability in both regions. So far the main threat to Western energy supplies from the FSU has come as a consequence of the economic crisis following its break-up into independent republics. However, a strategy of "divide and rule" would be an apt and natural policy objective in the West regarding any such developments towards greater producer linkages. Concerns over such motives behind the ECT have already been voiced in OPEC circles, with officials warning of a Western-instigated "investment beauty-contest". (McBride 1995)

13.2.3. Regionalization of energy?

The arguments in favour of a regionalization of energy markets, through either predetermined action or the natural responses of governments, firms and markets to exogenous events, are complementary and convincing. Attempts by a group of producers to exert control over the international oil market, in most scenarios embracing the major Gulf states, or simply consumers' fears over such developments taking place, could encourage major consumers and other producers to come to formal or informal arrangements guaranteeing exclusive market relations to the detriment of the prospective oligopoly. OECD indigenous productive capacity would most likely be protected in some way in order to maintain a low level of import dependency, and producers outside the low-cost Gulf core, either unwilling or unable to bear the costs of depressed prices, the only way of asserting short term control over the market, and thus reduced revenues, investment capabilities and investment opportunities, may prefer the security of guaranteed, preferential access to (lucrative) OECD markets (Odell 1994, pp. 109–113)

Regional economic cooperation is already a reality, with the North American Free Trade Area (NAFTA), embracing the USA, Canada and Mexico, the EU/European Economic Space in Europe and an embryonic free trade area built around Japan, ASEAN and Australasia becoming increasingly important integrative economic organizations. It would be neither difficult nor unreasonable for these groupings of developed/developing countries to attract proximate and prominent energy producers capable of meeting their oil and gas import requirements, e.g. in Central and northern South America for NAFTA, in the FSU, North and West Africa for Europe, and the Russian Far East and China on the Western Pacific Rim, energy crisis or not. OECD financial and technological strength through the multinational oil corporations (MNOCs), independent operators and public sector initiatives could provide the economic cement to the political expediency in all these regional arrangements.

13.3. EUROPE'S ENERGY BALANCE

Table 13.2. Western Europe's total primary energy requirement (TPER) by fuel, 1950–1994 (million tonnes/oil equivalent (MT/MTOE))

Fuel	1950	1960	1967	1973	1986	1994
Oil	62.5	210.0	453.7	749.0	585.1	652.5
N. gas	5.0	12.5	26.1	129.8	192.5	263.2
Coal	325.0	362.5	331.0	271.8	250.0	261.8
Nuclear	–	–	2.4	16.7	138.6	209.3
Hydro	31.8	87.5	25.1	88.7	101.1	42.4
Total	424.3	672.5	838.3	1256.0	1267.3	1429.3

Source: BP Statistical Review of World Oil/Energy 1961, 1968, 1974, 1987, 1995.

13.3.1. Oil

Over the past 50 years patterns of energy use in Europe have changed dramatically (Table 13.2). Post-War reconstruction in Western Europe was built initially on the recovery of indigenous coal mining capacity and the availability of cheap coal imports from the USA. During the 1950s and 1960s coal was increasingly priced out of the European market by imported oil, seemingly available in unlimited quantities and sufficient to meet rapidly rising demand both in conventional energy use, e.g. heating, industry and power generation, and in new refined-product markets, e.g. transportation and petrochemicals. The MNOCs' extensive exploration efforts in the Persian Gulf and elsewhere after the war had uncovered abundant low-cost-production oil fields capable of meeting substantial output increases at extremely low marginal cost to the producer. And though production was highly concentrated within a few geographical regions and controlled by a small number of companies, a variety of factors combined to keep crude oil prices low[3] and, therefore, competition from alternative energy sources subdued. By the end of the 1960s energy consumption in Europe was increasing by 10 per cent annually and imported oil met most of the rise. On the eve of the 1973 oil crisis, 60 per cent and 45 per cent of Western Europe's energy requirements were met by total imported and imported Middle Eastern oil respectively (Odell 1995, p. 2)

After the Arab members of the OPEC cartel introduced output controls and raised the posted price for oil, real oil prices expressed in 1990 dollars quadrupled between 1973 and 1974 then doubled between 1974 and 1980 (Adelman 1995). There were few options for the big consumers in Europe but to encourage more energy efficiency and the use of alternatives to oil/imported oil. As energy policy within the EU was still

---

[3] Conventional wisdom holds that US import controls left a greater surplus for consumption elsewhere. More importantly, once the Persian Gulf price became the effective world price, prices could have tumbled further. For political reasons prices were maintained at low, but still above-competitive, levels (Adelman 1995, pp. 47–50).

largely under national government control, disparate measures were pursued depending to a large degree on the domestic energy situation in any given country and its general economic fitness. Thus, for example, France, with little by the way of indigenous resources, intensified a programme of civil nuclear power generation, and Germany encouraged efficiency and diversity of supply sources and, in any case, being a major exporter benefited from the general increase in prices for consumer products on the heels of commodity price rises. The recently discovered petroliferous provinces of the North Sea, a godsend in terms of their safe, strategic location, became a magnet for MNOC investments as high oil prices made previously uneconomic fields more attractive for development.

By the early 1980s increased production outside of OPEC regions, mainly in the North Sea, Mexico and the USSR, stagnating demand for oil through greater energy efficiency in major consuming regions, the growing use and supply of alternatives, especially natural gas and nuclear power, and the increasing inability of OPEC producers to resist quota-hopping put continued downward pressure on prices, tumbling in 1986 after Saudi Arabia, OPEC's main producer, refused to maintain its position as swing producer[4]. Since 1981 prices have dropped by more than 70 per cent and remain more or less stable at $15–$18/bbl (per barrel), i.e. below 1974 levels and continually supportive of investment in higher-cost production areas.

Table 13.3. Oil balance in Western Europe (EU/EFTA) 1986–1994 (million tonnes)

Year	1973	1986	1994
Production	22.6	195.1	286.7
Consumption	749.0	602.6	652.5
Net imports	726.4	407.5	365.8
% Net imports	96	67.6	56.1
TPER (MTOE)	1256.0	1171.8	1429.3
Net oil imports as percentage of TPER	57.8	34.8	25.6

Source: BP Statistical Review of World Energy, 1974, 1987, 1995.

As a result of the price rises and subsequent consumer government responses of the 1970s, primary energy consumption in Europe has grown by a mere 12 per cent since 1973, while the average annual increase has been brought down to less than 0.5 per cent, even following the oil price collapse of 1986. Western Europe's indigenous oil production has increased almost 13-fold from 22.6 million to 286.7 million tonnes/annum between 1973 and 1994, helping to reduce dependence on imported oil from 57.8 per cent to 25.6 per cent of total primary energy consumption thus seriously curtailing its geopolitical exposure. And though still the world's largest net importer of crude and oil products at 365.8 million tonnes/annum, Western Europe's ability to meet supply shortfalls has been greatly enhanced through the availability of domestic

---

[4] The swing producer, usually that with the greatest capacity for production, shoulders the burden within a price-fixing cartel for the maintenance of an agreed level of output and hence price by adjusting its own production up or down, depending on the existing or expected level of supply on the global market.

surge capacity production and of stockpiled oil, at present meeting about 245 days of import requirements (Odell 1995, p. 2). Further, given the current state of over-supply in the global oil system, and the potential for conditions to remain so for some time, e.g. with resumption of Iraqi production and major exports expected from the FSU, producers' competitive efforts to retain, let alone increase market share ensures that Western Europe's present position remains one of strength in what must be considered a buyer's market.

13.3.2. Natural gas

Running concurrent to the surge in indigenous oil production in Western Europe came an up-turn in demand for natural gas. Natural gas can be substituted for oil in many areas and is available in large quantities both domestically, from the Netherlands and the North Sea, and from a variety of competing proximate external suppliers, notably Russia and Algeria. A more efficient fuel, retaining some 65 per cent of its calorific value, i.e. heat component not lost to the atmosphere or cooling after combustion, compared with 45 per cent for oil and 35 per cent for coal, gas is economically advantageous and environmentally attractive, producing negligible waste or pollution.

None the less, as a dilute fuel form gas is a far less flexible resource, particularly in transportation and, hence, more tied to infrastructure than oil. Extensive national and international pipeline networks have been developed to facilitate access for consumers and to transport internationally traded gas across considerable distances. Liquefied natural gas (LNG), the highly concentrated form obtained through extreme cooling, is used to transport gas by tanker but remains a hugely expensive, front-end, capital-intensive business and consequently still a marginal, if growing, component of the international energy trade.

Consequently, not only is gas a hostage to international politics, as is oil, but it is part of an inherently less flexible market where large-scale capital investments must be made with long-term implications for buyers and sellers and far less short-term room for manoeuvre. The massive growth in consumption in Europe since the early 1970s and the industry's continued expansion have been built up largely by monopoly state-run enterprises, often in control of the upstream and downstream ends of the market, or through long-term "take-or-pay" contracts between independent producers and distributors, where volumes are bought at a fixed price, usually following the price of oil, for the duration of a specific period. Though such stable market conditions have suited producers and consumers alike, with greater seasonal flexibility of gas purchases in the more mature markets (Estrada *et al.* 1995, p. 36), liberalization of the gas market, it is hoped, will increase competition within the industry, giving consumers better value and ensuring greater economic efficiency for the European economy in general. The UK market is already midway through this process and the pace and extent of change throughout the rest of the EU are rapidly coming to dominate debate on energy policy at the EU level.

Table 13.4. Natural gas balance in Western Europe (EU/EFTA countries) 1986–2010 (Million Tonnes Oil Equivalent)

Year	Production	Consumption	Net Imports	As percentage of total consumption
1986	154.8	201.7	46.9	23.3
1994	188.8	263.2	74.4	28.3
2010	348.9	521.1	172.2	33

Source: *BP Statistical Review of World Energy*, June 1995, Odell (1995).

Not surprisingly, given its economic and environmental attractiveness, demand is expected to rise from the present 21 per cent to upwards of 30 per cent of TPER by 2010, with all estimates pointing toward sustained expansion of gas use, particularly in electric power generation, and indigenous production with additional growth in imports. Moreover, as with oil, a more than adequate domestic capacity to meet much of demand, estimated at 67 per cent of the 2010 total (Odell 1995, p. 5), leaves external suppliers again competing for incremental growth in market share, both with other gas producers, the number and capacity of which are both expected to rise, and oil producers given the relatively high degree of substitutability between the two fuels.

13.4. EU ENERGY POLICY

There was much talk of the need for a common energy policy for Western Europe before the oil crises of 1973 and 1979 forced national governments to base energy policy decisions on short-term strategic national interests. In the 1990s, with international energy markets apparently more stable, the Single Market Program (SMP) now a decade under way, liberalization of the electricity and gas markets looming and the upsurge in the number of energy demand and supply linkages both within the EU and between the EU and its neighbours set to continue, conclusion of an integrated EU energy policy is again the focus of much debate within governments, EU institutions, businesses and consumer groups. The general momentum towards greater policy integration within the EU has been heightened by the 1992 TEU, article 3 of which specifies that the Community must pursue common policies or activities, including "measures in the sphere of energy" (Commission of the European Communities 1996, p. 54), ensuring either an institutional impetus to conclusion of an energy chapter in the revision of the TEU, scheduled for 1997–98, or at least further clarification of the Union's competencies in this vital sector.

13.4.1. Energy at Euro-level

Energy issues have been at the heart of the process of Western European integration since its beginnings in the 1950s, but never subordinated to the aegis of a balanced, single, energy policy. In 1952 the establishment of the European Coal and Steel

Community (ECSC) created a common market for coal and steel, with the former then amounting to some 75 per cent of the community of six's TPER (Swann 1992, p. 262). The High Authority of the ECSC, set up to oversee the market, was never really effective in supplanting national regulation of the coal or steel industries (Strange 1994, p. 193), nor potentially so to the European energy economy given the great changes taking place in Western Europe's TPER from the early 1950s onwards (See Table 2). Increasingly the ECSC, and later the EEC, would deal with the domestic coal sectors of Europe not primarily in terms of their contribution to TPER but in order to alleviate the internal political instability caused by regional decline and unemployment once mines began to close.

The ECSC is generally seen as the forerunner of the European Economic Community (EEC), founded in 1957 through the Treaty of Rome and, in the field of energy, given the responsibility for oil, gas, hydro-power and electricity. The Rome Treaty in general was oriented towards more competition in industry but also acknowledged the special place of the state-run utilities, especially in the gas and electricity sectors, in meeting public service obligations and retaining some of their monopolistic features. (McGowan 1994, p. 266). A separate treaty called Euratom established a pool for cooperation in nuclear technologies, reflecting the strongly held view of the time that nuclear power would be the panacea of the future.

Therefore, the three pre-1980s treaties on which the EC was built divided responsibility for energy policy, a rapidly changing and expanding sector of Europe's economy, helping ensure real policy tools would remain under the control of national governments. The perceived need for a common energy policy has wavered widely over time due to a number of important dynamics emanating from within the energy sector itself, the intensity of integrative efforts within the EU, and the guiding ideological current of the day, the relative importance of each having either surfaced only recently or fluctuated over time. These could be described as: (a) international supply and demand characteristics (see sections 13.2 and 13.3); (b) energy effects on the internal market project; and (c) economic efficiency and liberalization. Let's examine the last two points.

13.4.2. Energy and the Internal Market

Energy materials, like any other essential commodity, can be subject to price instability, though unlike other commodities such price instability affects the whole of the production cycle and hence the price of all goods and services right across the economic spectrum. Common market theory gives us some indication of how instability in energy markets can affect the EU's internal market for goods and services. Swann (1992, p. 262) cites two basic reasons why a common energy policy is thought necessary. First, distortions of competition arising through the pursuit of different national energy policies, e.g. state subsidy of the inefficient production of indigenous resources, low pricing policy, disparate taxation measures on consumption, etc., affect profit margins and run counter to some of the principles of free and fair competition laid out in Articles 85 to 94 of the Treaty of Rome. Second, in a situation of over-dependency on external suppliers by any number of member states, different national energy policies could well result in divergent crisis-management programmes, such as the development of strategic petroleum reserves or the expansion of storage facilities for stockpiling emergency supplies. In the event of a crisis, though the prudent, i.e. those with the more extensively developed contingency plans (reinforcement measures), would face fewer supply disruptions than the imprudent, they would nevertheless also be indirectly affected by the shortage as the importing and exporting capabilities of the imprudent would be severely diminished. In an integrated market some form of coordination between energy policy-makers clearly appears necessary to avoid such distortions taking place and jeopardizing the integrity of the SMP.

Accordingly, the creation through harmonization of an internal energy market with common standards and taxes and the removal of state subsidies is recognized as the priority energy task for the EU.[5] Indeed, specific energy-related issues, concerning economic efficiency and global competitiveness, the restriction of environmental damage and concerns over the security of energy supply, can only really be tackled at national level while the gas and electricity sectors of Europe remain structured on national lines. The policy instruments to conduct a common energy policy already exist in the relevant articles of the ECSC, Euratom and Maastricht treaties, but the existing variation between national energy structures, the threat to vested interests of tampering with them, as well as fears for consumers'/voters' welfare, have restricted movement forward. And while there is, more or less, a broad consensus within the Union in favour of more integration in these markets, the desired route is an object of some contention between the protagonists of greater liberalization, where the market does the work, and those favouring continued public sector participation with a harmonized regulatory structure under supranational scrutiny.

13.1.3. Intervention vs. liberalization

The ideological battle has effectively already been decided. Governments continue to turn away from Keynesian demand management in favour of *laissez faire* economics, a process tracing its origins back to the early 1970s. With a minimum of constraint on the private sector and the gradual elimination of "public ownership of the means of production", paraphrasing *Old Labour*, the view that the free market could better provide for societies, in principle if not always in practice, became the dominant economic creed in a growing global economy built on technological advance and, on a scale never before seen, the massive accumulation of wealth. As the major world economic powers, and decisively the USA, cut public spending and deregulated industry, services, financial markets and labour markets, aiming for healthy public balance sheets and low-cost competitive advantages for domestic companies, other governments found it increasingly difficult to maintain extensive macroeconomic

---

[5] "Market integration is the central, determining factor in the Community's energy policy, in its absence most other activities would lose their justification and would be done at national level" – EU Energy Commissioner Christos Papoutsis (Reuters, 13 Dec. 1995).

management without incurring financial instability in the form of exchange rate volatility and a consequent loss of competitiveness on international markets. Limits on state spending have been strictly enforced not only by the financial markets but also by the international financial institutions (IFI), i.e. IMF/World Bank, which can limit access to loans and damage a nation's credit rating if it is found to be failing to maintain budgetary constraint. The temptation then is to retreat from involvement in the economy through privatization of the public sector and deregulation of markets, especially when the private sector can act with greater impunity and without the constraint of public obligation, only the need for shareholder confidence and consumer loyalty.

Perhaps surprisingly considering its penetration into public policy statements, this neo-liberal agenda has not yet fully limited the ability of governments to influence markets. Though governments in Western Europe, with a strong history of intervention, still produce a hefty percentage of Gross National Product (GNP), on average 60 per cent in the EU and ranging from the lower end of about 40 per cent in the UK to a much larger 65–70 per cent in France, the trend towards more privatization and deregulation continues apace. And notwithstanding the growing popularity of privatization and its positive effect on balance of payments calculations, strong state involvement, both as operator in industry and especially in monitoring business practice through the regulation of markets and the work-place, remains pivotal to economic performance.

Energy, already dominated in large measure by the private sector in the form of the MNOCs, has, however, proved a prominent backdrop to the changes. It is a generally accepted principle that a capital intensive market structure, with the need for heavy front-end investment in an extensive distribution network such as the natural gas system, is best set up and brought to maturity by a state monopoly. It is likewise considered desirable if not inevitable that once past that stage it can thrive better under free market conditions (V. Thomas 1996, pp. 13–14). Privatization of the energy sector in the United Kingdom, first of the government's majority stake in British Petroleum and then the coal, gas and electricity sectors, has been plagued by problems ranging from the miners' strikes of the early 1980s to concerns over the procedural aspects of share flotation and the detrimental effects on consumers of creating private sector monopolies facing little in the way of serious competition. It is still too early to say for certain if liberalization of the energy sector in the UK, particularly in gas and electricity, has achieved the desired outcomes of improved efficiency through increased competition. To date the production of gas and electricity has attained a high degree of competitiveness but distribution and retail are still largely in the hands of monopolistic private companies with high profit margins and little obligation to make any but the most necessary of incremental investments. In applying such approaches to the EU as a whole, a major problem arises in the wide disparities between national structures, ranging from the very mature markets in Germany, the Netherlands, France, Italy and the UK, to the adolescents in Greece, Portugal and Spain. Unsurprisingly, the latter are concerned to first build up and strengthen not only market structures which benefit producers, consumers and distributors alike, but also national carriers which can also compete with the established operators in mature markets.

Next to privatization, a general programme of macroeconomic adjustment, the core issue in liberalization of the energy markets is centred on the introduction of competition to the gas and electricity markets through third-party access (TPA), favoured by private operators, the UK government and the Commission, and opposed by the continental utilities particularly in the Netherlands (Gasunie), Germany (Ruhrgas) and France (Gaz du France). Already facing problems in the UK and under experimentation in Italy, TPA would allow competitors right of access to national transmission systems, understandably resisted by the public operators given their long-term "take-or-pay" commitments and the threat mandatory TPA poses to their monopoly positions.

However, in the short run and probably more than anything else, it will be concerns over growing import dependency in Europe, substantiated or otherwise (see Tables 13.2 and 13.3), and the security of natural gas supplies which will influence just how far member states will allow deregulation of the markets to proceed. In the past and bearing the continental gas and electricity utilities in mind, so long as they continued to secure advantageous terms of trade for their countries, there monopoly positions within national markets would not be challenged (Estrada *et al.* 1995, p. 37). If the private sector can be seen providing the same guarantees, e.g. as oil companies, then certainly in the more mature markets liberalization will proceed further.

Accordingly, in the debate on EU energy policy there is a need to strike a balance between providing an impetus to integration of the energy sectors without scaring national governments/carriers and/or private sector operators with excessive regulation or deregulation of the emerging harmonized market structure (Baragona 1995).

13.4.4. Present policy objectives

13.4.4.1. Global economic competitiveness

In an increasingly competitive global marketplace, rationalizing the use, availability and cost of energy and, thus, improving the economic efficiency and competitiveness of the Union is a policy priority, fully supported by the underlying principles of the SMP. As early as 1959 the Community recognized the effect of energy prices on industrial competitiveness through the findings of its inter-executive committee on energy (McGowan 1994, p. 266). The EU's share of global markets has come under increasing strain in the past two decades because of advances made both by developing countries and by traditional competitors in established export markets. Given that the structure of European industry is considered overall too rigid, especially in excessive regulation of labour markets, and not always favourable to innovation, e.g. inefficient management in the public sector, an internal market for energy would rationalize energy use within the EU and cut costs for consumers, particularly large-scale end-users and electricity generating companies, making European exports cheaper and more attractive.[6]

13.4.4.2. Environmentalism

Sustainable development, also enshrined in the Maastricht Treaty, is the ability to maintain economic expansion without the risk of excessive environmental damage, and has become a goal much proffered in the industrialized world where, of course, the greater part of such environmental dangers originate. Most energy actions, and especially those involved in the larger part of TPER, have some negative effect on the environment, be it the burning of hydrocarbons, the disposal of waste nuclear materials, the construction of hydro-electric dams, etc. Controlling the emission of pollutants harmful both at the local level, e.g. sulphur dioxide, hydrocarbons and nitrogen dioxide, and at the global level, particularly CO_2, is essential if the targets set at the 1996 Berlin Conference on Climate Control are to be met by 2000.[7] The Commission has been supporting initiatives in R&D, especially of energy saving and energy efficiency technologies, for some time and rightly regards green technologies as a growth sector of the European economy with a strong export showing. The idea of a "carbon tax" has also been floated, but remains controversial as it would be detrimental to the competitiveness of European producers because of higher costs and seen as aggressive behaviour by energy producing countries which fear a further transfer of oil revenues from producer to consumer governments.

13.4.4.3. Security of supply

That the former two policy objectives even figure so highly in a region with such a major energy import requirement is definitely a sign of the market conditions that have "weaken(ed) the scarcity culture which had prevailed among suppliers, consumers, governments and the Commission" since the middle of the 1980s (McGowan 1994, p. 270) Conceptions of energy security, however, remain supply-oriented, and heavily influenced by the experience of the oil crises of the 1970s where exposure to a single source of imported energy, i.e. Middle Eastern oil, proved an difficult experience. There is still a great reluctance to let market forces meet the demand and supply requirements of consumers, the UK providing the exception to the rule. Security of supply should be a non-issue given Europe's energy balance and the real potential threats to supply, i.e. reliance on any one unstable external supplier (unnecessary as there are many competing ones), or the threat of external suppliers ever acting in tandem over a prolonged period to limit Europe's import options (unlikely where external suppliers are heavily dependent on their oil and gas revenues and inward investment, the number of suppliers is too great and, because of their other differences, regional interests in the Middle East, Central Asia, the Balkans, etc., their scope for concerted action is at present narrow). As present market conditions are very favourable for the energy situation in Europe, any policy aiming at continuing

---

[6] German manufacturing companies complain loudly that high domestic energy costs impair their standing in world markets. "Germany: Consumption grows as companies bicker about access". *Petroleum Economist*, Oct. 1996.

[7] Berlin Conference.

security of supply should encourage the maintenance of existing conditions. As Europe is marginally dependent on external suppliers of oil and gas, policies aimed at energy conservation remain appropriate, as does the promotion of local and global expansion of oil and natural gas production, and creation of suitable conditions for long-term social and political stability in regions that contribute to Europe's energy import requirement.

13.5. WESTERN POLICY TOWARDS THE EX-COMMUNIST BLOC

In the limited space available it would be impossible to give adequate measure or justice to the full range and direction that "Western policy" took, as a whole, towards Eastern Europe after the collapse of state-sponsored communism. However, the inception of the ECT must be seen in that broader context, given that its origins, aims and the methods adopted to try and achieve them are deeply rooted in policy decisions made by the major Western governments at the beginning of the 1990s and followed through right up to the present. Accordingly, it is necessary to make some general points about the focus of Western responses and to show that the Western-constructed "transitional model" was incorporated into the European Energy Charter and ECT processes.

When the Communist parties of Eastern Europe ceased to function as the principal tools of political and socio-economic organization, fragile post-communist societies reeling from the breakdown of the plan system needed aid, investment and access to Western markets to promote nascent indigenous economic forces and to bolster the democratic foundations of the new regimes. Western governments and international organizations could provide such incentives and enjoy the privileged role of guiding the transition to the free market as membership of the Western club was targeted early as the overriding policy objective of the new democracies. Private enterprise, a move to the free market and liberal democracy were not challenged as goals, only the means and the methods adopted to transform whole societies were up for discussion, either in the East or in the West. A choice between two basic models emerged in the West (Gowan 1995, pp. 6–7):

- a Franco-German proposal[8] to support the development of an Eastern European economic community, built on the existing trading relations between members of the Council for Mutual Economic Assistance (CMEA) and Western encouragement of the region as a whole though a regional development bank and the prospect of a pan-European free trade area embracing ECE, the FSU and the EU.
- an American/British-backed approach incorporating a complete break-up of the CMEA region, each country re-focusing its trade towards the West, liberalization of markets, the stimulation of export-led growth through foreign direct investment (FDI), massive Western aid for currency stabilization and eventual membership of

---

[8] The European Bank for Reconstruction and Development was the only fruit of this, but its original role as an organizer of finance for major public works was eventually toned down to conformity with the rest of the ST programme.

an enlarged and probably altered EU.

The latter course of "shock therapy" (ST) as outlined by the eminent Harvard Professor, Jeffery Sachs (1994) was adopted by the G7 group of leading industrialized nations in 1990, perhaps reflecting the growing German preoccupation with domestic matters, the general preference for neo-liberal approaches, hinted at above, and even more likely the direction of US leadership. In any case, the course of reform for a region of some 120 million in ECE and 250 million in the FSU had been decided upon from without, with the tacit support of Eastern élite groups. Western *economic-statecrafting*, a combination of carrots and sticks, e.g. IFI loans and assorted bilateral aid programs with strict conditions attached, exertion of leverage over indebtedness, deferred promises of eventual membership of the EU and the North Atlantic Treaty Organization (NATO), unilaterally negotiated (and generally unfavourable) trade and cooperation agreements with the EU, e.g. the Association/Europe Agreements, created the conditions for maximum penetration by Western operators of Eastern capital markets, industry and services, while simultaneously denying reciprocal treatment in EU markets, the natural focus for Eastern exporters. The role of Western(-dominated) institutions in this process was decisive, providing both incentive for and tutelage of the "transitional economies", as "inputs", e.g. loans, grant aid, trade-related aid *and* "outputs", e.g. trade concessions, organization membership, access to technology, were means and ends of transition, and totally dependent on the unbound reciprocity of Western governments and international organizations. Thus, though democracy and the market were conceived as goals, the latter, i.e. the rush to the market, was afforded the priority at the expense of the former, i.e. majority domestic support for ST.

Measurement of the social and economic costs and benefits of ST is difficult, and in any case unnecessary in the context of this chapter. However, in assessing the ECT it is important never to lose sight of this overriding Western strategy, combining incentivization and conditionality – tying macroeconomic aid, debt relief and market access to systemic transformation which maximizes openness to Western capital, ideas and influence.

13.6. THE ECT'S PROVISIONS

The basic thrust of the Charter was in line with Western policy towards the region following the collapse of Soviet power. Reform at the micro level, modernization of the energy sector, maximizing efficiency gains, improved safety and technical standards, sustainable environmental policies and enhanced security of supply would boost trade and were best facilitated by Western technology, know-how and finance. Creating a favourable environment for FDI was a prerequisite for trade-led growth of a substantial nature, a concept fully in line with ST dogma.

The preliminary signing of the European Energy Charter took place in The Hague in 1991, prior to which the negotiations on the "Basic Protocol", the ensuing ECT, had already begun and would give a legally binding element to the principles set out in the Charter. The negotiations concentrated on two key politico-economic issues –

investment and trade – and tentatively covered areas of specific concern in a series of ancillary provisions and protocols on the environment, competition, nuclear cooperation, technology transfers, and trade-related investment measures (TRIMs). By the time participants signed the legally binding treaty in Lisbon on 15 December 1994, without the participation of the USA and Canada, consensus had been reached in a number of areas. The most substantive developments were in the investment and trade provisions while the supplementary protocols were generally softened up. Only the protocol on energy efficiency was signed at Lisbon and limits the obligations to 'best efforts' (*Financial Times EC Energy Monthly*, "Russia Signs Energy Charter At Lisbon", 23 Jan. 1995, pp. 73–79).

13.6.1. Investment

It was clear that substantial investment in the energy sectors of the FSU would be needed, in particular to reverse the drastic fall in oil production since the late 1980s. The Soviet oil industry, once the world's largest, continues to suffer from a drastic production decline, an insurmountable technological deficit and innumerable environmental hazards as a result of "bureaucratized disorganization" and the mid-1980s fall in oil prices, where neglect of exploration and innovation, and an eventual lack of resources to maintain production of the highest yielding fields, have told.

A central political issue would be access to and development of resources, and the rights of investors before and after an agreement for development was made. The key for Western negotiators, and the American delegation in particular, was the principle of *national treatment* (NT) for foreign investors at all stages of exploration and production, and especially regarding capital flows, i.e. repatriation of profit. As in many Third World countries, and for that matter developed ones, foreign ownership of strategic natural resources is still regarded with a heavy degree of scepticism, especially in parts of the FSU where Marxist/structuralist thought is still heavily influential, especially when dealing with Western governments and operators. Undoubtedly, the circumstances under which the FSU representatives in particular, but also the ECE states, were negotiating put them at a disadvantage to their Western counterparts. Having only recently (re)gained their independence, they had an acute lack of experience in talks on international finance and trade, and of domestic legislation on which to base their expectations.[9] There was little by the way of precedent on matters of exceptions to treaty agreements in the fields of national sovereignty over energy resources, privatization, centre–periphery relationships and taxation. Economic depression and exchange rate volatility also made it difficult to evaluate assets and therefore to regulate foreign involvement in investment programmes such as privatization. This dislocation was eventually rectified through a Commission pro-

---

[9] "Many of the concepts of the Treaty come straight out of Western bilateral investment treaty and OECD practice – concepts founded in the international economic law of market economies with which the former socialist countries had no truck. Signing on to such concepts may often seem, to the CIS policy-makers, as the thing to do to become a market economy and part of the club of "civilised nations"; they may have only hazy notions of what the obligations will actually mean for them" (Waelde 1995, p. 9).

posal to adopt a two-stage approach to negotiations where the first treaty, covering post-investments, i.e. guaranteeing rights for investors after the negotiation and conclusion of an investment agreement, could be completed immediately leaving a transitional period of up to four years for the negotiations of a second treaty in which the formerly centrally-planned economies could introduce domestic legislation on energy and fiscal policies, and develop a set of exceptions, already well developed in the West, at the pre-investment stage, i.e. in guaranteeing rights for investors in actual international tendering for contracts.

Paradoxically, Western negotiators could hardly expect Eastern states to open up unconditionally to Western capital without reciprocal NT for foreign investors in their own energy industries. The initial *perceived* unidirectional nature of the Lubbers Plan (West–East investment flows for Eastern energy supplies) was, therefore, superseded during the course of the negotiations on the Treaty, to emerge re-worked within a multilateral framework incorporating a far broader range of international politico-economic relationships. Consequently, it is not sufficient to examine the ECT merely in terms of its impact on West–East energy patterns, as the East–West, West–West and East–East dimensions cannot be ignored (Andrews-Speed 1996, p. 373). Such developments were certainly neither intended nor foreseen by the early proponents of the plan, and consequently hitherto very restrictive regimes of national-based invest-ment guidelines required renegotiation. The extended duration of negotiations, initially estimated at 18 months to two years but eventually taking almost five years, was due in no small measure to the concerns of the USA and the EU, specifically, about liberalization made in investment or trade to the detriment and/or the benefit of one or the other (*EC Energy Monthly*).

13.6.2. Trade

Along with changes in investment patterns the liberalization, or at least transparency, of trading conditions for energy products and associated services is at least as impor-tant to the construction of an European EnCom. Many post-Communist governments, starved of hard currency and needing to rectify balance of payments and budget deficits, have developed extensive fiscal measures designed to maximize government revenues, through export/import tariffs, capital gains tax (especially on profit repa-triation) and other trade-restricting practices. At the same time they need to balance the needs of consumers and domestic businesses through subsidies, debt-rescheduling and other forms of social and corporate welfare during a period of great socio-economic upheaval. Such conditions can be disincentives for foreign companies with tight profit margins to make substantial investments in domestic energy markets, i.e. downstream, given that they would not benefit from the same level of subsidies, (if any) as domestic producers. Hence the emphasis on trade and exports. Progressive integration into the GATT/WTO international trading system was highlighted early as a positive framework for future free trade developments,[10] with Most Favoured

---

[10] All non-OECD participants, except Cyprus and Malta, were also non-GATT signatories.

Nation (MFN) status applying to signatories where bilateral or other multilateral agreements did not meet the same level of preferential treatment. This would help standardize trading practices on quotas, tariffs and Voluntary Import Restraints (VIRs), and bolster confidence.

In geopolitical terms the most crucial aspects of negotiations on trade concerned the security of energy supply and, specifically, transit guarantees. Supply disruptions have been most notable in the FSU where exports to non-paying customers have been restricted or even cut off because of non-payment, causing delays in exports destined for paying customers in Western Europe when in order to meet their own energy requirements those indebted third-party transit states access supplies intended for paying customers. The commonly cited example of this has been the disruption in supplies to Central and Western Europe of Russian and Turkmen natural gas deliveries by the indebted Ukrainians (Stern 1995, pp. 61–62). Article 7 of the Treaty deals with transit provisions where the concerns of producers and consumers were matched with devices for international arbitration when a contracting party does not take the necessary measures to facilitate energy transit "consistent with the principle of freedom of transit and on an indiscriminate basis" (paragraph 1). This vague phrase, when applied in conjunction with Article 7(2) which lists activities contracting parties agree to encourage, does offer some scope for action. These measures include "modernization, development and *operation of inter-regional transport facilities,* as well as the development of internal and cross-border connection facilities' (Baragona amd Butler 1995) (emphasis added). It is implied that contracting parties should promote such initiatives along the principles of freedom of transit, recognized in international law for many centuries, and at least guarantee the *status quo.* Further, the treaty has attempted to tackle the issue of national sovereignty in the transit of goods over sovereign territory by distinguishing between existing transit facilities and infrastructure, where the smooth continuation of international trade takes the precedent, and the creation of new or additional transit arrangements where issues of national sovereignty are greatest (art 7 (4 & 5)). Therefore, mirroring somewhat the distinction made between pre-investment and post-investment procedures, previously existing or agreed upon transit facilities are protected under the ECT but there is little by way of dispute settlement over the construction of new facilities that cannot be blocked by states concerned over their national sovereignty, or at least using sovereignty in that capacity for any objections it may have to such developments being made.

Article 7(7) tackles problems specifically associated with a transit state taking retaliatory action "to interrupt or reduce the existing transit" in the event of a reduction in its own supplies. Here the Treaty provides a dispute settlement procedure lasting up to 120 days and during which the General Secretary (of the ECT Secretariat in Brussels) must appoint an independent conciliator, who, in the event that no negotiated settlement can be reached, has the power to recommend a resolution to the situation which once the 120 days are up must be followed, either until final agreement can be reached, or for a period of 12 months, whichever comes sooner. Not only does this procedure provide real international arbitration of such transit disputes but it stipulates that contracting parties cannot interrupt supplies for the duration of the 120 day process. The efficacy or otherwise of this provision will certainly be of critical importance to the success of the Treaty, particularly in terms of its guarantees of energy supplies, addressing as it does the problems experienced in the delay of supplies from the FSU and enhancing the stability of the legal framework of the supply situation to Central and Western European markets.

13.6.3. Enforcement

The ECT would become fully legally binding once ratified by the governments of 30 of the signatory states to the final treaty and, until that time, the key investment and trade provisions of the Treaty would apply on a provisional basis. Part 5 of the ECT deals with dispute settlement "reinforcing the credibility of the legal framework...and representing an unprecedented set of sanctions applicable to a sectoral international agreement" (Doré and De Bauw 1995, p. 56). Resolution can be made through the courts of contracting parties, e.g. in the case of an investment, a host government can be prosecuted by its own judiciary or tribunal if found to be in breach of Treaty provisions, or in accordance with previously agreed procedures, i.e. in existing bilateral or multilateral treaties which take precedent, e.g. GATT, where international arbitration can be sought through the International Center for the Settlement of Investment Disputes (ICSID), authorities established under the Arbitration Rules of the United Nations Commission on International Trade Law, or the Arbitration Institute of the Stockholm Chamber of Commerce. The result of arbitration is final and legally binding on the parties to the dispute (ibid., p. 57).

13.7. CONCLUSION

Other analyses of the ECT have tended to concentrate solely on its provisions and their possible consequences for East–West energy linkages, and in particular the improvement in operating conditions for Western companies (Andrews-Speed 1996, Axelrod 1996, Doré and De Bauw 1995, Waelde 1995). The Treaty can only improve the fluency of such linkages as the breadth of states involved and the legal cover of the key investment and trade provisions give it real political weight. It is doubtful that the integrity of the Treaty would be compromised – it is the first multilateral treaty of its kind, in the field of energy and embracing (most of) the West and the new democracies. Consequently, in the greater part of this chapter I have tried to provide an outline of the major internal and external imperatives, energy-related and otherwise, which motivated the EU to take a strong lead in driving the ECT to a concrete conclusion. Grasping key characteristics of the IPE of energy, i.e. the importance of non-OPEC energy supply to global markets and the regionalization of energy markets, and stressing the EU's motivations in playing such a prominent role in its initiation and negotiation, allows some qualitative judgement on two levels. First, the ECT's impact on post-Cold War international politics in Eurasia, both for East–West relations and US–European relations. Second, evaluation of the ECT as a real foreign policy initiative of the EU, and its relative success or failure.

The ECT supports global expansion of investment and production outside OPEC regions, particularly in the FSU where such developments are already under way. However, the long-term stability of such undertakings as Western-backed Azeri and Kazakh oil production and export to world markets, and Russian natural gas exports, are enhanced by the improved investment conditions – safer guarantees in the post-investment stage, and, especially, the strengthening of transit conditions. If a second treaty covering pre-investment and TRIMs, i.e. in new pipelines, can be negotiated the results would certainly appear more tangible for Western operators in the short term. The persistent emphasis on improving conditions for Western operators misses the one essential point of the treaty in that the improvement in conditions for Eastern economies, and consequently Eastern operators, was, or should have been, at least as important a goal. Hopefully the treaty does afford some short-term protection for indigenous economic forces while at the same time providing an opening into an otherwise extremely unfairly balanced East–West energy structure.

Regionalization is to some extent encouraged by the ECT, potentially tying the producing regions of the FSU to the large consuming areas of Europe, supporting the ability of the European market to receive the majority of its energy supplies, of oil and gas, from outside OPEC well into the next millennium. However, in contemplating any scenarios about regionalization of energy and specifically a Euro-energy market, it is very important not to lose sight of one inalterable fact. Though all regional energy markets contain powerful indigenous economic forces, especially in Europe, the single most striking factor in all such formations concerns the still central role of the upstream and downstream operations of the American-dominated MNOCs. In this respect, the USA's absence from the list of signatories could be the death knell for the ECT should the overall East–West political climate become more confrontational and US-MNOCs be discouraged from FSU operations.

In terms of East–West relations the ECT can be viewed as an integral component of Western strategy, along with other EU, IMF, and World Bank initiatives, and bilateral agreements, in this case targeting specifically the energy sector within the producing regions of the FSU. Lubbers' EnCom suggestion came at an appropriate time: fitting neatly with the role assigned to the EU by the G7, it could fairly easily incorporate ST credentials, and force the pace of an issue at the heart of East–West economic relations, i.e. energy and access to resources. The irony is that had the ECT been brought to a more rapid conclusion and under a united Western approach it could have been more far-reaching in its ability to secure access for Western operators, as indigenous forces in the East, particularly in Russia, became stronger the longer the negotiations proceeded. Doctrinaire neo-liberal approaches to international agreements, it seems, are more palatable when unidirectional.

In fact the real consequences of the ECT will probably be felt more within the Western Alliance itself. A greater emphasis on energy imports from the FSU, especially Russian natural gas, implies a more prominent role for European energy companies and Russian security structures in energy supply security, potentially diluting the dominant role played by the USA and NATO in Europe. At present, it is US technological and military power which guarantees the supply of oil from the Middle

East (and elsewhere) to world markets, including Europe. The Gulf War proves beyond any reasonable doubt how far the USA is prepared to step in order to maintain supply and its own supervision over the market. In the initial suggestion of a "European" energy charter the Americans certainly saw an attempt by Europeans to exclude US companies from the FSU's oil and gas riches and promote an Eurasian energy network less dependent on the Middle East *and* the USA. In fact, US influence over development of FSU hydrocarbons potential will remain central, through the financial, technological and management resources of the MNOCs and the USA's superpower trappings, so long as the general international political climate still supports it, i.e. US–Russian/FSU relations do not deteriorate exponentially. Increased West European–Russian energy linkages will have only long-term consequences for the security architecture of the Atlantic Alliance if present arrangements become unstable or more palatable alternatives emerge – both highly unlikely. Alternatively, in finance, monetary union in Europe combined with increased gas use could de-link gas prices from oil prices and the US dollar, reinforcing the regional Euro-energy market. However, though gas use is predicted to rise greatly, imports are unlikely to assume the important position in Europe's TPER that imported oil once did, resulting in only minor broader economic and security implications. More general political and economic developments outside of energy will matter more in respect of security and US–EU relations. In this sense the negotiations and outcome of the ECT have only highlighted some of the contradictions in the dominant neo-liberal/free-trade movement as espoused both in the USA and in Europe.

The EU's involvement in the ECT has all the hallmarks of EU foreign economic policy-making. The *internalization* of external processes, i.e. Western policy towards the East, and *externalization* of internal processes, i.e. EU energy policy, are common signs of such activity, particularly in those areas where the EU has most authority, such as agriculture and trade (Smith 1994, p. 463). A European EnCom actively internalizes Western policy and is consistent with all EU energy policies and broadly supportive of the key objective of harmonization of European energy market structures. That the three main policy goals of economic efficiency, environmentalism and security of supply can be mutually exclusive does not detract from this but does entail a certain "fudging" of the first two in favour of the last within the ECT process. Security of supply, the most easily recognizable "foreign" energy policy, has been enhanced considerably through improved investment and trading conditions, and simply through the ECT process itself. The EU is already highly influential in ECE, for instance where prospective EU candidates have begun to introduce legislation in line with EU environmental standards independently of binding multilateral or bilateral agreements, has forced the pace and character within ECE and the FSU on general energy, environmental and natural resources legislation, encouraging harmonization and stability of the market across the region. Its influence over this aspect of the Treaty will remain especially strong as long as the USA is absent from active public involvement. Such developments in the East could even provide an external stimulus to internal EU liberalization. Harmonization and the creation of an IEM have also been aided particularly by the improved investment conditions but also by forcing liberalization of Euro-energy markets higher up on the political agenda.

Voluntary TPA, shut out of the ECT early on, has become a reality during recent months: an improbable development had the ECT not prompted a higher priority for energy in EU affairs.

Consequently, not only can the ECT be characterized as a foreign policy of the EU but it is a largely successful one, strengthening the role of the EU in the ex-Soviet Bloc and meeting to varying degrees the primary objectives of EU energy policy.

13.8. REFERENCES

Adelman, M.A. (1995). *The Genie Out Of The Bottle*. Cambridge, MA: MIT Press.

Andrews-Speed, P. (1996). "The Energy Charter Treaty: Its Importance to Western European Energy Companies". *Oil and Gas Law and Taxation Review*, Sept.

Axelrod, R.S. (1996). "The European Energy Charter: Reality or Illusion?". *Energy Policy 24*, No. 6.

Baragona, K.C. (1995). "Debate On The Need For An Energy Chapter". *The Petroleum Economist*, June.

Baragona, K.C. and R. Butler (1995). "Special Report on International Energy Law – Transit Rights under the Energy Charter Treaty". *The Petroleum Economist*, May.

British Petroleum (BP) (1991–1996). *BP Statistical Review of World Oil/Energy*. London.

Commission of the European Communities (CEC) (1995a). *Energy In Europe 26*. Brussels, Dec.

Commission of the European Communities (CEC) (1995b). *An Energy Policy For Europe (White Paper)*. COM(95) 682 final, Brussels, 13 Dec.

Commission of the European Communities (CEC) (1996). *Energy in Europe to 2020: A Scenario Approach*. Brussels, Spring.

Doré, J. and R. De Bauw (1995). *The Energy Charter Treaty*. London: RIIA.

Estrada, J., A. Moe and K.D. Martinsen (1995). *The Development of European Gas Markets: Environmental, Economic and Political Perspectives*. Wiley.

Gowan, P. (1995). "Neo Liberal Theory and Practice For Eastern Europe". *The New Left Review*, No. 5.

Gray, D. (1995). Reforming the Energy Sector in Transition Economies. *World Bank Discussion Paper*, No. 296, Washington, DC.

Harvie, C. (1995). *Fool's Gold: The Story of North Sea Oil*. London: Penguin.

International Energy Agency (IEA) (1995). *The Energy Charter Treaty: A Description of Its Provisions*. IEA (109). Paris: IEA/OECD.

International Energy Agency (IEA) (1996a). *Energy Policies of IEA Countries, 1996 Review*. Paris: IEA/OECD.

International Energy Agency (IEA) (1996b). *World Energy Outlook, 1996 Edition*. Paris: IEA/OECD.

McBride, J. (1995). "OPEC Sees Scope for Links with Ex-Soviet Producers". Reuters, 23 Feb.

McGowan, F. (1994). "EC Energy Policy". In: A. El-Agraa (ed.) *The Economics Of The EC*, 4th edn. Hemel Hempstead: Harvester Wheatsheaf.

Mitchell, J. (1995). "EU Energy Policy, Foreign Policy and Geopolitics: Three Causes That Have Not Found One Another". *Geopolitics of Energy 17*, No. 8, Aug.

Odell, P.R. (1994). "World Oil Resources, Reserves And Production". *The Energy Journal*. Special Edition H.J. Frank (ed.) "The Changing World Petroleum Market". IAEE. 1994 pp. 89–144.

Odell, P.R. (1995). "The Geopolitics of Western Europe's Energy, From Problems to Opportunities". *Geopolitics of Energy 17*, No. 10, Oct.

Sachs, J. (1994). "Analysing Shock Therapy". *Social Market Foundation*.

Smith, M. (1994). "The European Community: Testing the Boundaries Of Foreign Economic Policy". In: R. Stubbs and G.R.D. Underhill (eds) *Political Economy and the Changing Global Order*. London: Macmillan.

Stern, J.P. (1995). "The Russian Natural Gas 'Bubble': Consequences For European Gas Markets". London: RIIA.

Strange, S. (1994). *States and Markets, 2nd Edition*. London: Pinter.

Streifel, S.S. (1995). "Review and Outlook for the World Oil Market". *World Bank Discussion Papers*, No.

301, Washington, DC, Aug.

Swann, D. (1992). *The Economics of the Common Market*, 7th edn. London: Penguin.

Tempest, P. (1995). "Latest Oil Data, Trends And Prospects". *World Petroleum Congress*, London.

Thomas, P. (1996). "The Caspian – Nitty Gritty, Nuts and Bolts". *FT Energy Economist*, Dec., 182/2–7.

Thomas, V. (1996). "Europe Drags Its Heels behind Stumbling UK". *The Petroleum Economist*, Oct.

Waelde, T.W. (1995). "International Investment under the 1994 Energy Charter Treaty". *Journal of World Trade 29*, May.

CHAPTER 14

Protectionism in a globalized food system: the impact of the Common Agricultural Policy on the world market

Marjoleine Hennis

14.1. INTRODUCTION

The Common Agricultural Policy (CAP) is one of the most developed policies within the EU. Since the start of the EEC it has been one of the few policy domains on which considerable agreement could be achieved. It has therefore often been regarded as an example for other policy domains in the process towards complete European integration.

At the same time, the CAP has created divergences between member states, between different policy domains, and between the EU and other trade blocs. Conflicts at the EU level have mainly concerned the surpluses the CAP has generated through its market and price support policy, its high budget costs, and its distorting effects on the world market for food and farm products due to the high level of protection and export subsidies.

Under pressure from both inside and outside the EU, the CAP has undergone some important changes. Yet criticism persists. A renationalization of the CAP, or further liberalization of trade, forms the centre of the debate on the alternatives. Agricultural policy with a common character therefore seems more and more difficult to maintain. Both for the process towards European integration and for the international food system, this will have serious implications.

This chapter seeks to explain which developments have led to the present situation. It starts with a brief historical overview of the CAP, indicating first the relativity of its "common" nature and second the dominant role of the member states in the policy process. It continues by showing how this situation has led to a rather static policy which basically remained unchallenged until 1992. Section 14.3 deals with the links of the European agricultural sector with other parts of the global food system and the role of the CAP herein. Section 14.4 discusses how the CAP and its support system have been gradually dismantled and why criticism nevertheless persists (section 14.5). In section 14.6, the main alternatives to the CAP are described. Finally, some conclusions are drawn on the consequences of the present situation and its alternatives for the role of the member states in the EU, and for the position of the EU internationally, in the framework of the process of European integration.

A. Cafruny and P. Peters (eds.), The Union and the World, 271–283

14.2. HISTORY OF THE CAP

14.2.1. Member states and the CAP

The origins of the Common Agricultural Policy (CAP) can be understood in the framework of the European integration process. The implementation of the CAP was, certainly from an administrative point of view, an important step in the process towards European unification. The integration of six national agricultural policies, which initially were organized in very different ways, into a common system provided an opportunity for gaining experience in decision-making at the European level. The protectionist character of the CAP with respect to third countries contributed further to the awareness of being part of the European Community.

However important this "common" character, the CAP is, and has always been, highly member state-based as the most fundamental decisions are negotiated in the Council of Ministers.[1] The Treaty of Rome, the founding document of the European Community which was signed in 1957 by Belgium, France, Germany, Italy, Luxembourg and The Netherlands, established a programme of economic cooperation and harmonization, and a common external tariff. The impulse for a common policy for the agricultural sector came primarily from those member states which already had solid organized agricultural sectors and which were characterized by strong government intervention. Each country sought to support farm incomes by keeping the internal prices of primary farm products above the price level of the world market. Once the EEC came about, it was the conviction of the six prospective member states that the integration process of their national economies could succeed only if the special position of the agricultural sector was taken into account. Thus, the official reason for establishment of the CAP was that it served to reconcile disparate national agricultural interests and differences in market organization schemes, and that concerted action towards European integration would be easier. In point of fact, it created a possibility for organized states such as The Netherlands and France to expand their markets, while maintaining the mechanisms of support for their farmers. This provided them the opportunity to delegate the financial responsibility for farmers' support to the European level while keeping farmers (representing a significant electorate) satisfied at the domestic level.

The decision about the CAP and its content was a direct result of a trade-off between Germany and France. Germany, which concentrated mainly on the reconstruction of its industry, was served by open trade and a stable food supply. France, on the other hand, had to deal with a farm structure consisting of both a large amount of small farms and influential middle and large farms which were all organized in the FNSEA. The FNSEA was most influential in French agricultural policy and its plea for generous price support (especially for wheat and sugar beet) was soon adopted.

---

[1] This argument is based on a theoretical framework which combines parts of Institutional Intergovernmentalism with an analysis of the underlying economic forces in the agro-industrial production chain in order to understand the outcome of the CAP process. According to the same argument, changes in the European agricultural structure influence the CAP through changes in domestic policy. For an extensive discussion of this framework see PhD thesis of the author (Hennis, forthcoming).

Thus, when designing the CAP, France stressed the necessity of strong market regulation for as many products as possible, while Germany managed to safeguard stable food supply and relatively high agricultural prices. Dutch demands were met through the implementation of the CAP: the improvement of the agricultural structure was to be achieved through modernizing agricultural holdings and regulation of agricultural prices and markets. The former especially suited The Netherlands, as its agricultural structure was already relatively modernized and its expansion, given its limitations of space, depended largely on the application of technology and intensification.

These proposals were studied in 1958 by the Commission. In 1960 they were translated into concrete directives for a market and price policy, and in 1962 the first market regulation was put into practice. Thus, the road to a gradual introduction of market intervention, linked to a system of protection, which separated the European market from the world market, was taken.

14.2.2. A static policy

For a long time, this policy has proved very hard to change. An explanation can be found within the member states. The position of the member states was based on the strong relations between bureaucracy and farmers' organizations on the national level.[2] It led to a bargaining situation in the Council where in general each national Minister of Agriculture defended the standpoint of the most important agricultural organization in its country with which it had developed strong relations. Giving up this standpoint would happen only if the buy-off price was very high.

The development of tight links between organized interests and governments within the national policy-making processes has tended to prevent the development of a European perspective in the CAP. These links frustrated Euro-wide interest representation of agricultural producers, and led to rigid bargaining positions of the member states in the Council. The bargaining process in the European Council, in turn, has been favourable to the maintenance of this situation. Due to the technical nature of many issues regarding the CAP it has been rather difficult for outside decision-makers to get a hold on the CAP. Furthermore, the meetings of the Council of Agricultural Ministers are not prepared by the Committee of Permanent Representatives (COREPER) but rather by a special committee on agriculture (Keeler 1996, p. 137).

This led to a situation in which the initial design of the CAP could be preserved over a long period. Until 1992, the CAP reflected the power balance among the member states during the EC's founding years: French policy aimed at a combination

---

[2] This part of the argument states that the links between decision-making and policy in the agricultural policy of the Member states have for a long time been characterized by corporatist relations, i.e. that the social–political structure of interest articulation and policy formation is based on a political–economic consensus between interest organizations with a representative monopoly on the one hand and the state on the other hand, in which organizations assure the discipline of their members in return for participation in policy formation and implementation (Frouws, 1994, p. 47). For the agricultural sector these relations are characterized by an institutionalized exchange of benefits and services between the state and farmers' organizations.

of integration in the European context with concerted action to stabilize world markets (Delorme 1994); Germany insisted on generous support measures (Hendriks 1994); The Netherlands aimed at a model of agricultural development which gave incentives to modern, high-tech and capital-intensive farms; whereas a strong advocate of liberal policy was still absent (Great Britain was not yet a member of the EC at the establishment of the CAP) (Keeler 1996, p. 136). The result was a delicate compromise of preferences of the strongest member states which could be maintained for many years thanks mainly to an increase of financial flows.

14.3. THE CAP AND THE WORLD

14.3.1. Globalization of the food system

The first way in which the CAP is linked to third countries is through the integration of European agriculture with the international food system. The global character of food production has led to a situation in which all parts of the global food chain are highly interlinked. This has determined the nature of development of the agricultural production structure in Europe, whereas third countries have been affected by the European agricultural sector and its common policy.

The global food production chain started in, and was led by, the USA (Friedman 1993). The American model of production was designed as part of the New Deal and provided the initial context for the regeneration of US agriculture and its technological transformation. It aimed to ensure relatively cheap, abundant and secure food supplies for the industrial labour force. At the same time, the industrial labour force was regarded as an expanding market for manufactured consumer goods.

The process towards the globalization of agricultural production was characterized by replication and integration. Replication means that the US model of both agricultural production and consumption, together with a policy of price support, trade restriction and competitive dumping, was "exported" to other countries. This model was adopted by the EC in the 1960s. The implementation was achieved through the CAP, based on a system of price and market support. Integration has taken place in the form of growing connections between especially European and US agro-food sectors via industrial inputs and processing which was facilitated through free trade of capital (Friedman 1993, pp. 36–37). During the 1970s the increased replication and integration of the US model of production started to show some problems. The growth of surpluses within the continents which had adopted the model was the most important. Moreover, the developed consumption pattern which demanded more meat production required the involvement of other countries. The solution found for those problems was the export of surpluses and part of the production process to other parts of the world. Maintenance of the production model was only made possible by the supply of cheap raw materials from mostly developing countries. Especially in Europe and the USA, these developments have influenced the relations among production forces by making agro-industry relatively powerful with respect to agricultural producers.

14.3.2. Agricultural structure and the CAP

The process of globalization should not be seen as an apolitical process characterized simply by adaptation to technologically driven change. On the contrary, the CAP partially regulates and has helped to shape changes in internationalization which were subject to the constraints of economics and technology. The impact of the CAP is felt in two ways. First, through its functioning it has had a considerable impact on the way the European agricultural structure has developed. The CAP is based on three principles: market unity,[3] community preference[4] and common financial responsibility.[5] The last principle found its expression in the foundation of the European Agriculture Guidance and Guarantee Fund (EAGGF), the Commission's budget for agriculture. These principles were to be achieved mainly through a market and price policy.

The market and price policy made up more than two-thirds of the agricultural budget. Until the beginning of the 1990s it was the main pillar of the CAP through which the CAP's objectives of self-sufficiency and a fair income for farmers were to be achieved. The idea behind this policy is based on the concept that producers should receive their income through the price for their products and not through direct income support or payments related to the amount of the stock or crop. In this way the CAP transferred the income from consumers to producers through high prices of agricultural products. Thus, net-importing countries for food transferred income to net-exporting countries through trade and through the Common budget.

It is clear that this mechanism of support encouraged member states to increase domestic production either in order to maximize net recipients or to minimize their net contribution to the budget. Given the fact that this support mainly went to commodities produced on relatively modernized holdings, this soon led to surpluses in production. Also, the policy gave an incentive to the enlargement of farms and to increased use of capital through the provision of high and stable prices. As larger, commercial farms have higher net returns per unit of land, these support prices increased access to credit and lowered its cost to the larger farmers, providing an incentive to bid up the price of land and to increase further the size of their farms (Johnson 1995, p. 34). Through these mechanisms, the supply of for example livestock and livestock products soon rose above the level of self-sufficiency.

For products for which the CAP gave relatively high support, this has had another

---

[3] Market unity means that products can freely circulate in all member states. Trade among member states may not be hindered by customs duties or other protective measures.

[4] Community preference means that on the internal market, products from member states are given priority over products from non-member states. In practice this is achieved by levying a variable tariff on imports from non-member countries.

[5] Expenses incurred as a result of the CAP are financed by the Community. All tax revenue generated by the CAP is regarded as revenue of the EU. In accordance with the latter principle, the budget of the Community is formed by a system of own means, employed to the implementation of a Common policy. The main part of this budget is directed towards EAGGF (until 1992 two third of total EC expenditure was spent by it of which the largest part went to market and price support). Apart from these contributions from member states , EAGGF is financed through means of the Union such as variable levies on imports, production levies and contributions for storing sugar and revenues via milkquotas.

effect concerning relations within the food chain.[6] Through price support, the above-mentioned larger and modernized farms obtained a much more competitive position with respect to processing industries. Having more financial resources for investments in the latest technology and high quality inputs, they could more easily adapt to the demands of processing industries for standardized, homogeneous agricultural products. Links between agro-industry and agricultural producers therefore developed mostly with this type of farm holding. As a result, differentiation increased between small-scale farmers producing more directly for the market on the one hand, and larger, modernized holdings on the other hand.

This situation was consolidated by the financial flows of the FEOGA to non-farm activities. In spite of the fact that in the Treaty of Rome its support system aimed at benefiting the income of farmers, a significant part of the costs incurred by price intervention or support systems went to other parts of the economy. For example, the costs for storage of the surpluses of agricultural products largely went to those who supplied the storage space and services (Johnson 1995, p. 30). Furthermore, the cost of distilling wine to make alcohol, or the subsidy to processing industries for the use of milk powder, went to non-farmers. Agro-industry thus benefited considerably from the CAP, and from the situation of surpluses in particular. Its position with respect to the CAP has therefore often been in favour of these policies.

The CAP has thus contributed to the modernization of the European agricultural sector, which in turn has caused a situation of surpluses and differentiation among European farmers. Due to the integration of the European agricultural sector with the global food system, third countries are confronted with the effects and fluctuations of those changes in the European agricultural sector and its policy.

14.3.3. The CAP as a "foreign policy"

The second way in which the CAP considerably affects the relations of the EU with the outside world is through the principle of Community preference, in other words, through its system of protectionism. Being the second largest exporter in the world for agricultural commodities, after the USA, the EU is a major actor on the world market and the CAP thus has far-reaching implications for third countries. The system of support which has turned the EU from net-importing to net-exporting, together with all kinds of protection, of which import barriers are the most important, have restricted the possibilities of other exporting countries (the USA, Australia, New Zealand, Canada and developing countries). Exports from developing countries to the EC are limited because of the distorted competition whereas higher exports from the EC to third countries limit the export possibilities among those countries. Moreover, the CAP tends to depress world market prices. The increase of domestic production leads to a reduction of the EC's imports and an increase in its exports. As a consequence, the supply on the world market is higher than it would normally be, which reduces the

---

[6] The food chain, according to Gray (1989, p. 31) is "all the economic interests involved, from the production of agricultural raw materials to the consumption of food by the final consumer....".

price on the world market. The most important commodities subject to this are sugar, dairy and wheat. Developing countries, which depend on exports to the world market, suffer especially from the resulting low prices and uncertainties. Furthermore, the high export subsidies paid by the EU often make it very difficult for other exporting countries to compete with products from the EU. Conflicts arise especially where tropical products are substitutes for products grown in temperate zones (sugar and tropical oils and fats) (Buckwell 1991, p. 237).

An example of how, through the global integration of the food system, domestic distortion can spread from one sector to another and from one country to another is given by Buckwell (1991, p. 233), who points at the system of very high protection of sugar in the USA. This has discouraged food manufacturers from using sugar and has led to the development of corn syrup industries as a cheap substitute. Corn syrup's by-product, maize gluten, is exported to Europe. There, it is used as an important source of protein in feed compounds for mainly pigs, poultry and dairy cows. Since the price of maize gluten in the EU is much lower than the usual feed compounds, its use contributes to a further expansion of European livestock sectors. The result is a surplus of milk powder, butter and meat which is exported to the world market (with subsidies), depressing the world market prices for those products.

A second example of the links in the global food system, this time with respect to developing countries, refers to the same substitute. Another way to avoid the high grain prices in compounding fodder in the EC is through replacing it by soybeans and tapioca. Large amounts have been imported from Brazil and Thailand. However, due to its protection barriers and subsidies, this kind of integration has created a one-sided dependency relation between the EU and developing countries: as soon as the internal prices of grains were reduced (in 1992), imports of tapioca decreased extensively, causing serious problems of overproduction and economic loss in Thailand.

14.4. THE CAP UNDER ATTACK

The effects of the globalization process which had been encouraged by the market and price policy at a certain point led to an untenable position of the CAP. There were three factors in this: first, the financial burden of the CAP internally, together with the lack of transparency of its working; second, the tensions it created on the world market in a period in which neo-liberalism and proponents of free trade gained in importance; third, the growing awareness of the environmental problems the agricultural way of production promoted by the CAP brings about. These gave a strong impulse to plans for reform of the CAP. These problems and its criticism, from inside as well as outside the EU, culminated in 1992. In that year, not only was the European Internal Market to be completed, but the GATT negotiations were at a decisive stage, while at the same time an agreement was reached about the reform of the CAP itself.

14.4.1. The Internal Market

The establishment of the Internal Market basically meant the removal of national barriers to commerce within the EC. It aimed at strengthening the position of Europe in the global economy while placing more of the regulatory levers at the European level. This also affected agro-industry. The Internal Market led processing industries to seek to broaden their sources of supply to remain competitive with respect to other firms in the same markets. Moreover, mutual recognition of disparate national health regulations, together with harmonized labelling, packaging, and additives legislation, which came with the Internal Market, encouraged the food industry to operate at a Community-wide level, even if many food markets continued to be regional. Moreover, food industries saw regulation (at the European level) increase, while the benefits from the CAP diminished for them. Accordingly, pressure from this side on the CAP, aiming at a reduction of EC price levels and an increase of access to imports, increased (Josling 1992). This pressure, together with criticism of the amount of agricultural spending, which was considered a threat to stability in the EC and an obstacle in the GATT negotiations, created the possibility for reforms in the CAP to take place.

14.4.2. Reform of the CAP

The reform of the CAP aimed at a control of the surpluses and a reduction of the cost of support for the European taxpayer. At the same time, it sought to satisfy the demands in the GATT negotiations through a reduction of the prices of some products, and through direct income aids for farmers.

The crops subject to the decoupling of the price and market policy were grains, oilseeds and protein crops. With this and with a measure for compulsory set-aside, an attempt was made to eliminate one of the most important incentives for a continuous increase of production under the market and price policy. There was a new attempt to redistribute support to the benefit of more vulnerable enterprises with a measure of compensation for lower prices and the setting aside of arable land. The quotas for sugar and milk were maintained.

The choice of a decrease in prices in order to tackle the budget problems indicates the most significant part of the reform, the gradual dismantling of the old support system. This paved the way for an agreement in the GATT negotiations in order to assure a competitive position for the EU in a free multilateral trade environment.

14.4.3. The GATT

The GATT negotiations further dismantled the CAP. The Uruguay Round was initiated in a period of rising protectionism and bilateralism in the early 1980s in which the CAP stood in the foreground. The aim of the negotiations was to counter these trends. The main elements of the outcome of the GATT negotiations were: a 20 per cent drop in internal support (production aid or prices) compared to 1986–1988, for all products, with direct aid under the CAP reform and American aid being excluded from this; a quota for the oilseed production area, which was consistent with the CAP reform; a 21 per cent reduction in the volume of subsidized exports over 6 years, product by product; and additional import duties (market access) to reach eventually 5 per cent of the consumer market.

The agreement reflects a clear shift away from increasing agricultural protection among the agreeing partners in both trade blocks since the mid-1950s. Furthermore, it was the first time that quantitative restrictions on imports and subsidies for exports were brought under some significant degree of control.

14.5. CONTINUOUS PRESSURE ON THE CAP

14.5.1. Moderate changes

These events undoubtedly mark a fundamental attack on the basis of the CAP and on agricultural support policies in general. Yet, although the reform of the CAP is viewed by many people as a historic change, others blame it for not having gone far enough. A frequent argument against the reform is that it did not apply to those sectors with the largest surpluses and that it did not sufficiently decrease production in other sectors.

In fact, one could argue about the impact of the reform. First, the effect of the lower prices, which struck mainly efficient, large-scale holdings, has been relatively limited. This is mainly due to an income compensation which moderated the effects of the lower prices, i.e. a decrease in output (for example in stock farming of 15 per cent). Large farms producing the established limit of volume (92 tonnes of grains) were compensated for setting aside arable land which would cause the 92 tonnes to be exceeded, while at the same time they tried to increase their income by more intensive production on the remaining production land. Yields (kg per ha of cereals) have increased with respect to 1992 (Commission 1996, p. T/51). On top of that, some sectors such as the dairy sector, which remained completely untouched, got an incentive to increase their production as they benefited from the lower prices of grain for fodder. According to many, what the reform basically lacked was the establishment of a direct link between internal prices and those prevailing on world markets (Kjeldahl and Tracy 1994, p. 5).

Also, the GATT outcome proved less radical than the initial proposal of the USA had intended. The resistance to the GATT, in particular that of the French farmers, had to be overcome. This was done by rescheduling the period over which the cuts were to be made to a period which was more convenient for cereals producers (Grant 1995, p.163). Furthermore, the most protected sectors in the EU, i.e. the dairy and sugar sectors, were excluded from the agreement, and the domestic agricultural subsidies were exempted from most challenges in the GATT. Also, direct income aid was not classified as "trade distorting", which left a possibility for farmers' support to be continued.

14.5.2. Change in position of member states

Thus, the adjustments have not been able to silence criticism of the CAP. The modifications do show, however, that the power equilibrium in the Common Agricultural Policy process has changed, which will undoubtedly lead to further reform of the CAP.

For one thing, the positions of the member states with respect to regulation and support of the agricultural sector have shifted. The traditional strong support of national farm sectors has been considerably weakened by the structural changes which have taken place in the European agricultural sector in general. The process of differentiation among farmers has weakened the general farmers' organizations. Consequently, it has become more difficult to sustain farmers as one group in the policy process. Besides, as the national state has gradually become a facilitator of transnational capital, while agro-industry represents this more and more within the agro-industrial production chain, farmers' interests have increasingly become marginal for the member states. Hence, in the Council of Ministers, there is less willingness to support the interests of the agricultural sector if this would induce a conflict.

Already during the GATT negotiations it had become apparent that the general climate within the EU had changed, in favour of an agreement towards free trade. In Germany, the general aspiration of a liberal trade policy had won over the specific demands from the national farm sector (Hendriks 1994). It had moved to the side of Trade Commissioner Sir Leon Brittan when he urged flexibility on the French. The German request for market access was assisted by the fact that there existed an overwhelming feeling among the majority of member states that the benefits of an agreement far outweighed the costs to specific sectors or groups. In this climate, the old system of farmers' support was not important enough for the position of the EU to be sacrificed in the GATT negotiations and beyond.

At present, the situation of declining support of the agricultural sector is reinforced by the increased transparency of the costs of financial support. The shift from price support to direct payments to farmers gives a much better insight into the expenditures for the agricultural sector, and makes it easier for political opposition to accuse the farming sector of using too large a share of the EU budget. This will put considerable strains on the CAP and will form an incentive to further revision.

Finally, future enlargement of the EU to Eastern Europe will contribute to the continuous pressure for a further reform of the CAP. It will be very hard to sustain a policy of subsidies of the present dimensions when those states, with large agricultural sectors, become members of the EU. Also, compensation in the form of higher world market prices is unlikely as Eastern European countries will start producing more efficiently and will take their products to the world market.

The CAP and its support system are thus still being reconsidered. The shift in preference of the member states, among other things, has brought to light the relative importance of the agricultural sector with respect to other sectors at the domestic level. The defensive attitude towards pressure from outside on the CAP will most likely be abandoned gradually.

14.6. ALTERNATIVES

Given this climate and the persisting criticism, it is likely that further reform will take place, or even that the "common" character of agricultural policy will disappear. Two main discussion topics can be distinguished: a further liberalization of trade and deregulation of the agricultural sector, and a renationalization of agricultural policy.

14.6.1. Deregulation and renationalization

With the establishment of the WTO, which came into operation at the start of 1995 as a result of the ratification of the Uruguay Round agreements, the trend towards liberalization as agreed in the GATT has continued. Internationally the pressure will increase. The USA, which also in the framework of NAFTA has far-reaching plans for further reform of its agricultural sector, will continue to put pressure on the EU. The USA aims at five-year plans, which, through considerably lower support ceilings, will prepare the American agricultural sector for the world market. They will demand the same from their trade partners. Also, Australia and New Zealand, both major exporting countries, have become more harsh in the negotiations and threaten to put the EU in front of the new dispute panels of WTO. Furthermore, WTO will impose a total package which means that if agreement about agriculture cannot be reached, negotiations over other issues will not continue.

This trend also sets the tone for the debates within member states and at the European level. For one thing, the influence of the new member states in the Council, and their broadly free trade views, will continue to shift the centre of the debates in that direction. More importantly, besides the shift towards a free trade policy in Germany, a gradual change in the position of France is taking place. Whereas the policy of the latter formerly focused on conservation of the principles of the CAP and adjustments of quantity (instead of price adjustments), the dominant school of thought is now a liberal one, with some influence of ruralists (who aim at digressive aids) (Delorme 1994, p. 57). Furthermore, large agro-industries increasingly see themselves confronted with the choice of expanding outside the EU or staying within a EU without protectionist measures. That these developments are taken seriously reflects a recent debate in France. The French are increasingly concerned as to whether they can maintain their position on the world market for grains. At present, it seems that they are becoming willing to give up support measures, under certain conditions. Finally, also at the European level, the trend towards lowering prices seems to be gaining ground; Fischler, the present Commissioner of Agriculture, has announced that a review of the quota system for the dairy sector will be on the agenda of 1997.

The member states, in addition to their role in the Council of Agricultural Ministers, have always controlled the implementation of the CAP (even if on instruction of the Commission). The same is true for agricultural advisory services, research or social security for farmers (Tracy 1994, p. 1). Financial support has always remained the competence of the EU. However, in practice, financial renationalization of the CAP is already taking place. This possibility is created by the Accompanying Measures implemented under the Internal Market. One of these measures is environmental aid (regulation 2078/92) which can be interpreted in such a broad way that member states apply it to finance the agricultural sector (up to 25 per cent). It is a form of state aid (Article 92, 3c), which is allowed by the Commission. This type of (financial) renationalization is still increasing (Wilkinson, 1994).

Apart from this, the debate on a further renationalization is gaining ground. The arguments in favour of this solution are led first by considerations about the financial pressure of the CAP on the EU budget, second by the possibility of decreasing the administrative burdens, and third by the demand for more flexibility of agricultural policy so as to consider the needs of the different regions (Berkhout and Meester 1994, p. 82). In France, for example, those responsible for policy and finance see a solution in renationalization in order to avoid the extra costs of the system of direct payments, and of the maintenance of the structurally weaker farms in the South of Europe (Delorme 1994, p. 48). Also in The Netherlands, with its traditionally liberal approach towards the agricultural sector and moderate support of regulation, a considerable part of the reform debate is now, with a view to the enlargement of the EU, dominated by those in favour of renationalization.

14.7. CONCLUSION

How should these developments be interpreted? It can be stated that farm support policies have been re-oriented towards the world market sphere. Within the member states the agricultural sector has lost its relative importance, which has made this re-orientation possible. Furthermore, a process of restructuring of the agricultural sector, due to the globalization of the food system, has shifted the power balance towards (transnational) food companies. The latter, with their strategy of incorporating regions into global production and consumption relations, have undermined the institutional bases of domestic farm policies. Linked to that, general CAP policy is driven by mostly non-farmer motivations. Regulatory institutions are consequently intended to disappear and make way for a free trade doctrine. Thus, the CAP as a "foreign policy" increasingly gives importance to the comparative advantage of the EU, instead of to the protection of the European agricultural sector as a whole. This is what McMichael (1994, p. 165) calls "a shift away from national coherence towards national competitiveness" (where "national" stands for EU).

In the case of trade liberalization, a large share of the EU trade pattern would be taken up by the USA, which shows the importance of the USA as an exporter of agricultural products but indicates also the competition between these two trade blocks for shares of the world market (Frohberg *et al.* 1989, p. 43). The terms of trade would improve for almost all developing countries. It would even be likely that, in the long run, the unprotected northern (metropolitan) farmers would lose competitiveness *vis-à-vis* lower-cost southern peripheral producers (Buttel 1989, p. 68). However, the ones to gain most from this trend would probably be transnational food companies, "since it would enhance and reward capital mobility and reduce costs precisely by de-regulation of national farm policies" (McMichael 1994, p. 176).

The shift towards renationalization of the CAP can be interpreted as part of the same process. On the one hand, member states will seek to fill the gap at the national level which has been created by deregulation of European policy. On the other hand, a foreign agricultural policy which aims at improving the comparative advantage of the EU in general will push member states to support especially their economically most viable sectors.

Finally, a differentiation of finances (renationalization), together with the EU agricultural policy of competitiveness, will leave regions with less favourable resources behind. An increase in regional disparities will probably be the result, while regions (not member states) will become key actors in an increasingly competitive global (food) system. It remains to be seen whether the reduced role of European institutions, in the case of the scenario described above, will allow them to perform successfully their only remaining task, i.e. to guarantee a minimum of cohesion.

14.8. References

Berkhout, P. and G. Meester (1994). "Dutch agricultural policy objectives". In: *Renationalisation of the Common Agricultural Policy?* Belgium: Agricultural Policy Studies

Buckwell (1991). "The CAP and World Trade". In: Ritson, C. and D. Harvey (eds) *The Common Agricultural Policy and the World Economy, Essays in Honour of John Ashton.* UK: C.A.B. International.

Buttel, F. (1989). "The US farm crisis and the restructuring of American agriculture: domestic and international dimensions". In: Goodman, D. and M. Redclift (eds), *The International Farm Crisis.* New York: St. Martin's Press.

Commission (1996). *The Agricultural Situation in the European Union, 1995 Report.* Brussels: European Commission.

Delorme, H. (1994). "French agricultural policy objectives". In: *Renationalisation of the Common Agricultural Policy?* Belgium: Agricultural Policy Studies.

Friedman, H. (1993). "The Political Economy of Food: a Global Crisis". *New Left Review*, Sept.

Frohberg, K., G. Fischer and K.S. Parikh (1989). "International Effects of CAP Trade Liberalization". In: *Agricultural Trade Liberalisation and the EC.* Oxford: Clarendon Press.

Frouws, J. (1994). Mest en macht: Een politiek-sociologische studie naar belangenbehartiging en beleidsvorming inzake de mestproblematiek in Nederland vanaf 1970. Wageningen: Landbouw Universiteit Wageningen.

Frouws, J. (1995). "The Social Regulation of Agriculture, Reflections from a Politico-sociological Perspective". Paper prepared for Conference on the Agrarian Question, Agricultural University Wageningen.

Hendriks, G. (1994). "German Agricultural Policy Objectives". In: *Renationalisation of the Common Agricultural Policy?* Belgium: Agricultural Policy Studies.

Johnson, D.G. (1995). *Less than meets the eye: the modest impact of CAP reform.* London: Centre for Policy Studies, cop. 1995.

Josling, T. (1992). "Emerging Agricultural Trade Relations in the Post Uruguay Round World". Paper presented at the University La Sapienza, Rome.

Keeler, J.T.S. (1996). "Agricultural Power in the European Community, Explaining the Fate of the CAP and GATT negotiations". *Comparative Politics*, Jan.

Kjeldahl, R. and M. Tracy (eds) (1994). *Renationalisation of the Common Agricultural Policy?* Belgium: Agricultural Policy Studies.

McMichael P. (1994). "GATT, Global Regulation and the Construction of a New Hegemonic Order". In: Lowe, P. *et al.* (eds) *Regulating Agriculture.* London: David Fulton Publishers.

Wilkinson, A. (1994). "Renationalisation, an Evolving Debate". In: *Renationalisation of the Common Agricultural Policy?* Belgium: Agricultural Policy Studies.

CHAPTER 15

EU telecommunications policy and the WTO

Juliette Enser[1]

15.1. INTRODUCTION

On 15 February 1997, 69 countries agreed to open their basic telecommunications markets to foreign competition, in particular, by abolishing monopolies over service supply and removing restrictions on foreign ownership of telecommunications suppliers. The 69 countries, which included all advanced industrial nations and many developing countries, cover over 90 per cent of the world's telecommunications revenues.[2] Their agreement marked the conclusion of negotiations which have been taking place since 1994, in the context of the World Trade Organization's General Agreement in Trade in Services (GATS). The liberalization commitments made by the participating governments should come into effect on 1 January 1998, subject to the successful completion of any necessary domestic ratification procedures. Among the principal participants in the negotiations were the European Community and its member states, which committed themselves to substantial market opening in the telecommunications field. These negotiations were the first successful sector-specific negotiations under the auspices of the recently created World Trade Organization.

So far, little research has been conducted on the process or outcome of the WTO negotiations on basic telecommunications, or their implications for EU foreign policy. Hence this chapter constitutes a first attempt to examine the interplay between the actors at the multilateral level during these negotiations, with a view to determining the extent to which these negotiations can be said to illustrate the pursuance of a common trade policy by the European Community following an agenda established in essence by the EC Commission, the protector of the "Community interest". The chapter will begin with a brief description of recent developments in telecommunications policy at the EU and the WTO level. Next, the evolution of the EU's programme for an internal market in telecommunications and the WTO negotiations on basic telecommunications will be discussed in more detail. Finally, some tentative conclusions will be drawn about the current position of the EU as an actor in global telecommunications policy, and how that position may develop in the future.

---

[1] I would like to thank Dr Wolf Sauter, Ms Miriam Gonzalez Durantes and Mr Nicholas Robson for their assistance with this chapter. Any mistakes are, of course, solely my own responsibility.

[2] The major exceptions are China and Russia, which are not members of the WTO.

A. Cafruny and P. Peters (eds.), The Union and the World, 285–296

15.2. UNDERSTANDING EU TELECOMMUNICATIONS POLICY AT A GLOBAL LEVEL: THE FUNDAMENTALS

Telecommunications policy in the European Union is a relatively recent creation. It was not until the mid-1980s that the first steps were taken by the Community, driven by Commission activism, to institute a policy of gradual or "phased" liberalization in this sector. Until then, the EU telecommunications markets were the domain of largely state-owned monopoly postal and telecommunications operators, or "PTTs". Global coordination of telecommunications policy, as required by the inherent technical and functional needs of international communications, was carried out through the International Telecommunications Union (ITU), of which the member states (but not the EC) were members. Regional cooperation took place through the Conférence Européene des administrations des Postes et des Télécommunications (CEPT), the members of which are the national PTTs of the member states and other European countries.

However, in 1987 the EU embarked on a gradual dismantling of the PTT's monopolies and introduction of competition. This initiative was led by the European Commission, using its autonomous legislative powers under Article 90(3)EC, with the support of some influential sections of industry. This was a novel approach, and represented the first instance where these powers were used in this manner, although their legal basis had already been established in the original Treaty of Rome of 1957. The reaction of the member states to the Commission initiative varied from support (from, for example, the UK which had independently embarked on its own liberalization programme) to outright opposition (in particular from states strongly committed to public enterprise and public ownership, such as France, Spain, Italy and, in a less outspoken manner, Germany). However, in the face of the affirmation by the Court of Justice of the Commission's powers under Article 90(3), there was little that the member states could do to prevent the Commission's drive towards liberalization.

Concurrently with the moves towards internal liberalization in the EU, negotiations were taking place in the framework of the Uruguay Round which aimed, for the first time, to establish multilateral rules governing trade in services. Initially, the results in respect of trade in telecommunications services were limited. In December 1993, at the time of the successful conclusion of the GATT/WTO negotiations, many participants committed to allowing a degree of market access in the "value-added" telecommunications sector, which covered the most innovative services but represented only a small proportion of the overall market. However, participants were unable to agree to market opening commitments in the considerably more valuable "basic" telecommunications sector, and instead agreed to extend the negotiations on a sector-specific basis. This was largely because, as described below, at least one major actor, the EU, was unable to commit to liberalization in 1993 because it had not yet determined the contours of its internal liberalization. From an EU perspective, no effective third country market access could be negotiated before the legislative framework was in place for internal liberalization that would allow member states access to each other's markets.

On the EU side, the participants in these sector-specific negotiations were both the

Community and its member states. For the reasons described below, neither the EU nor the member states were solely competent to negotiate and conclude an agreement on basic telecommunications. Thus the Commission, as the EU negotiator, had no mandate to offer market-opening measures beyond those agreed by, or indeed forced on, individual member states. Conversely, the WTO negotiations were an opportunity for the Commission to further its internal market-opening ambitions since the widespread desire for a successful conclusion of the negotiations increased the pressure on individual member states to accept liberalization.

The evolution of EU telecommunications policy on a global scale cannot be understood without an appreciation of the dynamics of the EU's internal liberalization programme. Hence, this chapter will briefly describe those dynamics, as well as the developments in the EU's negotiating position within the GATS.

15.3. THE EU LIBERALIZATION PROGRAMME

Prior to the 1980s, telecommunications had been considered a "natural monopoly" in most countries, on the basis of arguments of economics and public interest. However, this position changed in the EU (and elsewhere) due to the interplay of a number of factors, including technological advances, the spill-over of international regulatory change (in particular deregulation in the US), the internal market programme, reform in certain member states, and the pressure of industrial lobbies.[3]

In 1987, the Commission published a landmark Green Paper on the Development of the Common Market for Telecommunications Services and Equipment, entitled "Towards a Dynamic European Economy".[4] This policy paper set out the principle that the market for value-added services and terminal equipment should be opened immediately, but that the PTTs would retain their monopoly over public voice telephony and network infrastructure for the immediate future, in order to enable them to continue to fulfil their public interest universal service obligations. Concurrently, sector-specific regulation would be adopted at Community level on the basis of Council (and, later, European Parliament) Directives under Article 100A EC. This was clearly a push to extend the fundamental logic of the internal market to a sector which had been hitherto exempt. It was also an attempt by the Commission to foster a pro-liberalization agenda by means of coalition-building between sections of industry (large consumers, equipment manufacturers, telecommunications service-providers) and certain member states. Finally, it represented an attempt to lever telecommunications into economic growth.

Although the member states agreed to the principles set out in the Green Paper, in practice they stalled and failed to enact the required legislative framework. In the face of continued resistance to liberalization among a number of member states, the Commission revised its legislative strategy. Emboldened by the impetus of its internal

---

[3] For a description of the forces leading to the EU liberalization programme, see Sauter (1995). European Law Journal Vol 1. No. 1 March 1995, p.96.
[4] COM(87) 290, 30 June 1987.

market programme and the success of its coalition-building efforts, the Commission acted on the principles set out in the Green Paper and issued Commission Directives based on Article 90(3) which required member states to abolish special and exclusive rights in the area of terminal equipment and value-added services. Because of their legal base, these Directives did not require the assent of either the Council or the European Parliament. The novel use of Article 90(3) in this manner was challenged before the Court of Justice by several member states in two landmark cases,[5] but the Court of Justice affirmed the Commission's autonomous power to legislate for the dismantling of the national telecommunications monopolies.

In 1992 the Commission, as required by the legislation it had enacted under Article 90,[6] conducted a further review of telecommunications policy, including several rounds of elaborate industry consultation, and concluded that a specific timetable should be set for the abolition of the remaining exclusive and special rights over public voice telephony, and that consideration should be given to liberalization of the underlying infrastructure. At the time it was noted by the Commission's consultees that "an early definition of a clear schedule would reinforce the international position of the Community in particular in the context of the GATT negotiations".[7] The Commission suggested 1 January 1998 as the date for full liberalization of public voice telephony, a date which, in a key compromise with France and Germany, was accepted by the Council in its Resolution 93/C213/EEC.[8] However, as a side-bargain for the peripheral member states, the Council Resolution stated that those Member States with less developed networks, i.e. Spain, Ireland, Greece and Portugal, would be given an additional transition period of up to five years in order to prepare for competition.[9]

Thus in 1993, when the GATS negotiations were concluded, the Community had only just established a timetable for intended liberalization of basic voice telephony. Moreover, the Community position in relation to other key subsectors of the telecommunications market, such as infrastructure or mobile services, remained open in numerous crucial respects. In other words, in spite of apparent agreement on general principles by 1993, no internal market yet existed in basic telecommunications services. This effectively prevented the Community from making any meaningful commitments in the context of the GATS. In the words of Karl Falkenberg, the Commission's negotiator from external relations DG I in the services field:

In basic telecommunications, within the Community we still have monopolistic structures that we have to break up. Within the Community we have taken the de-

---

[5] Case C-202/88 *French Republic v. Commission* (1991) ECR I-1223, Joined Cases C-271/90, C-281/90 and C-289/90 *Spain, Belgium and Italy v. Commission* (1992) ECR I-5833.

[6] For example, Article 10 of Commission Directive 90/388 of 28 June 1990 on competition in the market for telecommunications services (O.J. L192/10, 24 July 1990).

[7] Communication to the Council and European Parliament on the consultation on the review of the situation in the telecommunications services sector COM(93) final, 28 April 1993.

[8] Council Resolution 93/C213/01 on the review of the situation in the telecommunications sector (O.J. 1993 C213/1).

[9] Luxembourg, as a Member State with a very small network, was given an extra transition period of a maximum of two years.

cision to do that by 1998, and in mentioning this date you will understand why I have a problem as a trade negotiator to commit myself as of today, what the Community's position in basic telecommunications trade can be, when I know that all the de-regulation, de-monopolization in this sector for the Community is still to be achieved in the future.[10]

By early 1996, the basic legislation requiring full liberalization of the Community telecommunications market was in place. The Article 90(3) Commission Directives liberalizing public voice telephony, infrastructure provision, mobile and satellite services had been adopted, and the necessary Council and European Parliament harmonizing legislation had also been adopted or was in the pipeline. Finally, the timetable for liberalization was, to a large extent, clear. Indeed, some member states perceived a "first mover" advantage and proceeded to liberalize ahead of time. However, the legislation had embodied the principle set out in Council Resolution 93/C213/EEC that the "derogation countries" (Spain, Ireland, Greece and Portugal) could apply to the Commission for a derogation from various liberalization obligations on the grounds that their markets were not sufficiently developed to allow full competition without threatening the viability of the universal service operator. For example, abolition of exclusive and special rights over public voice telephony could be delayed for a maximum of five years (i.e. until 2003).[11] These potential derogations (which, on the internal plane, had not seemed crucial since they concerned national markets which were, by definition, marginal) were to prove problematical in the context of the WTO negotiations on basic telecommunications. Remarkably, however, the Commission was able to turn external leverage to its advantage in resolving the "derogation problem".

15.4. THE GENERAL AGREEMENT ON TRADE IN SERVICES

At the outset of the most recent round of GATT negotiations (which also led to the establishment of a new institution governing world trade, the WTO), Ministers gave the multilateral negotiators the remit of establishing a framework of principles and rules to govern trade in services under conditions of gradual liberalization. The result was the GATS, which establishes multilateral rules for the conduct of trade in services among members of the WTO (which include both the Community and its member states). The GATS is one of the fundamental agreements within the remit of WTO which all WTO members must sign and ratify. It is governed by the WTO dispute settlement mechanism, so violations can be brought before an independent panel. It provides, in particular, that all WTO members are to offer service suppliers from another member MFN treatment (i.e. to offer service suppliers from other WTO members, on a non-discriminatory basis, the best treatment they offer to any foreign

---

[10] Falkenberg, "Services Trade after the Uruguay Round – The European Perspective", http://www.ucd.ie/~sirc/Falkenberg.html.

[11] See Commission Directive 96/19/EC of 13 March 1996 amending Directive 90/388/EEC with regard to full competition in telecommunications markets (O.J. L74/14, 22 March 1996) at Article 1.2.2.

service supplier). This MFN obligation was subject to a one-off possibility for WTO members to negotiate express derogations from the MFN obligation. Further, the GATS provides for members to negotiate "specific commitments", binding themselves to providing a degree of market access and/or national treatment to service suppliers from other WTO members in a specific services sector.

In their Schedule of Specific Commitments in the GATS (i.e. the schedule setting out the extent of market access and national treatment to which the WTO members agreed to bind themselves), the EC and the member states[12] made specific commitments to remove almost all restrictions on market access and national treatment as regards trade in "value-added" telecommunication services, such as electronic mail and voice mail. Many other WTO members made similar commitments. All WTO members also agreed to allow foreign service suppliers access to and use of the public telecommunications networks on reasonable and non-discriminatory conditions, in circumstances where such access was required to offer a service for which a specific commitment was made.[13] However, as previously indicated, because of internal problems, the EU and its member states were unable to make any commitments on basic telecommunications at this stage and participants, partly for this reason, agreed to prolong these negotiations for a further two years.

15.5. COMMUNITY COMPETENCE

During the Uruguay Round, the member states had contested the competence of the Community to conclude agreements in all the trade-related areas under discussion, and particularly in relation to trade in services and intellectual property. This caused the Commission, in 1994, to request the ECJ to give its opinion on the scope of the Community's competence over external trade relations. No doubt to the disappointment of the Commission, the ECJ held that, for the most part, GATS was a matter of "mixed" competence.[14]

As a framework for their "specific commitments", the Uruguay Round participants had agreed to divide each service sector according to four different modes of supply: "cross-border", "consumption abroad", "commercial presence", and "presence of natural persons". Thus, for example, a country could agree to allow service-suppliers from other WTO members to open subsidiaries in its territory, while permitting only limited access to foreign employees of that service-supplier. The ECJ held that, while cross-border trade in services (the first mode of supply covered by GATS) fell within the scope of the Community's exclusive competence under Article 113, the remaining modes of supply were within the Community's exclusive competence only to the extent that Community internal legislative provisions dealt with the treatment of third country nationals, or achieved full harmonization of the rules governing access to an

---

[12] Although the EC and the member states are all members of the WTO, the member states made their GATS commitments in one Schedule of Specific Commitments entitled "the Schedule of Specific Commitments of the European Communities and their Member States".

[13] See the GATS Annex on Telecommunications, Article 5.

[14] See Opinion 1/94, 1994 (ECR) I-5265.

activity. This was not the case in relation to telecommunications (where, as mentioned above, many matters were still regulated at member state level, including licensing of foreign service suppliers). Therefore, at least in theory, the participants in the negotiations on basic telecommunications should have been both the EC and the member states. In reality, as described below, the Commission none the less took the lead in shaping the evolution of the EU negotiating strategy.

15.6. NEGOTIATIONS ON BASIC TELECOMMUNICATIONS 1994–1997

In 1994, a limited group of WTO members (which included all the major telecommunications players) commenced negotiations for specific commitments in trade in basic telecommunications services, which were scheduled to be completed by April 1996. The negotiations covered "basic telecommunications" services, which were treated as including all the major subsectors of telecommunication (whether offered on a facilities-based or a resale basis, whether wireless or wireline). The objective of the negotiations was to achieve a "critical mass" of offers, such that the participants in the negotiations and in particular the US would be prepared to open their national markets on an MFN basis by abolishing monopolies and foreign ownership restrictions. The prospects for the negotiations appeared hopeful in view of the emerging trends towards liberalization both in the European Union and world-wide. However, in case the negotiations failed, the WTO members reserved the right[15] to take MFN exemptions in order to preserve the possibility of using unilateral or bilateral market-opening measures. Hence, while engaging in multilateral talks in an attempt to build up momentum towards an inclusive global deal, the participating countries kept open a back door for a system of reciprocity.

15.7. THE EMERGENCE OF THE EU NEGOTIATING POSITION

Once the member states had been forced to accept the principle of full competition for the internal EU telecommunications market, broad support emerged for the concept of global liberalization in the context of the GATS. The EU did not appear in favour of seeking market access in third countries by the use of unilateral measures.[16] It was

---

[15] See the GATS Annex on Negotiations on Basic Telecommunications.

[16] The Commission's proposal for a European Parliament and Council Directive on a common framework for general authorizations and individual licences in the field of telecommunications services (COM/95/545 Final) (O.J. C90/5 27 March 1996) contained certain mechanisms for achieving reciprocal access (Article 18). However, it is understood that this provision did not reflect any real desire by the Commission or member states for such a regime, but was merely a fall-back in case the negotiations failed. Indeed, in its Common Position on this Proposal the Council agreed merely that the Commission could, if given an appropriate mandate, commence negotiations with third countries where Community operators were experiencing difficulties in obtaining market access (Common Position (EC) No. 7/97 adopted by the Council on 9 December 1996 with a view to adopting Directive 97/.../EC of the European Parliament and of the Council of ..., on a common framework for general authorizations and individual licences in the field

perhaps felt that, as regards trade in services, the leverage that could be gained by using reciprocity measures was small since, on the whole, developing countries had comparatively little to gain from obtaining market access to foreign markets at the expense of opening up their domestic markets to competition. Further, the legal mechanics of the EU's single market regime would have made it very difficult for member states, acting on an individual basis, to block access to third country service suppliers once the EU single market in telecommunications was in place. In addition, it can be assumed that the industry actors which had been extremely influential in bringing about the internal EU liberalization were also supportive of global liberalization.

In order to achieve the objective of successfully completing the negotiations, the Community and the member states had to ensure that their offer was sufficient to satisfy the US, without whose participation a global telecommunications deal would have been unthinkable. In principle, the Community, once the internal framework was in place, was in a position to offer unrestricted market access from 1 January 1998. Despite this opportunity, the EC offer of April 1996 was relatively restricted. Greece, Ireland, Portugal and Spain sought to delay the granting of market access, generally until the end of the maximum transition period they could obtain under the derogations from the internal market programme (e.g. until 2003 for public voice telephony), and even beyond the internal transition period for some subsectors. Further, Belgium, France, Portugal and Spain maintained foreign ownership restrictions.[17] The delayed market access detracted considerably from the EC offer, especially in view of the size of the Spanish market and the strong position of Telefonica, the incumbent Spanish operator, in third country markets in South America. In any event, the US was generally unsatisfied with the level of the offers on the table in April 1996 and, under pressure from certain sectors of its domestic industry, refused to strike a deal. Instead, the participants in the negotiations, led by the US and the EC, agreed to extend the negotiations until February 1997.

In general, where the interplay between the "internal" and "external" dimensions of EU policy are concerned, the Commission cannot be regarded as a unitary actor. In fact, the Commission is made up of a number of Directorates-General, with differing responsibilities and falling within the portfolios of different Commissioners. Thus, for example, Commission participation in the negotiations on basic telecommunications was the responsibility of DG I, the Directorate-General of the Commission which deals with multilateral trade relations. The internal market programme in telecommunications, on the other hand, was largely the responsibility of the Directorates-General responsible for competition (DG IV) and telecommunications (DG XIII). However, in the case of telecommunications liberalization, internal and external policy objectives coincided and the responsible DGs acted together in pursuance of this common objective.

---

of telecommunications services (O.J. C41/48 10 February 1997)). A similar evolution can be seen in relation to the Community's legislation on interconnection.

[17] The compatibility of some of these foreign ownership restrictions with applicable EC law must be questionable, in so far as they were stated to be applicable as against EC companies with third country parents.

By 1996 it was clear from DG I's perspective that an improved EC offer would be required to complete the deal, both to satisfy pressure from the US and to encourage other participants to improve or table offers. This also coincided with DG IV's objective of limiting, to the greatest extent possible, the derogations from the internal timetable. That the EC and its member states were able, in the end, to table a greatly improved offer by February 1997 illustrates the extent to which, despite the "mixed" competence of the GATS, the Commission set the EU agenda in relation to the WTO basic telecommunications negotiations, as it had done in respect of internal liberalization. Indeed, the Commission was able to use the basic telecommunications negotiations to consolidate its position in relation to the internal market in telecommunications. Perhaps the starkest indicator of the Commission's role is seen in the case of Spain – the most recalcitrant of the member states in this respect – which will be discussed below.

15.8. THE SPANISH COMMITMENTS

In the initial EC offer Spain had refused to offer market access for public voice telephony and facilities-based services before 2003 and had restricted mobile operators to use of Telefonica's infrastructure until 2003. This was consistent with its attitude to a derogation from the internal liberalization programme.[18] Fortunately for the Commission, DG IV had at hand an instrument to exert pressure on the Spanish Government, as DG IV was handling Telefonica's application, under the EU competition rules, for clearance of its participation in the Unisource alliance of telecommunications operators. DG IV had, in respect of an earlier alliance between the telecommunications operators of France and Germany, clearly established the precedent that competition clearance could be made conditional on market-opening measures by member states.[19] DGIV made it clear to the Spanish government that the same analysis would be applied in the Telefonica–Unisource case. The link between DG IV's attitude and the ongoing WTO negotiations was obvious, as illustrated by a press release issued by the Commission in October 1996 following a Commission meeting during which the derogations were discussed:

> The liberalization of telecommunications within the European Union can also have a major impact on the international telecommunications negotiations taking place within the World Trade Organization. The European Union's deadline must be as close as possible to 1998 in most Member States since that year is also the target date for global liberalization.... Special attention was paid to recent developments in Spain. In line with the approach taken in the Atlas/Global One case, Mr Van

---

[18] In fact, Spain brought annulment actions regarding three relevant Article 90 Commission Directives, claiming that the additional transition periods were automatically granted to Spain under Community law and that the Commission had no power to expressly grant or deny derogations under the Article 90 Directives (Cases C-11/96, C-123/96 and C-199/96).

[19] See Commission Decision of July 17, 1996 relating to a proceeding under Article 85 of the EC Treaty and Article 53 of the EEA Agreement (O.J. L239/23, September, 19, 1996).

Miert [the Commissioner responsible for competition] made the point that an alliance between dominant operators was not acceptable in the context of a market still closed to competition. Spain is also particularly important in the context of the WTO negotiations given the size of its domestic market and the presence of its dominant operator in several countries of Latin America.[20]

In the circumstances, and in light of parallel pressure from US regulators, Spain agreed to table a substantially improved offer in the WTO telecommunications talks and substantially to forgo any derogation.

15.9. THE RESULTS OF THE NEGOTIATIONS

The EC's improved offer was matched by an improved offer from the US, and from other participating countries, with the result that in April 1996, an agreement was reached which, for the first time, binds the 69 countries to provide market access and national treatment to service suppliers of basic telecommunication services from any WTO member. Most industrialized countries have agreed to offer significant market access as from 1 January 1998 with only limited restrictions on foreign ownership. Developing country commitments, on the other hand, have tended towards delayed market access, presumably in order to allow domestic suppliers to develop and modernize their infrastructure before facing competition (mirroring the internal EC position as regards derogations). In addition, most participants agreed to abide by a series of fundamental regulatory principles, such as the separation of regulatory and operating functions, and the application of mandatory interconnection to the network of "major suppliers" on non-discriminatory, transparent, cost-based terms, thereby laying the basis for the facilities-based competition which is generally seen as the final blow to a monopoly situation.

The major failure, from the EC point of view, in these negotiations was the last-minute decision by the US to table an MFN exemption for satellite transmission of DTH and DBS television services and of digital audio services, thus retaining for itself some possibility of using unilateral action to force market-opening. At the time the EC response was relatively forceful, including threats to challenge the legality of the exemption.[21] But the EC none the less agreed to conclude a deal, apparently in order to avoid jeopardizing the success of the talks, which was badly needed to prove the viability of the new WTO structure. This raises the question of whether a more unified EC would have been able to dissuade the US from insisting on the MFN exemption. However, it is not immediately obvious what further measures could have been taken by the EC, or that the EC response was anything less than coordinated. The press statements, at least, indicate that the Council endorsed the position enunciated by Sir Leon Brittan concerning the potential illegality of the US MFN exemption. By reserving the right to challenge the measure, the EU also raised the perhaps more interesting question of whether initiation of dispute settlement proceedings in relation

---

[20] Commission Press Release IP/96/958 of 24 Oct. 1996.

[21] See e.g. *Agence Europe*, 18 Feb. 1997.

to a "mixed" agreement requires unanimity among the member states. If this is the case, it remains to be seen whether such unanimity will ever be obtainable in practice.

15.10. CONCLUSION

The GATS negotiations on basic telecommunications saw the EC and in particular the Commission performing as a highly effective actor in the complex arena of global telecommunications liberalization. The EC objective of securing a global liberalization pact on basic telecommunications was eventually secured despite the fact that the April 1996 conditional offers had failed to satisfy the US constituency. The only cloud on the horizon was the last-minute US MFN exemption. The case of Spain clearly shows the Commission setting the agenda for the EU's policy in the negotiations, and also illustrates the complex interplay between the EU's internal and external relations.

However, the battle over the Community's role in relation to trade in services is still not over. At the time of writing, the member states have just declined, at the Amsterdam Summit of June 1997, to extend the exclusive competence of the Community over the common commercial policy under Article 113 of the Treaty to cover trade in services. On the other hand, they have expressly preserved the Community's existing competences and have agreed that the scope of Article 113 can be extended to cover services by unanimous decision of the Council without the necessity of a Treaty amendment.[22] Although this position can hardly be regarded as a great leap forward, at a minimum it should allow the Community to respond to international developments without awaiting a further Intergovernmental Conference.

15.11. REFERENCES

Arkell, J. (1995). "The General Agreement on Trade in Services (GATS). Liberalisation Concepts, Structures and Modalities". In: Bourgeois *et al.* (eds) *The Uruguay Round Results. A European Lawyer's Perspective.*

Hilf, H. (1995). "The ECJ's Opinion 1/94 on the WTO – No Surprise, but Wise?". *European Journal of International Law 6*, No. 2, 245.

Kuijper, P. (1995). "The Conclusion and Implementation of the Uruguay Round Results by the European Community". *European Journal of International Law 6*, No. 2, 222.

Petersmann, E. (1995). "The Transformation of the World Trading System through the 1994 Agreement Establishing the World Trade Organisation". *European Journal of International Law 6*, No. 2, 161.

Sandholz, W. (1996). "The Emergence of a Supranational Telecommunications Regime". Working Paper 2.43, Center for German and European Studies, Berkeley, California.

Sauter, W. (1995). "The Telecommunications Law of the European Union". *European Law Journal 1*, No. 1, March, 92.

Sauter, W. (1997). "International and EU Telecommunications Liberalisation". *Utilities Law Review 8*, No. 3, 71.

---

[22] Ironically, it is understood that one of the arguments deployed by the member states to resist an extension of the Article 113 competence was that the Commission's success in the basic telecommunications negotiations demonstrated that no extension of Community competence was necessary.

Scott (1996). "Institutional Competition and Coordination in the Process of Telecommunications Liberalisation". In: Britain *et al.* (eds) *International Regulatory Competition and Coordination*.

Zacher (1996). "The International Telecommunications Regime". In: Zacher and Sutton (eds) *Governing Global Networks*. Cambridge University Press, Cambridge.

PART FIVE

CONCLUSIONS

CHAPTER 16

Towards a European foreign policy? Evidence from the case studies and implications for the next decade

Alan Cafruny and Patrick Peters

The contributors to this volume were charged with the task of assessing the extent to which the European Union has forged a communitarian foreign policy, and seeking to understand the impact of this policy on the rest of the world. A communitarian policy was defined as one which was initiated and managed primarily by the Union's institutions. In principle, it is possible to assert two ideal typical EU foreign policies: At one extreme, a purely communitarian policy would mean that states have conceded all authority to Union institutions. At the other extreme, a purely intergovernmental policy would either paralyse Union institutions or compel these institutions to establish their *raison d'être* by mediating among the member states.

As this volume makes clear, none of the Union's foreign policies occupy the extremes of this spectrum. In the final analysis, because the Union is a result of a Treaty, and not a Federation, the Union's foreign policy negotiators are ultimately responsible to the member states, even if they enjoy a great deal of day-to-day latitude. Yet, in all the cases examined in this volume, there is at least some element of communitarianism. Thus, even where policy is largely shaped by the member states, the Union's institutions matter.

The case studies in this volume indicate clearly that the extent to which a communitarian policy has developed depends greatly on the issue. The EU's policy towards former Yugoslavia most closely conforms to an intergovernmentalist model of European great power diplomacy. Yet even here some significant aspects of supranationalism were identified. At the opposite end of the spectrum, commercial policies show the strongest elements of communitarianism. Nevertheless, states continue to influence commercial policy, even if they do so indirectly and with great subtlety, and with obligatory references to harmonization.

The reluctance of states to surrender national sovereignty provides one obvious explanation for the limits of communitarianism, even if it has been widely recognized that a communitarian policy can serve national objectives. Yet many contributors to this volume have sought to identify institutional and bureaucratic characteristics of the Union which generally constrain, but at times might also enhance, the communitarian dimension of policy. Competition within the European Commission has opened up

A. Cafruny and P. Peters (eds.), The Union and the World, 299–302
© 1998 *Kluwer Academic Publishers. Printed in Great Britain.*

new areas of Union foreign policy. At the same time, however, the decentralization of policy that is endemic to the Commission – and indeed the EU in general – also limits the Union's bargaining power and leverage in world affairs. Competition among and within institutions has caused the EU to be a difficult and occasionally unreliable partner. As a result, it is hard for either the member states or third-country states and actors to consider the EU as sovereign.

A number of factors help to explain the low level of institutional efficiency. The inter-institutional division of labour within the EU places great constraints on the bureaucracy. Moreover, EU policy-makers are themselves seeking to enhance their powers and prerogatives in relation not only to the member states, but also to other supranational institutions and agencies. Foreign policy coordination is difficult and often contradictory, thereby exacerbating problems of identity and leadership. For example, it is unclear to many third countries how the Union can uphold its opposition to the Helms Burton Act and strengthen the WTO while continuing to maintain the CAP and a dollar banana policy that contradicts the spirit of the WTO. With power diffused, it is difficult for third countries to identify the responsibility at the international level, and easier for member states to assert their primacy. Thus even in the area of trade policy, where the communitarian dimension is strongest, Henry Kissinger's provocative question (see the Introduction) remains unanswered.

The increasingly influential position of the Commission and the Court in trade and commercial policy makes these institutions a breeding-ground for the establishment of a tradition of communitarian foreign policy. It is clear that when these institutions become involved, as they increasingly tend to do, foreign policy becomes embedded in a framework of rules and agreements which limits the expression of national sovereignty. Clearly, a nascent constitutionalization of foreign policy in trade and commerce is taking place. As many of the contributors to this volume suggest, not only the common approach to the WTO negotiations, but also successive sectorial negotiations and agreements (financial services, telecommunications, energy and transport) are tending to elicit predictable behaviour of the Union in international affairs. The constitutional process is also driven forward by the tendency of business organization to become pan-European, as exemplified by the European automobile industry. That such behaviour does at times provoke conflict with third countries or actors does not limit the impact of this achievement. It is clear that commercial policy, trade-related policies, issues of investments and multilateral relations and, possibly, monetary relations will be the cornerstone of EU foreign economic policy.

As legal guardian of European law and treaties, the increasingly influential European Court is guided by communitarian norms which animate the treaties of Rome and, more recently, the SEA and the Treaty of Maastricht. In its various interpretations of commercial and trade policy the Court in particular has shown that it is capable of acting against the will of member states and willing, albeit within certain limits, to allow the principle of communitarianism to supersede that of sovereignty. The interpretation given by the Court to community legislation has enhanced the role of the Parliament and the Commission, often against the will of the Council and some member states. Thus not only the Commission, but also the Court now seek to uphold communitarian principles against those of sovereignty.

To assert the establishment of a process of expansion of communitarian norms and practices is not to ignore the salience of institutional deadlock or the potency of national interest. We do not contend that the EU is an embryonic state in the Weberian sense: the striking lack of bureaucratic rationality documented in so many of the chapters in this volume is itself greatly reinforced by the unwillingness of states to abandon their sovereign prerogatives. This is readily apparent in the analysis of high foreign policy and military security.

It is easier to anticipate the rationalization of institutions than the withering away of the nation state. The EU has adopted two strategies for overcoming inter-institutional deadlock. One is to define more clearly an institutional hierarchy; a second is to limit institutional authority in sectors where interests have clashed. At the Maastricht IGC, for example, both the Parliament and the Commission sought to expand their authority at the expense of the Council. At the Amsterdam IGC (see below) there was a re-definition of authority; a decision was made to expand the CFSP within the context of an intergovernmental framework, with an enhanced role for the Council's secretary general, and to continue to pursue defence policy within the NATO framework. Thus Amsterdam represented a significant retreat from the principle of communitarianism that guided Maastricht. A second (potential) example of redefinition of authority is the case of agricultural policy, which may be experiencing aspects of renationalization. Like defence policy, agricultural policy is too sensitive for nation states. Anti-trust policy is also an area with strong external implications in which the Commission is encroaching on the traditional primacy of the Council, as German and British objections to Commission initiatives indicate.

EU FOREIGN POLICY AFTER AMSTERDAM

Significant developments in the EU's foreign policy have arisen out of the dynamics of incremental changes in the European and global political economy. But these changes have received institutional and legal expression in the Union's intergovernmental conferences. The driving force of the SEA of 1987 was economic liberalization taking place both regionally and globally. The most important external dimension of the SEA was *structural*, and not a result of institution-building: European business had achieved a sufficient degree of regional organization to make the internal market attractive as a single unit. Through a series of mergers European firms achieved the necessary critical mass to compete at a world level, and the responsibilities and power of the Commission increased dramatically to include sectors such as telecommunications, energy, and services.

The Maastricht Treaty on European Union of 1991 (ratified in 1993) sought to establish the institutional expression for Europe's expanded global reach. The planned monetary union, itself a communitarian strategy to enhance Europe's global role, would demand greater political and institutional cohesion. Hence Maastricht buttressed the position of the Parliament and the Commission. The co-decision procedure made the Parliament an effective player in foreign policy. The Commission entrenched its role in trade policy. It was expected that a common foreign and security policy (CFSP) would complement these developments, but the Maastricht Treaty did not establish a clear line between the competing principles of sovereignty and communitarianism.

Yet, the war in former Yugoslavia quickly showed that it was impossible to fashion an effective CFSP on the basis of these competing principles. At the same time, Europe's structural unemployment crisis has called the establishment of EMU into question. The mood of cautious realism at the Amsterdam IGC of June 1997 thus contrasted greatly with the optimistic expectations of Maastricht. Europe's leaders could hardly contemplate ambitious new initiatives as they confronted the twin spectres of an angry French electorate and an equally stubborn Bundesbank.

Thus, not surprisingly, Amsterdam did not provide new answers. The clearest winner was the Parliament, which won the right to greater participation under the co-decision procedures.[1] But the Parliament did not dramatically increase its power, and no major institutional reforms were undertaken. The reluctance of small countries to re-weight their votes in exchange for the expansion of majority voting was disappointing, but understandable. Yet such a re-weighting, with its clear Federalist implications, is a precondition of greater communitarianism in foreign policy.

A future "zone of freedom, security, and justice"[2] does show that the Union will continue to pursue communitarian goals. In the third pillar of justice and home affairs, more issues have become communitarian even if Schengen remains intergovernmental and an opt-out on border controls was obtained by the UK and Ireland. [Asylum] policy, visas, and immigration were included within the communitarian pillar, paving the way for the greater involvement of the Commission and the Court.

The CFSP will remain largely unchanged. While the Commission will carry out the negotiations on enlargement to the East, a credible CFSP remains at the blueprint stage because of the failure to incorporate the WEU and to define the EU's relationship with NATO. Moreover, Monsieur Pesc has become a civil servant taking orders from the Council, and not a high-ranking politician capable of providing leadership and visibility.

Not surprisingly, the Amsterdam IGC made it clear that the EMU, and not the CFSP, will dominate the EU's agenda for the foreseeable future. Thus the question "Who speaks for Europe?" will remain unanswered. In the longer run, however, the Union's external role can only be expected to increase, generating a continuing momentum for a stronger communitarian policy. The Commission, the Parliament and the Court have all established their place in the making of EU foreign policy, and it is likely that they will seek to expand their role in the coming years.

---

[1] *Financial Times*, 19 June 1997, p. 2.

[2] This proposed "zone of freedom" will take five years to be established. Prior to its establishment most decisions will be taken by unanimity. Thus it is becoming more likely that the political Union, once proposed by Germany and the Benelux countries, is no longer a necessary condition for Economic and Monetary Union.

Index

A. Cafruny and P. Peters (eds.), The Union and the World, 303-310
© 1998 *Kluwer Academic Publishers. Printed in Great Britain.*